EARS THAT HEAR

EXPLORATIONS IN THEOLOGICAL INTERPRETATION OF THE BIBLE

Edited by

Joel B. Green

and

Tim Meadowcroft

SHEFFIELD PHOENIX PRESS

2017

Copyright © 2013, 2017 Sheffield Phoenix Press
First published in hardback, 2013
First published in paperback, 2017

Published by Sheffield Phoenix Press
Department of Biblical Studies, University of Sheffield
45 Victoria Street
Sheffield S3 7QB

www.sheffieldphoenix.com

All rights reserved.
No part of this publication may be reproduced or transmitted in any form or by any means, electronic or mechanical, including photocopying, recording or any information storage or retrieval system, without the publishers' permission in writing.

A CIP catalogue record for this book
is available from the British Library

Typeset by Forthcoming Publications
Printed by Lightning Source

ISBN 978-1-907534-77-5 (hardback)
ISBN 978-1-910928-35-6 (paperback)

Ears That Hear

Contents

Acknowledgments	vii
Abbreviations	ix
List of Contributors	xiii

INTRODUCTION: AN INTERPRETIVE CONVERSATION
   Tim Meadowcroft   1

1
THEOLOGICAL INTERPRETATION AND THE
PROBLEM OF METHOD
   Murray Rae   11

2
THE PROBLEM OF 'HISTORY'
IN RECENT THEOLOGICAL COMMENTARY
   Seth Heringer   26

3
THEOLOGICAL INTERPRETATION OF SCRIPTURE
IN SERMONIC MODE: THE CASE OF T.F. TORRANCE
   Myk Habets   43

4
INTERPRETING THE BIBLE ON LANGUAGE:
BABEL AND RICOEUR'S INTERPRETIVE ARC
   Allan Bell   70

5
THE ASCENT OF THEOLOGICAL READING:
ICONOCLASM AND THE DIVINE EVENT OF MAKING READERS
   John C. McDowell   94

6
LEX ORANDI, LEX VIVENDI: A THEOLOGICAL INTERPRETATION
OF DISCIPLESHIP IN THE GOSPEL OF MATTHEW
   Marianne Meye Thompson   114

7
'HE ASCENDED INTO HEAVEN':
JESUS' ASCENSION IN LUKAN PERSPECTIVE, AND BEYOND
   Joel B. Green   130

8
THE ANABAPTIST VISION OF THE CHURCH AND FAITH
IN THE EPISTLE TO THE HEBREWS
   Matthew C. Easter   151

9
1 TIMOTHY 3.16 AS A PROTO-RULE OF FAITH
   Paul Trebilco   170

10
'EXEGESIS AS LOVE':
ENCOUNTERING TRUTH IN JOHN 14.15-26
   Tim Meadowcroft   191

11
THEOLOGICAL INTERPRETATION AND THE BOOK OF LAMENTATIONS:
A POLYPHONIC RECONSIDERATION
   Miriam J. Bier   204

12
HISTORY, HERMENEUTICS, AND THEODICY IN LIGHT
OF ISRAEL'S TRADITION OF PROTEST
   James E. Harding   223

13
RESPONSE: THEOLOGICAL INTERPRETATION ON DISPLAY:
TRAJECTORIES AND QUESTIONS
   Joel B. Green   253

14
RESPONSE: READING AS FORMATION
   Murray Rae   258

Bibliography   263
Index of References   285
Index of Authors   292

Acknowledgments

This volume of essays, *Ears That Hear*, had its genesis in a colloquium on the theological interpretation of Scripture, held at Laidlaw College, Auckland, New Zealand, in August 2011. Apart from the commissioned essays by Marianne Meye Thompson and Paul Trebilco, each of the contributions herein arose in response to the theme of the colloquium. We are grateful to the contributors to this volume of essays, but also to all who presented material and engaged with the topic at the colloquium. The occasion was sponsored by the Laidlaw–Carey Graduate School of Theology in Auckland and the Department of Theology and Religion at the University of Otago, Dunedin. Murray Rae and Joel Green led the colloquium as keynote speakers, and now as respondents as well as contributors in this collection. Our thanks go to the sponsoring institutions and to Rae and Green for their support both of the colloquium and of the subsequent publication. We note also with gratitude the work of Benjamin Lappenga on the bibliography and Timothy Reardon on the indices. The editors also acknowledge with thanks the publishers, Sheffield Phoenix Press, and in particular David Clines for his response to our publication. We offer this collection as a contribution to the ongoing task of the theological interpretation of Scripture.

The Editors
September 2012

ABBREVIATIONS

I. *General Abbreviations*

ch(s).	chapter(s)
ed(s).	editor(s); edited by
edn	edition
ET	English translation
HB	Hebrew Bible
NS	New Series
NT	New Testament
OT	Old Testament
p(p).	page(s)
rev.	revised; revised by
trans.	translated
vol(s).	volume(s)

II. *Modern Literature*

AB	Anchor Bible
ABD	David Noel Freedman (ed.), *The Anchor Bible Dictionary* (6 vols.; New York: Doubleday, 1992).
AbNTC	Abingdon New Testament Commentary
ABR	*Australian Biblical Review*
AcBib	Academia Biblica
ACW	Ancient Christian Writers
AJL	*Australian Journal of Liturgy*
ANF	Ante-Nicene Fathers
ANRW	H. Temporini and W. Haase (eds.), *Aufstieg und Niedergang der römischen Welt: Geschichte und Kultur Roms im Spiegel der neueren Forschung* (Berlin: de Gruyter, 1972–).
ANTC	Augsburg New Testament Commentary
AsTJ	*Asbury Theological Journal*
BCOTWP	Baker Commentary on the Old Testament Wisdom and Psalms
BDAG	Walter Bauer, *et al*. *A Greek–English Lexicon of the New Testament and Other Early Christian Literature*, 3rd ed., rev. and ed. Frederick William Danker (Chicago: University of Chicago Press, 2001).
BETL	Bibliotheca ephemeridum theologicarum lovaniensium
BI	*Biblical Interpretation*
BIS	Biblical Interpretation Series
BHS	*Biblia hebraica stuttgartensia*
BK	*Bibel und Kirche*
BNTC	Black's New Testament Commentary

BSac	*Bibliotheca sacra*
BSTBT	Bible Speaks Today, Bible Themes Series
BT	*The Bible Translator*
BTB	*Biblical Theology Bulletin*
BTCB	Brazos Theological Commentary on the Bible
BZNW	Beihefte zur Zeitschrift für die neutestamentliche Wissenschaft
CBQ	*Catholic Biblical Quarterly*
CCSS	Catholic Commentary on Sacred Scripture
CIT	Current Issues in Theology
CSEL	Corpus scriptorum ecclesiasticorum latinorum
CTJ	*Calvin Theological Journal*
ECC	Eerdmans Critical Commentary
ESV	English Standard Version
ExAud	*Ex auditu*
ExpTim	*Expository Times*
GPBS	Global Perspectives on Biblical Scholarship
HNT	Handbuch zum Neuen Testament
HTR	*Harvard Theological Review*
HvTSt	*Hervormde teologiese studies*
IBS	*Irish Biblical Studies*
ICC	International Critical Commentary
IJST	*International Journal of Systematic Theology*
Int	*Interpretation*
ITC	International Theological Commentary
ITQ	*Irish Theological Quarterly*
JBL	*Journal of Biblical Literature*
JETS	*Journal of the Evangelical Theological Society*
JPS	Jewish Publication Society
JPTSup	Journal of Pentecostal Theology Supplement Series
JR	*Journal of Religion*
JSNT	*Journal for the Study of the New Testament*
JSNTSup	*Journal for the Study of the New Testament Supplement Series*
JSOT	*Journal for the Study of the Old Testament*
JSOTSup	Journal for the Study of the Old Testament Supplement Series
JTI	*Journal of Theological Interpretation*
JU	Judentum und Unwelt
KEK	Kritisch-exegetischer Kommentar über das Neue Testament (Meyer-Kommentar)
KJV	King James Version
LCC	Library of Christian Classics
LHB/OTS	Library of Hebrew Bible/Old Testament Studies
MM	James Hope Moulton and George Milligan, *The Vocabulary of the Greek Testament* (Grand Rapids: Eerdmans, 1963).
NABC	The New American Bible Commentary
NASB	New American Standard Bible
NCB	New Century Bible
NDT	S.B. Ferguson and D.F. Wright (eds.), *New Dictionary of Theology* (Leicester: Inter-Varsity Press, 1988).

NEB	New English Bible
NET	New English Translation
NETS	New English Translation of the Septuagint
NIBC	New International Biblical Commentary
NICNT	New International Commentary on the New Testament
NIDOTTE	Willem A. VanGemeren (ed.), *New International Dictionary of Old Testament Theology and Exegesis* (5 vols.; Carlisle: Paternoster, and Grand Rapids: Zondervan, 1997).
NIGTC	New International Greek Testament Commentary
NIV	New International Version
NJB	New Jerusalem Bible
NJPS	New Jewish Publication Society Translation
NovT	*Novum Testamentum*
NovTSup	Novum Testamentum Supplements
$NPNF^2$	Nicene and Post-Nicene Fathers, Series 2
NRSV	New Revised Standard Version
NRTh	*La nouvelle revue théologique*
NTG	New Testament Guides
NTL	New Testament Library
NTS	*New Testament Studies*
OGIS	*Orientis graeci inscriptiones selectae*
OTG	Old Testament Guides
OTL	Old Testament Library
PNTC	Pelican New Testament Commentaries
PRSt	*Perspectives in Religious Studies*
PTMS	Pittsburgh Theological Monograph Series
QR	*Quarterly Review*
RevistB	*Revista bíblica*
RB	*Revue biblique*
RSV	Revised Standard Version
SANT	Studien zum Alten und Neuen Testament
SemeiaSt	Semeia Studies
SBL	Society of Biblical Literature
SBLDS	Society of Biblical Literature Dissertation Series
SBLSymS	Society of Biblical Literature Symposium Series
SBT	Studies in Biblical Theology
SJT	*Scottish Journal of Theology*
SNTSMS	Society for New Testament Studies Monograph Series
SP	Sacra pagina
STL	Studia theologica lundensia
TDNT	Gerhard Kittel and Gerhard Friedrich (eds.), *Theological Dictionary of the New Testament* (G. W. Bromiley [trans.]; 10 vols.; Grand Rapids: Eerdmans, 1964–1976).
THNTC	Two Horizons New Testament Commentary
THOTC	Two Horizons Old Testament Commentary
TJ	*Trinity Journal*
TPI	Trinity Press International
TynBul	*Tyndale Bulletin*

VT	*Vetus Testamentum*
VTSup	*Vetus Testamentum*, Supplements
WBC	Word Biblical Commentary
WestBC	Westminster Bible Companion
WTJ	*Westminster Theological Journal*
WUNT	Wissenschaftliche Untersuchungen zum Neuen Testament
ZAW	*Zeitschrift für die alttestamentliche Wissenschaft*
ZNW	*Zeitschrift für die neutestamentliche Wissenschaft*

III. *Ancient Literature*
Pseudepigrapha

1 En.	*1 (Ethiopic) Enoch*
2 Bar.	*2 (Syriac) Baruch [= Apocalypse of Baruch]*
3 Macc.	*3 Maccabees*
Jub.	*Jubilees*
Pss. Sol.	*Psalms of Solomon*

Other Early Jewish and Christian Literature

Acts Pet.	*Acts of Peter*
Ap. Jas.	*Apocryphon of James*
b. Shabb.	Babylonian Talmud, *Shabbat*
Barn.	*Barnabas*
Did.	*Didache*
Ep. apost.	*Epistula apostolorum*
Gos. Pet.	*Gospel of Peter*
Ignatius, *Phld.*	Ignatius, *Letter to the Philadelphians*
Ignatius, *Smyrn.*	Ignatius, *Letter to the Smyrnaeans*
Irenaeus, *Adv. haer.*	*Adversus haereses* (*Against Heresies*)

LIST OF CONTRIBUTORS

Allan Bell is Professor of Language and Communication, and Director of the Institute of Culture, Discourse and Communication at Auckland University of Technology, Auckland, New Zealand. He has held research appointments at a number of international and New Zealand universities. His contributions in language and communication include the Audience Design theory of style, and pioneering work on media language and discourse, and on New Zealand English. His research interests cover biblical discourse, media discourse, New Zealand languages, language style and social and linguistic aspects of the internet. He has published many papers and authored or co-edited six books, including *The Language of News Media* (Blackwell, 1991), *Approaches to Media Discourse* (co-authored, Blackwell, 1998) and *Languages of New Zealand* (co-edited, Victoria University Press, 2005). He is co-founder and editor of the international quarterly *Journal of Sociolinguistics*.

Miriam Bier, a recent graduate of the University of Otago, is now Lecturer in Old Testament, London School of Theology, London. Her research interests include Lamentations, feminist and evangelical readings of Old Testament texts, and dialogic and theological hermeneutics. Her publications include 'Colliding Contexts: Reading Tamar (2 Sam 13:1-22) as a 21st Century Woman' in *Tamar's Tears* (Pickwick, 2011), and 'Is There a God in This Text? Violence, Absence, and Silence in 2 Samuel 13:1-22' in *Reconsidering God and Gender* (Pickwick, 2010). She is currently co-editing a collection of essays on the theology and practice of lament (Wipf & Stock, forthcoming).

Matthew Easter recently completed a doctoral thesis entitled '"Let Us Go to Him": The Story of Faith and the Faithfulness of Jesus in Hebrews' in the Department of Theology and Religion, University of Otago, Dunedin, New Zealand. He is currently Adjunct Professor of Bible, Missouri Baptist University, St Louis, Missouri, and Small Groups Pastor, Canaan Baptist Church, St Louis. His publications include '"Certainly this Man was Righteous": Highlighting a Messianic Reading of the Centurion's Confession in Luke 23:47' (in *Tyndale Bulletin*, 2012) and 'The *Pistis Christou* Debate: Main Arguments and Responses in Summary' (in *Currents in Biblical Research*, 2010).

Joel B. Green is Associate Dean for the Center for Advanced Theological Studies and Professor of New Testament Interpretation, Fuller Theological Seminary, Pasadena, California. His research and writing have focused especially on Luke–Acts, the interface of science and theology, and theological interpretation of Christian Scripture. He has authored or edited more than thirty-five books, including most recently *Practicing Theological Interpretation* (Baker Academic, 2011) and *Wesley, Wesleyans, and Reading Bible as Scripture* (Baylor University Press, 2012). He is also the editor of the New International Commentary on the New Testament (Eerdmans), co-editor of Studies in Theological Interpretation (Baker Academic) and of the Two Horizons Commentary on the New Testament (Eerdmans), and editor-in-chief of the *Journal of Theological Interpretation*. He is an ordained elder in The United Methodist Church.

Myk Habets is Lecturer in Systematic Theology and Head of Carey Graduate School, Carey Baptist College, Auckland, New Zealand. He has published a number of articles and edited collections on the Trinity, pneumatology, Christology, Reformed Theology, the theology of Thomas F. Torrance, and theological ethics. His books include *Theosis in the Theology of Thomas Torrance* (Ashgate, 2009) and *The Anointed Son* (Pickwick, 2010); among his edited works is a co-edited volume on *Evangelical Calvinism* (Pickwick, 2012). He is currently working on a volume of essays on the theology of Torrance, and editing a set of ecumenical perspectives on the *filioque* for T. & T. Clark. He is registered as a Minister of the Baptist Churches of New Zealand.

James E. Harding is Senior Lecturer in Hebrew Bible/Old Testament Studies, Department of Theology and Religion, University of Otago, Dunedin, New Zealand, where he has taught since 2003. His research has been primarily on the Qumran scrolls and the book of Job, but he has also recently completed a major monograph on the David and Jonathan narrative, *The Love of David and Jonathan* (Equinox, 2012). He is one of the founding editors of the journal *Relegere*, as well as serving on the editorial board of the Library of Hebrew Bible/Old Testament Studies Monograph Series. He is an Anglican priest in the Diocese of Dunedin.

Seth Heringer is a doctoral candidate at Fuller Theological Seminary, Pasadena, California, where he is researching a theological understanding of historiography. His publications include 'The Practice of Theological Commentary' (in *Journal of Theological Interpretation*, 2010) and 'Forgetting the Power of Leaven: The Historical Method in Recent New Testament Theology' (forthcoming in *Scottish Journal of Theology*). He currently serves as an Adjunct Professor in the Theology Department of Fuller Theological Seminary and in the Biblical Studies Department of Azusa Pacific University.

John C. McDowell has been the Morpeth Chair of Theology and Religious Studies since 2009 at the University of Newcastle, New South Wales, Australia. Among other publications, he is the author of *Hope in Barth's Eschatology: Interrogations and Transformations beyond Tragedy* (Ashgate, 2000) and *The Gospel according to Star Wars* (Westminster John Knox, 2007). He has edited *Philosophy and the Burden of Theological Honesty: A Donald MacKinnon Reader* (T. & T. Clark, 2011), and co-edited *Conversing with Barth* (Ashgate, 2004).

Tim Meadowcroft is Senior Lecturer in Biblical Studies and currently Head of School: Theology, Mission and Ministry, Laidlaw College, Auckland, New Zealand. His research is focused on biblical texts of the Second Temple period and hermeneutical questions, on both of which he has written and edited extensively. Apart from a range of articles, his recent publications include the Readings commentary on *Haggai* (Sheffield Phoenix, 2006) and *The Message of the Word of God* (Inter-Varsity Press, 2011) in the Biblical Themes series. He has also co-edited and contributed to a volume entitled *Gospel, Truth, and Interpretation: Evangelical Identity in Aotearoa New Zealand* (Archer, 2011). He is an honorary priest assistant in the Anglican Diocese of Auckland.

Murray Rae is Professor of Theology at the University of Otago and Head of the Department of Theology and Religion, where he teaches courses in Systematic Theology and Ethics. His research interests include the work of Søren Kierkegaard, theological hermeneutics, Māori engagements with Christianity, and theology and the built environment. He is editor of the Journal of Theological Interpretation Supplement Series. His publications include *Kierkegaard's Vision of the Incarnation* (Clarendon, 1997), *History and Hermeneutics* (T. & T. Clark, 2005) and *Kierkegaard and Theology* (Continuum, 2010). He is an ordained minister of the Presbyterian Church (NZ).

Marianne Meye Thompson is the George Eldon Ladd Professor of New Testament at Fuller Theological Seminary, Pasadena, California. She is author of a commentary on *Colossians and Philemon* (Two Horizons New Testament Commentary; Eerdmans, 2005), *The God of the Gospel of John* (Eerdmans, 2001), and *The Promise of the Father* (Westminster John Knox, 2000), and co-author of *Introducing the New Testament* (Eerdmans, 2001).

She has also published numerous articles and reviews in scholarly journals and various volumes focusing particularly on God, Jesus, the Gospels, and the Gospel of John. She is currently working on a commentary on the Gospel of John for Westminster John Knox Press. She is an ordained minister of the Presbyterian Church (USA).

Paul Trebilco is Professor of New Testament in the Department of Theology and Religion at the University of Otago, Dunedin, New Zealand. His research has focused on Jewish and Christian groups in Western Asia Minor, on the Pastoral Epistles and the Johannine Literature, and on issues related to the development of early Christian theology and identity. His publications include *Jewish Communities in Asia Minor* (Cambridge University Press, 1991), *The Early Christians in Ephesus from Paul to Ignatius* (Mohr Siebeck, 2004; paperback Eerdmans, 2007), *1 Timothy* (co-authored, Asia Theological Association, 2006), *2 Timothy and Titus* (co-authored, Asia Theological Association, 2009), and *Self-Designations and Group Identity in the New Testament* (Cambridge University Press, 2012). He is also General Editor of the Society for New Testament Studies Monograph Series, published by Cambridge University Press. He is an ordained minister of the Methodist Church of New Zealand.

INTRODUCTION:
AN INTERPRETIVE CONVERSATION

Tim Meadowcroft

There is a growing corpus of material that seeks consciously to do and/or to think about doing theological interpretation of the Bible.[1] Consider, for example, the *Journal of Theological Interpretation*, in its sixth year of production at time of writing, or the introductory volume edited by Kevin Vanhoozer.[2] These are supplemented by a range of other works that with varying degrees of intentionality make an attempt on 'theological interpretation'.[3] This volume of essays is a further contribution to that growing corpus. The cautious denotation in the book's subtitle of this set of essays as 'explorations in...' indicates, however, an awareness that we write into a debate and context in which a clear consensus or set of literary or methodological characteristics has not yet emerged. This collection is, in that respect, a contribution to a process of emergence. Accordingly, in this introduction I propose to do three things: (1) to expand on my comment above about the debate and context with an overview of what seems to me to be happening under the rubric of 'theological interpretation';[4] (2) to affirm the importance

---

1. I use the phrases 'interpretation of the Bible' and 'interpretation of Scripture' interchangeably, while recognizing that one is more focused on the body of literature being interpreted—interpretation of the *Bible*—while the other is a little more interested in the process being undertaken—*interpretation* of Scripture.

2. K.J. Vanhoozer (ed.), *Dictionary for Theological Interpretation of the Bible* (Grand Rapids: Baker Academic, 2005). From a slightly different tack, see also E.F. Davis and R.B. Hays (eds.), *The Art of Reading Scripture* (Grand Rapids: Eerdmans, 2003), an outcome of the Scripture Project based at the Center of Theological Inquiry in Princeton.

3. See for example D.J. Treier, *Introducing Theological Interpretation of Scripture: Recovering a Christian Practice* (Grand Rapids: Baker Academic, 2008); R.W.L. Moberly, 'What Is Theological Interpretation of Scripture', *JTI* 3 (2009), pp. 161-78.

4. My survey is idiosyncratic rather than exhaustive, but nevertheless I hope is roughly representative of the state of affairs. I am not including the study of the doctrine of Scripture in this survey, although that theological task is clearly an important companion to theological interpretation. See below on Webster and the *viva vox Dei*.

of the exploratory enterprise by making a tentative proposal of my own, as to what might be the key elements in a theological interpretive conversation; and (3), in concluding, to locate the contents of this monograph into the landscape of theological interpretation now and as it may become.

Theological Interpretation

Perspective or Method?

A number of questions continue to rumble around the practise and theory of 'theological interpretation'. A key one asks whether it may properly be spoken of as a methodology. Generally speaking, practitioners and theorizers steer clear of methodological claims concerning theological interpretation, although it is occasionally referred to as a model.[5] Mostly, though, it is conceived of as a mindset or perspective or approach to Scripture.[6] Caution around making methodological claims for theological interpretation reflects the possibility that any such claims have the potential to create an unresolveable tension between the aim of interpreting Scripture in its own theological and literary terms, and the possibility that any methodology of interpretation is capable of creating an interpretive straitjacket, which then inhibits the possibility of the reader hearing the voice of God in Scripture (on which see further below). That is why practitioners prefer to think in terms of perspective or approach rather than method.

This does not mean, however, that there is no place for methodological comment, in that a theological perspective on the interpretation of Scripture is likely to develop a range of methodological preferences in the service of the reading goal of hearing the voice of God. And these need to be thought about and assessed. The ongoing challenge to any attempt at theological interpretation, of course, is that preferences become biases, which in their turn inhibit rather than amplify the voice of God in Scripture. Methodological comment in the context of theological interpretation is therefore important.

Reading the Bible as a Theological Source Book

Below that global comment, however, there are a range of practises that could claim to be theological interpretation. The first of these that I would identify is an approach that seeks to identify the theological truths—truths

---

5. See for example S.E. Fowl, *Engaging Scripture: A Model for Theological Interpretation* (Eugene, OR: Wipf & Stock, 2009).

6. A number of works could be referenced, but this point emerges particularly strongly in the opening chapter by Murray Rae in this volume; and see Moberly, 'Theological Interpretation', pp. 169-75.

about God—that may be found in the reading of particular texts.[7] While it is true that the Bible is about God (!), any reading of Scripture undertaken with a view to knowing more about God is to be commended. But to call that enterprise 'theological interpretation' hardly advances the matter. For one thing, it is self-evident to any faith-oriented reading of Scripture. For another, it does not make a meaningful differentiation from the traditional task of Old and New Testament Theology. But, more importantly, it does not recognize that there is a difference between knowing about God and encountering the voice of God.[8] Furthermore, it does not comment sufficiently on how the medium and nature of Scripture might affect the manner in which Scripture is interpreted. In other words, it does not answer the question that continues to keep the proponents of the theological reading of Scripture awake at night: how might the fact that this is a body of texts which presents itself as one within which we expect in a unique way to hear the voice of God, impact the way we handle that text?[9]

Thematic Approaches
A closely related, but not identical, approach is to read Scripture in order to filter out what are felt to be the key theological terms and concepts present in particular texts. This is a valid and important exercise, without which any commentary on Scripture is incomplete. But to present it as 'theological interpretation' is problematic in that it is not clear what such readings may be doing that any number of Old and New Testament introductions have not done before. Notwithstanding the excellent programmatic remarks by Kevin Vanhoozer prefacing his introduction to theological interpretation,[10] this is a criticism that I think may fairly be levelled at some of the contributions within that volume.[11] It could be that the very format of a book-by-book

7. This is what appears to be argued, albeit in a highly nuanced way, by J.E. Goldingay, 'The God of Grace and Truth', in M.A. Rae, J.E. Goldingay, C.J.H. Wright, R.W. Wall, and K. Greene-McCreight, 'Christ in/and the Old Testament', *JTI* 2 (2008), pp. 7-11. For Goldingay, 'Reading the OT Christologically…enables us to see aspects of what is there in the way the OT talks about God that we might otherwise miss' (p. 10).
8. In that respect, K.J. Vanhoozer, 'Introduction: What Is Theological Interpretation of the Bible?', in Vanhoozer (ed.), *Dictionary for Theological Interpretation of the Bible*, p. 24, does not go far enough when he says: 'Theological interpretation…is biblical interpretation oriented to the knowledge of God'.
9. This subsection has revealed the assumption that pervades this introductory essay, namely, that theological interpretation of Scripture is interpretation that expects to hear the voice of God. For an extended argument in this direction, see T.J. Meadowcroft, *The Message of the Word of God: The Glory of God Made Known* (BSTBT; Leicester: Inter-Varsity Press, 2011).
10. Vanhoozer, 'Introduction'.
11. See T.J. Meadowcroft, review of K.J. Vanhoozer (ed.), *Theological Interpretation of the Old Testament: A Book-by-Book Survey* (Grand Rapids: Eerdmans,

approach tends towards a thematic and militates against a genuinely theological reading, for it is a characteristic of theological interpretation that it must be free to range beyond the immediate texts that are taken as starting points of reading.

It also, no doubt unintentionally, does not quite read Scripture on its own literary terms. For it still carries with it a trace of the older propositionalist approaches characterized by such neo-evangelical authors as Carl Henry,[12] for whom the task of interpretation was to distil the propositions carried by the narrative. What theological approaches to the interpretation of Scripture have in common is a determination to read the text in its own terms. If that text is primarily cast in a narrative mode, as is arguably the case, exclusively thematic approaches ultimately become ironic denials of the literary nature of the Bible.[13]

Christological Approaches
In that light, a theological reading of Scripture is one that takes into account the self-perception of Scripture that it conveys and signposts the living voice of God, and attempts to read and interpret in those terms.[14] In doing so, it takes into account both the texts themselves and the form in which they are couched. Apart from the brief allusion above to narrative form, which is beyond the scope of this reflection, the form of Scripture has a theological coherence around the expectation that God continues to speak in Scripture. Accordingly, a theological reading will both read on that basis and allow the manner of reading to reflect that expectation. In that respect, such readings are more complete responses to the theological challenge than are the more thematic approaches.

Three types of readings in particular may be highlighted. The first is what might be called christological readings, and a notable case in point is the

---

2008), *Colloquium* 41 (2009), pp. 223-25. This is a review of material duplicated from the *Dictionary for Theological Interpretation of the Bible*.

12. For a critique of which, see M. Habets, 'Beyond Henry's Nominalism and Evangelical Foundationalism: Thomas Torrance's Theological Realism', in T.J. Meadowcroft and M. Habets (eds.), *Gospel, Truth, and Interpretation: Evangelical Identity in Aotearoa New Zealand* (Auckland: Archer, 2011), pp. 206-208.

13. Note the link drawn between narrative and theological appreciation by R.B. Hays, 'Can Narrative Criticism Recover the Theological Unity of Scripture?', *JTI* 2 (2008), pp. 193-212.

14. There is a fine distinction between 'reading' and 'interpretation'. In one sense all reading is interpretation, although to speak of 'interpretation' is to speak of a greater intentionality around discerning meaning and implication. In this essay, I use 'interpretation' of that intentional process as distinct from 'reading', while at the same time assuming that interpretation is included in my comments on reading.

work by Murray Rae in his *History and Hermeneutics*.[15] I return to this work below, but note at this point that it assumes that the Bible—both Old and New Testaments—is fundamentally a witness to the life and significance of Jesus. Therefore all of Scripture is read in light of what is made know to us of God in Christ, including and perhaps especially his incarnation, suffering and resurrection. As well as impacting the meaning that emerges from reading, this also has an epistemological effect on how one reads.[16] As one example and as the title of Rae's book suggests, historiography becomes informed by a christological reading of the Bible in that the modernist parking of the resurrection into a separate, non-historical category of event is simply unsustainable when the resurrection is seen as the key to history. Such a theological approach to the Bible is much more than an extraction of what we may know about Jesus and the God revealed in Jesus from Scripture; it also informs the assumptions that are brought to the reading.

Trinitarian Approaches
In the context of this discussion, trinitarian approaches to interpretation of Scripture need not be distinguished from the christological, except perhaps as a point of emphasis. The centrality of Christ is supplemented by the broader emphasis already mentioned that the Bible has to do with encountering God, as understood in various trinitarian formulations.[17] Of particular interest to me, though, is the reminder made by trinitarian approaches that a theological reading—a reading undertaken that is informed by God and expectation of encountering God—must have a strong pneumatological element. The Holy Spirit is present in the Scriptures themselves and in each

---

15. M.A. Rae, *History and Hermeneutics* (London: T. & T. Clark, 2005).

16. For an early hint on this aspect of theological interpretation, see W. Vischer, *The Witness of the Old Testament to Christ*. I. *The Pentateuch* (trans. A.B. Crabtree; London: Lutterworth Press, 1949), p. 14: 'In their fleshliness, in their temporal contingency and historical fortuitousness, the writings of the Old and New Testament bear witness to the incarnation'. N.T. Wright, 'Resurrection: From Theology to Music and Back Again', in J. Begbie (ed.), *Sounding the Depths: Theology through the Arts* (London: SCM Press, 2002), pp. 207-208, draws a more explicit epistemological link: 'I…cautiously agree with those theologians who have insisted that the resurrection, if true, must become not only the corner-stone of *what* we know but also the key to *how* we know things, the foundation of all our knowing, the starting point for a Christian epistemology' (emphasis original).

17. See for example D.W. Congdon, 'The Trinitarian Shape of πίστις: A Theological Exegesis of Galatians', *JTI* 2 (2008), pp. 231-58, a study undertaken in conversation with the Christology of Barth and Hays. Congdon argues 'that the trinitarian shape of faith in Galatians confirms the christological insights of both Hays and Barth while at the same time providing a more robust account of divine agency that clarifies the relation between the christological and the anthropological' (p. 239).

part of the process between their writing and their taking up residence as the voice of God in the heart and mind of the believing reader.[18]

The Regula fidei *Tradition*

Another approach or set of approaches to theological interpretation is to look behind the Western epistemology of doubt explicitly challenged by christological readings to the earliest understandings of the nature of Scripture and the means of its interpretation. This is a self-conscious perspective in that it is intentional about the importance of the historical task of recovering early interpretations and understanding well the mindset behind them.[19] It is a quite explicit attempt to recover and apply what came in the early church to be known as the *regula fidei*, or the 'rule of faith'.[20] It is saying that the guiding truths for which the early church fathers and the councils struggled over the first five to eight centuries of our era should be reprised in the contemporary enterprise of encountering God in Scripture.

Implicit and explicit in this approach is the proposition that the 'rule of faith' that emerged in the early church has much to teach contemporary readers of the Bible as we seek to shake off the shackles of several centuries of Enlightenment assumptions. Part of the argument goes further than that also to suggest that the interaction of early interpretation with the formation of the canon itself gives particular reason to pay close attention to the leadership of the 'rule of faith' in matters of interpretation. From a methodological perspective, notable within the 'rule of faith' is the notion of 'spiritual exegesis', which contributes to the presupposition with which this volume is working: that the Bible is read in order that the voice of God may be heard.[21]

Beyond the more particular, even specialist, attempt to recapture the 'rule of faith' of the early church for interpretation today, is the more general application of the notion of tradition—understood in its best sense—to reading and interpretation. This is the axiom, variously applied, that each of us reads out of a faith tradition that has been informed by Scripture and continues to guide the reading of Scripture. It is inevitable that this is the case, and

---

18. See for example M. Habets, 'Reading Scripture and Doing Theology with the Holy Spirit', in M. Habets (ed.), *The Spirit of Truth: Reading Scripture and Constructing Theology with the Holy Spirit* (Eugene, OR: Pickwick, 2010), pp. 89-106.

19. See for example Joel B. Green, *Practicing Theological Interpretation: Engaging Biblical Texts for Faith and Formation* (Grand Rapids: Baker Academic, 2011), pp. 71-98, who calls for 'the work of biblical interpretation [to be] placed in a dialectical relationship with Scripture that is mutually informative' (p. 97).

20. B. Demarest, 'Creeds', in *NDT*, pp. 179-80.

21. For a more contemporary expression of this idea, see the work cited by me in ch. 10 of this volume, C.C. Black, 'Exegesis as Prayer', *Princeton Seminary Bulletin* 23 NS (2002), pp. 131-45.

it is an important means by which to bring a spiritual and theological cohesion to our 'spiritual exegesis' of the word of God encountered in the Bible. I return to this below.

A Theological Conversation

In light of the range of practices that jostle for ownership of the rubric 'theological interpretation of the Bible', I propose a four-way conversation, which may be thought of as structured in a particular way. I suggest that the necessary conditions for good theological interpretation of the Bible are most likely to be set in place when a conversation is maintained between (1) christological/trinitarian approaches and (2) the 'rule of faith' and/or a more general notion of tradition; when this is moderated by (3) a theology of Scripture as the *viva vox Dei*, the living voice of God; and when (4) a strong backdrop of methodological reflection is sustained, for the development of awareness of the natural intellectual handmaidens to reading to hear the voice of God.

For an idea of what that might look like I assume the fourth element—methodological consideration—but expand below on each of the first three in turn.

Christological/Trinitarian

First, one approach to the reading of Scripture theologically is to do so in the light of Christ, in whom is expressed all the fullness of God and to whom the Scriptures bear witness. As indicated above, Rae has articulated one form of this approach in his monograph on *History and Hermeneutics* and I am taking my lead from him. He writes,

> This is the point of the incarnational narrative. In the incarnate life of Jesus Christ, the Word of God and second person of the Trinity graces our history with his own presence, thus confirming its goodness, and showing it to be the medium through which God's loving purpose is worked out. In Jesus Christ, God's relation to the world takes the form of his becoming a subject within it.[22]

On this reasoning the culmination of the revelation of God to humanity is in the incarnation of God in Christ and in his death and resurrection. All else is understood in the light of that person and those events, for it is in them fully and finally that we see what God is like. All aspects of God's story are then read against an assumption of God's fundamental goodness and loving relatedness to God's creation, as demonstrated in the life and work of Jesus. Therefore it is in the light of that goodness and love that we are able to read theologically.

---

22. Rae, *History and Hermeneutics*, p. 59.

While the task of Scripture, then, is to bear witness to Christ, it is also the case that Scripture is read in the light of Christ. This potentially involves a theological critique of aspects of Scripture as part of the evolving story of God with respect to humanity and the cosmos. There are aspects of that story that need to be read as culturally conditioned and/or limited in perspective and so needing to be re-appreciated in some way. At the same time, it is necessary to work with an understanding of the Holy Spirit as active in ensuring that such a critique remains rooted in the God revealed in Christ. A christological reading needs also to be trinitarian. As it is so, it is able to bring the fresh voice of God to each generation of readers and reading context.

Tradition or 'rule of faith'

There is always a danger, however, that christological reading becomes hijacked by the human tendency to read a 'canon within a canon'. It is at this point that the notion of tradition—which may also incorporate the historical understanding of the 'rule of faith'—becomes useful. I am taking the use of tradition as broadly expressive of the idea that we read in the context of the church and may usefully and legitimately be guided by how the community of faith has read and interpreted, through the centuries and into the present. There are various ways of describing tradition, understanding its function and relating it to Scripture itself.[23] One is that of James McClendon, who focuses on particular creeds and statements that have punctuated the life of the church and which he describes as

> cairns, trail-marks that indicate where the people of God have been on their journey through time. In this sense they tell us how Scripture has been (then and there) read, and invite us to read it that way if we can.[24]

Tradition is valuable in that it draws the reader into a comprehensive reading community that helps to make sense of the Bible as it has been experienced over time. That in its turn lends a confidence that apprehensions of God in the reading of the text are not merely individual or idiosyncratic. At the same time, it offers broader insights that may not necessarily emerge simply with christological reading. As a matter of historical theology, it may also reintroduce broad assumptions about reading and interpretation that have become buried under the modernist context of the last few centuries.

---

23. For one fine, extended exploration of the value of tradition, see J. Pelikan, *The Vindication of Tradition* (New Haven, CT: Yale University Press, 1984).

24. J.W. McClendon, Jr, *Doctrine: Systematic Theology*, II (Nashville: Abingdon Press, 1994), pp. 470-71.

But McClendon goes on to caution against too heavy a reliance on tradition. In a similar vein, John Webster insists on a differentiation between 'Holy Scripture' and tradition in the sense that tradition can only be a hearing of Scripture and does not in any sense participate in the speaking of Scripture.[25] There is also a danger that theological tradition gives permission not to do the hard work of reading and interpreting into the questions of the present age, or even stultifies the attempt to do so. It is at that point that the fresh voice of Christ, who comes to complete the law—who says, 'you have heard that it was said...but I say to you' (Mt. 5.21)—must be allowed to question the tradition in which the reader stands.

Viva vox Dei, *The Living Voice of God*

If tradition can lead into too easy a disengagement from the questions of our age, so reading christologically may lead into too easy a jettisoning of aspects of God of which we do not approve. Both types of reading need to take place in conversation with one another. And the conversation is made possible by the presence of a third voice: a lively appreciation of the living word of God wherever in the Bible it is encountered. Accordingly, I assert with Webster in his reading of Bonhoeffer that 'Holy Scripture is the *viva vox Dei*, and that this living voice demands an attitude of ready submission and active compliance',[26] even at points, I suggest, where it is difficult or even indefensible to do so. There are voices within Scripture that strike discordant notes to our post-Christendom Western ears, but they too are part of the chorus of God. However difficult it might be, we are compelled to include them, and indeed are helped to include them as we listen for the living voice of God by reading in the light of God as revealed in Christ and in the light of the traditions that have shaped us.

Locating the Conversation

The following set of essays is but one example of what such a conversation might look like. It is a somewhat unformed and in some respects incomplete conversation at this point—an 'exploration' in fact. But all of the conversation partners identified above are present, and the non-prescriptive nature of the set of essays is at least reflective of the state of play with respect to scholarly reflection on the notion of the theological interpretation of the Bible. But this is also arguably reflective of the nature of the case when it comes to theological interpretation; it is never going to be tidy, and if it ever

---

25. J. Webster, *Holy Scripture: A Dogmatic Sketch* (CIT; Cambridge: Cambridge University Press, 2003), p. 51.
26. Webster, *Holy Scripture*, p. 80.

becomes so it is likely to have been captured by method at the cost of openness to the fresh wind of the Spirit of God informing the reading.

We find herein some methodological discussion, not only to rebut the hegemony of any one method, but also to consider the natural companions to theological reading. We find a steady turn to the christological in reading, as well as an openness to wider trinitarian influences in reading. We find also an intentional turn for guidance to early interpreters and the 'rule of faith' that they encapsulate, as well as a listening to how more contemporary readers of Scripture read constructively within a tradition. And we find all of this moderated by a regular listening to the (sometimes discordant) living voice of God, both for its own sake and for how it may instruct in more acute listening to that voice.

We invite the reader into the interpretive conversation.

1

THEOLOGICAL INTERPRETATION AND THE PROBLEM OF METHOD

Murray Rae

Engaging Scripture

Although there are many scholars today committed to the 'theological interpretation' of Scripture, the question, 'What is theological interpretation?' remains a matter of debate. The *Journal of Theological Interpretation*, for instance, ran an article in 2009 by Walter Moberley with the title 'What Is Theological Interpretation of Scripture?' suggesting, clearly, that there is still a need for clarification of what theological interpretation is.[1] Likewise, the question of how theological interpretation ought to be pursued is a subject of ongoing discussion and debate, so much so, in fact, that some have worried that those involved in promoting theological interpretation of Scripture talk rather too much about what theological interpretation is and about method without actually engaging with Scripture itself. A glance at the back issues of the *JTI* reveals a significant proportion of articles dealing with the question of how one might go about interpreting the Bible theologically but that do not themselves actually do it—or so it appears.[2] Along the same lines, a frequently heard criticism of John Webster's widely read book *Holy Scripture* is that Webster writes extensively about the nature of Scripture without actually engaging directly with the text of Scripture.[3] Walter Moberly makes this point in the *JTI* article I have mentioned, as does Richard Briggs in his recent book, *The Virtuous Reader*.[4]

---

1. Walter Moberly, 'What Is Theological Interpretation of Scripture?', *JTI* 3 (2009), pp. 161-78.
2. This observation is not meant as a criticism of the *JTI*. I am myself a member of the journal's editorial board and believe that its attention to methodological issues is timely and important.
3. John Webster, *Holy Scripture: A Dogmatic Sketch* (CIT; Cambridge: Cambridge University Press, 2003).
4. See Moberly, 'Theological Interpretation', pp. 169-70; Richard S. Briggs, *The Virtuous Reader: Old Testament Narrative and Interpretive Virtue* (Studies in Theological Interpretation; Grand Rapids: Baker Academic, 2010), pp. 168-70.

For myself, I prefer to frame the point as an observation rather than a criticism, for there is much in Webster's book and in the *JTI* itself that helps to clarify in a highly contested environment both what Scripture is and how we should read it, and does so in ways consistent with and informed by Scripture itself, albeit there is little direct engagement with Scripture's text. Like the *JTI* articles, Webster's book is profoundly reliant upon Scripture and engaged with it, but not in exegetical mode. Nevertheless, I intend in this chapter to take seriously the point that Moberly and Briggs have made and will attempt in what follows to develop an account of the nature and task of theological interpretation through direct engagement with the text of Scripture itself.

One further preliminary remark is in order before we begin that task. I take theological interpretation to be concerned above all with the self-communication of God through Scripture. Kevin Vanhoozer, in his 'Introduction' to the *Dictionary for Theological Interpretation of the Bible* puts it thus: 'Those who seek to interpret Scripture theologically want to hear the word of God in Scripture and hence to be transformed by the renewing of their minds ([Rom.] 12:2)'.[5] Accordingly, the theological interpreter of Scripture, whether a scholar or not, is one who reads Scripture in order to live by it.[6]

The Instruction to Listen!

With that statement of what we are about, let us begin. I do so with a familiar parable recorded in Mk 4.1-9 (NRSV here and throughout):

> [1]Again [Jesus] began to teach beside the sea. Such a very large crowd gathered around him that he got into a boat on the sea and sat there, while the whole crowd was beside the sea on the land. [2]He began to teach them many things in parables, and in his teaching he said to them: [3]'Listen! A sower went out to sow. [4]And as he sowed, some seed fell on the path, and the birds came and ate it up. [5]Other seed fell on rocky ground, where it did not have much soil, and it sprang up quickly, since it had no depth of soil. [6]And when the sun rose, it was scorched; and since it had no root, it withered away. [7]Other seed fell among thorns, and the thorns grew up and choked it, and it yielded no grain. [8]Other seed fell into good soil and brought forth grain, growing up and increasing and yielding thirty and sixty and a hundredfold.' [9]And he said, 'Let anyone with ears to hear listen!'

---

5. Kevin J. Vanhoozer (ed.), *Dictionary for Theological Interpretation of the Bible* (Grand Rapids: Baker Academic, 2005), p. 22.

6. I take the point from Henri de Lubac, 'Spiritual Understanding', in Stephen E. Fowl (ed.), *The Theological Interpretation of Scripture: Classical and Contemporary Readings* (Cambridge, MA: Blackwell, 1997), p. 16.

The audience, we are told, is 'a very large crowd'. We learn soon afterwards, in v. 10, that the twelve recently appointed disciples (3.13-19) were also present. That turns out to be important, as we will see. Jesus began to teach them 'many things in parables' (v. 2). And his teaching begins with an instruction: *Akouete*, 'Listen!' Jesus calls for careful attentiveness. I recommend that we take this instruction as a methodological proposal for the theological interpretation of Scripture.

Listen! That is not as easy as we might suppose. Those readers who have children will be familiar with the experience of telling one's children something that passes in one ear and out the other while leaving little trace on that part of their brain responsible for obedient or considered action. The sound waves have penetrated their ear canals but our children have not listened. This failing is not unique to children, of course. Inattention afflicts us all and manifests itself in numerous forms. It may be that we are simply oblivious to what is being said; our minds are somewhere else. Or it may be that we are sure we know already what a speaker wishes to convey. We 'run on ahead' in our minds presuming ourselves to have grasped the point already; but often, it turns out, we have taken the wrong road. A third form our inattention may take I will call, for want of a more elegant term, presuppositional clutter. We take in the words that we are hearing, but in our processing of them the sense gets distorted. Our prior certainties, beliefs, commitments get in the way of the new thing we are being told so that the new thing cannot do its work of transforming our minds. Instead, we transform the 'new thing' so that it fits our prior beliefs, our commitments, our supposed certainties. The new wine is poured into old wineskins—and is spoiled.

Given our human propensity not to listen, Jesus issues an instruction. To understand this little part of Scripture at least, this parable of the sower, we must listen. So the author requires. Whether the author of this instruction is Mark or Jesus himself need not concern us for the moment. Either way, the authority I appeal to in taking the instruction as a methodological proposal for theological interpretation is the Bible itself. The Bible itself calls for a particular kind of attention to the text.

The parable concludes by repeating and embellishing the instruction, 'Let anyone with ears to hear listen!' (v. 9). What does it mean to have ears to hear? At this point in the narrative we can only speculate, but we may surmise on the basis of the embellished instruction that listening is not a skill given to all. A proper hearing of the parable, and of the biblical text, requires a particular kind of listener—one with ears to hear! We will return later to the question of how one might become that kind of listener. Meanwhile let us focus our attention on the parable itself.

The Obscurity of Scripture

A sower went out to sow. 'And as he sowed, some seed fell on the path… other seed fell on rocky ground…' and so on. We who read the parable now are quick to identify the sower with Jesus and the seed with the word. The various hindrances to growth, likewise, are quickly identified with the cares of the world, the lure of wealth, barrenness of heart, the interference of Satan and so on. But none of these interpretations are supplied within the parable itself. They come later in vv. 13-20 when Jesus or Mark or the early church interprets the parable for us. The parable as it stands is rather enigmatic. Its meaning is far from obvious. Is the seed supposed to represent anything at all? Is the sower supposed to be identified with anyone in particular? Or might it be that the focus of Jesus' concern rests neither with the seed nor with the sower but with the abundance of the harvest, a harvest that is not threatened by the fact that some seed came to nothing, and a harvest for which, in the recent calling of the disciples, Jesus has now appointed his labourers? If that is the point, then it stands without the seed having to represent anything. It probably does require, however, that we understand Jesus or the Father or the Spirit, or all three, as the sower. But we do not know if that is intended or not. And the point only stands if the harvest is somehow representative of the kingdom, or of the fruitfulness of God's purposes. But we do not actually know that either. We stand with the crowd and with the twelve disciples as those summoned to listen, but if we set aside the interpretive accretions of tradition and place ourselves in the position of its first hearers, the parable is a puzzle. It does not give up its meaning straightforwardly at all.

The ambiguity of the parable taken by itself is illustrated by C.E.B Cranfield who, in his commentary on Mark's Gospel, lists five possible interpretations ventured by scholars. I will come later to the question of whether there might be some legitimacy in multiple interpretations, but for the meantime my purpose is simply to draw attention to the hermeneutical puzzle presented to us by the parable. The puzzle led Rudolf Bultmann to conclude that the original meaning of the parable can no longer be determined.[7] As it turns out, Bultmann is in good company for in v. 13 we are told that even the twelve disciples do not understand.

Faced with the parable as it stands there are some things the standard methods of biblical interpretation can help us with. Attention to historical context, for instance, yields the insight that the sower in the parable was following standard farming practice in Palestine at the time. It was not

---

7. See Rudolf Bultmann, *History of the Synoptic Problem* (trans. John Marsh; Oxford: Basil Blackwell, 1963), p. 200.

customary to till the ground first and confine one's sowing to the cultivated area. Rather the seed was sown along the beaten path, on thin soil with underlying rock, among thorns. Only after the sowing was the seed then ploughed in.⁸ So the sower in the parable was not being quite as careless as it might seem. I guess that Jesus' original audience would have understood that well enough but that knowledge, while interesting, apparently does not diminish to any significant degree their (or our) perplexity about the meaning of the parable. We may also discover, through careful attention to the Greek text, that there are nuances in the Greek that are lost in English translation.⁹ The Greek verb *epheren*, for instance, used to speak of the abundant harvest, indicates 'a continuous productivity which is repeated over and over'.¹⁰ Philological scholars can no doubt tell us whether there is an Aramaic expression conceivably used by Jesus that does the same trick. If so, then we may again suppose that the original audience readily understood this point. The continuing abundance of the harvest is interesting to be sure, and potentially important, if only we knew what the parable was about. Philological analysis, however, while potentially enhancing our understanding and appreciation of the parable, still cannot tell us, more fundamentally, what the parable is supposed to be about.

Further critical analysis of the context in which the parable appears in Mark's Gospel may at first glance make the problem worse. The parable is followed by a short pericope in which Jesus confirms that he speaks in parables precisely so that 'those outside' (v. 11) will not understand. In and of themselves, Jesus suggests, the parables are enigmatic, difficult to understand. According to the text, Jesus then provides an explanation of the parable for the disciples but biblical scholars commonly observe that the interpretation of the parable presented in vv. 13-19 probably does not come from Jesus himself but is the contribution either of Mark or of the early Christian church. That prompts the question whether the interpretation offered here is a legitimate interpretation or not of the parable teller's intent. We will come back to that matter below.

If readers, or hearers, now feel with respect to the interpretation of this parable that they have little clue as to its meaning, that seems to be just what Jesus intended. That realization brings us to vv. 10-12:

---

8. See, e.g., Eduard Schweizer, *The Good News according to Mark* (Atlanta: John Knox Press, 1970), p. 90.

9. Admittedly the present participles 'growing up' and 'increasing' preserve something of that continuous sense for us, but 'brought forth' does not capture the unfinished sense of the imperfect Greek verb.

10. Schweizer, *Mark*, p. 90.

> ¹⁰When [Jesus] was alone, those who were around him along with the twelve asked him about the parables. ¹¹And he said to them, 'To you has been given the secret of the kingdom of God, but for those outside, everything comes in parables; ¹²in order that "they may indeed look, but not perceive, and may indeed listen, but not understand; so that they may not turn again and be forgiven."'

Jesus suggests here that the parables are designed to confound at least 'those who are outside'. He makes the point by citing parts of Isa. 6.9-10. Thus in two places now—Isaiah and Mark—Scripture itself confirms that the word of the Lord is not perspicuous to all. Its meaning is not self-evident but is given only to some: to those who have ears to hear, and, more specifically in Mark's account, to those who have been given the secret of the kingdom.

Who Has 'Ears to Hear'?

Verses 10-11 suggest that the group to whom 'the secret of the kingdom' has been disclosed, and who, in time, will have ears to hear, comprises, specifically, those who were around him and the twelve, or, to qualify it further, those with whom he was alone, apart from the crowds. Mark's earlier references to this group indicate that they were those who, like Simon and Andrew, had left their nets to follow him (1.16-20), or who were like Levi who had left his tax booths to follow (2.13). Or, as in 3.13-14, they are those who answered his call to come to him, a group more extensive apparently than just the twelve. It is to these followers that the secret of the kingdom is given and to whom, before long, the meaning of the parable will also be given. Here we may venture a tentative answer to the question posed earlier about how one becomes a person with ears to hear. Mark's account of things, as it unfolds, suggests that one becomes a hearer of the word by also being a follower. I suggested earlier that we take the instruction to 'listen', to be attentive, as a methodological proposal for the theological interpretation of Scripture. On the basis of what we are discovering in Mark 4, I want to add now the further suggestion that listening be accompanied by following. However, the 'method' for theological interpretation here emerging is perhaps better described, as Richard Hays has done, as a set of practices, a set of practices involving faith, discipleship and obedience.[11] As Hays also points out, these practices are 'self-involving'. 'Interpreters who read the Bible theologically approach the text with an awareness that we are addressed and claimed by the word of God that is spoken in the text, and we understand ourselves to be answerable to that word.'[12] This position

---

11. See Richard B. Hays, 'Reading the Bible with Eyes of Faith: The Practice of Theological Exegesis', *JTI* 1 (2007), pp. 5-21.

12. Hays, 'Reading the Bible', p. 12.

contrasts with the scholarly prerogative to remain detached and uninvolved. One could say as a scholar that this is what the disciples or Mark or the early church believed, but it has nothing to do with me. Such a scholar could get tenure, gain promotion and become the editor of a prestigious scholarly journal of biblical studies. Theological interpretation, however, is concerned above all with what the text has to do with us. Or to put it more exactly, it is concerned with what God through the text has to say to us.

Let me tease out the logic of this a little further. Recall again Vanhoozer's contention that '[t]hose who seek to interpret Scripture theologically want to hear the word of God in Scripture and hence to be transformed by the renewing of their minds'. The point we have reached in our reading of Mark 4 is that those who have ears to hear are those who keep company with Jesus. Notice now that Jesus indicates to those around him that the secret of the kingdom has been given to them. In Mark, Jesus' public ministry begins with the announcement of the kingdom of God. The announcement that the kingdom of God has come near is the very first thing that Jesus says in Mark's Gospel (1.15) but the subsequent sayings and parables of Jesus that refer to the kingdom are enigmatic when taken on their own. They give a hint of what the kingdom may be like, but the only way to learn more of this kingdom is to become a participant in it. And that means, again, to become a follower of the one in and through whom the kingdom is brought near. Put another way, the content of the gospel is not a teaching, a philosophy or even a worldview. It is not a piece of sage advice that can be abstracted from the new form of life commended by Scripture itself. It is to be understood just insofar as the reader participates in the new reality of the kingdom of God brought about in and through Jesus himself. Accordingly, there is no way to understand this reality except from the inside. To those outside, Jesus says, everything comes in parables; in order that 'they may indeed look, but not perceive, and may indeed listen, but not understand; so that they may not turn again and be forgiven' (v. 12). In biblical terms, perception of the reality of the kingdom, a true understanding of things, and even forgiveness, are bound up with a new way of being, a transformation of our minds and hearts.

The same logic requires us to recognize that the theological interpretation of Scripture, hearing aright the word of God addressed to us through Scripture, likewise involves a new way of being. Although it may and should make use of scholarly techniques, theological interpretation is not itself a scholarly technique. That is to say, it is not a tool wielded by the scholar to gain mastery over the text. Theological interpretation is better conceived as a form of attentiveness in which we relinquish hermeneutical control and subject ourselves to the transforming power of the word. This entails, as Hays points out, that theological interpretation must be done 'from a posture of prayer and humility before the word'.[13] From this posture the valuable work of biblical scholarship is also likely to be transformed. It will no longer have use for certain presumptions about the detached objectivity of the reader, about the necessity to set faith aside, about the requirement that theological commitments have no place in the work of scholarship, or about the separation of academy and church. Theological interpreters of Scripture will conceive the work of biblical scholarship, suitably transformed, as an instance of *ministerium verbi divini*, service of the divine word.

The Teaching of the Lord

We come now, at last, to the interpretation of the parable of the sower. As yet, we have merely noted the puzzlement of those who first heard the parable, including those who were around Jesus along with the twelve. We have learned too that the secret of the kingdom and understanding of the parables is given only to those who keep company with Jesus. In Mark's account of things, however, understanding has not been given yet. Thus v. 13 continues, 'Do you not understand this parable? Then how will you understand all the parables?' For these twelve, and for those who were around Jesus, puzzlement at the parable of the sower has not yet been dispelled. There is a further step in the process of interpretation that has yet to take place. And so Jesus explains (vv. 14-20):

> [14]The sower sows the word. [15]These are the ones on the path where the word is sown: when they hear, Satan immediately comes and takes away the word that is sown in them. [16]And these are the ones sown on rocky ground: when they hear the word, they immediately receive it with joy. [17]But they have no root, and endure only for a while; then, when trouble or persecution arises on account of the word, immediately they fall away. [18]And others are those sown among the thorns: these are the ones who hear the word, [19]but the cares of the world, and the lure of wealth, and the desire for other things come in and choke the word, and it yields nothing. [20]And these are the ones sown on the good soil: they hear the word and accept it and bear fruit, thirty and sixty and a hundredfold.

It seems obvious to note here that the question, 'how will you understand all the parables?', is in fact answered by Jesus himself as he proceeds to interpret the parable for them. They will understand because Jesus tutors them. But this obvious point yields a crucial and perhaps surprising conclusion. Interpretation is not our job! Our task, in humility and in prayer, is to be attentive to the hermeneutical work of the one whose word Scripture is. Theological interpretation involves attentiveness as I have said, but it

---

13. Hays, 'Reading the Bible', p. 15.

requires us to be attentive not only to the text itself, but also to the interpretation of it given by the Lord. The exhortation to listen, I suggest, directs us not only to the ancient text, but also to the voice of the one who by the Spirit is present and communicative still. Karl Barth has put the matter thus:

> ...if Scripture as testimony to Jesus Christ is the Word of God...who then can expound Scripture but God himself? And what can man's exposition of it consist in but once more in an act of service, a faithful and attentive following after the exposition which Scripture desires to give itself, which Jesus Christ as Lord of Scripture wishes to give Himself?[14]

There is nothing new in this observation, forgetful of it though the modern academy has sometimes been. Barth is following the advice here of the Bible itself, as, for instance, in the Lord's promise, reported in John's Gospel, that,

> I still have many things to say to you, but you cannot bear them now. When the Spirit of truth comes, he will guide you into all the truth; for he will not speak on his own, but will speak whatever he hears, and he will declare to you the things that are to come. He will glorify me, because he will take what is mine and declare it to you. All that the Father has is mine. For this reason I said that he will take what is mine and declare it to you. (Jn 16.12-14)

The promised guidance of the Spirit was long held in Christian tradition, in the period we call 'premodern', to be the necessary condition for the understanding of Scripture. Through the tutoring of the Spirit, interpreters arrived at what was called the 'spiritual meaning', a meaning that is not divorced from the literal or historical meaning, but that, instead, properly illuminates the literal sense and historical reference of the text. Premodern readers typically believed too that the process of spiritual understanding, that is, the process of attentiveness to the Spirit was identical to the process of conversion. To put it as Augustine did, *Intellectus spiritualis credentem salvum facit* (Spiritual understanding saves the believer).[15]

Henri de Lubac explains,

> The Word of God, a living and effective word, acquires true fulfillment and total significance only by the transformation which it effects in the one who receives it. This is why the expression 'passing on to spiritual understanding' is equivalent to 'turning to Christ'—a conversion which can never be said to have been fully achieved.[16]

---

14. Karl Barth, *The Knowledge of God and the Service of God according to the Teaching of the Reformation* (London: Hodder & Stoughton, 1938), pp. 180-89, cited in Webster, *Holy Scripture*, p. 101.
15. Augustine, *In Psalmum 33*, sermon 1, n. 7, cited in de Lubac, 'Spiritual Understanding', p. 13.
16. De Lubac, 'Spiritual Understanding', p. 13.

De Lubac's observation coheres precisely with the portrayal of events that we have been following in Mark's Gospel. Unable to understand the parable of the sower when first they hear it, the disciples turn to Christ with the plea that its meaning may be disclosed. Those familiar with the Gospel of Mark will realize that the conversion of the disciples' hearts and minds remains a work in progress throughout the Gospel. Their conversion, as ours also, can never be said to have been fully achieved—at least until that day when the Son will hand over all things completed to the Father. Seeking transformation of their understanding, however, the disciples turn to Christ who proceeds to explain the parable.

'The sower sows the word,' Jesus begins. Familiar though this explanation is to us, it was by no means clear to the original hearers, as we have seen. If any of the crowd who listened to Jesus on the lakeshore got the point, we are not told so. We *are* told that the small circle of those around Jesus, including the twelve, did not get it. Their understanding is wholly dependent upon the Lord's explanation. The explanation, when it comes, supports, I suggest, my contention at the outset that the injunction to listen may be taken as a methodological proposal for the theological interpretation of Scripture. The explanation of this parable is, precisely, an explanation of the conditions under which the word may be rightly heard, an explanation both of what kind of hearers we need to be and of where true hermeneutical authority lies. Recall once more Vanhoozer's claim, 'Those who seek to interpret Scripture theologically want to hear the word of God in Scripture and hence to be transformed by the renewing of their minds....' In his explanation of the parable of the sower, Jesus makes clear what is involved in our doing just that. The process begins with listening, with attentiveness to the one who explains his word.

Jesus explains, however, that many obstacles lie in the way of a true hearing. Some seed falls on the path where it has no protection from the wiles of Satan (v. 15). For some hearers, apparently, the seed of the word fails to penetrate and makes no impact on them. For our purposes here, that point requires no further elaboration. There are those who hear or read the word, but remain disinterested, and unchanged. A second type of response is initially more promising.[17] The word falls on rocky ground and is received with joy. But on rocky ground it cannot take root and endures only for a while, but then when trouble or persecution arises on account of the word, immediately these hearers fall away (vv. 16-17). Effective hearing of the word requires deeper soil, a soil provided perhaps by the community of faith, a fledgling community in Jesus' own time and uncertain about its continuity with Israel, but identifiable nevertheless as 'those around him along with the

---

17. I follow here the reading of R.T. France, *The Gospel of Mark: A Commentary on the Greek Text* (Grand Rapids: Eerdmans, 2002), p. 205.

twelve' (v. 10). Contemporary readers of Scripture can now set their roots in a longer tradition and in the long established practice of gathering in the company of the triune God to receive the nourishment of sacrament and word.

With this in mind, advocates of the theological interpretation of Scripture consistently point out that such interpretation takes place first and foremost within the context of the church. Stephen Fowl's book, *Engaging Scripture*, for example, gives sustained attention to this theme, while Hays proposes that the first of twelve identifying marks of theological exegesis is that it is '*a practice of and for the church*'.[18] Similarly, fifteen scholars involved in the 'Scripture Project' at the Center of Theological Inquiry in Princeton from 1998–2002 included among 'nine theses on the interpretation of Scripture' the claim: 'Faithful interpretation of Scripture invites and presupposes participation in the community brought into being by God's redemptive action—the church'.[19] It is undoubtedly an extrapolation beyond the text of Mk 4.17 to suggest as I have done that the fertile ground in which the seed of the word can take root may be identified with the community brought into being by God's redemptive action, but the point seems well justified by the biblical record as a whole, and, as has already been observed, by the narrative setting of this parable in which Jesus gathers around him a community of disciples to whom the meaning of the parable is disclosed. It is worth pointing out in this regard that Mark's telling of the story preserves the possibility that there were some in the crowd, outside the community of disciples, who also had ears to hear. We are not told whether there were or not. I recommend as a matter of considerable importance however that the identification of the church as the *primary locus* of theological interpretation be stated in such a way that it not preclude the work of God's Spirit taking place also outside the church.[20] The Spirit blows where it wills!

We come in vv. 18-19 to the third category of the word and its hearers:

> [18]And others are those sown among the thorns: these are the ones who hear the word, [19]but the cares of the world, and the lure of wealth, and the desire for other things come in and choke the word, and it yields nothing.

---

18. Hays, 'Reading the Bible', p. 11 (italics original). The same point is made by many others including for instance Francis Watson, *Text, Church and World: Biblical Interpretation in Theological Perspective* (Edinburgh: T. & T. Clark, 1994), p. 3; Daniel J. Treier, *Introducing Theological Interpretation of Scripture: Recovering a Christian Practice* (Grand Rapids: Baker Academic, 2008); Joel B. Green, *Seized by Truth: Reading the Bible as Scripture* (Nashville: Abingdon Press, 2007).

19. See 'Nine Theses on the Interpretation of Scripture', in Ellen F. Davis and Richard B. Hays (eds.), *The Art of Reading Scripture* (Grand Rapids: Eerdmans, 2003), p. 3.

20. I am inclined therefore to modify slightly the cited theses of Hays and of the 'Scripture Project' so as to allow for this possibility.

Here we learn that a proper hearing of the word ought to yield something, something in contrast, apparently, with 'the cares of the world, the lure of wealth, and the desire for other things'. The point is confirmed in discussion of the fourth category of hearers who 'hear the word and accept it and bear fruit' (v. 20). The lesson to be learned here is that the process of hearing the word is not concluded with the announcement that we have understood. Nor could it be concluded with a complete statement of the findings of biblical scholarship, even were that statement correct in every detail. The process of hearing the word involves, *essentially*, the fruitfulness of faithful discipleship, enabled by the Spirit, and ever dependent upon divine forbearance and grace.

The argument I have been developing here is that the parable of the sower, along with its narrative setting and interpretation in Mark's Gospel, offers us an account of what is involved in hearing the word of the Lord that can serve also as a description of the task of theological interpretation. Theological interpretation involves attentiveness, not simply to the word of Scripture but to the self-communicative presence of the one whose word Scripture is. It requires also that we be a particular kind of people, a people participant in the community of faith, tutored by the Lord and transformed by his word. It involves discipleship, the day-to-day business of having our lives shaped by the redemptive word and work of God.

The Fruits of Theological Interpretation

Finally, theological interpretation involves fruitfulness. We have noted that, but have said nothing about what the fruitfulness entails. Readers familiar with the parable of the sower and, more especially, with the interpretation offered by Jesus will know that there is an ambiguity in this interpretative passage. It is suggested first that the seed is the word. The sower sows the word. But as Jesus describes the various kinds of ground into which the seed falls, what is sown appears no longer to be the word but the people who hear the word. 'These are the ones sown on rocky ground', Jesus says, 'when they hear the word they immediately receive it with joy….' The word is what is sown, we were told to begin with—that is, the seed—but now, it appears the hearers are the seed rather than the word itself. Some commentators take this confusion to be evidence of an incompetent interpreter and so attribute the explanation of the parable, not to Jesus but to the early church. It seems unlikely, however, that such incompetence, if that is what it is, would have escaped the gospel writer's eye. What would be the point in preserving an explanation that is problematic and confused? A more likely explanation, I suggest, is that we are invited to ponder more deeply the relationship between the word and its hearers, between these two forms of the seed. The word of God is such that it transforms those who hear, makes a new person of them, conforms them more and more to its own reality, so that, more and more, the hearers themselves become instruments of God's communicative presence in the world. Beyond Mark's Gospel there is much biblical support for this idea. John's Gospel for instance makes much of Jesus' gift of the word to those he loves. In his prayer for the disciples in John 17, Jesus repeatedly speaks of his having given the disciples his word. It is on account of his word being in them that the world now hates them (Jn 17.14), and by virtue of their having being given the word they are now sent into the world (Jn 17.18) where they are likely to encounter the mixed reception of which the parable of the sower speaks. It is apparent in John's account that hearers of the word also become bearers of the word. Their hearing is also a commissioning.

Thus may the parable of the sower be read in two ways. It speaks first of our reception of the word, probes our hearts and our lives, enquires after the kind of soil that we are and asks what has become of the word that has been given us. And further, it enjoins us to do as the letter of James enjoins us to do: 'be doers of the word, and not merely hearers who deceive themselves' (1.22). In becoming doers of the word, however, in becoming a fruitful people, we become ourselves bearers of the word, bearers whose proclamation of it will be subject to the same very mixed response described in the parable itself.

The dual reference of the seed to the word itself and to those who hear the word is like one of those pictures portraying a Gestalt switch. Now we see a duck and then a rabbit. Or now we see an old woman, and then a young one in the same picture. In the parable of the sower we are invited to see ourselves first as hearers of the word, as those who receive the seed, and then as sowers, enjoined to become bearers and proclaimers of the word.

Theological interpretation works within the same matrix. 'Those who seek to interpret Scripture theologically', we have said, 'want to hear the word of God in Scripture and hence to be transformed by the renewing of their minds'.[21] The transformation and renewal spoken of here makes disciples of those engaged in such hearing, and as disciples they become also bearers of the word, people engaged in proclaiming the gospel both in word and in deed. That is the end towards which theological interpretation is directed.

Multiple Interpretations

Observation of the double duty done by the parable of the sower takes us back to a question I raised earlier and promised to return to, namely, the question of whether there might be multiple interpretations and multiple

---

21. See citation above of Vanhoozer, 'Introduction', p. 22.

meanings of a text. My answer to this is Yes. I do not subscribe to the determinate view of biblical interpretation whereby the task of the interpreter is to determine the single, original meaning of the text, usually to be identified with the author's intention. Nor, however, do I accept the indeterminate or anti-determinate view, according to which we may make of a text whatever we like. I believe that readers of texts have a certain responsibility toward authors and their intentions, however difficult those intentions may be to establish in many cases. Because texts are modes of communication, however, we have a duty to attend to what the communicator intends to convey. Texts may well convey *more* than the author's intention—indeed they often do—but disregard of authorial intention amounts, in my view, to semantic vandalism and a violation of the other.

Although my own position differs in some respects from that advocated by Fowl, I accept in general terms his proposed alternative that biblical interpretation should be underdetermined.[22] 'Underdetermined interpretation,' he explains, 'recognizes a plurality of interpretive practices and results without necessarily granting epistemological priority to any of these.'[23] Although I have defended a version of this alternative more fully elsewhere, the key point I wish to make here is that an underdetermined model of interpretation, allowing for multiple readings of a text but within some limits, serves best theological interpretation's understanding of Scripture as the Word of God. If Scripture is to be understood as an instrument by which God communicates with his people, then we must allow, I think, that God is free to use Scripture in whatever way best suits God's purpose. That means that God is not constrained by what we might say was the original meaning of the text. Particular texts in the books of Exodus and Deuteronomy, for example, upon which Israel's celebration of the Passover is founded, had, and retain to this day, quite specific meanings for the people of Israel. But that did not preclude Jesus from turning those texts to a new purpose when he took bread at a Passover meal and broke it and said, 'this is my body given for you'. It is important to recognize, however, that in turning the texts to a new purpose Jesus nevertheless remained faithful to the original intent of the author to bear witness to the saving work of God. Authorial intention is being respected even as Jesus exercises an extraordinary degree of hermeneutical freedom, even as he has the text do work that the authors of Exodus and Deuteronomy could never have envisaged themselves. The bread of affliction, referring to the unleavened bread prepared in haste

---

22. Unlike Fowl, I think it possible and advisable to retain the category of the 'meaning' of a text. For my defence of this view, see 'Texts in Context: Scripture and the Divine Economy', *JTI* 1.1 (2007), pp. 23-45, or *History and Hermeneutics* (London: T. & T. Clark, 2005), pp. 131-40.

23. Stephen E. Fowl, *Engaging Scripture* (Malden, MA: Blackwell, 1998), p. 33.

before Israel's flight from slavery, has a new referent. 'This is my body', Jesus now says. The ancient word of Scripture is pressed by Jesus into service of the new thing that God is doing. My preference for underdetermined interpretation recognizes the Lord's prerogative to do just that.

Recognition of the Lord's prerogative to speak afresh through the word of Scripture, to speak indeed to the context and challenges of our own day, brings me again to 'the problem of method' referred to in my title. Those who read the Bible as theological interpreters, who read it thus in prayerful expectation that the voice of God is to be heard through Scripture, should not be surprised that the *viva vox Dei* is not beholden to precisely specified methods of interpretation. The ineffable sovereignty and freedom of God in the event of divine self-communication itself confounds the academic desire to bring interpretation under strict methodological control.

Conclusion

I hope that it has become clear through my account of theological interpretation that it is best understood not as a method or tool to be wielded alongside other methods of biblical interpretation. Theological interpretation is not a scholarly tool like the historical critical method, or redaction criticism, or philological analysis. Although it may learn from and utilize some of these scholarly tools itself, theological interpretation is better described as a mode of discipleship or set of practices rather than a scholarly method.[24] It is one more instance of faith seeking understanding.

In case the mention of faith should tempt the scholarly community to suppose that it can set itself apart from theological interpretation, however, and proceed with its work unhindered by the dogmatic claims and pious practices of faith, we need to be clear that the theological interpretation of Scripture is premised upon a claim about what the Bible really is, namely, an instrument of God's self-communication. If that claim is true, as the church has held it to be throughout the church's history, then those who read Scripture seeking to hear and to understand it aright cannot proceed as though God has no part in the process. As we have seen in the parable of the sower, it was only as those around Jesus, along with the twelve, kept company with the Lord and attended to his instruction, that the meaning of the word became clear. As it was for them, so also will it be today for those seeking ears to hear.

---

24. See citation above of Hays, 'Reading the Bible'.

2

THE PROBLEM OF 'HISTORY' IN RECENT THEOLOGICAL COMMENTARY

Seth Heringer

The genre of theological commentary has recently become an active and growing field with three series standing out as making substantial contributions. The earliest of these three has its roots in a book edited by Joel Green and Max Turner entitled *Between Two Horizons: Spanning New Testament Studies and Systematic Theology*, which sets out the general methodology of the Two Horizons New Testament Commentary Series.[1] Brazos followed in 2005 with the Brazos Theological Commentary on the Bible. Not to be left out, in 2010 Westminster John Knox Press began publishing its series, entitled Belief: A Theological Commentary on the Bible. Between 2005 and 2011 thirty-one theological commentaries from these series were published.

Each of these series differentiates itself from traditional historical-critical commentaries. In one of their methodological essays, Green and Turner argue that a new type of commentary is needed because

> the great commentary series have become increasingly detailed and methodologically complex, and many individual volumes are now so exhaustive that they are virtually inaccessible to all but the most well trained. The reader often finds it difficult to see the theological wood for the exegetical trees.[2]

They structure their series to correct this problem by having the commentaries focus less on historical issues and more on examining the theology of the original context and helping readers interpret it in the context of

---

1. Joel B. Green and Max Turner (eds.), *Between Two Horizons: Spanning Biblical Studies and Systematic Theology* (Grand Rapids: Eerdmans, 2000). Eerdmans published the first two books from this series in 2005: Stephen E. Fowl, *Philippians* (THNTC; Grand Rapids: Eerdmans, 2005), and Marianne Meye Thompson, *Colossians and Philemon* (THNTC; Grand Rapids: Eerdmans, 2005). Eerdmans added to this series in 2008 by releasing The Two Horizons Old Testament Commentary series with different editors but the same format.

2. Joel B. Green and Max Turner, 'New Testament Commentary and Systematic Theology: Strangers or Friends?', in Green and Turner (eds.), *Between Two Horizons*, pp. 2-3.

twenty-first century theology. Similarly, in the preface to the Brazos series, R.R Reno contrasts the series with modern interpretation of Scripture that removes doctrine from interpretation. He explains this contrast by writing that the series 'was born out of the conviction that dogma clarifies rather than obscures.... Doctrine...is a crucial aspect of divine pedagogy, a clarifying agent for our minds fogged by self-deceptions.'[3] The Belief series also distinguishes itself from historical-critical commentaries when its general editors identify themselves as sharing

> Karl Barth's concern that, insofar as their usefulness to pastors goes, most modern commentaries are 'no commentaries at all but merely the first step toward a commentary.' Historical-critical approaches to Scripture rule out some readings and command others, but such methods only begin to help theological reflection and the preaching of the Word.[4]

This practical focus emphasizes their desire to move beyond historical-critical work to theological interpretation.

Although these series set themselves up as something different from historical-critical commentaries, and certainly they achieve difference in many areas, this essay will argue that the individual commentaries do not free themselves from the bonds of historical criticism with enough methodological precision. This deficiency is caused by their not giving the relation of history and theology its methodological due.[5] Thus, an unclear methodological mixture arises that accepts and rejects historical criticism *ad hoc*. Even though these commentaries generally accept and use the knowledge gained by the historical-critical method, they often press back on its most theologically problematic aspects. Because these instances of pushback are widespread, when taken together, they show that the historical-critical method is not appropriate for theological commentary. Currently, Murray Rae's *History and Hermeneutics* offers the most theologically sophisticated alternative to the historical method traditionally understood and practiced, providing a way to bring some methodological clarity to theological commentary.[6]

---

3. R.R. Reno, 'Series Preface', in *Genesis* (BTCB; Grand Rapids: Brazos, 2010), pp. 11-12.
4. William C. Placher and Amy Plantinga Pauw, 'Series Introduction', in William C. Placher, *Mark* (Belief; Louisville, KY: Westminster/John Knox Press, 2010), p. ix.
5. This statement is not true of the book-length methodological work done by Green and Turner (*Between Two Horizons*). Even with multiple chapters dealing with the relationship between history and theology, however, the book does not resolve the problem.
6. Murray A. Rae, *History and Hermeneutics* (London: T. & T. Clark, 2005).

Ernst Troeltsch's Principles of the Historical Method

Ernst Troeltsch gives one of the most-cited formulations of the historical method in his 1898 essay 'Historical and Dogmatic Method in Theology'.[7] In this essay he argues that religion can no longer use the dogmatic method in its historical investigations and must recognize the overwhelming power of the historical method. Troeltsch formulates three principles that serve as the foundation of the historical method: criticism, analogy, and correlation. The impetus behind *criticism* is Troeltsch's belief that academic history is being wrongly influenced by tradition, theology, and the church. To prevent this outside influence, thereby letting scholarship produce pure results, Troeltsch invokes criticism to force all historical claims onto an even playing field. No historical claims, even those with church authority behind them, are allowed a special status; all must fall equally under the critical eye of the historical method. Thus, as Troeltsch says, there can no longer be historical surety, only probability: 'In the realm of history there are only judgments of probability'.[8] Under this principle, Christian claims concerning the resurrection, Jewish stories of sea-crossings, and American legends about the battle of Gettysburg are all investigated using the same historical method.

Once all historical claims have been leveled, tools are needed that can distinguish the probable from improbable claims. To do this, Troeltsch moves to the principles of analogy and correlation. Troeltsch refers to *analogy* as the 'instrumentality that makes historical criticism possible'.[9] Analogy functions just as is expected from its name: something unknown is compared with something known. Specifically, the unknowns of history are compared with the known (or historically probable) of history and personal experience. Christian history is thereby made analogous to all history. Thus, the probability of the resurrection of Jesus is determined by comparing it to the known events of history and personal experience to see if analogous events can be found. If such a confirmation is not possible, the probability of the event drops precipitously.

Finally, Troeltsch refers to *correlation*, simply understood as cause and effect through time. Troeltsch defines correlation in this manner:

> This concept implies that there can be no change at one point without some preceding and consequent change elsewhere, so that all historical happening

---

7. In this essay I will use the terms 'historical method', 'historical-critical method', and 'historical criticism' interchangeably, as this follows Troeltsch's usage.

8. Ernst Troeltsch, 'Historical and Dogmatic Method in Theology', in *Religion in History* (Minneapolis: Fortress Press, 1991), p. 13.

9. Troeltsch, 'Historical and Dogmatic Method', p. 13.

is knit together in a permanent relationship of correlation, inevitably forming a current in which everything is interconnected and each single event is related to all others.[10]

For Troeltsch, the historical method works within a closed system of cause and effect, with each effect having a natural and explainable cause. In relation to religion, the teachings of Jesus or the Torah cannot be the injection of the divine into the closed world system; rather, they must be fully explainable based on the natural development of ancient near eastern religion, or in Jesus' case, on the combination of Jewish, Greek, and Roman religious influences.

These three principles, although formidable alone, gain overwhelming power when combined. Troeltsch describes their mutual interaction in this way:

> The historical method itself, by its use of criticism, analogy, and correlation, produces with irresistible necessity a web of mutually interacting activities of the human spirit, which are never independent and absolute but always interrelated and therefore understandable only within the context of the most comprehensive whole.[11]

The result of such a web is that the 'inner logic' of the principles 'drives us forward; and all the counter-measures essayed by theologians to neutralize its effects or to confine them to some limited area have failed, despite eager efforts to demonstrate their validity'.[12] For Troeltsch, these three principles form a system that cannot be broken apart or stopped halfway. Like leaven, they seep everywhere and overcome all other methods, 'transforming everything and ultimately exploding the very form of earlier theological methods'.[13]

These three principals have significant consequences for Christianity. First, criticism destroys the authority of the church, tradition, and doctrine by denying them a place of privilege. Moreover, without church or doctrinal authority the canon can no longer function as a whole, for it was formed by theological decisions made well after the individual books were written.[14] Thus there is no theological unity to the books, only individual works written at various times and places from different perspectives. The proper context for these books, then, is their immediate literary and historical

---

10. Troeltsch, 'Historical and Dogmatic Method', p. 14.
11. Troeltsch, 'Historical and Dogmatic Method', p. 15.
12. Troeltsch, 'Historical and Dogmatic Method', p. 18.
13. Troeltsch, 'Historical and Dogmatic Method', p. 12.
14. I understand that this position is somewhat controversial and argued against specifically in Peter Balla, *Challenges to New Testament Theology: An Attempt to Justify the Enterprise* (Tübingen: Mohr Siebeck, 1997; repr. Peabody, MA: Hendrickson, 1998).

surroundings, not a grouping decided on hundreds of years after they were written. Second, analogy and correlation work together to deny historical appeals to God's ability to act in the world. As alluded to above, the principle of analogy limits the types of events that are allowed in history, thereby making miracles historically improbable because no other examples from history or experience can be verified.[15] Similarly, correlation rules out God's affecting history by rejecting any event or interpretation not fully explainable by the chain of cause and effect through time. Since any divine activity would lie outside this closed system, God cannot be considered as a cause of any world event.

The Use of History in Theological Commentary

Theological commentaries are generally unclear when dealing with history. Before going further, however, let me offer two caveats. First, the nature of essays that overview large bodies of work from various authors forces any synthetic claims made to remain somewhat general, and this is a characteristic of this essay. Although I give examples to illustrate the points made, these examples do not reflect every theological commentary. Nevertheless, I maintain that the positions in this essay fairly portray the genre taken as a whole. Second, although I point to a methodological weakness of theological commentary, I strongly support the field and the work done so far.

A good place to begin is Rusty Reno's *Genesis* commentary, in part because he is a general editor of the Brazos series, but also because it serves as a good representative of how theological commentary interacts with historical criticism. After giving a lengthy list of both critical commentaries and theological works that influenced his book, he cautions that he has 'pointed things to say about modern historical-critical study of the Bible'. He continues:

> In the main, I find modern historical-critical scholarship sometimes helpful, sometime maddeningly myopic, and sometimes irrelevant to the sorts of questions I find myself asking about Genesis. So, in this commentary I do not reject historical-critical exegesis. I am happy to consult it when helpful. I am

---

15. Troeltsch sees the problems with this position and thus admits the existence of 'contingent' and 'new' events that do not fit with universal laws, or possibly, fit with laws not yet discovered (Ernst Troeltsch, 'Contingency', in James Hastings [ed.], *Encyclopedia of Religion and Ethics* [12 vols.; Edinburgh: T. & T. Clark, 1911], IV, pp. 87-89); 'Modern Philosophy of History', in *Religion in History* [Minneapolis: Fortress Press, 1991], pp. 285-88). Despite this openness to the unexpected, Troeltsch retains the principle of analogy as a criterion separating the probable from improbable events based on their adherence to the interpreter's experience.

only irritated by its unsustainable claims to an exclusive interpretive authority. As a tradition of scholarship, historical-critical cannot provide us with all the resources necessary to interpret the Bible as the living source for Christian faith.[16]

In this passage Reno gives a criterion and a warning for the use of historical criticism. The criterion is that he will use historical criticism 'when helpful', but warns that it is not the supreme authority and cannot provide Christian interpretation with all the necessary interpretive tools. One of those missing tools is the theological insight to properly identify the 'enemies' of Christian interpretation. The greatest danger for interpreters of Genesis lies not with historical-critical questions but Gnosticism and the degradation of the body.[17] This focus on theological insight fits well with his overall interpretive strategy of choosing to limit his commentary to texts he finds theologically telling. In selecting these texts he admits to having 'no single rule or principle' to guide his judgment and does not 'follow a consistent method or pattern of exegesis'.[18] His method consists, then, of finding interesting texts, offering a theological interpretation of them, and using the historical-critical method when he finds it helpful.

Despite this claim to allow room for historical criticism, Reno's commentary seldom asks historical questions and sticks mainly to narrative and theological interpretation. One of the few places I could find a concern with how well the story of Genesis matches historical reality comes in his rejection of a conflict between the creation accounts and science. He attempts to overcome this difficulty by reading the accounts in a non-temporal way that avoids 'a false conflict between creation and science'.[19] Even here, however, interpretation is ruled by doctrine and not science or historical criticism, for he argues that any idea of creation must cohere with the doctrine of *creatio ex nihilo* because 'any reading that contradicts the doctrine of creation out of nothing will undermine our capacity to read the Bible as a whole in a theologically coherent fashion'.[20]

Moreover, even when Reno switches from the 'figures and events' of Genesis 1–11 that have a 'timeless, archetypical feel of myth or legend' to the 'particular' man of Abraham where God 'injects a new possibility *into* the flow of history', his method does not match the new historical focus of the text. Reno never questions the historical existence of Abraham or the later movement of Israel to Egypt. More specifically, instead of asking

---

16. Reno, *Genesis*, p. 26.
17. Reno, *Genesis*, pp. 26-27.
18. Reno, *Genesis*, p. 21.
19. Reno, *Genesis*, p. 35.
20. Reno, *Genesis*, p. 46.

historical questions about the destruction of Sodom and Gomorrah or Lot's wife's being turned into a pillar of salt, Reno turns to a theological understanding of God's judgment and the consistent biblical witness against 'turning back' from a life with God.[21] Throughout the commentary, in its coverage of what Reno identifies as both the mythical and the historical parts of Genesis, historical questions are passed over.

In his commentary on Mark, William C. Placher also claims to use historical criticism only when helpful. During his discussion of what text he will use for exegesis, he invokes the authority of historical criticism:

> I will comment on the best scholarly guess as to the 'original autograph'—the text someone back in the first century wrote.... At every stage, I will be dependent on the work of modern historical-critical scholars to illumine many features of the text. I am in awe of their learning.

This high praise for historical criticism is immediately followed by a warning as to its limitations:

> Still, I confess that their work often strikes me, as Karl Barth said of the biblical commentaries of his time, as 'no commentary at all, but merely the first steps toward a commentary.' To put the matter more colloquially, they often seem to stop just when they get to the good stuff.[22]

Placher accepts the knowledge gained by historical criticism but wants to add to it, to press further into theological construction. Despite this acceptance, he also thinks that historical knowledge can distort, for sometimes the 'most historically reliable details may not be at all the most characteristic'.[23] Thus the Jesus Seminar, he says, may get the historical details correct but still create the wrong picture of Jesus. With this understanding of narrative's relation to history, Placher trusts that

> Mark thought he knew what was really important about Jesus, and I want to listen to what he has to say—all of it, set down the way he chose to tell it—even if I doubt some of what he tells happened at all as he describes.[24]

Thus Placher wants to keep a place for history but let it be overruled by the narrative of the text when it offers a better understanding of Jesus.

Placher is more willing than Reno to raise questions about the historical reality of the events related in the text, but he does not use the historical method to answer them. Instead, he argues for the philosophical possibility of God's actions in the world, thereby creating a world where the miracle

---

21. Reno, *Genesis*, p. 188.
22. Placher, *Mark*, p. 12.
23. Placher, *Mark*, p. 4.
24. Placher, *Mark*, p. 5.

stories could have happened. In fact, his arguments rely more on the limitations of human knowledge than positive argumentation for miracles. As one example, in an excursus on demons in Mark, Placher rejects Bultmann's rejection of a 'NT worldview' by arguing that we may never know if Jesus really drove out demons or 'to what extent that was the explanation accommodated to their understanding'.[25] This argumentation from ignorance also appears when considering nature miracles. After Placher questions the historical reality of Jesus calming the winds and waves in Mk 4.35-41, he stops for an excursus on miracles and argues that anything is possible when Jesus is seen as Creator: 'If one accepts that premise, it would not be surprising if some quite remarkable things happened around him. At least one did: Jesus was raised from the dead.'[26] He uses this same logic of the unknown regarding the historical reality of Jesus' feeding of the 5,000 in Mk 6.30-44. On the feeding he says, 'I do not know what happened in that deserted place', but proceeds again to posit that 'if the Creator of the universe was walking around Galilee in the first century, it seems plausible that some quite unusual things might have happened in his immediate vicinity'.[27] Taken together, these examples show that Placher is interested in the question of the historical reality of these events but does not use the historical-critical method to answer such questions.

Stephen Fowl also asks questions about the nature and importance of historical investigation, considering it the job of a theological commentary to discern how historical questions can help or harm theological inquiry. His idea of 'historical', however, has nothing to do with Troeltsch's method. This characteristic can be seen in his understanding of modern commentaries as 'historical' since they focus on putting texts into their 'original historical context as best and as fully as one can'. Fowl is interested in background material relating to the text, not in trying to determine the historical reality of the events related in the text based on historical-critical principles.[28] He then contrasts this modern historical aim with the pre-modern commentaries where 'theological concerns regulate all others'. It is the task, then, of theological commentaries to discern when one approach is more helpful than the other, or differently, 'to discern how and in what ways to present

---

25. Placher, *Mark*, p. 66.
26. Placher, *Mark*, p. 79. Placher also questions whether miracles should be seen as the breaking of natural laws—a position that places God outside of nature. In addition, he leaves open the possibility for psychosomatic explanations of healings (p. 78).
27. Placher, *Mark*, p. 97.
28. Fowl, *Philippians*, p. 4. For a helpful typology that sets up three types of historical inquiry, see Joel B. Green, *Practicing Theological Interpretation: Engaging Biblical Texts for Faith and Formation* (Grand Rapids: Baker Academic, 2011), pp. 43-50.

historical concerns in ways that enhance rather than frustrate theological inquiry'.[29]

Fowl gives an example where he finds the historical context helpful and one where it is distracting. It is helpful, he argues, to know the local practices of giving and receiving gifts while reading Phil. 4.10-20. Such knowledge can help the reader better understand the motives behind the carefulness with which Paul thanks the Philippian church. Fowl's example of where contextual information can be distracting is the controversy surrounding whether Phil. 2.6-11 is a hymn. Even here, however, a passage where he says that the historical background of the text can 'get in the way of theological inquiry', he spends much time investigating the contextual evidence for his own positions.[30] Both of these examples show that Fowl is concerned with a type of history, but one that is quite different from the historical-critical method.

Rejecting the Principles of the Historical Method One-by-One

The previous section examined the understanding and use of history in three theological commentaries judged to be typical examples of the genre. This section will focus on places where theological commentaries challenge specific principles of the historical method. These challenges, however, never amount to a concerted attack on the web created by the principles taken together; rather, they result from problems that arise when theological commentary is confronted with the ramifications of the historical method.

Against Criticism

As we have seen, Troeltsch's principle of criticism levels all historical arguments, destroying the authority of the church, doctrine, and religion. Everything must be treated equally in historical discussions with no outside influences affecting historical investigations. These claims, however, directly contradict the stated purpose of much theological commentary. Again Reno serves as a good example. Discussing historical criticism, he states that history and criticism are not problematic in themselves; what is detrimental is antitraditionalism:

> The problem is not historical consciousness. Nor is it the critical cast of the mind, which, in any event, is well represented in the church fathers, the medieval Scholastics, and the Reformers. The problem is a collective self-impoverishment that stems from the antitraditionalism implicitly endorsed by most modern biblical scholars. Stripped of the interpretations developed over

---

29. Fowl, *Philippians*, p. 5.
30. Fowl, *Philippians*, p. 4; see pp. 88-117.

the course of a long tradition of biblical reading, we end up with small pieces of text, which, however carefully surrounded by sophisticated reconstructions of historical context, we cannot bring into synthesis with the other parts of the Bible or with current Christian practice or even with the most basic requirements for a cogent view of God. The end result of the modern historical critical tradition is therefore painfully obvious: a great deal of valuable but localized philological and historical knowledge, combined with crude generalizations and vague theological gestures.

Reno here shows that the principle of criticism impoverishes, not improves, theological interpretation by casting aside years of Christian understanding. It picks apart the canon, destroying the possibility of a larger theological synthesis. As a solution, he reintroduces traditional authority so that scholars can 'stop trying to reinvent interpretation', and let the wisdom that has accumulated over two thousand years of Christian reflection be available and authoritative for theological commentary.[31] This strategy is enacted in his concern that *creatio ex nihilo* be a part of any understanding of creation because of its doctrinal implications.

Problematizing criticism from a different angle, Allen Verhey and Joseph S. Harvard, in their commentary on Ephesians, argue for the importance of ecclesial locatedness when interpreting Scripture. They do so by pointing out that the creation of the canon was a church-dependent move, requiring theological decisions of the church to classify these diverse writings as Scripture. Thus, they argue, 'without the church the writing called "Scripture" would not exist. It was the church that gathered these documents into a collection, a whole, a canon, because in them the church found the story of its life'. Because of the correlative relationship between church and Scripture, Verhey and Harvard attempt 'to read [Ephesians] within the Christian community and to read it as part of that whole called "canon"'.[32] This methodological move is part of their larger vision to read Scripture in service of the church and with the church's help. This means the church is active in turning Scripture into script, into a document that shows the church how to live. Putting this principle into practice, Verhey and Harvard used the experience of teaching Ephesians in a Sunday School class as part of their writing process, a misguided practice in the eyes of historical criticism.

Canonical readings of Scripture are pervasive throughout theological commentaries. Robert Jenson shows the perspective of theological commentary on the canon succinctly when he says, 'Theological commentary presupposes that scripture tells the truth about God in his history with us; and

---

31. Reno, *Genesis*, p. 45.
32. Allen Verhey and Joseph S. Harvard, *Ephesians* (Belief; Louisville, KY: Westminster/John Knox Press, 2011), pp. 3-4.

this supposition includes that the Holy Spirit, the living breath of God that moves all history, does this regularly "by the prophets'".[33] The text for theological interpretation is 'the canonical text presented by the church and not a putatively original or earlier text constructed by a scholar—though determining what may be a plausibly canonical text sometimes requires considerable critical thought'.[34] Theological commentary is thoroughly canonical, valuing the narrative coherence of the whole and the theological insight that can be gained from it.

Each of these interpretive moves—traditional, ecclesial, and canonical readings—challenge the principle of criticism by allowing something outside of history (as this is determined by the historical method) to influence interpretation. They do so by claiming that church tradition can affect both interpretation and historical probability, that there is more to interpretation than reconstructing what the original hearers might have understood the text to mean, and that the proper context for a biblical book is not merely its historical contemporaries but a larger scriptural collection chosen by the church. These interpretive claims all have historical ramifications—ones that contradict the accepted norms of historical criticism.

Against Analogy and Correlation

Because analogy and correlation both reject considering in historical study the idea of an active God who works in the world, the ways that theological interpretation pushes back on these principles will be considered together. It does so mainly by questioning the assurance of a closed universe. An example of such questioning is Justo González's use of random theory: 'the modern view of the world, which by definition excludes miracles, is not unassailable. The world is not as closed or as rational as modernity would have us think.' One of the reasons for the pervasiveness of a closed system in modern biblical interpretation is that the nature of miracle has been misunderstood. Thus, González argues, when Luke speaks of miracles he is not speaking about an interruption of a closed order; rather, he is saying that miracles are an 'irruption of the true order—the order of the creator God—into the demonic disorder of the present world. It is a sign of God's victory over the powers of evil'.[35] This seemingly strong stance on miracles, however, is weakened when nature miracles are considered. While interpreting Jesus' quieting of the storm, González points to the literary significance of water as a symbol for chaos and the symbolic connections of this story to Jonah. He concludes:

33. Robert W. Jenson, *Ezekiel* (BTCB; Grand Rapids: Brazos, 2009), p. 18.
34. Jenson, *Ezekiel*, pp. 22-23.
35. Justo L. González, *Luke* (Belief; Louisville, KY: Westminster/John Knox Press, 2010), p. 83.

> When we put these various elements together, what emerges is a vision in which the storm at sea is an expression of the power of the demons of destruction—and a reminder of the corruption of all of creation as a result of sin and the fall. It is an indication of the power of Jesus over the demons that threaten to sink the boat. But above all it points to the connection between God's saving work in Exodus and God's saving work in Jesus.[36]

González hedges his historical bets, focusing on the passage's narrative and theological connections over questions of historicity. While never denying the historical reality of the stories, he nevertheless does not champion the importance of their historicity.

Writing on Matthew's Gospel, Stanley Hauerwas takes a stronger stance on the historicity of miracles. For him, miracles are to be expected if the story of the Bible is to be taken seriously. When considering the historicity of the virgin birth, he says it is all a matter of one's view of the Creator God:

> Virgin births are not surprising given that this is the God who has created us without us, but (as Augustine observes) who will not save us without us. What the Father does through the Spirit to conceive Mary's child is not something different than what God does through creation. God does not need to intervene in creation, because God has never been absent from creation. Creation is not 'back there,' but is God's ongoing love of all he has willed and continued to will to exist.[37]

If one sees the world as a place where God is upholding his creation with love, Hauerwas argues, then there is no problem with God's interaction with the world. This is because God is already present in it and can affect it at will. The deeper problem with modernity is that it has lost sight of the miraculous nature of life itself and speaks the language of science and machines. 'We use the analytic language that gives power to experts and fails to designate what is being described. As a result, the world has been reclassified from creature to machine, making us strangers to our own lives.'[38] This specific example fits with Hauerwas's overall theme of accepting the possibility of miracles because of God's involvement with the world. Hauerwas does not, however, get caught up in historical investigation, but seeks to understand the purpose behind God's action at that time and place.

Another way some commentators have critiqued the notion of a closed universe is by arguing for ideas of space and time that do not fit with the normal scientific worldview. In his work on Ezra and Nehemiah, Matthew Levering, for example, contrasts his view of history with a 'normal' view that focuses on identifying authors and assigning plausibility to historical events:

36. González, *Luke*, pp. 107-108.
37. Stanley Hauerwas, *Matthew* (BTCB; Grand Rapids: Brazos, 2006), p. 34.
38. Hauerwas, *Matthew*, p. 140.

> Theological commentary on scripture, however, recognizes a second and deeper dimension of human history, one that completes and enriches the first (linear) dimension of history—namely, from eternity the Creator God, the Trinity, brings forth time with its fulfillment already in view, and so in God's knowledge earlier persons and events relate to later ones in ways that escape the historian's tools. Likewise, later persons and events have connections to earlier ones that would appear anachronistic from a strictly linear or horizontal perspective that is unaware of the inner relationality of history.[39]

By using this principle of cross-chronological relationality Levering is able to make claims that appear as nonsense to historical criticism. For instance, he has no problem with the claim that Moses and the first-century believers in Jesus share the same faith. He can make such claims because 'what appears to be an anachronism is in fact a fundamental truth about the non-chronological interrelationships that belong to persons who live in widely variant times and places, due to the active presence of the triune God's work in human history'.[40] For Levering humans from various times and places participate in the same world created by a God not bound by time and space, thus allowing relationships that surpass what is considered to be the normal working of cause and effect. Clearly this principle conflicts with the principle of correlation, which does not allow for such an idea of causation.

Another such attack on a closed universe comes from Jenson. His position is best understood by looking at an example from his exegesis of Ezek. 26:1-21. This passage, he believes, contains a prophecy that Nebuchadnezzar would sack Tyre and completely destroy it. The problem is that Tyre was never destroyed. Jenson then asks, 'What are we to make of prophecy that seems to be straightforwardly unfulfilled and thereafter unfulfillable?' His answer stretches the bounds of time and space by saying that no matter what happened in history, if God 'has indeed spoken that settles the matter: Tyre will hear the word of her fall and will fall to Nebuchadnezzar, for "the word of our God will stand forever" (Isa. 40:8)'.[41] By this strong endorsement of God's faithfulness he is positing a view of the world where God is not limited to normal causation. Thus he argues:

> The Word of God is not impeded by time or space, for he is the second identity of the God who creates both space and time (John 1:1).... If a word from God has not yet been fulfilled, indeed if it cannot be fulfilled within the time and space of this age, we may nevertheless depend on it. For when the word of God is spoken, time and with it space do not display the linearity we in our finitude and fallenness assume. Christian thinking has for two

---

39. Matthew Levering, *Ezra and Nehemiah* (BTCB; Grand Rapids: Brazos, 2007), p. 22.
40. Levering, *Ezra and Nehemiah*, p. 23.
41. Jenson, *Ezekiel*, pp. 211-12.

laborious millennia been learning—and forgetting and relearning—to interpret time by biblical phenomena such as this: the man Jesus, born many centuries after Abraham's death, can say, 'Before Abraham was, I am' (John 8:58).[42]

A universe with a God unbounded by space and time, who can work freely in the world connecting the unconnected and bringing about the fulfillment of prophecy separate from the working of time—this is a universe unrecognizable to the principle of correlation.

Theological Commentary and the Loss of History

The previous section identified trends in theological commentary that challenged the principles of the historical method. Nevertheless, these challenges never rise to a complete rejection of Troeltsch's principles and the formulation of new ones. Instead, the commentaries remain mostly ambivalent, accepting some facets of historical criticism and rejecting others. This methodological fuzziness regarding history leads theological interpreters to downplay historical questions in order to pursue narrative interpretation. In this manner, theological commentaries are able to keep their canonical, ecclesial, and doctrinal positions while remaining uncommitted on questions of history.

An example of this approach to historical questions is González's choice not to discuss contextual questions in his commentary:

> While taking into account current discussions among scholars on matters such as sources, genre, date, and so on, in this commentary I do not deal with them. The main question I seek to address is, What does the text mean to us?[43]

This question coheres with his overall focus on the narrative of Luke rather than attempting to reconstruct the history behind the text. An example of this narrative emphasis is apparent when he sets aside questions about the historical reality of the virgin birth to focus on its narrative function of showing Jesus as the fulfillment of Israel's history. Despite a willingness to overlook some historical questions, González does see the necessity for a historical core to Luke. Thus, to allow the historical validity of some events he distinguishes between primary and secondary events in Scripture. Therefore, the exact historical details of the Gospels do not matter.

> What was important was to affirm that Jesus Christ was indeed born, that he suffered and died on the cross, that he was raised from the dead, that all this

---

42. Jenson, *Ezekiel*, p. 212.
43. González, *Luke*, p. 11.

was done for our salvation, that it is the fulfillment of God's ancient promises to Israel. The rest—how many people Jesus fed, what were his exact words from the cross, and the like—was secondary.[44]

In this way he is able to keep a historical core without getting bogged down in the details of history.

Another example of such a move is Jaroslav Pelikan's discussion of miracles in Acts. When considering miracles, he argues, one must place them in their historical context, in a world where people thought the divine could and often did intervene in history. Despite this openness, he states, 'The primary interest here in Acts…was not in these "extraordinary miracles"…as spectacles, but in the sovereignty of God the Creator over his creation (→17:24-29) and over its laws'.[45] This practice of focusing on the theology of a passage rather than its historical probability continues in his discussion of angels—both in Acts and throughout the Bible. He concludes:

> Even from all these and other biblical references to angels taken together, it is a considerable distance to the speculative constructs of Pseudo-Dionysius the Areopagite (17:34) and of later Scholastics in both East and West about the ranks of the celestial hierarchy. But it is a much longer way to the dismissal of angels altogether in so much of modern theology.[46]

His discussion includes a warning on both sides: extensive speculation on angels does not fit with Scripture, but neither does their outright rejection. A mediating position is found again, one that neither rejects nor accepts the historical reality of things that fall outside the bounds of historical criticism.

A Unified Theological Vision of History

This essay has argued that theological commentaries have not given the relationship between history and theology enough methodological attention; thus, despite wanting to retain the historical reality of the stories told in Scripture, they revert to narrative and theological interpretations when events do not fit within the boundaries of historical criticism as articulated by Troeltsch. But we have also seen places where theological commentary pushes back on the principles of the historical method, with each principle being attacked from various angles. None of these commentaries has presented a sustained and thorough criticism of the historical method; never has an alternative method with different principles been used. These factors together point to the pressing need for a new historical method in theological commentary, one that allows it to retain its unique characteristics while also

---

44. González, *Luke*, p. 15.
45. Jaroslav Pelikan, *Acts* (BTCB; Grand Rapids: Brazos, 2005), p. 97.
46. Pelikan, *Acts*, p. 147.

making claims about historical reality apart from the hegemony of the historical-critical method.

Murray Rae has constructed such a theological understanding of history in his *History and Hermeneutics*. Although there is not space here to go into the specifics of Rae's proposal, I will set out its most important principles and overarching method. Rae offers an unabashedly theological account of history and space-time: 'I offer an account of history drawn from the Bible itself in which history is recognized as the space and time given to humankind to be truly itself as the covenant partner of God'.[47] With this base, he begins his account with the beginning of the biblical narrative: creation. Rae sees creation as showing that the world and history were created separate from God but with a God-given purpose. This purpose is revealed through the pattern of promise and fulfillment in Scripture, where God uses the particulars of history to accomplish his plans. One particularly important fulfillment was accomplished with the resurrection of Jesus, an event that changes our understanding of the world. For Rae, the resurrection changes how we see history:

> The resurrection...brings about a new understanding of the way reality is constituted. If this is true, then the old paradigms of historical and scientific enquiry will be inadequate for the task of apprehending this reality. 'Seeing' the resurrection, therefore, is not possible within the prevailing canons of historical-critical enquiry, not, as we shall argue, because the resurrection is not an historical event, but rather because history itself has been misconceived by historians as a causal series from which God is necessarily excluded.[48]

Rae explicitly rejects the principles of correlation and analogy here, saying that the resurrection shows us that the world cannot fit into the narrow view offered by them. With this broader view of the world in place, Rae offers alternative ways of thinking about history through testimony, tradition, and the church. Christianity, he argues, relies on testimony, and that is not a bad thing, for scholars increasingly see its historical value. Tradition is important for it takes into account the communal nature of human knowledge and the clarity that can come from passing knowledge down through time. Connected with this communal focus, Rae argues that the ecclesial community is the right interpretive setting for reading Scripture, for it can offer correctives when interpretation goes astray.

With these moves Rae has rejected the historical-critical method and replaced it with a theological understanding of history. He has offered theological commentary a much needed alternative to historical criticism. By incorporating such a method, theological commentary can begin reclaiming

---

47. Rae, *History and Hermeneutics*, p. 2.
48. Rae, *History and Hermeneutics*, p. 68.

historical judgments. This reclamation does not mean the lessening of narrative or theological approaches; rather, it means the addition to them of theologically based historical judgments. Moreover, rather than undermining narrative and theological interpretations, adding Rae's vision for theological history will add to the depth of those strategies by tying them to the historical reality of a God-created world.

Although Rae's vision of history should be integrated into theological commentary, I do not believe it is a panacea to all historical questions that will arise. For example, questions of how to interpret seemingly contradictory accounts in the Gospels remain. Also, once a closed view of the universe is rejected, how once again to place limits on historical inquiry is unclear. For instance, questions of how to allow for the resurrection of Jesus but not for Moroni's giving of the golden tablets to Joseph Smith, or for the miracles of Honi the Circle Drawer, remain unanswered. These questions point to the need for theologians and biblical scholars to continue working together to seek methodological precision in their discussions of the relationship of history and theology.

3

THEOLOGICAL INTERPRETATION OF SCRIPTURE IN SERMONIC MODE: THE CASE OF T.F. TORRANCE

Myk Habets

What Is a Theological Interpretation of Scripture?

Readers of Scripture have long known that hermeneutics alone cannot be the path to true understanding of texts—divine or human.[1] Theological interpretation of Scripture is the latest attempt to articulate and form communities of readers which can utilize the latest in critical biblical scholarship and at the same time, read Scripture as a holy text for disciples of Christ, filled with the Spirit. In order to do this, advocates of theological interpretation of Scripture draw on reading strategies of the past, such as the *regula fidei*, and present hermeneutics, such as speech-act theory or realist approaches to the biblical narrative, which lend themselves to dramatic readings of the *historia salutis*. Thus theological interpretation of Scripture is both new and old.

Perhaps the most succinct definition of theological interpretation of Scripture is that it is, in the words of Kevin Vanhoozer, '...reading Scripture in and for the community of the faithful'.[2] Vanhoozer is quick to point out that this does not mean theologians may simply read their own confessional theology into the text in an uncritical way. It is, rather, recognition of the fact that 'there are some interpretative questions that require theological, not hermeneutical, answers.'[3] Stephen Fowl succinctly summarizes this as follows: 'In brief, I take the theological interpretation of Scripture to be that practice whereby theological concerns and interests inform and are informed

---

1. I am grateful to Robert T. Walker for helpful comments on an earlier draft of this essay.
2. K.J. Vanhoozer, 'Introduction: What Is Theological Interpretation of the Bible?' in K.J. Vanhoozer (ed.), *Dictionary for Theological Interpretation of the Bible* (Grand Rapids: Baker Academic), p. 19.
3. Vanhoozer, 'Introduction', p. 19.

by a reading of Scripture'.[4] And in Francis Watson's words: 'The text in question is the biblical text; for the goal is a theological hermeneutic... within which an exegesis oriented primarily towards theological issues can come into being'.[5]

Markus Bockmuehl expresses the same thought with his own rhetorical flourish:

> Here I claim no crystal ball with which to prognosticate. It merely seems worth considering from the outset that an interpretation of Scripture determined to operate wholly without reference to the historic Christian ecclesial context is particularly prone to misapprehend the nature and purpose of its very object of study.[6]

Here Bockmuehl and others are rightly reacting to the modern dominance of critical hermeneutics and the postmodern ascendancy of ideological theory, radically imported into biblical studies. In relation to modern critical hermeneutics Bockmuehl likens its approach to 'restricting the study of a Stradivari to the alpine softwood industry of Trentino', which 'can be intellectually respectable and may even have a certain complementary scientific or sociological interest. But it has by definition little light to shed on the instruments actually played by a violinist like Itzhak Perlman or a cellist like Yo-Yo Ma.'[7] In short, what Bockmuehl is calling for is for biblical scholars to operate out of an explicitly theological stance. Bockmuehl is not alone in this criticism of biblical studies and exegesis, of course. It may be a slight exaggeration but it would appear to be the case that what is now called theological interpretation of Scripture is wining the day amongst Christian biblical scholarship. Or perhaps just within theological approaches to the text.

In his introduction to theological interpretation of Scripture, Daniel Treier notes that for many of its advocates, theological interpretation of Scripture is perhaps the latest redemption of a biblical theology, with key modifications.[8] While not rejecting the grammatical-historical approach of contemporary evangelical exegesis, theological interpretation of Scripture does not limit

---

4. Stephen E. Fowl, 'Introduction', in Stephen E. Fowl (ed.), *The Theological Interpretation of Scripture: Classic and Contemporary Readings* (Blackwell Readings in Modern Theology; Oxford: Blackwell, 1997), p. xii.

5. Francis Watson, *Text, Church and World: Biblical Interpretation in Theological Perspective* (Edinburgh: T. & T. Clark, 1994), p. 1.

6. Markus Bockmuehl, *Seeing the Word: Refocusing New Testament Study* (Studies in Theological Interpretation; Grand Rapids: Baker Academic, 2006), p. 76.

7. Bockmuehl, *Seeing the Word*, p. 77.

8. Stephen Fowl has more to say of biblical theology in his perceptive little work, *Theological Interpretation of Scripture* (Cascade Companions; Eugene, OR: Cascade, 2009), pp. 20-21.

interpretation to these 'rules'. Theological interpretation of Scripture takes a canonical approach to Scripture and asks genuinely theological questions such as, What difference does Christ make to an understanding of each and every text (including, of course, the Old Testament)? As such this approach is church-centred, hermeneutically and methodologically flexible, and credally orthodox.[9] Finally, theological interpretation of Scripture is interdisciplinary and as such it seeks to break down but not eliminate the distinctions between the various disciplines of biblical theology, systematic theology and practical theology.

In order to progress the state of theological interpretation of Scripture, Vanhoozer supplied ten theses on theological interpretation in a 2009 address at Gordon–Conwell Theological Seminary.[10] His ten points are worth recounting:

1. The nature and function of the Bible are insufficiently grasped unless and until we see the Bible as an element in the economy of triune discourse.
2. An appreciation of the theological nature of the Bible entails a rejection of a methodological atheism that treats the texts as having a 'natural history' only.
3. The message of the Bible is 'finally' about the loving power of God for salvation (Rom 1:16), the definitive or final gospel Word of God that comes to brightest light in the word's final form.
4. Because God acts in space-time (of Israel, Jesus Christ, and the church), theological interpretation requires thick descriptions that plumb the height and depth of history, not only its length.
5. Theological interpreters view the historical events recounted in Scripture as ingredients in a unified story ordered by an economy of triune providence.
6. The Old Testament testifies to the same drama of redemption as the New, hence the church rightly reads both testaments together, two parts of a single authoritative script.
7. The Spirit who speaks with magisterial authority in the Scripture speaks with ministerial authority in church tradition.
8. In an era marked by the conflict of interpretations, there is good reason provisionally to acknowledge the superiority of catholic interpretation.

---

9. Daniel J. Treier, *Introducing Theological Interpretation of Scripture: Recovering a Christian Practice* (Nottingham: Apollos, 2008), p. 115. Fowl makes the same points in *Theological Interpretation of Scripture*, pp. 32-35, while specifically suggesting that a Christian reading of Scripture is one in which Christ is the *res* of all Scripture, and the notion that Christ is the *telos* of the law.

10. Kevin J. Vanhoozer, 'Interpreting Scripture between the Rock of Biblical Studies and the Hard Place of Systematic Theology: The State of the Evangelical (Dis)union' (delivered at Renewing the Evangelical Mission Conference, Gordon–Conwell Theological Seminary, 13–15 October 2009).

9. The end of biblical interpretation is not simply communication—the sharing of information—but communion, a sharing in the light, life, and love of God.
10. The church is that community where good habits of theological interpretation are best formed and where the fruit of these habits are best exhibited.[11]

Several significant features impress in these succinct points: first, the persuasive influence the doctrine of the Trinity has on any theological interpretation; second, the ecclesial context within which theological interpretation is conducted, both in its traditional and contemporaneous senses; third, the prioritization of the theological over the strictly philosophical-hermeneutic, in any Christian reading of Scripture;[12] and finally, the goal of communion with God as the controlling purpose in theological interpretation. In conformity with Vanhoozer's overview, Fowl reminds us of the following:

> The practice of theological interpretation is, at its core, an activity of Christian communities. The triune God, to whom scriptural texts bear witness, calls us into such communities. Hence, Christian communities provide the contexts whereby we learn, as the body of Christ through the power of the Holy Spirit, to interpret and embody Scripture in ways that enhance rather than frustrate our communion with God and others.[13]

Before turning to the theological interpretation of Scripture offered by Thomas F. Torrance, I want to suggest that a viable precursor of the theological interpretation of Scripture movement is in fact the history of what we now call systematic theology, and that one example supremely exhibits this: John Calvin's *Institutes of the Christian Religion*.[14] In the preface to the 1559 edition Calvin explains his intent in writing the *Institute,* how it relates to his *Commentaries*, and then how it relates to Scripture. This is instructive, I think, for our own purposes here. In his note to the reader Calvin clarifies the relation between the *Institutes*—theology—and Scripture when he writes:

---

11. For similar lists see Richard B. Hays who presents a list of twelve identifying marks in his 'Reading the Bible with Eyes of Faith: The Practice of Theological Exegesis', *JTI* 1 (2007), pp. 5-21; and Michael Gorman who provides a list of eight principles for theological interpretation of Scripture in his *Elements of Biblical Exegesis: Revised and Expanded Edition* (Peabody, MA: Hendrickson, 2009), pp. 148-55.

12. In relation to the priority of the theological over the hermeneutical Fowl argues that, 'In short, we should not ask philosophy to do the church's work' (*Theological Interpretation of Scripture*, p. 51).

13. Fowl, *Theological Interpretation of Scripture*, pp. 51-52.

14. Of course, the division and specialization of biblical studies and systematic theology is a recent invention, thus one could legitimately argue that biblical studies has exemplified something of a theological interpretation of Scripture in the premodern period as well. Not disregarding this recent specialization, it is still true to say that biblical studies and systematic theology have been distinguished since the early church.

> Moreover, it has been my purpose in this labor to prepare and instruct candidates in sacred theology for the reading of the divine Word, in order that they may be able both to have easy access to it and to advance in it without stumbling. For I believe I have so embraced the sum of religion in all its parts, and have arranged it in such an order, that if anyone rightly grasps it, it will not be difficult for him to determine what he ought especially to seek in Scripture, and to what end he ought to relate its contents.[15]

In short it was Calvin's belief that his theology was derived from Scripture and would in turn enable his readers better to understand Scripture.[16] A form of circular reasoning may be detected here, although I would personally prefer to see this more as a hermeneutical spiral than a circle.[17] From at least the time of Tertullian and Irenaeus theology has been constructed from Scripture as a means for reading Scripture.[18] The scaffolding for such an enterprise is not a philosophical hermeneutics but, rather, use of the *regula fidei* or *depositum fidei*. According to Robert Wall, we may define the Rule of Faith as 'the grammar of theological agreements which Christians confess to be true and by which all Scripture is rendered in forming a truly Christian faith and life'.[19] Clearly the ecumenical creeds are central here and constitute the Apostolic Faith; however, we may extend this definition to include the specific theological traditions within which a theologian worships and

---

15. John Calvin, 'John Calvin Note to the Reader', in *Institutes of the Christian Religion* (1559 repr.; ed. J.T. McNeill; trans. F.L. Battles; Library of Christian Classics; Philadelphia: Fortress Press, 1960), XX, p. 4.

16. There was also the goal to which the use of Scripture was oriented. See Brian C. Dennert, 'John Calvin's Movement from the Bible to Theology and Practice', *JETS* 54 (2011), pp. 345-65, where Calvin's views on church government are the focus of the study.

17. From the vantage point of biblical studies see Grant R. Osborne, *The Hermeneutical Spiral: A Comprehensive Introduction to Biblical Interpretation* (Downers Grove, IL: InterVarsity Press, 1991); and for a theological account see Trevor Hart, 'Tradition, Authority, and a Christian Approach to the Bible as Scripture', in J.B. Green and M. Turner (eds.), *Between Two Horizons: Spanning New Testament Studies and Systematic Theology* (Grand Rapids: Eerdmans, 2000), p. 191.

18. The difference between Irenaeus' use of the *regula fidei* and Torrance's is that Torrance makes explicit what Irenaeus does not, namely, that the truth or reality of God as revealed in the incarnate Son is what the Rule of Faith discloses, is what is revealed through Scripture, is expressed doctrinally, and is subsequently practiced in ecclesial contexts, in which activity the believer communes with God through their union with Christ. Irenaeus' use of the *regula fidei* can thus look entirely circular, whereas Torrance's use of it more approximates an ascending spiral. See Thomas F. Torrance, 'The Deposit of Faith', *SJT* 36 (1983), pp. 1-28. See further below.

19. Robert W. Wall, 'Reading the Bible from within our Traditions: The "Rule of Faith" in Theological Hermeneutics', in J.B. Green and M. Turner (eds.), *Between Two Horizons*, p. 88.

ministers.[20] Thus Calvin, to take this one example, reads Scripture as a catholic and *Reformed* theologian and this is what guides his interpretative decisions. As we shall see below, Thomas Torrance does the same. Wall argues later in his essay, 'In my judgment the church's Rule of Faith is narrative in shape, Trinitarian in substance, and relates the essential beliefs of Christianity together by the grammar of christological monotheism'.[21] This is an important clarification of the compatibility of a theological interpretation of Scripture with the *regula fidei*, something that we shall see is central in the theological interpretation of Thomas Torrance.

Calvin continues to explain the relation between theology and Scripture in the preface to the 1560 French edition of the *Institutes* when he writes:

> Although Holy Scripture contains a perfect doctrine, to which one can add nothing, since in it our Lord has meant to display the infinite treasures of his wisdom, yet a person who has not much practice in it has good reason for some guidance and direction, to know what he ought to look for in it, in order not to wander hither and thither, but to hold to a sure path, that he may always be pressing toward the end to which the Holy Spirit calls him.[22]

Thus, Calvin believed his *Institute* would provide 'a key to open a way for all children of God into a good and right understanding of Holy Scripture',[23] a worthy goal of all dogmatics, one would suggest. Calvin then explains the relation between the *Institute* and his *Commentaries* specifically.

> If, after this road has, as it were, been paved, I shall publish any interpretations of Scripture, I shall always condense them, because I shall have no need to undertake long doctrinal discussions, and to digress into commonplaces. In this way the godly reader will be spared great annoyance and boredom, provided he approach Scripture armed with a knowledge of the present work, as a necessary tool. But because the program of this instruction is clearly mirrored in all my commentaries, I prefer to let the book itself declare its purpose rather than to describe it in words.[24]

He then makes his rather comical assertion (given the subsequent length of his *Commentaries*): 'Thus, if henceforth our Lord gives me the means and opportunity of writing some commentaries, I shall use the *greatest possible brevity*, because there will be no need for long digressions, seeing

---

20. Wall also accepts this contention and thus suggests the Rule of Faith is in practice 'a richly variegated confession' ('Reading the Bible from within our Traditions', p. 102).
21. Wall, 'Reading the Bible from within our Traditions', p. 101.
22. John Calvin, 'Subject Matter of the Present Work: From the French Edition of 1560', in *Institutes of the Christian Religion*, XX, p. 6.
23. Calvin, 'Subject Matter of the Present Work', p. 7.
24. Calvin, 'John Calvin Note to the Reader', pp. 4-5.

that I have here treated at length almost all the articles pertaining to Christianity'.[25]

One may turn a millennium earlier to the works of Augustine to find the same thing, expressed most typically in his *De doctrina christiania*, the four books on Christian doctrine, where he develops essentially the same position as Calvin.[26] In his preface we read:

> There are certain rules for the interpretation of Scripture which I think might with great advantage be taught to earnest students of the word, that they may profit not only from reading the works of others who have laid open the secrets of the sacred writings, but also from themselves opening such secrets to others. These rules I propose to teach to those who are able and willing to learn....[27]

Chief among such 'rules' for interpreting Scripture explicated in book 2, chapter 7 are fear, piety, knowledge, resolution, counsel, purification of heart, stop or termination, and wisdom.[28] What Augustine explicitly adds to those insights gleaned from Calvin are what we may term the 'practices' of the theological interpreter of Scripture.[29]

It is in this tradition of theological interpretation of Scripture that Thomas Torrance stands. Torrance echoes similar thoughts to Calvin in the way he defines Christian dogmatics and its relation to Scripture. According to the interpretation of Robert Walker, 'Christian dogmatics is the discipline which attempts to express the essential content of Christian faith and doctrine as an aid to the church in her teaching and preaching'. Like biblical theology, dogmatics is faithful to Scripture but has three further features: i) it thinks

---

25. Calvin, 'Subject Matter of the Present Work', p. 7 (italics added). Calvin was, of course, alluding to commentaries such as those of Bucer, which were anything but brief and contained lengthy disquisitions on doctrine.

26. Augustine, *On Christian Doctrine* (ed. P. Schaff; 2 vols.; Nicene and Post-Nicene Fathers, first series; Grand Rapids: Eerdmans, 1956), II, pp. 517-97.

27. Augustine, 'Preface', in *On Christian Doctrine*, II, p. 519.

28. Augustine, *On Christian Doctrine*, II, pp. 537-38. Fowl, *Theological Interpretation of Scripture*, pp. 66-70, provides his own list of indicative practices, namely truth seeking/telling, repentance, forgiveness and reconciliation, and patience.

29. For an example of Augustine's theological interpretation of Scripture, see Keith E. Johnson, 'Augustine's "Trinitarian" Reading of John 5: A Model for the Theological Interpretation of Scripture?', *JETS* 52 (2009), pp. 799-810. Fowl reminds us of an image Augustine used when he spoke of Scripture as a vehicle to carry us to our true home, although he was aware that we might find the vehicle of biblical studies so plush and the ride so smooth that we would forget we were on a journey and not a joy ride (*Theological Interpretation of Scripture*, p. 39). While no reference is given by Fowl I assume he is referring to Augustine, *On Christian Doctrine*, I, p. 533, under a discussion of 'The fulfilment and end of the Scriptures is the love of God and of our neighbour'. I am indebted to Ivor Davidson for directing me to this text.

with the saints in the tradition of the church and in faithfulness to apostolic tradition, church creeds and ecumenical decisions on doctrine; ii) it recognizes that such church tradition must always be subject to Scripture; and iii) it endeavours to express faithfully the doctrine of Christ and to bring all doctrine, preaching and ministry of the church into agreement with Scripture and above all with Christ.[30] Clearly, this is an affirmation of the central tenets of a theological interpretation of Scripture.[31]

In outlining his own perspective on theological interpretation of Scripture, Fowl suggests that the urgent task is to see more actual theological interpretation of Scripture.[32] He goes on to suggest that this may be done in a variety of contexts: the commentary, monographs and scholarly articles. However, when patristic and medieval sources are consulted it is evident that the sermon is one of the primary exemplars of theological interpretation of Scripture in the pre-modern period. Fowl thus issues a challenge: 'the future of theological interpretation concerns how and in what ways sermons can become a mode for serious scholarly theological interpretation'.[33] In what follows we shall introduce Thomas Torrance as a theological interpreter of Scripture and then proceed critically to examine his lectures and sermons for evidence of how well he evinces such an approach.

Torrance's Theological Hermeneutics

That Thomas F. Torrance is a proponent of theological interpretation of Scripture is without question.[34] If the brief account above of what constitutes

---

30. Robert T. Walker, 'Editor's Introduction', in Thomas F. Torrance, *Incarnation: The Person and Life of Christ* (ed. Robert T. Walker; Milton Keynes: Paternoster; Downers Grove, IL: InterVarsity Press, 2008), p. xxiii. See Thomas F. Torrance, 'The Place of Christology in Biblical and Dogmatic Theology', in *Theology in Reconstruction* (Grand Rapids: Eerdmans, 1965), pp. 128-49.

31. Robert Walker has described the Edinburgh lectures as 'effectively an extended theological commentary on the Bible' ('Editor's Introduction', in *Incarnation*, p. xi).

32. Fowl, *Theological Interpretation of Scripture*, p. 71.

33. Fowl, *Theological Interpretation of Scripture*, p. 73.

34. An article published in 1980 was already identifying Torrance as a theological interpreter in a way which specifically parallels what is today termed theological interpretation of Scripture. See Bryan J. Gray, 'Towards Better Ways of Reading the Bible', *SJT* 33 (1980), pp. 301-15. Gray compared Torrance's theological hermeneutics with that of Paul Ricoeur, and noted significant parallels in their respective work. Torrance receives passing mention as a theological interpreter in Brevard S. Childs, 'Toward Recovering Theological Exegesis', *ExAud* 16 (2000), p. 122; and David S. Yeago, 'The New Testament and the Nicene Dogma: A Contribution to the Recovery of Theological Exegesis', in Stephen Fowl (ed.), *The Theological Interpretation of Scripture: Classical and Contemporary Essays* (Oxford: Blackwell, 1997), p. 96 n. 17.

theological interpretation of Scripture is accurate, then Torrance clearly exemplifies this method. In a sermon on Jn 1.19-51, for instance, Torrance affirms his theological interpretation of Scripture as follows:

> In this very Gospel, for example, it is John who is speaking and bearing witness to Jesus, and I am expounding what John has said, not simply in the light of what I think he said but in the light of what I have learned together with others in the Church of the meaning of the Gospel. I am influenced in my witness by the witness of others in the history of the Church, so that as we meditate upon this passage and seek to listen to its message, we do that 'with the saints', in the communion of the Spirit. But in that very communion it is Jesus Christ Himself alive, acutely and personally near, who speaks to us, and we hear and know Him face to face, invisibly as yet, but nonetheless directly and intimately. That is the perpetual miracle of the Gospel wherever it is preached.[35]

By way of overview I suggest that Torrance is an exponent of theological interpretation of Scripture on the following grounds: first, it is well known that for Torrance the doctrine of the Trinity is that which controls all others and it is this which structures his approach to Holy Scripture; second, he rejects the dominance of any historical-critical hermeneutic in favour of a christological hermeneutic; third, Christ is acknowledged as the subject matter or *res* of all Scripture, including the Old Testament, and Christ is also considered the end or *telos* of the law; fourth, Torrance interprets Holy Scripture within the constraints of the *regula fidei*; fifth, in his acknowledgment that Holy Scripture is a divine and human book he adopts a realist epistemology; and finally, reading Holy Scripture is a churchly activity in which the goal is to commune with God. As such, certain practices are required in order rightly to order our service and worship of God, including our performance of Holy Scripture. In these six ways at least, Torrance is an exemplar of theological interpretation of Scripture. What follows is an attempt to justify and illustrate this claim with reference to his theological method, his doctrine of Scripture, his exegesis, and his preaching of the Word written.[36] In a lengthy citation Torrance summarizes his position as follows:

---

35. Thomas F. Torrance, 'The Lamb of God', in *When Christ Comes and Comes Again* (London: Hodder & Stoughton, 1957), p. 57. The citation continues: 'It is preached by very fallible human beings, but through their witness and in spite of their mistakes, Christ Himself comes and meets with sinners directly and enters into conversation with them just as He entered into conversation with these disciples at the very beginning of the Gospel'.

36. For an account of the similar view of Scripture by Thomas's brother James Torrance, see Alan J. Torrance, 'The Bible as Testimony to our Belonging: The Theological Vision of James B. Torrance', in G.S. Dawson (ed.), *An Introduction to Torrance Theology* (London: T. & T. Clark, 2007), pp. 103-19.

In seeking to interpret God's trinitarian self-revelation through the medium of the gospels and epistles we have to do with an altogether deeper dimension in knowledge. But here it holds true that it is through personal dwelling in Christ and interiorising his Word within us that we enter into a cognitive union with him as God incarnate, and are thereby admitted to an intimate knowledge of God's self-revelation in its intrinsic wholeness and are enabled to discern the truth of his self-revelation as we could not do otherwise. By indwelling the Scriptures of the New Testament and interiorising their message we become drawn into the circle of God's revelation of himself through himself. Spiritually and theologically regarded, this kind of indwelling, in Christ and his Word, involves faith, devotion, meditation, prayer and worship in and through which we are given discerning access to God in his inner Communion as Father, Son and Holy Spirit. Any faithful interpretation of the Scriptures operates on different levels, the linguistic and the conceptual level, but unless the interpreter participates in the movement of God's unique self-revelation through Christ and in the Spirit which gave rise to the Scriptures and has left its imprint upon them, he or she will fail to understand them in their deep spiritual dimension and will be blind to their essential truth content. Hence if we are to interpret the Holy Scriptures we must cultivate the habit of tuning into them as a whole in order to penetrate into their centre of meaning, so that the spiritual realities and truths of divine revelation to which they testify may be allowed to govern our knowing and shape our understanding of them. It is when we interpret different passages and statements in the light of the whole that their real meaning and force become apparent.[37]

Realist Hermeneutics

With this basic structure in place Torrance considers more specifically how theological interpretation is to be done.[38] According to Torrance this is where a form of critical realism is to be aligned with Christology. If Jesus Christ is the Word of God, the true Object and Subject, then he must reveal himself in any theological interpretation of Scripture. And this is exactly what happens. 'Only as we enter into the relation of resemblance set up between us and God through the Incarnate Word and Work of his Son do we discern the validity of our theological terms and expressions, which we

---

37. Thomas F. Torrance, *The Christian Doctrine of God: One Being Three Persons* (Edinburgh: T. & T. Clark, 1991), p. 38. I am indebted to Bobby Grow for reminding me of this citation.

38. Although Torrance outlines a broad hermeneutical method, he never actually presents a detailed discussion of how he understands a legitimate hermeneutics. He comes closest to this in Thomas F. Torrance, *Reality and Evangelical Theology* (Downers Grove, IL: InterVarsity Press, 2nd edn, 1999); and the somewhat ambitiously titled *Divine Meaning: Studies in Patristic Hermeneutics* (Edinburgh: T. & T. Clark, 1995). In this area as in so many others, Torrance's efforts were distracted by clearing epistemological issues first and never quite getting round to constructively building on that epistemological foundation.

employ on the basis of revelation, to be ontologically as well as soteriologically rooted'.³⁹ Because of the incarnation, theological activity is a participation in the act whereby God in Christ assumes our human nature into union with himself. Here in Christology theology can penetrate into the inner *ratio* and *necessitas* of the object of our knowledge in order to achieve a clarification in the whole field of theological inquiry. Only God can reveal himself!

This explains Torrance's dissatisfaction with modern forms of historical-critical hermeneutics.⁴⁰ As he explains:

> [T]his is why the theologian knows that he cannot get very far *theologically* with historico-critical and historico-analytical methods, which can be of help to him only at comparatively superficial and formal levels of thought. Important and essential as they are at those levels, they are unable to cope with the all-important integrative process which is of an onto-relational and empirico-theoretical kind, but tend rather to dismantle the in-depth structure upon which the semantic focus finally depends.⁴¹

The theologian reads Scripture in order to see what Scripture points to. Attention is directed along the line of the witness of Scripture to the self-revealing and reconciling God, which inevitably means that Scripture has a subsidiary status in the face of what is apprehended *through* Scripture—the truth itself.⁴² Torrance summarily concludes: 'What really makes Scripture a transparent medium is the divine light that shines through it from the face of Jesus Christ into our hearts'.⁴³

---

39. Thomas F. Torrance, *Karl Barth: An Introduction to his Early Theology 1910–1931* (1962 repr.; Edinburgh: T. & T. Clark, 2000), p. 194. Unfortunately, Torrance does not fully develop the constitutive role of the Holy Spirit in his depth exegesis. Without this corresponding work of the Spirit Torrance's depth exegesis is somewhat distorted and undeveloped.

40. Torrance is critical of contemporary hermeneutical methods in a number of places, most notably in Thomas F. Torrance, *Space, Time and Resurrection* (1976 repr.; Edinburgh: T. & T. Clark, 1998), pp. 1-21, 159-93; *Preaching Christ Today* (Grand Rapids: Eerdmans, 1994), pp. 1-11; and '"The Historical Jesus": From the Perspective of a Theologian', in W.C. Weinrich (ed.), *The New Testament Age: Essays in Honor of Bo Reicke* (2 vols.; Macon, GA: Mercer University Press, 1984), II, pp. 511-26. In this regard, see the analysis of Paul D. Molnar, *Divine Freedom and the Doctrine of the Immanent Trinity: In Dialogue with Karl Barth and Contemporary Theology* (London: T. & T. Clark, 2002), pp. 174-75; 'God's Self-communication in Christ: A Comparison of Thomas F. Torrance and Karl Rahner', *SJT* 50 (1997), pp. 294-96.

41. Torrance, *Space, Time and Resurrection*, p. 12. Note the situation of Barth also in his break with the liberal theology and critical methodology of his day in his pastoral work at Safenwil. In his own way Torrance is himself reliving what his great mentor went through nearly sixty years earlier.

42. Consult Thomas F. Torrance, 'Truth and Authority: Theses on Truth', *ITQ* 39 (1972), pp. 215-42.

43. Torrance, *Space, Time and Resurrection*, p. 12.

It is not to be understood from this that the theologian leaves the Scriptures behind for their own ideas or opinions. *Anathema*! This is made clear when Torrance outlines a basic four-step process of what is involved in hermeneutics: first, the scope of the Bible is Christ; second, a realist account of the economic condescension of the Son in the incarnation; third, an interpretative framework of thought; and fourth, the canon of truth.[44] Torrance concludes, 'The implication of this is that we may know God and interpret his self-revelation only in the attitude and context of worship and within the fellowship of the church, where to the godly reason God is more to be adored than expressed'.[45]

Torrance reminds us:

> Although the Scriptures have a subsidiary role in the human and earthly coefficient of divine revelation, that is nevertheless essential to the reciprocity which the revealing and reconciling God creates between us and himself, for without all that the Scriptures in the saving purpose of God have come to embody, we would not be able to know God or to have intelligible communion with him within our continuing human and historical existence.[46]

Because we are unable to know God except on the basis of the biblical witness we never leave behind the written Word of God. 'Torrance's concern', writes Elmer Colyer, 'is that while we cannot attain knowledge of God apart from the Bible, when we focus just on the text it can lose its in-depth significance in its grounding in the realities and events of God's self-revelation and its semantic function of directing us to them'.[47] In Torrance's estimation:

> This means that the church must always turn to the Holy Scriptures as the immediate source and norm of all revealed knowledge of God and of his saving purpose in Jesus Christ. Since all doctrinal formulations of the Church take shape within the matrix of the biblical revelation where they have their kerygmatic and didactic basis, regular examination and interpretation of the Holy Scriptures are in order, so that the Church may clarify and purify its knowledge of God's self-revelation mediated through them, and put all its biblical exposition, all preaching of the Gospel, and all theological statements about its understanding of the content of God's self-revelation into question through referring them back to their divine ground.[48]

---

44. These points are largely derived from his original essay on the hermeneutics of Athanasius (Torrance, *Reality and Evangelical Theology*, pp. 101-20). See Elmer M. Colyer, *The Nature of Doctrine in T.F. Torrance's Theology* (Eugene, OR: Wipf & Stock, 2001), pp. 64-68.

45. Torrance, *Reality and Evangelical Theology*, pp. 119-20.

46. Torrance, *Space, Time and Resurrection*, pp. 12-13.

47. Colyer, *Nature of Doctrine*, p. 156. Cf. Thomas F. Torrance, *Karl Barth: Biblical and Evangelical Theologian* (Edinburgh: T. & T. Clark, 1990), p. 117; *Theological Science* (Oxford: Oxford University Press, 1969), p. 192; and *Reality and Evangelical Theology*, p. 96.

48. Torrance, *Divine Meaning*, pp. 5-6.

Theological language is clearly conceived by Torrance as the vehicle of analogical reference.[49] Heltzel points us to this fact in his statement,

> In itself [theological language which is analogical] is radically unlike God, the extralinguistic object to which it refers, but by grace it is able to transcend itself, attaining a sufficient likeness or adequacy to its object. 'The being of God is either known by grace or it is not known at all', writes Barth (*CD* II/1: 27). Thus, by God's grace, our language by analogy truly refers to God in an actual way.[50]

It is this analogical condition of Scripture that lies behind Torrance's theological hermeneutics.[51] Analogical reasoning is based on the assumption that God is both the ultimate source of all truth and the ultimate interpreter of all truth.[52] Human interpretations are thus second-order reflections upon the self-revelation of God to humanity in his Word. Analogical reasoning is, especially in light of a theological realism, self-consciously dependent on God who is the ultimate point of predication.[53] As a result God's knowledge

---

49. See especially Torrance, *Divine Meaning*, p. 7: 'There is thus analogical unlikeness as well as likeness in the relation between the divine and human in Christ and the relation between the divine (that is, Christ himself) and the human in the Bible'. Cf. Torrance, 'Truth and Authority', thesis seven, p. 216.

50. Peter Heltzel, 'Thomas Torrance', in *Dictionary of Modern Western Theology*. No pages. Cited 28 August 2012. Online: http://people.bu.edu/wwildman/WeirdWildWeb/ courses/mwt/ dictionary/mwt_themes785. Barth's adoption and use of analogical reference is clearly articulated in George Hunsinger, 'Beyond Literalism and Expressivism: Karl Barth's Hermeneutical Realism', in *Disruptive Grace: Studies in the Theology of Karl Barth* (Grand Rapids: Eerdmans, 2000), pp. 210-25 (especially p. 217). In rejecting literalism and expressivisim Barth adopts the category of realism and with it analogy over a univocal or equivocal referent function of language.

51. A similar analogical relationship is employed in Torrance's understanding of the sacraments. See Thomas F. Torrance, *Theology in Reconciliation: Essays towards Evangelical and Catholic Unity in East and West* (London: Geoffrey Chapman, 1975), pp. 82-83. Cf. George Hunsinger, 'The Dimension of Depth: Thomas F. Torrance on the Sacraments of Baptism and the Lord's Supper', *SJT* 54 (2001), pp. 155-76.

52. See Michael S. Horton, 'A Vulnerable God apart from Christ? Open Theism's Challenge to the Classical Doctrine of God', *Modern Reformation Magazine* 10.3 (2001), p. 33.

53. Torrance deals with the anthropomorphic nature of Scripture in T.F. Torrance, 'The Christian Apprehension of God the Father', in A.F. Kimel (ed.), *Speaking the Christian God: The Holy Trinity and the Challenge of Feminism* (Grand Rapids: Eerdmans, 1992), pp. 120-43, especially pp. 127-29. For surveys of Reformed attitudes to analogical language and its wider context, see Michael S. Horton, 'Hellenistic or Hebrew? Open Theism and Reformed Theological Method', *JETS* 45 (2002), pp. 317-41; John M. Frame, *The Doctrine of the Knowledge of God: A Theology of Lordship* (Phillipsburg, NJ: Presbyterian & Reformed, 1987); and Alvin Plantinga and Nicholas Wolterstorff (eds.), *Faith and Rationality: Reason and Belief in God* (Notre Dame, IN: University of Notre Dame Press, 1983).

is archetypal, theological statements are ectypal; analogous thinking means bringing our creaturely thoughts into accord, but not into identity with, God's divine thoughts.

Torrance's use of analogy can only be understood fully within his wider epistemic concerns, especially those having to do with the stratification of truth which must be coordinated through various levels of thought.[54] A summary of his position is that Scripture contains truth statements but not the Truth, which is exclusively the being and act of God himself. Theological concepts, including Scripture, point beyond the statements themselves to the Truth and do so through three levels of cognition: the level of experience, the theological level and finally the meta-scientific level. These levels are coordinated together in such a way that each is open to the other and is 'translogically' related to it at certain boundary points in which the higher level is capable of explaining more fully the lower level. Torrance applies these levels of cognition to the analogical nature of Scripture:

> It is, I believe, within this open hierarchical structure of levels of thought, that we are able to cope with the problem of analogy and truth-reference, in a way that our predecessors were not able to do. The main point to remember is that there is no one-to-one or point-for-point correspondence between the concepts on one level and their counterparts on another level, but they are analogically related through the translogical relation between the different levels to which they belong and by which they are defined.[55]

In order further to explain the analogical function of Scripture and its depth dimension Torrance draws on Calvin's analogy of the Bible as

---

54. On Torrance's theological method of cognitive stratification, see Thomas F. Torrance, 'The Stratification of Truth', in *Reality and Scientific Theology* (Edinburgh: Scottish Academic Press, 1985), pp. 131-59; *Christian Doctrine of God*, pp. 88-111. See a discussion of these levels in Colyer, *Nature of Doctrine*, pp. 181-87; and an overview in A.G. Marley, *T.F. Torrance: The Rejection of Dualism* (Edinburgh: Handsel, 1992), pp. 15-16. For a wider perspective which draws particularly upon Nicolai Hartman and Roy Bhaskar, see Alister E. McGrath, 'Stratification: Levels of Reality and the Limits of Reductionism', in *The Order of Things: Explorations in Scientific Theology* (Oxford: Blackwell, 2006), pp. 97-116.

55. Torrance, 'Truth and Authority', p. 234. He goes on to illustrate with reference to the analogical relation between human fatherhood and the Fatherhood of God, 'the concept of the Fatherhood of God which is defined by the supreme level is in the nature of the case not open to any reductionism to or definition from below, although the open structure from below through its analogical and translogical reference is necessary for *our* apprehension of the divine Fatherhood. At the same time the representational content of what we mean by a human father does not as such correspond to anything in the divine Fatherhood, although it is conceptually co-ordinated with it in this open way through the hierarchy of levels' (pp. 234-35). For a full-length discussion on the topic consult Torrance, 'The Christian Apprehension of God the Father'.

'spectacles' which enable the wearer to see and know God, something the Reformers termed the 'perspicuity' of Scripture.[56] According to Calvin, the Bible functions as an aid to seeing and knowing God's self-revelation. Following Calvin, Torrance argues that proper hermeneutics does not focus 'myopically' on the biblical text but rather on the reality and truth of God which sounds and shows through them. It is this function of sounding or showing through that accounts for Torrance's language of a depth exegesis.

The Epistemological Role of the Holy Spirit

An often overlooked aspect of theological hermeneutics is the epistemological role of the Holy Spirit.[57] In Torrance's work this comes in for special, though limited, consideration.[58] A key function of the Spirit is to mediate knowledge of God to human creatures through the incarnate Word.[59] In so doing Christ and the Spirit mutually mediate one another. This held true throughout the Incarnation as it does post-Pentecost through the church, especially through the sacraments and the Scriptures. As Colyer explains,

> Through the Spirit, we come to share in the incarnate Son's knowledge of God the Father realized in Christ's vicarious humanity. In the incarnation God adapts knowledge of God to our creaturely structures of knowledge and adapts those structures to knowledge of God. In the Holy Spirit God utilizes those creaturely structures as the means by which we apprehend God and know God in God's divine reality as Triune.... Thus doctrine and the nature

---

56. Calvin, *Institutes*, 1.7.1; 1.14.1. See Torrance, *Reality and Evangelical Theology*, pp. 64, 144; and *Transformation and Convergence in the Frame of Knowledge: Explorations in the Interrelations of Scientific and Theological Enterprise* (Grand Rapids: Eerdmans, 1984), p. 310.

57. See Myk Habets, 'Reading Scripture and Doing Theology with the Holy Spirit', in Myk Habets (ed.), *The Spirit of Truth: Reading Scripture and Constructing Theology with the Holy Spirit* (Eugene, OR: Pickwick, 2010), pp. 89-104; and the retroactive hermeneutic described in *The Anointed Son: A Trinitarian Spirit Christology* (Eugene, OR: Pickwick, 2010), pp. 103-12.

58. Despite this focus, Torrance only developed the role of the Spirit in certain, limited directions. He did not, for instance, spend much time examining or explicating the role of the Spirit on the theological interpreter. In a 2009 essay Darren Sarisky provides an appreciative critique of Torrance's theological hermeneutics, in which one of his main criticisms is the inattention Torrance pays to the reader, who appears to be passive in his depiction of scriptural interpretation. Sarisky recommends Barth's ethics of interpretation in *Church Dogmatics* 1/2 of *explicatio* (determining the sense of the text), *meditatio* (reflecting on the sense or the words), and *applicatio* (appropriating the Bible's message) ('T.F. Torrance on Biblical Interpretation', *IJST* 11 [2009], p. 345). See Karl Barth, *Church Dogmatics* 1/2 (Edinburgh: T. & T. Clark, 1956), pp. 722-40. The closest Torrance comes to such practice is, in Sarisky's opinion, in his sermons.

59. See Thomas F. Torrance, *God and Rationality* (1971 repr.; Eugene, OR: Wipf & Stock, 1997), p. 174; and Molnar, *Divine Freedom*, p. 175.

of doctrine are conditioned by the way in which they are related to Christ through the Apostolic foundation of the Church and the Scriptures *in* the Spirit.[60]

Because of Torrance's application of the dynamic nature of revelation, the Holy Spirit becomes central to understanding the dynamics of his doctrine of Scripture and the theological interpretation of it. The relation between God's self-revelation and the Scriptures is dynamic and ontological in origin but also in its ongoing relation, for it is one which God sustains through the mediation of the Holy Spirit as God's sovereign freedom to be present in the creaturely structures of the Word written through the mutual mediation of the Word and the Spirit.[61]

It is the divine presence of both Word *and* Spirit which renders Scripture an abiding and authoritative Word of God to humanity and it is this dynamic presence which Torrance considers to be the true content of a dynamic concept of verbal inspiration.[62] Torrance writes,

> All Scripture given by divine inspiration is and becomes what it really is through the presence and advocacy of the Holy Spirit. The Spirit of God is God in his freedom to be present to what he has brought into being through his Word and to realise its true end in himself through a relation of himself to himself.[63]

It is not to be assumed that the active presence of the Spirit changes Scripture in any way in the dynamic of revelation and reconciliation. Rather, 'through the Spirit God makes himself present to man and thereby acts from within him to make him subjectively open and ready and capable for God, and thus to realise his revelation in him'.[64] Based on the transcendent freedom of God in his Spirit to be present with us, Torrance adopts Barth's notion of the 'contingent contemporaneity' of the Word and act of God,[65] and concludes that 'it is that kind of divine creative and sustaining Presence which makes the Bible what it is and what it ever becomes as the written Word of God'.[66] The important point of this dynamism is that, consistent with

---

60. Colyer, *Nature of Doctrine*, p. 152. Cf. Torrance, *Reality and Scientific Theology*, pp. 185-86, 192; and *Theological Science*, p. 52.

61. See Colyer's excellent treatment of these themes in *Nature of Doctrine*, pp. 154-55.

62. For a comparative account, see John Webster, *Holy Scripture: A Dogmatic Sketch* (CIT; Cambridge: Cambridge University Press, 2003), pp. 30-39.

63. Torrance, *Karl Barth*, pp. 91-92.

64. Torrance, *Karl Barth*, p. 92.

65. Torrance, *Karl Barth*, p. 92. Cf. Barth, *CD* I/1, p. 145.

66. Torrance, *Karl Barth*, p. 92. For an analysis of this in Barth's theology, see the useful essay by Trevor A. Hart in which he compels the reader to look for the human and divine aspects within the three-fold Word in Barth's theology. When we do so we see, to

Torrance's scientific theology as a whole, God is the only proper revealer of himself. Following Barth, this is a fully Trinitarian concept of revelation: 'Hence it may be said that the Bible is what it is as the written Word of God precisely through the divinely ordained bond between its creaturely form and God's self-revelation', states Torrance.[67] Recall here Vanhoozer's earlier insistence upon Triune discourse.

Torrance and Theological Interpretation of Scripture

Torrance as a Precursor to the Modern Theological Interpretation of Scripture Movement

Theological interpretation of Scripture is a major feature of contemporary biblical-theological studies and has the potential to revitalize Christian readings of Holy Scripture in ways which are church-affirming and God-honouring. The approach to Scripture adopted by Torrance has been shown to prefigure the recent move to theological interpretation of Scripture. As John Webster once stated, 'Well before the recent revival of interest in precritical hermeneutics and in theological interpretation of Scripture, Torrance was pondering classical Christian modes of interpretation and discovering in them a resource for extricating the interpretation of the bible from captivity to historical and literary phenomenology'.[68] This is borne out in several ways. In his interaction with the Fathers more than with the moderns Torrance's hermeneutic is clearly premodern.[69] Second, it is self-consciously

---

use christological terms, a relationship between the humanity and divinity of Scripture and preaching that is more of a Nestorian union than a Chalcedonian one ('The Word, The Words and the Witness: Proclamation as Divine and Human Reality in the Theology of Karl Barth', in *Regarding Karl Barth: Toward a Reading of his Theology* [Downers Grove, IL: InterVarsity Press, 1999], pp. 28-47 [esp. p. 35]). This is why Barth and Torrance both prefer on occasion the analogy of John the Baptist to that of the humanity of Christ. John's role is to point away from himself to Christ and to bear witness to his hidden identity: 'he must increase but I must decrease'. See also Torrance, 'Truth and Authority', p. 242. Where Torrance does use the christological analogy for Scripture, see the discussion by Robert T. Walker, 'Editor's Introduction', in Thomas F. Torrance, *Atonement: The Person and Work of Christ* (ed. Robert T. Walker; Downers Grove, IL: InterVarsity Press, 2009), pp. lvii-lx; and the comments later in the same work by Torrance, 'The Biblical Witness to Jesus Christ', pp. 336-39, where Torrance appeals to a notion of the *communicatio idiomatum* between the written word and the incarnate Word, technically a *communicatio operationum*.

67. Torrance, *Karl Barth*, p. 93.
68. John Webster, 'T.F. Torrance on Scripture' (keynote address at the annual meeting of the T.F. Torrance Theological Fellowship, Montreal, 6 November 2009), p. 24.
69. Vanhoozer correctly points out that theological interpretation of Scripture is not simply precritical ('Introduction', p. 1).

a *church* dogmatics, to use Barth's terminology, and not a theology for the academy as if this were an end in itself. Torrance's commitments to his Reformed heritage, along with the Patristic consensus, and his ecumenical reading of Scripture in dialogue with the East all attest to this fact.[70] One of the central tenets of theological interpretation of Scripture is context; it is a reading of Scripture which is 'aimed at shaping and being shaped by a community's faith and practice'.[71] In this regard too, Torrance's hermeneutics and depth-exegesis fit nicely as he adopts, as we have seen, Polanyian themes such as indwelling, tacit knowledge and commitment to his approach to Scripture. The critical research university context where belief can actually be considered an impediment to genuine theology is something to which Torrance is squarely opposed. A perfect illustration of this is the time when, in 1939, Torrance was interviewed for a teaching position at Princeton University. In his interview for the position it was pointed out to Torrance that he would be required to teach theology on an 'objective basis' and in a 'dispassionate way'. Torrance responded by declaring that he could only teach theology as a *science*. When asked to elaborate on this statement he explained that in science

> you don't think in a detached way; you think as you are compelled to think by the evidential grounds upon which you work. It's a much more rigorous way of thinking, but it is a much more objective way of thinking because all your thinking is controlled by the realities you are inquiring into.[72]

Torrance was, to his surprise, appointed to the position.[73] By means of such a 'scientific' theology Torrance meant a theology born from within the faith community and for the faith community.[74]

Examples of Torrance's Theological Exegesis
From what has been said so far it is clear that Torrance can be considered a precursor to and an example of one who utilizes theological interpretation of Scripture. That much is clear. But how good an interpreter was he in

---

70. An especially clear example of each of these commitments can be found in Thomas F. Torrance, 'Trinity Sunday Sermon', *Ekklesiastikos pharos* 52 (1970), pp. 191-99.
71. Fowl, 'Introduction', p. xix.
72. Thomas F. Torrance, 'A Pilgrimage in the School of Faith—An Interview with T. F. Torrance', by John I. Hesselink, *Reformed Review* 38 (1984), p. 54.
73. He subsequently turned it down due to the impending outbreak of World War II. See Alister E. McGrath, *T.F. Torrance: An Intellectual Biography* (Edinburgh: T. & T. Clark, 1999), pp. 57-58.
74. For a fascinating study that expresses similar concerns and themes, see John Webster, *Holiness* (Grand Rapids: Eerdmans, 2003), pp. 8-30. When read in light of the fact that Webster was in the process of leaving the University of Oxford for the University of Aberdeen, his comments on 'the university' take on added significance.

practice? Several appreciative readers of Torrance's work have offered critical conclusions regarding his theological hermeneutics. Webster believes Torrance pays little attention to the literary forms used by interpreters of the Bible—most of all the commentary; that pneumatological interests are inadequately addressed; and he questions the relation of the semantic and the syntactic in Torrance's articulation.[75] In relation to this final criticism Webster notes,

> If it is true that '*no syntactics contains its own semantics*'...it is also true that inquiry into the syntactical features of the text is not only a necessary condition for grasping its semantic features but is itself the means of discerning its semantics.... The Word's relation to the text is more than asymptomatic, and so to read the text as natural sign *is* to hear the divine Word in (not only behind or beneath) its textual surface.[76]

Webster speaks for many when he wishes Torrance had adopted a more commentorial rhetoric.

Webster's point is well taken and is shared by others who wish Torrance had provided more examples of his exegesis in action. It should be noted that Torrance did want to write a theological commentary on the epistle to the Colossians and another on the epistle to the Hebrews, but they never eventuated. He also says that before he went to New College he did write a theological commentary on the epistle to the Philippians, only to destroy it later. He then states:

> Ever since then I have felt the urge to write a theological commentary. After having worked through so many of Calvin's commentaries, I felt that I would like at least to have a hand at trying to do some doctrinal exposition to show how theological interpretation of a book of the New Testament can be done without betraying either the biblical exegesis or retreating from high theology.[77]

Mark 4: The Parable of the Soils
Bryan Gray examines one of the few explicit examples of depth exegesis Torrance does offer in his works.[78] In *Theological Science* Torrance provides exegetical notes on Mark 4 (the parable of the soils). He sees the teaching of Jesus as being given on two interrelated levels of meaning, thus requiring the theological interpreter to penetrate beneath the surface form of the parable to the deeper interpretation in another form. As Torrance states,

---

75. Webster, 'T.F. Torrance on Scripture', pp. 24-27.
76. Webster, 'T.F. Torrance on Scripture', p. 26 (italics original).
77. Torrance, 'A Pilgrimage in the School of Faith', pp. 61-62.
78. Gray, 'Towards Better Ways of Reading the Bible', p. 313.

> Considered from the point of view of theological inquiry the parable (*parabolē*) is the concrete form which Jesus throws (*ballein*) alongside of or parallel to (*para-*) His Word in order to bring it to bear upon our understanding and to apply it to our actual human life.[79]

Torrance argues that one must distinguish between and look through the text of Mark reporting on Jesus' teaching to the real or original text, Jesus' teaching itself.[80] In so doing one moves from the moral and social level to the deeper theological level where meaning becomes evident in the light of the incarnation of the divine Word.[81]

Colyer's study of the nature of doctrine in Torrance's theology draws the conclusion that his

> understanding of the character of Scripture means that for Torrance, the Bible is properly understood only as we focus both on the text and the realities to which it bears witness. We do not attempt to penetrate into the subjective states of biblical writers (or even Jesus); rather we share with the writers their orientation away from themselves in the Spirit through Jesus Christ to the living God.[82]

This, it seems to me, is a fair conclusion to make regarding Torrance's doctrine of Scripture. But is it finally acceptable? For instance, it is out of step with the majority of biblical exegetes, past and present, and as such does not appear to be a very good example of theological interpretation of Scripture at all. What it does illustrate is a certain form of early twentieth-century Barthian biblical scholarship that, in the wake of Barth and his reaction to liberal anthropological readings of Scripture, shied away from asking (and thus answering) the questions of what Jesus knew and when he knew it.[83]

---

79. Torrance, *Theological Science*, p. 275. The comment on Mark 4 is no doubt due to the fact that Torrance learnt much of this approach from his former teacher William Manson, who dealt with Mark at length in his *Jesus and the Christian* (London: James Clarke, 1967), especially pp. 32-49, 58-66.

80. Torrance, *Theological Science*, pp. 274-77.

81. Torrance, *Theological Science*, pp. 275-76.

82. Colyer, *Nature of Doctrine*, p. 156. Cf. Torrance, *Reality and Evangelical Theology*, pp. 96, 104.

83. It is undoubtedly an issue that goes much wider than the question of 'Barthian' readings, but it is these 'Barthian' inspired readings of Scripture I am most interested in here when analysing Torrance's theology. Cf. Paul W. Meyer, 'The Problem of the Messianic Self-Consciousness of Jesus', *NovT* 4 (1960), pp. 122-38, for the classical issues involved in this question. Gray, 'Towards Better Ways of Reading the Bible', p. 315, believes Torrance 'moved little from the position of the early Barth, so we look in vain for methodological paths to follow'. We see Torrance's explicit aversion to approaching anything like an anthropology, as opposed to a Christology, when in an introduction to a collection of sermons he speaks of the then popular practice of preach-

As Stanley Porter wrote on this topic,

> If we believe that the social-scientific methods that we have developed, including psychology and sociology, have any explanatory power, and if we believe that human nature, despite its changing surroundings, has at least a minimal constant element, then there is the opportunity to ask probing and personal questions of ancient personages—including Jesus—regarding what they thought of themselves and others. These questions can be asked in such a way as to examine what they said and what they did, and, more importantly, to penetrate into the internal cognizance that must have existed behind such statements and actions. This is an area that bears renewed attention in study of the Jesus of history as we refine our methods for historical exploration under the influence of complementary models, such as those developed in the social sciences, and as we learn to benefit from the advances made in other historically based disciplines.[84]

It is apparent that what Porter recommends and what patristic theologians exemplified is the sort of depth exegesis Torrance was committed to but did not finally bring himself actually to do on a consistently explicit basis. It was also not his primary calling, as he understood it.[85]

Torrance's theological hermeneutic actually invited him to reflect on the self-identity of Jesus as the Messiah, rather than claiming this was an illegitimate approach to Scripture.[86] It is just such an approach that one finds in classic treatments of Christ, texts from which Torrance was fond of drawing. One thinks of Athanasius's *On the Incarnation*, or the various Cappadocian contributions. More to the point, when Torrance does comment on the life

---

ing people's experiences, or cultural interpretations, rather than the substance of the gospel, something which inevitably leads, in his opinion, to 'give the people anthropology instead of Christology, or to preach the Church instead of Christ in His Church and so to give the congregation the traditions of men instead of Incarnation, Atonement, Resurrection, Ascension, and Advent' ('Preface', in *When Christ Comes and Comes Again*, p. 8; see further in Torrance, *Incarnation*, pp. 34-35).

84. Stanley E. Porter, 'Foreword', in Michael F. Bird, *Are You the One Who Is to Come? The Historical Jesus and the Messianic Question* (Grand Rapids: Baker, 2009), p. 8. Porter makes this point in the foreword to Bird's monograph, which explores the issue of Jesus' self-consciousness regarding his identity as the Messiah.

85. On Torrance's description of his academic motivations, see Torrance, 'A Pilgrimage in the School of Faith', pp. 49–64.

86. I prefer to use the language of 'identity' rather than psychology in regard to how we are led to believe Jesus thought of himself. In this I have been highly influenced by Richard Bauckham's 'Christology of Divine Identity' as found in his *Jesus and the God of Israel: God Crucified and Other Studies on the New Testament's Christology of Divine Identity* (Grand Rapids: Eerdmans, 2008), especially pp. 182-232. Since 'the mental states and psychological profiles of individuals from antiquity are beyond the bounds of historical inquiry', Bird prefers 'Messianic self-understanding' over 'Messianic self-consciousness' (*Are You the One Who Is to Come?* p. 29).

of Christ as it is narrated in the Gospels he *does* indulge in answering the question of Jesus' self-identity, along with a host of related issues.

Rather than being some sort of anthropologically driven quest to find a fictitious Jesus of history separate from the Christ of faith, this approach merely asks what clues there are in the text which alert us to Jesus' messianic status, clues of which Jesus himself was no doubt aware. As such, the depth dimension of the Gospel narratives actually invites us to penetrate beneath any narrated 'objective' history of Jesus down into perceiving the Truth inherent in such a history. History then, as far as we have it in the Gospel accounts, is as much biography, narrative, and theological interpretation as it is history.[87] It is this, arguably, that William Manson exemplified in his *Jesus and the Christian*, with which Torrance was so enamoured. 'Who is this Jesus?' Torrance asks, 'He is the Jesus of Bethlehem, the Jesus of Calvary, the Jesus of the Resurrection. It is identically the same Jesus as the historical Jesus who will come again. Let us think abut the significance of that.'[88] Indeed, let us do so primarily by means of Torrance's lectures and sermons.

John 4.43-54: The Healing of the Nobleman's Son
We find Torrance penetrating into the subjective state of Jesus numerous times throughout his sermons. In 'The Healing Word', a sermon on the healing of the nobleman's son in Jn 4.43-54, Torrance tells the congregation that Jesus cannot resist a father's agony over his child before going on to say, 'But there is an agony too at the heart of Jesus. It tears at His soul, it crucifies Him, to see that such hot passionate prayers come only when we are driven to our knees by illness or hurt or desperation.'[89]

The Son of Man
In his lectures on the Incarnation, amidst a discussion of what it means for Jesus to be the incarnation of the Son become servant, Torrance discusses the motif of Adam, the Son of God as it is applied to Jesus and concludes, 'I cannot help but feel that the concept of Adam lies in Jesus' own name for himself, the "Son of Man" (the Son of God as man)…'.[90] Here we see but one example of Torrance seeking to penetrate into the self-understanding and messianic identity of Jesus in order to explicate his self-understanding as the Messiah. In my opinion this is a perfectly legitimate thing to do and

---

87. Porter continues to say that 'We may wish to shy away from over psychologizing our knowledge of Jesus, or any other person, ancient or modern, for that matter. That should not necessarily inhibit us from realizing the intentions that legitimately lie behind particular words and actions' ('Foreword', p. 10).

88. Torrance, 'When Christ Comes to the World', in *When Christ Comes and Comes Again*, p. 17.

89. Torrance, 'The Healing Word', in *When Christ Comes and Comes Again*, p. 79.

90. Torrance, *Incarnation*, p. 72.

entirely consistent with theological interpretation of Scripture. It is, however, contrary to certain emphases found within Torrance's stated method.

The Virgin Conception
Similarly, in his ubiquitous references to the virgin conception of Christ, Torrance repeatedly draws theological conclusions from the text of Scripture at the same time that he reads theological commitments into it. One particularly interesting and informative example of this is Torrance's contention that in the Gospel of Mark there are direct allusions to the supernatural conception of Jesus of Mary, despite the fact that Mark does not speak of the human conception and childhood of Jesus.[91] Torrance believes that Mk 6.3 and 12.35-37, when read in conjunction with the parallel texts in Matthew and Luke, definitely lean 'toward a witness to the virgin birth, and in stronger ways than Matthew or Luke....'[92] Similarly, Torrance sees in Jn 1.13 an explicit mention of the virgin conception of Jesus, despite most commentators not seeing this. Torrance translates the text as follows: 'born not of bloods, nor of the will of the flesh, nor of a husband, but of God'.[93] To substantiate this claim Torrance appeals to the Greek: *andros* is used, not *anthrōpou*. And he looks to the manuscript evidence, notably the Verona Old Latin and patristic precedent, citing Tertullian, Irenaeus, Justin Martyr, *Epistola apostolorum*, Hippolytus, Clement of Alexandria, Ambrose, Augustine and Leo the Great (albeit ambiguously), as well as a number of codices such as 10, 14, 36, and 37. Torrance then links Jn 1.13 with the doctrine of baptism when he argues that in Christian baptism we are born from above, because in baptism we are incorporated into the one who was born of the Spirit from above. Thus baptism 'reposes upon the virgin birth of Christ as well as upon his death and resurrection'.[94] This is a clear instance of theological interpretation of Scripture.

John 2.23–3.15: The New Birth
We find a related argument in one of Torrance's sermons, 'The New Birth', where the dialogue with Nicodemus in Jn 2.23–3.15 is theologically interpreted.[95] Drawing in part on the Jerusalem Talmud, Torrance exegetes the phrases 'born from above' and 'born anew of water and of the Spirit'. While Nicodemus understood the language Jesus was using, he did not understand the meaning he was giving to it, thus Nicodemus provides a rare example of a biblical character doing a depth exegesis of Jesus' words. Torrance writes,

91. Torrance, *Incarnation*, pp. 88-104, especially pp. 88-89.
92. Torrance, *Incarnation*, p. 89.
93. Torrance, *Incarnation*, p. 90.
94. Torrance, *Incarnation*, p. 91.
95. Torrance, 'The New Birth', pp. 61-75.

> If Nicodemus is to understand he must listen to the Truth as it is communicated to him from above; he must enter inside the Kingdom and see it from its inner and heavenly side, and then he will really see....[96]

What we are meant to see, argues Torrance, is that behind or beneath the language of new birth and being born anew of water and Spirit is 'a heavenly reality, a heavenly secret'.[97] Perhaps 'mystery' would technically be closer to the truth, for the heavenly reality that lies behind the birth of water and Spirit is the descent of the Son of Man from above. 'In other words, John wants us to understand that behind all that Jesus has been saying there lies the fact of His own birth and incarnation.... In other words, it is in Christ and through Christ only that we are born again.'[98] For Torrance, Jesus alone is born of the Spirit from above, and through water baptism believers are granted the right to be called sons and daughters of God, but in Christ's name. By way of summary, Torrance concludes, 'In St John and St Paul it is evident that the doctrine of the virgin birth is woven into the very texture of their theology which shows its inner importance: but that is just what we would expect'.[99]

Luke 22.42: Gethsemane

A further example of Torrance's practice of theological interpretation of Scripture may be seen in his account of Gethsemane, a pericope he returns to often in his theological explication of the Mediator. In a section on the life and faithfulness of the Son towards the Father, Torrance delves into the motivations of Jesus' obedience. Rightly setting up further discussion, Torrance perceives,

> We have to think of all this not only in terms of passive obedience but of active obedience also, not only in terms of forensic and judicial righteousness and obedience, but in terms of positive communion and filial life, and of worship.[100]

---

96. Torrance, 'The New Birth', p. 64.
97. Torrance, 'The New Birth', p. 72.
98. Torrance, 'The New Birth', p. 72. Further, 'To be incorporated by baptism into Christ is to partake of his Spirit of sonship which he is able to bestow on us men and women because of his own coming into existence of a woman, as a real man' (*Incarnation*, p. 93).
99. Torrance, *Incarnation*, p. 94. Torrance sees Paul arguing the same thing in his epistles. Based upon 1 Cor. 15.22 and Gal. 4.4, 23, 24, 29, Torrance argues Paul only ever uses the word *ginesthai* for Jesus' human generation, never *gennan*, the word used for all other human generation but that of Adam (1 Cor. 15.22). See Rom. 1.13; Phil. 2.7; Gal. 4.4. 'In other words, in reference to Jesus' birth [Paul] refuses to use the only word the New Testament uses of human generation...that is the strongest disavowal of birth by ordinary human generation in regard to the birth of Jesus' (p. 93).
100. Torrance, *Incarnation*, p. 114.

To do this Torrance adopts an image he returns to often, that of Jesus undoing the curse of Adam through his step-by-step, minute-by-minute, 'blow-by-blow' vicarious life—that is, by use of the notion of *prokopē* (Lk. 2.52).[101] 'Thus Jesus enacted in human flesh and human life, in his sinless solidarity with sinful man, the will of God to be one with man and to gather men and women into the heart of God'.[102] We see this most acutely in Jesus' Gethsemane words, 'Not my will, but yours be done' (22.42). Here Jesus' prayer is essentially a redemptive activity. Jesus prays this standing in our place, from within our rebellion, alienation and independence. Jesus offers from out of our disobedience, a prayer of obedience. As such his entire life is redemptive, as Jesus perfects and actualizes communion between God and humanity. It is here that Torrance moves behind the text to provide something of an extended commentary on Jesus' psychological state:

> Therefore all the powers of evil launched their attack upon Jesus; fearful temptations and assaults fell upon him, all in order to isolate him from God, to break the bond of fellowship between them, to snap the life of prayer and obedient clinging to the heavenly Father; to destroy the life of obedience to God's will and word, and so to make impossible any meeting between God and man in Jesus; to destroy the ground of reconciliation, to disrupt the foundation for atonement being laid in the obedience and prayerful life of the Son of Man.[103]

The question of whether this is right or wrong aside, one has to ask how Torrance knows this, if he is not attempting to get beneath or behind the text of Scripture, and into the subjective states of biblical writers and of Jesus himself.[104]

Matthew 18.20: Where Two or Three Are Gathered

Torrance's theological interpretation of Scripture was not always exemplary, as for instance when he lets the christological focus swamp or negate the linguistic and contextual features of the Bible. An instance of this may be seen in his eisegesis of Mt. 18.20, 'Where two or three have gathered together in my name, I am there in their midst'. After establishing the wider literary context of this saying Torrance asks why the text says two or three

---

101. See Torrance, 'The New Birth', p. 73, where we read that Jesus 'bent our perverted humanity back to the divine will'.
102. Torrance, *Incarnation*, p. 107.
103. Torrance, *Incarnation*, p. 119.
104. Torrance seeks to penetrate beneath the text to John the seer's motivations-psychology, when he wonders if in Revelation 7 John (who Torrance believes was John the Apostle) has in mind Jesus' words in Mt. 20.22 about his impending baptism and crucifixion. See Torrance, 'Angels behind the Scenes', in *The Apocalypse Today* (London: James Clarke, 1960), p. 65.

witnesses and not one or two. He provides two answers. First, the presence of Christ is not experienced individually or exclusively, but corporately and communally. Second, the Word must be communicated to us and thus cannot be heard individualistically.[105] Rather than appeal to the legal customs of the day, as most commentators do, and see that it was Jewish legal custom to have two or three witnesses to ratify a legal proceeding and validate an eyewitness account,[106] Torrance adopts a christological and spiritualized reading of the text. He then summarizes the account in this way:

> So in the Church or the Family of Christ He saves us in such a way that He plants us in fellowship with one another, and to deny that fellowship or to withdraw from it is to cut at the very root of our salvation.[107]

Torrance then proceeds to apply this to Thomas the disciple and to psychologize his experience. He argues on the basis of Thomas's absence from the upper room when Jesus appeared to the disciples on Easter evening, that Thomas could not receive a revelation of Jesus until he returned to the fellowship of the disciples in the upper room; only then could Jesus reveal himself to Thomas. 'That precisely is what He meant and what He still promises to do for us in these words: "Where two or three are gathered together in my name, there am I in the midst of them"'.

Torrance concludes an important section of his *Atonement* lectures, 'The Biblical Witness to Jesus Christ', with the following, telling comments:

> When theology turns to the holy Scriptures and in exegetical and theological interpretation seeks to articulate the content of the word of God, how does it handle the text of the New Testament Scriptures? The New Testament text is the glass or window in and through which we look at the basic text which underlies all the New Testament writings, all the apostolic tradition which they enshrine. That basic text is the text which the apostles themselves 'read', studied, interpreted, and expounded directly—their text was a living text, the

---

105. This point is made often, for instance in Torrance, 'Christ in the Midst of His Church', in *When Christ Comes and Comes Again*, p. 114; and especially in the same work, 'The Cleansing of the Fellowship', p. 145, where we read: '...we are not able ultimately to disentangle the Word of God from our own desires and wishes, and even when we read the Bible privately we are accustomed to tell ourselves what we think the Bible says rather than to listen to what it says against our own preconceptions and assumptions'.

106. That Torrance knows of this tradition of interpretation is without dispute, and we may only refer to Calvin's Commentaries edited by Torrance (*Calvin's New Testament Commentaries* [ed. D.W. Torrance and T.F. Torrance; 12 vols.; Grand Rapids: Eerdmans, 1959–72]), to prove this. See Calvin, *Commentary on a Harmony of the Evangelists: Matthew, Mark, and Luke* (trans. William Pringle; Ages Digital Library Edition), II, pp. 263-64.

107. Torrance, 'The New Birth', p. 115.

words and deeds and life of Jesus Christ all woven into one seamless pattern, in which word, deed, life are inseparable in the person of Jesus Christ. *The basic text is the obedient humanity of Jesus Christ alone.*[108]

Conclusion

Torrance's reading of Scripture is a distinctly rational process but only fully practicable by one who is in Christ, led by the Spirit, and a participant in the church. Consequently, true theological interpretation is a distinctly communal event through which God speaks to the church. Theological interpretation of Scripture is thus worship, 'where to the godly reason God is more to be adored than expressed'.[109] Only within the fellowship of faith and the constant meditation on the Holy Scriptures does a believer come under the creative impact of God's self-revelation and gain spiritual perception or insight which enables them to discriminate between conceptions of truth and the Truth itself.[110]

Torrance's doctrine of Scripture, bound up intimately as it is with a doctrine of revelation, brings us back to Trinitarian foundations—to know God is to participate in Christ through the Holy Spirit. To know the Word written is to have the 'mind of Christ' empowered by the Holy Spirit. The event of revelation is bound to reconciliation within this Trinitarian context: we come to know God as Father in and through our knowing of and sharing in the life of the incarnate Son, empowered and sustained by the anointing Spirit. The event of revelation carries with it the consequence of reconciliation which draws us into the centre of God's triune life: into knowledge of the Father's love for the Son by the Spirit and the love of the Son for the Father in the Holy Spirit. What Torrance achieves is the groundwork upon which other theological interpreters of Scripture may profitably build.

---

108. Torrance, *Atonement*, p. 340 (italics original).
109. Torrance, *Reality and Evangelical Theology*, pp. 119-20.
110. Torrance, *Reality and Evangelical Theology*, p. 120. While not giving the creeds the same authority as Scripture, Torrance does apply the same hermeneutic to the creeds, given his understanding that the creeds operate as *regula fidei*, witnesses to the Truth. See Torrance, *Reality and Evangelical Theology*, pp. 121-56; Colyer, *Nature of Doctrine*.

4

Interpreting the Bible on Language: Babel and Ricoeur's Interpretive Arc[*]

Allan Bell

The French philosopher Paul Ricoeur wrote extensively on the interpretation and analysis of texts. He was active through most of the second half of the twentieth century in France and the United States, and much of his later work dealt with the concerns of hermeneutics. Most of these writings are philosophical rather than text-analytical, but—as a French Protestant—most of his engagements with actual texts were biblical interpretations.[1] Ricoeur himself is reasonably well known in biblical studies,[2] although the hermeneutical arc which I adapt below is not.

I define hermeneutics as 'the theory and practice of interpreting texts'. Ricoeur's own clearest summation of how he views his hermeneutical method and enterprise is:

---

[*] A much longer version of this article appeared as Allan Bell, 'Re-constructing Babel: Discourse Analysis, Hermeneutics and the Interpretive Arc', *Discourse Studies* 13 (2011), pp. 519-68. That article was the focus paper of a theme issue on 'Hermeneutics and Discourse Analysis', and offers a good deal of detail not presented here. I am indebted to the editor Teun van Dijk for agreement to reuse some of that material. My thanks go also to the scholars whose commentaries on the paper were published in that issue. Thank you too to the three colleagues who read the original manuscript: Sharon Harvey, Philippa Smith and Tim Meadowcroft—whom I also thank for his guidance into Old Testament studies. I acknowledge my debt to John B. Thompson's translations of Ricoeur, and to Walter Brueggemann's reinterpretation of Babel. Most of all, I pay tribute to the remarkable thought and engagement of Paul Ricoeur himself, whose work I encountered too late to allow personal interaction.

1. Paul Ricoeur, *Essays on Biblical Interpretation* (ed. Lewis S. Mudge; Philadelphia: Fortress, 1980).

2. E.g. Craig Bartholomew, Colin Greene and Karl Möller (eds.), *After Pentecost: Language and Biblical Interpretation* (Carlisle: Paternoster Press, 2001); Anthony C. Thiselton, *New Horizons in Hermeneutics: The Theory and Practice of Transforming Biblical Reading* (Grand Rapids: Zondervan, 1992); Kevin J. Vanhoozer, *Biblical Narrative in the Philosophy of Paul Ricoeur: A Study in Hermeneutics and Theology* (Cambridge: Cambridge University Press, 1990).

The kind of hermeneutics which I now favor starts from the recognition of the objective meaning of the text as distinct from the subjective intention of the author. This objective meaning is not something hidden behind the text, rather it is a requirement addressed to the reader. The interpretation, accordingly, is a kind of obedience to this injunction starting from the text.... What has to be interpreted in a text is what it says and what it speaks about, i.e., the kind of world which it opens up or discloses.[3]

Only occasionally does Ricoeur lay out his approach in a transparent or linear fashion, and much of what I present below has been distilled and interwoven from different publications. His central concept is the hermeneutical arc: 'The activity of analysis then appears as one segment on an interpretive arc extending from naïve understanding to informed understanding through explanation'.[4]

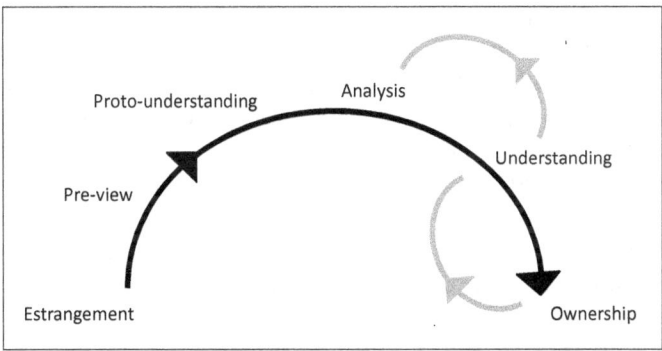

Figure 1. The Interpretive Arc
(including dialectic of Analysis–Understanding–Ownership)

My approach adapts Ricoeur's hermeneutical arc—which he describes but never diagrams—into the six-phase Interpretive Arc, displayed in Figure 1. As well as movement along the arc, there is a dialectical circling back and forth between later phases. Most of Ricoeur's terms are translations of German-language originals, several of which I re-gloss.[5] Most of the primary works I cite come from five English-language collections of Ricoeur's translated essays generated across about thirty years from 1960 on. I illustrate the Interpretive Arc by applying each step to the story of Babel (Gen. 11). This choice of text is not random. Babel is a narrative whose

---

3. Paul Ricoeur, *The Philosophy of Paul Ricoeur: An Anthology of his Work* (ed. Charles E. Reagan and David Stewart; Boston: Beacon Press, 1978) p. 90.
4. Paul Ricoeur, *From Text to Action: Essays in Hermeneutics*, II (trans. Kathleen Blamey and John B Thompson; Evanston, IL: Northwestern University Press, 1991), p. 130.
5. See Bell,'Re-constructing Babel', for detail and rationale on this.

focus is understanding and non-understanding, and we can therefore expect its content to offer matter directly relevant to issues of text interpretation.

I need to preface the chapter with a caveat: I am a discourse analyst and sociolinguist, not a philosopher nor a biblical scholar nor a theologian. I therefore come as an outsider to the conversations and conventions of these disciplines, including hermeneutical philosophy. My encounter with Ricoeur's thinking, and with the text of Babel, remains a work in progress. Importing ideas from one discipline to another is a prime source of refreshing the recipient field, but it also offers an unfamiliar author plenty of occasion to demonstrate ignorance and misunderstanding. I hope the undertaking furnishes more promise than perils.

The Interpretive Arc offers an approach that is congenial to theological interpretation of the Bible because it treats interpretation as only completed in 'ownership' of the word—in transformation of the self by the text. Also underlying much of the discussion throughout the chapter is an issue that faces all interpreters, including those whose text is the Bible: what is the validity of the interpretations we offer? How do we position ourselves between interpretive determinacy—that a text has only one single meaning—and unbounded indeterminacy—that there are no limits to the number of alternative readings? How do we warrant our fair dealing with a text? We shall see that the meaning of biblical texts is neither determinate nor indeterminate. While there may be no one meaning, neither are there unlimited meanings.

The Estrangement of the Text

The first phase of the Interpretive Arc is Estrangement—the translation I prefer above the awkward 'distanciation', which is the English adoption of the French translation of German *Verfremdung*. As readers our experience is one of Estrangement from the written text. Ricoeur writes: 'Distanciation... is constitutive of the phenomenon of the text as writing'.[6] While speech is instantiated in dialogue—involving the presence of an interlocutor and occurring in a context—the writer of a text is absent from its reading, and the reader is absent from the act of writing.[7]

Such distancing makes writing fundamentally of a different order from speech, Ricoeur argues. Compared to spoken language, there is an upheaval of all the relations among writer, reader, text and their contexts.[8] The result

---

6. Paul Ricoeur, *Paul Ricoeur: Hermeneutics and the Human Sciences: Essays on Language, Action and Interpretation* (ed. and trans. John B. Thompson; Cambridge: Cambridge University Press, 1981), p. 139.
7. Ricoeur, *Hermeneutics and the Human Sciences*, p. 146.
8. Ricoeur, *Hermeneutics and the Human Sciences*, p. 147.

is a three-fold autonomy of the text: it is uncoupled from the writer, from the original readers, and from its original social context.[9] Most obviously, readers are estranged from the author, and the text is no longer bound to the author's intention. The text and its interpretation are also autonomous of its first readers or addressees; it does not necessarily and only mean what its first audience took it to mean. And thirdly, it is independent of the socio-cultural context in which it was produced (and probably received), having moved into a new context. All three of these claims are contentious in biblical interpretation, and I return to them below.

Authors write, Ricoeur argues 'for anyone who can read'.[10] A text transcends its original addressee and attracts to itself an audience to address.[11] Emancipated from its author and original situation, Ricoeur says, a text is then liberated to become embedded in a new situation in the act of being read. This emancipation is the 'birth' of the text. A text is therefore opened to unlimited potential readings in different sociocultural conditions, Ricoeur writes.[12] This represents a radical and controversial uncoupling from the role and intentions of the author, and we will revisit the validity and range of that uncoupling below.

Pre-view

Ricoeur calls our first approach as readers of a text 'pre-understanding'[13] or 'naïve understanding'.[14] I believe the dual terms reflect two distinct stages in our activity: Pre-view, which is the second phase of the Interpretive Arc, and Proto-understanding, the third phase.

Pre-view is our state of knowledge or opinion in that moment just *before* we engage with a text—when we pick up a book or newspaper, for example. This is the starting position that we first touch a text from, and it is important not to confuse it with our actual first reading (proto-understanding). We make even a first approach to an unknown text as positioned human beings, with knowledge and views relevant to what the texts are about—e.g. knowledge of the site of a disaster that is in the news, or acquaintance with biblical literary forms. We come to a text from our own existing position in a tradition, a history, a culture, a church.[15]

---

9. Ricoeur, *Hermeneutics and the Human Sciences*, p. 91.
10. Ricoeur, *Hermeneutics and the Human Sciences*, p. 182.
11. Ricoeur, *Hermeneutics and the Human Sciences*, p. 202.
12. Ricoeur, *Hermeneutics and the Human Sciences*, p. 139.
13. Ricoeur, *Hermeneutics and the Human Sciences*, p. 243.
14. Ricoeur, *From Text to Action*, p. 130.
15. Ricoeur, *Hermeneutics and the Human Sciences*, p. 243.

It is virtually impossible for a reader to bring no kind of prior knowledge relevant to a text, otherwise we could not begin to understand it. This is of course supremely so in the case of biblical texts, in which many Christians have been immersed from a young age. Very many such texts will be familiar, or at least representatives of familiar genres. Uncoupling our reading from our pre-view—what we already know or think we know about the text or its world—is a challenging but necessary task.

To some texts, such as canonical pieces of literature or folktales, everyone within a culture comes with prior knowledge at some level. This holds for some biblical texts, including the story of Babel. Potential readers of the story, whether Jewish, Christian or other, will approach it with existing ideas, although possibly most in the third group may never have read the actual text. Their ideas are drawn from the repository of cultural knowledge within which they have been socialized, which will usually include a set of associations with the term 'Babel', and some idea of the story itself.

Proto-understanding

What I termed 'pre-view' above is the state we are in just before engaging with a text. Proto-understanding—Ricoeur's 'pre- or naïve understanding'—is the next step, the fruit of our initial encounter with the text itself. At this point we form a first, pre-analytical impression of the text, almost a visceral response to it. We are, Ricoeur says, making a 'guess' about what the text means: 'To construe the meaning…is to make a guess'.[16] The guess is at this initial stage independent of analytical evidence, and possibly even of conscious reflection. We have to 'guess' the meaning because we have no access to the author's intention; and even if we did, it would not control our own meaning-making process, because the meaning taken may be other than the meaning given, diverging from or surpassing the author's intent.

A proto-understanding is not one that brings no prior knowledge or positioning to a text. Rather it is one that is not—yet—informed by the analytical work of the interpreter. It is a pre-analytical state of impressionistic reading, which is in practice where all hermeneutics, including biblical interpretation, begins. The concept of the guess seems to me a useful admission for biblical interpreters. I doubt that our first approach to a text is ever initially an analytical one. It would be a rare piece of interpretation that was not preceded by an impressionistic reading—usually by several.

Ricoeur maintains that there are 'no rules for making good guesses'.[17] First impressions may not be lasting ones, they may or may not be confirmed

---

16. Paul Ricoeur, *Interpretation Theory: Discourse and the Surplus of Meaning* (Fort Worth, TX: Texas Christian University Press, 1976), p. 76.
17. Ricoeur, *Interpretation Theory*, p. 76.

by closer inspection or the analytical work of validation. The guesses which constitute our proto-understanding of a text need to be brought to the analytical steps of explanation before they can become fuller understandings.[18]

Proto-understanding Babel

Many texts we may approach with no direct knowledge at all, of the author, of the first audience, or of the originating context or society. With many others we have varying degrees of social or cultural information as a backdrop to the text—our pre-view. Regardless of how much we bring, a first reading is a unique opportunity for immediate, unexamined understanding—proto-understanding. The New Revised Standard Version of Gen.11.1-9 is shown in Text 1.

Text 1: The Story of Babel, Genesis 11:1-9 (NRSV)

[1] Now the whole earth had one language and the same words. [2] And as they migrated from the east, they came upon a plain in the land of Shinar and settled there. [3] And they said to one another, 'Come, let us make bricks, and burn them thoroughly'. And they had brick for stone, and bitumen for mortar. [4] Then they said, 'Come, let us build ourselves a city, and a tower with its top in the heavens, and let us make a name for ourselves; otherwise we shall be scattered abroad upon the face of the whole earth'. [5] The Lord came down to see the city and the tower, which mortals had built. [6] And the Lord, said, 'Look, they are one people, and they have all one language; and this is only the beginning of what they will do; nothing that they propose to do will now be impossible for them. [7] Come, let us go down, and confuse their language there, so that they will not understand one another's speech.' [8] So the Lord scattered them abroad from there over the face of all the earth, and they left off building the city. [9] Therefore it was called Babel, because there the Lord confused the language of all the earth; and from there the Lord scattered them abroad over the face of all the earth.

A 'commonsense' proto-understanding based on a first reading—at least by a white Western middle-class male like me, reared in the prevailing Christian and cultural interpretation of Babel—makes the story look like a polemic against overweening human ambition, possibly even against urbanism, certainly against mortals trying to 'make a name for ourselves' and to preserve it in concrete, trying to reach heaven and act like God. God comes across as a somewhat peevish local deity, afraid of being outshone by a group of ambitious humans, and taking steps to mess them up so massively that they will never again be a challenge. And, most particularly for a view

---

18. Ricoeur, *Hermeneutics and the Human Sciences*, p. 93.

of language, it positions the proliferation of languages and the resulting non-comprehension as a punishment and curse for humankind.

I can at this juncture, of course, no longer recapture my own naïve reading of Babel. But I can say that a few years ago I had committed myself to giving a talk based on Babel, without having looked at the text at all recently. I still recall that my new reading of Babel, with the refreshed 'proto-understanding' it engendered, appalled me. What was I going to do with the manifestly primitive cosmology and theology that presented itself here? And, as a linguist, with the negativity of this explanation of origins—this 'etiology'—of multilingualism? In accord with my quote from Ricoeur above, I had found there was indeed no rule for making a good initial guess about this, and I could only hope that my proto-understanding (paraphrased in Text 2 below) would be turned into something more tractable by the next phase on the Interpretive Arc—the analytical work of 'explanation'.

Text 2: A Traditional Christian and Western Interpretation of Babel

1. At the time, the known earth spoke a single language.
2-3. Some migrating people settled on a plain and learned to build.
4. The people decided to secure their unity and power by building a city with a tower that would reach right up into heaven.
5. God saw this construction
6. and believed the unity of the people and their language could challenge God's own supremacy.
7. God concluded that confusing their language could prevent this attempted rebellion.
8. God punished the people by scattering them, and they stopped building the tower.
9. The confusion of many languages in the world today results from the curse of God on human ambition and rebellion.

Analysis

Proto-understanding, as we have seen, is prior to Analysis (in Ricoeur's terms 'explanation' for the German *Erklärung*), which is the pathway along the Interpretive Arc towards (fuller) Understanding. Ricoeur characterizes this phase as the process of 'validation' of the guesses which constitute proto-understanding. He treats analysis/explanation and understanding as complementary and reciprocal.[19] Understanding is mediated by explanation/analysis, which is fulfilled in understanding. There is then a dialectic, a back-and-forth movement, a '…balance between the genius of guessing and the scientific character of validation'.[20]

19. Ricoeur, *Hermeneutics and the Human Sciences*, p. 150.
20. Ricoeur, *Hermeneutics and the Human Sciences*, p. 212.

There can of course be no return to the 'naïve' state of proto-understanding. But analysis is enveloped on the hermeneutical arc by understandings, preceded by proto-understanding and followed by (fuller) understanding. Ricoeur gives priority to understanding over explanation/analysis. Analysis is a necessary means, not the end. This situates—rightly, I believe—the weight and value of hermeneutical work in the interpreters' insightfulness more than in their analytical skills. Analysis is prerequisite to understanding, and the more skilful the better, but it is not interpreters' analytical cleverness but the quality of their insights that determines the worth of their contributions. This truth holds for biblical interpretation. Three approaches to interpretation are challenged by Ricoeur's hermeneutics:

The Author's Intention Does Not Determine Meaning
The thrust of nineteenth century hermeneutics was that 'the ultimate aim of hermeneutics is to understand the author better than he understood himself'.[21] Ricoeur argues trenchantly and repeatedly that hermeneutics should not try to deduce the intentions or psyche of a text's original author. In the debate between those who believe a text 'really' means what its author intended, and those who believe it means what readers take from it, Ricoeur leans to the side of the readers. 'What the text says now matters more than what the author meant to say', Ricoeur writes, largely aligning himself with 'anti-historicist' approaches to literary interpretation.[22] This puts him at apparent odds with Vanhoozer,[23] who otherwise draws heavily on Ricoeur: 'We reject the idea, rampant among some postmoderns, that meaning and reference are radically indeterminate, as well as the related idea that the author is "dead" or irrelevant to the process of interpretation'.[24]

I believe Ricoeur's point here is not so much a total discounting of the author as ensuring that the meaning of a text is not equated simplistically with what the author intended, thus reducing interpretation to the divination of that intention: 'the problem of the right understanding can no longer be solved by a simple return to the alleged intention of the author'.[25] Authors are not sovereign over their texts' meanings, Ricoeur argues; their 'intention is often unknown to us, sometimes redundant, sometimes useless, and sometimes even harmful'.[26] My own view is congruent with this, but less radical:

---

21. Paul Ricoeur, *The Conflict of Interpretations: Essays in Hermeneutics* (ed. Don Ihde; Evanston, IL: Northwestern University Press, 1974), p. 397.
22. Ricoeur, *Hermeneutics and the Human Sciences*, p. 201.
23. Kevin J. Vanhoozer, 'From Speech Acts to Scripture Acts', in Bartholomew, Greene and Möller (eds.), *After Pentecost*, pp. 1-49.
24. Vanhoozer, 'From Speech Acts to Scripture Acts', p. 6.
25. Ricoeur, *Hermeneutics and the Human Sciences*, p. 211.
26. Ricoeur, *Interpretation Theory*, p. 76.

author intention is a factor in interpretation but not the determining one. The author's intention is not the final arbiter of a text's meaning, but it may cast light on meaning.

Analysis Does Not Itself Yield Meaning
Ricoeur argued against the self-sufficiency of the structuralist analysis, with its positivist illusion of objectivity, which was in its heyday in France during his career.[27] His reasoning can also apply to the standard tools of biblical analysis over the past century. Historical, form-critical or redactional analyses are limited tools which cannot themselves produce understanding. Ricoeur saw analytical procedures as stopping short of understanding, as indeed the servant of understanding. More severely, without progressing on to understandings such analysis is just 'a sterile game' which does not address the fundamental nature and purpose of texts. It is reductionist unless it leads on to depth interpretations.[28]

Texts Limit their Own Meanings
The third approach to which Ricoeur's hermeneutics speaks, but which it addresses less explicitly, is the unlimited polysemy espoused by some constructivism and criticized by Vanhoozer above.[29] Constructivist approaches were just gaining strength at the time of Ricoeur's later writings but had not yet attained their current hegemonic position in the social sciences and textual analysis. Ricoeur is against the objectivist readings of structuralism, but he equally opposes limitless polysemy of texts. He is on the side of the reader, but does not believe that all interpretations are equally valid.

Validating our Guesses
How then do we proceed with analysis in the service of understanding? The form and reception-context of a text limits the possible constructions that can be put on it, and interpreters can advance arguments to arbitrate between competing interpretations. While there may be no rules for making good guesses, Ricoeur writes,[30] 'there are methods for validating those guesses we do make':

> The logic of validation allows us to move between the two limits of dogmatism and scepticism. It is always possible to argue for or against an interpretation, to confront interpretations, to arbitrate between them and to seek agreement, even if this agreement remains beyond our immediate reach.[31]

27. E.g. Claude Lévi-Strauss, *La pensée sauvage* (Paris: Librairie Plon, 1962).
28. Ricoeur, *Interpretation Theory*, p. 87.
29. Vanhoozer, 'From Speech Acts to Scripture Acts', p. 6.
30. Ricoeur, *Interpretation Theory*, p. 76.
31. Ricoeur, *Interpretation Theory*, p. 79.

Ricoeur's most concrete operationalization of this is in terms parallel to Karl Popper's thesis of the falsifiability of scientific theories.[32] Popper contends that scientific 'facts' cannot actually be proved, only disproved. A fact becomes scientific by virtue of being capable of falsification. Ricoeur applies this to the hermeneutical task, proposing that one way of proceeding with textual explanation is through procedures of *in*validation. An interpretation must be more probable than competing interpretations. The superior interpretation is the one that has stood up better than its competitors to attempts to invalidate it. There is promise in this as a process. As interpreters, we know that we are not actually able to prove that our reading of a text is the 'right' or even the best one. But we can try to demonstrate that competing readings are less valid or probable than the alternative.

Analyzing Babel

So, what is Analysis to make of the apparently intractable surface of the Babel story? How much of the 'guess' of my proto-understanding that I outlined above can be validated through analytical explanation? Babel has been the subject of much biblical scholarship, and space does not allow any kind of full analytical exposition here,[33] but the work of biblical scholars together with my own textual analysis lays the basis for a fuller understanding of Babel. Like most lay readers, I am working with a translated text, dealing with the original at second hand, reliant on the glosses provided by linguists and translators, and commentary by specialists in the language.

The Babel Narrative

The Babel text dates from the tenth century BCE, although with later revisions.[34] On a scale of chronological estrangement from the present, 3,000 years is hard to beat. Less obvious is the distance that existed already at the time of the original text. Babel as recorded in Genesis is already a story told at a considerable distance from its origin. It was written in Israel, but was located in distant Mesopotamia and up to a thousand years before its

---

32. E.g. Karl R. Popper, *The Logic of Scientific Discovery* (London: Hutchinson, 1959).

33. For detail see Bell, 'Re-constructing Babel'.

34. Walter Brueggemann, *Genesis* (Interpretation; Atlanta: John Knox Press, 1982); Arie van der Kooij, 'The City of Babel and Assyrian Imperialism: Genesis 11:1-9 Interpreted in the Light of Mesopotamian Sources', in André Lemaire (ed.) *Congress Volume: Leiden, 2004 (Papers from the XVIIIth Congress of the International Organisation for the Study of the Old Testament)* (VTSup, 109; Leiden: Brill, 2006), pp. 1-17.

appearance in Genesis. It also reflects customs and materials that were culturally alien: Israel built in stone, not bricks.[35]

Intertextual Context

Intertextual analysis is a focal point of some approaches to discourse analysis[36] and to biblical interpretation,[37] and is an essential part of our approach to Babel. Genesis 11 is the closing chapter of the prehistorical section of the book. The previous chapters (6–9) tell the story of the great flood of Noah, which forms the backdrop to Babel. Chapter 10 narrates the dispersion of Noah's children and their descendants across the known earth. The Babel narrative follows immediately and recounts one strand of the settlement that occurred during this migration. The story appears to cover a long period, perhaps many centuries, from the discovery of bricks and bitumen as building materials through to their use in the construction of numerous and substantial structures (v. 5). Three horizons of the intertextual context are relevant:

'Scattering' in the prior text of Genesis. The 'scattering' of Babel occurs against the background of the mandates given to humankind by God at creation and after the flood to 'be fruitful and multiply and fill the earth' (9.1). The word *pws* used approvingly to describe these peoples 'spreading abroad' after the flood (10.18) is the same term applied to the 'scattering' from Babel.[38]

'Listening' in the prophetic tradition. The use of *shema'* in v. 7 is significant in the context of the prophets who were to follow. Translated as 'understand' here, it can also mean 'listen'. An alternative translation of v. 7 could read 'not listen to each other' rather than 'not understand'.[39] The prophets were constantly rebuking the people for failing to listen to God (e.g. Jer. 7.13).

'Comprehending' at Pentecost. The New Testament account of Pentecost forms the horizon of Christian—and traditional Western—interpretations of Babel. On the day of Pentecost the disciples spoke in many different

---

35. Robert Alter, *The Five Books of Moses: A Translation with Commentary* (New York: Norton, 2004), p. 58.
36. E.g. Norman Fairclough, *Critical Discourse Analysis: The Critical Study of Language* (Harlow: Pearson Education, 2nd edn, 2010).
37. Although not necessarily under that label, see Michael Fishbane, *Biblical Interpretation in Ancient Israel* (Oxford: Clarendon Press, 1985).
38. Brueggemann, *Genesis*, p. 98.
39. Brueggemann, *Genesis*, p. 103.

languages. This has traditionally been interpreted as a reversal of Babel. It is not: reversing Babel would mean that speakers returned to speaking a single language. At Pentecost speakers talked and listeners understood in a great variety of languages (thirteen are listed). It was not the diversification of languages itself that was reversed, but the resultant incomprehension. The languages remained different, but they were understood.

Lexicon
Overall the vocabulary appears meticulously chosen, and intentionally repetitive of key terms.[40] The punchline (v. 9) involves a three-fold actualization of the language confusion that is its subject. The situation is (1) described with the Hebrew word *balal* 'confuse', which is (2) the subject of a code-switch pun with the Akkadian name 'Babel', which is (3) given a patently false etymology in the Hebrew *balal*. The linguistic care with which the story as a whole is worded makes it unlikely that the misleading etymology is a mistake rather than deliberate word play.

Word Play
The story is notable for the number of linguistic devices it puts to work, on the micro as well as the macro level. There is a great deal of lexical and phono/graphological play in the Hebrew. *Khemar* 'bitumen' links to *khomer* 'mortar', and *sham* 'there' to both *shamayim* 'heavens' and *shem* 'name' (v. 4).[41] The people's statement *nilbenah* 'let us make' (bricks) (v. 3) and God's response *navlah* 'let us mix up' (v. 7) realize the foreshadowed mixing of the language through the shuffled order of the graphemes in the word itself.[42]

Structure
All analysts agree that Babel is a carefully crafted narrative: 'a short but brilliant example of Hebrew story telling'.[43] The narrative is structured in an envelope of parallel and converse expressions. It begins and ends with the phrase 'all the earth': in v. 1 regarding the speaking of one language, and in v. 9 the dispersing throughout. There are symmetries between the v. 1 orientation and the v. 9 coda, and within the developing action of vv. 3-4 compared to vv. 7-8.[44] In v. 4, the people declare they will build a city and a

    40. Alter, *Five Books of Moses*, p. 59.
    41. Alter, *Five Books of Moses*, p. 60.
    42. Gordon J. Wenham, *Genesis 1–15* (WBC, 1; Nashville: Thomas Nelson, 1987), p. 234.
    43. Wenham, *Genesis 1–15*, p. 234
    44. Terence E. Fretheim, 'The Book of Genesis: Introduction, Commentary, and Reflections', in Leander E. Keck (ed.), *The New Interpreter's Bible* (12 vols.; Nashville: Abingdon Press, 1994), I, pp. 410-14.

tower to prevent themselves being scattered. In v. 8, God scatters them. The phrase 'Come let us' is repeated three times at turning points of the narrative, twice of the people: 'Come let us make bricks' (v. 3); 'Come let us build a city and a tower' (v. 4). The third usage is attributed to God and initiates the resolution of the action: 'Come let us go down and confuse their language' (v. 7). Text 3 below presents a 'bare' précis of the Babel story which attempts to leave unstated any linkages of cause or fault, representing the kind of gloss we might put on the story at the end of (a first round of) the analytical phase of the Interpretive Arc.

Text 3: *A Bare Précis of the Babel Story*

1. At the time, the known earth spoke a single language.
2-3. Some migrating people settled on a plain and learned to build.
4. The people decided to maintain their unity by building a city with a tall tower.
5. God saw this construction
6. and believed the unity of the people and their language could lead to unlimited achievements.
7. God concluded that mixing up their language could prevent this.
8. God scattered the people and they stopped building the city.
9. The many languages in the world today result from this dispersion across the earth.

Understanding

What then is the Understanding that we move towards through the labour of textual analysis? Ricoeur's approach can be distilled like this:

> To understand is
> to place ourselves in front of the text
> so we can unfold or disclose
> the matter or injunction of the text
> (in order to make it our own).

In Front of the Text

The central task of hermeneutics, according to Ricoeur in multiple rephrasings, is to 'unfold the world which is in front of the text'.[45] The first of Ricoeur's images is that our understanding comes from *in front of* the text. Readers stand figuratively before a text. They are confronted by it, addressed by it, engaged by its matter. To Ricoeur, the text is an active participant in such encounters, not passively at the behest of the readers. A text creates the audience that it wishes to address,[46] and the act of reading that ensues is an

---

45. E.g. Ricoeur, *Hermeneutics and the Human Sciences*, p. 111.
46. Ricoeur, *Hermeneutics and the Human Sciences*, p. 202.

event. It is almost an interpersonal encounter, a meeting between two subjects, in which the reader and the text interact. This is most obvious in liturgical traditions where the public reading of Scripture may be accompanied by ceremony that embodies both the opening of the text and its confrontation with believers. It may be held up high to view, it may be blessed or consecrated, it may be processed into the middle of the people, who may stand and turn to face it.

Unfolding the Text
From this place in front of the text, to understand is to *unfold—disclose—open up—reveal—lay open—discover* the world of the text, picking up on the range of terms that Ricoeur applies. What does it mean to unfold the world of the text? Two images (mine not Ricoeur's) may enlighten this. The first is that of opening up a large, folded document such as a map (which is a type of text). We—literally—unfold and spread the map out so that what is on it can be disclosed to us. If we do not unfold it, we do not see what is on it. If we try to refold it to reveal just one section, the process is both clumsy and partial. We can't get in control of the physical document, and we can't get a hold on what the whole means. This images our interpreter task as unfolding and laying out what the text says. So it is with Scripture: we open the pages, and the text is revealed in front of the book, in front of us. A related image is a biblical one, 'opening' a text. As Jesus 'opened the scriptures' on the road to Emmaus (Lk. 24.32), so preachers are said to follow suit for their congregation, with the intention that the hearers appropriate that knowledge to their own lives.

The Matter of the Text
What our unfolding reveals is the 'matter of the text', its gist.[47] To return to our map image: unfolding discloses the matter of the map—literally the world portrayed by this particular cartography. The text offers a world, and it is the interpreter's task to open up the nature of that world—the 'heart' of the text. This is especially the case for biblical interpreters; our prime task is to unfold the matter of the texts we analyse, in all the analytical and critical richness which that requires. This includes expecting a text to be 'plurivocal', its matter to be multiple: 'This plurivocity is typical of the text considered as a whole, open to several readings and to several constructions'.[48]

---

47. Note Elvey's use of this phrase as a title for her engagement with the materiality of biblical texts (particularly the scroll), their physicalness and relationship to the sense. See Anne F. Elvey, *The Matter of the Text: Material Engagements between Luke and the Five Senses* (Sheffield: Sheffield Phoenix Press, 2011).
48. Ricoeur, *Hermeneutics and the Human Sciences*, p. 21.

The Injunction of the Text

Ricoeur also characterizes the text as providing its own injunction for how it is to be understood. Punning on the ambiguity of the French *sens* as both 'sense/meaning' and 'path/direction',[49] he pictures a text as having a given direction, as leading down a particular path: 'to interpret is to follow the path of thought opened up by the text'.[50] A related image is the 'arrow' of meaning, which leads the interpreter to think in accordance with the text.[51] The text both *is* dynamic and *has* a dynamic.

To Say Again What the Text Said

Finally, Ricoeur believes that the text and its features limit the plausible constructions that can be put upon it: 'If it is true that there is always more than one way of construing a text, it is not true that all interpretations are equal. The text presents a limited field of possible constructions.'[52] One construction may be more probable than another on the grounds that it 'takes account of the greatest number of facts furnished by the text'.[53] It is my view that a congruence of evidences converge towards a few likely interpretations, or even to a single probable reading. Our constructions will be based on the clues which the text itself offers: 'A clue…contains at once a permission and a prohibition; it excludes unsuitable constructions and allows those which give more meaning'.[54] Our highest calling as biblical interpreters is then to 'say again' what the text has already said. In the midst of all our analysis and critique, we remain answerable to the text's own matter.

Understanding Babel

How then do we apply this to Babel? How do we unfold this text to disclose its matter and its injunction? How do we 'say again' what the Babel story says? Our concern here is to interpret what the story of Babel means in the light of textual analysis and biblical scholarship rather than cultural myth or even Christian tradition. My own proto-understanding, derived from the traditional in-culture interpretation of Babel, was spelled out in Text 2 above, which 'says Babel again' in accordance with this view. Has this reading been validated or invalidated by my analysis above? The key question is this:

---

49. Ricoeur, *Hermeneutics and the Human Sciences*, p. 30.
50. Ricoeur, *Hermeneutics and the Human Sciences*, p. 162.
51. Ricoeur, *Hermeneutics and the Human Sciences*, p. 192.
52. Ricoeur, *Interpretation Theory*, p. 79.
53. Ricoeur, *Hermeneutics and the Human Sciences*, p. 175.
54. Ricoeur, *Hermeneutics and the Human Sciences*, p. 175.

What Was the Offence of Babel?

The traditional Jewish, Christian and Western understanding—both lay and scholarly—has been that the people of Babel were attempting to challenge God by building their tower, and they were accordingly punished for their pride and rebellion.[55] This goes back to the earliest surviving Christian observations on Babel, from Theophilus of Antioch in the late second century CE.[56] Wenham exemplifies this still predominant traditional reading, albeit in extreme form, in describing the judgment of Babel as 'fierce condemnation of mankind's sinful folly'.[57] His conclusion for the story's etiology of multilingualism is that 'the multiplicity of human languages is a reminder of divine retribution on human pride'.[58]

By contrast, my very 'plain' précis in Text 3 above does not in fact identify an obvious trigger for God's action against the people, for the simple reason that this remains inexplicit in the story itself. The general Christian and cultural understanding of Babel assumes as cause something which is not actually said by the text. It is not obvious what the fault may have been. The nature of the fault is, however, the main issue in the story, the key to unfolding the 'matter' of this text. What did they do so wrong that God's response was so severe, to scatter them and confuse their language? It is precisely the text's inexplicitness about the people's fault that opens it to divergent readings.

They Were Not Challenging God

There are, elsewhere in the Scriptures, intertextual counter-arguments to the traditional Western reading:

- It is not the establishment of a city in itself that was wrong. Biblical writings recognize the potential that cities have for good as well as evil.[59] The city is often a positive concept, from the prophets' visions for Zion through to the holy city in Revelation.
- Nor was the building of the tower necessarily a problem. This may have been a defensive tower,[60] but even if it was a ziggurat, the description 'with its top in the heavens' was a conventional

---

55. P.J. Harland, 'Vertical or Horizontal: The Sin of Babel', *VT* 48 (1998), pp. 515-33.

56. Christoph Uehlinger, *Weltreich und 'eine Rede': Eine neue Deutung der sogenannten Turmbauerzählung (Gen 11, 1-9)* (Göttingen: Vandenhoeck & Ruprecht, 1990), p. 258.

57. Wenham, *Genesis 1–15*, p. 245.

58. Wenham, *Genesis 1–15*, p. 244.

59. Brueggemann, *Genesis*, p. 101.

60. E.g. Claus Westermann, *Genesis 1–11: A Commentary* (trans. John J. Scullion; London: SPCK, 1984), p. 547.

hyperbole.⁶¹ The judgment was not directed against the tower.⁶² The city was left unfinished, but the text is silent about the fate of the tower. Perhaps it was completed.
- Lastly, not even the wish to 'make a name' is necessarily problematic in the biblical context. King David is not disapproved of for making a name for himself (2 Sam. 8.13).

These three possibilities do not seem reason enough for the scale of response God visited on the people of Babel. They are proto-understandings of causes which are therefore not validated under closer evidence.

They Were Refusing to Spread through the Earth

In recent decades, some Old Testament scholars, Jewish and Christian, have come to alternative and linked interpretations of Babel very different from the received cultural reading. The key to understanding the story, according to Brueggemann, lies in the preceding matter of Genesis.⁶³ The people of Babel built the city and the tower because 'otherwise we shall be scattered abroad upon the face of the whole earth' (v. 4). The phrase is a clear echo—and contradiction—of the mandate that God gave to humankind at creation and after the flood. Van Wolde argues that God's action was less *against* the city and tower than *on behalf of* the earth.⁶⁴

The fault of Babel is that the builders were trying to anchor themselves in one place, not so much out of any positive motivation but out of fear of being scattered. Their building activity took no regard for the intention and needs of the wider creation or even for their fellow-humans. They were therefore putting the development of creation at risk. Whereas the traditional Western imputation is that the people of Babel were overstepping the mark by challenging God, the alternative view is rather that they were *understepping* what was expected of them.⁶⁵

In the light of this interpretation, the judgment of vv. 7-9 is in fact entirely appropriate and logical. The punishment rectifies the crime. It forces the Babel builders out of their self-imposed limits and makes them disperse across the earth as God had always intended.⁶⁶ The story therefore concludes

---

61. Nahum M. Sarna, *Genesis* (JPSTC; Philadelphia: Jewish Publication Society, 1989), p. 83.
62. Westermann, *Genesis 1–11*, p. 536.
63. Brueggemann, *Genesis*, p. 98.
64. Ellen van Wolde, *Words Become Worlds: Semantic Studies of Genesis 1–11* (Leiden: Brill, 1994), p. 102.
65. Fretheim, 'Genesis', p. 412.
66. The Babel text has a bet each way on whether physical dispersion triggered linguistic dispersion, or vice versa. Verse 7, spoken by God, prioritizes language mixing, while v. 8 narrates that God acted to scatter them. The v. 9 coda has both of these—

with a judgment which is simultaneously a blessing. This matter as unfolded is paraphrased in Text 4.

Text 4: *A Re-interpretation of Babel*

1	At the time, the known earth spoke a single language.
2-3	Some migrating people settled on a plain and learned to build.
4	The people decided to maintain their unity by building a city with a tall tower.
5	God saw this construction
6	and believed the unity of the people and their language could stop them spreading through the earth as God had intended.
7	God concluded that mixing up their language would prevent them remaining isolated in one place.
8	God scattered the people and they stopped building the city.
9	The mix of many languages in the world today results from the blessing of God on human dispersion and diversity.

Validating Babel

Texts limit their own readings, Ricoeur has maintained. But some texts set more limits than others. The analyses of the Babel text in the earlier section leave its interpretation under-determined. The lack of direct expression of cause and motive in the Babel story (as shown in Text 3) renders it open to a range of understandings that are, at the extremes, directly contradictory. Nor can the issues be settled by appeal to the arbitration of authorial intentions. Ricoeur's observation that the text is the place where the author appears applies wholly to the Babel story.[67] Interpretation of the text itself is our only path to guessing what either the divine or human authors intended with this story. There is no separate road to the deduction of intent than the one we have already taken.

My initial guess/proto-understanding of Babel, based largely on a culture-derived pre-view (Text 2), has not stood up robustly under the scrutiny of validation procedures. Babel can be understood as signifying something quite different from the traditional interpretation. To a linguist, the most striking conclusion from the analysis is that the text can be read as a positive rather than negative account of the origins of multilingualism (Text 4).

However, in the spirit of seeking counter-evidence that might falsify my own interpretation (à la Popper), what are the textual evidences against it? They mainly involve a chain of inference that triggers a succession of negative readings, none of which need be so. One of the two 'punishments'—*fwts* 'scatter'—has been shown also to have positive meanings intertextually.

language mixing, and geographical scattering. There is a likely sociolinguistic dialectic here; migrations lead to language mixing, and mixing leads to migration.
67. Ricoeur, *Hermeneutics and the Human Sciences*, p. 149.

Even the twice-repeated, negatively loaded 'confuse' has an alternative translation as the neutral 'mix up' (see Texts 3 and 4). Such a gloss leaves the story open to either a positive or negative interpretation.

Lastly, an interpretation of Babel as a fulfilment of dispersal and diversity seems to me to receive strong support from the linguistic findings of the analysis phase, taken holistically. The narrative instantiates the linguistic richness that is its outcome; the form of the story is itself a celebration of linguistic variety. The cross-language punchline pun on *balal/Babel* is only possible because of language difference. It is itself the direct fruit—as well as the emblem—of Babel. I argue, then, that the form of the story *as a whole* is one of those clues that, Ricoeur maintains, direct us to think in accordance with the gist of this text.[68] It is hard to square the rich linguistic diversity of the Babel text with a reading that presents multilingualism as a curse. But it is entirely congruent with a *positive* view of language diversity as blessing.

Ownership

Our encounter with the matter of the text, our following of the injunction of the text, moves seamlessly into and concludes with Ownership (my preference to the usual translation of *Aneignung* as 'appropriation'). This is the last phase of the Interpretive Arc—'the final brace of the bridge, the anchorage of the arch in the ground of lived experience'.[69] The significance of ownership/appropriation is that understanding the text is not its own end. It is a means to ownership of meaning and the understanding of one's self. Understanding which does not move on to ownership is as reductionist as is analysis which does not move on to understanding: 'an interpretation is not authentic unless it culminates in some form of appropriation'.[70]

The Text and a New Self

The text, says Ricoeur, is 'addressed to me'.[71] Therefore understanding of the text is meshed with self-understanding, so that 'to understand is *to understand oneself in front of the text*'.[72] The dialectic between analysis and understanding is succeeded by—or better, interwoven with—a dialectic of understanding and ownership. We therefore do not reach an interpretation solely or even primarily as something out there, distanced from ourselves: 'in hermeneutical reflection—or in reflective hermeneutics—the constitution of the *self* is contemporaneous with the constitution of *meaning*'.[73]

---

68. Ricoeur, *Hermeneutics and the Human Sciences*, p. 175.
69. Ricoeur, *Hermeneutics and the Human Sciences*, p. 164.
70. Ricoeur, *Hermeneutics and the Human Sciences*, p. 178.
71. Ricoeur, *Interpretation Theory*, p. 92.
72. Ricoeur, *Hermeneutics and the Human Sciences*, p. 143 (emphasis original).
73. Ricoeur, *Hermeneutics and the Human Sciences*, p. 159 (emphasis original).

Central to this is the opportunity that a text offers a reader of something fresh, 'a new way of looking at things'.[74] This is why it is important to grasp the matter and injunction of the text in their own right, so that our pre-views do not mask its gist: 'Only the interpretation which satisfies the injunction of the text, which follows the "arrow" of meaning and endeavours to "think in accordance with" it, engenders a new *self*-understanding'.[75] The self that emerges from encounter with the text is in principle a new or different or 'enlarged' self. However it may be a reinforced rather than a reshaped self. It is possible for the text or our reading of it to serve only to solidify our current stance. In that case, we will have refused an opportunity for renewal, but will not be unchanged—our existing positioning will have been hardened.

Disowning through Ideological Critique

As part of the process of appropriation/owning, readers must pass through 'disappropriation/disowning' by means of an ideological critique of their own positioning and that of the text. The biblical text critiques us and our pre-views. Ideological critique is an essential part of the ownership phase of the Interpretive Arc, looping back in a dialectic with Analysis and Understanding. Ideological critique is necessary both to address the social issues immanent in texts, and to avoid the capture of interpretation by the prejudice of the individual reader.[76] Ricoeur argues that it need not be the case that the reader takes possession of the text, depriving it of its own standing. To interpret is not to project oneself into the text, but to understand oneself in front of the text.[77] It is to 'own up to' one's own preconcepts and disown them.

Owning Babel

How then are we to reach a new understanding and self understanding from the matter of the Babel text? What new selves does it engender? Bringing together what we have discussed above under analysis and understanding, let me identify five material issues that appear to me to be part of what we can 'own' today from Babel.

A Primeval Call to Sociocultural Diversity

Babel, on the basis of the evidence presented earlier, is not about direct human rebellion against God but about refusal to diversify in the manner the

---

74. Ricoeur, *Interpretation Theory*, p. 88.
75. Ricoeur, *Hermeneutics and the Human Sciences*, p. 192 (emphasis original).
76. Ricoeur, *Interpretation Theory*, p. 94.
77. Ricoeur, *Hermeneutics and the Human Sciences*, p. 178.

Creator ordained for the good of humanity and of the earth. This involves physical dispersion, sociocultural diversity and linguistic variety. Babel's call to diversity is then interpretable as a polemic against empire—that centripetal human undertaking that seeks to enforce monoculturalism, monolingualism, unity and unanimity. Parallels are suggested between Babel and the fate of Sargon II of the savage Neo-Assyrian empire, whose capital city Dur-Sharrukin was abandoned unfinished on his death.[78] The story of Babel stands as a critique of such exercises of centralized, homogenizing domination. It is a history written by the disadvantaged and oppressed who are hopeful of their liberation.

A Primeval Call to Linguistic Diversity
Ancient empires clearly had an impetus to monolingualism that will look familiar to modern eyes. The Neo-Assyrian empire nurtured probably the world's first imperial languages,[79] initially Akkadian, then Aramaic—which was still the lingua franca of the Near East a thousand years later and the first language of Jesus. At times it appears to have pursued a policy of enforced monolingualism. 'One speech' was part of Assyrian kings' ideology and rhetoric of domination, abolishing language variety and bringing people under one language and rule.[80]

Contemporary Empire
Today's commentators often apply the words 'fortress mentality' to Babel.[81] The city and tower were isolationist, a means of seeking security at the expense of human relations. The Argentinian liberation theologian José Míguez-Bonino holds that the story's main matter is to condemn imperial dominion and achieve the liberation of nations with their own place and languages.[82] The Babel story holds a dialectic of unity and scattering, according to Brueggemann.[83] We tend to think of unity as good and dispersion as bad, but both of these have the potential for either good or bad. Monolingualism was part of the identity of the people of Babel, and that identity marker was lost in their scattering. Brueggemann comments that religion can serve to bolster a wrongful unity, and notes the difficulty that

---

78. Uehlinger, *Weltreich und 'eine Rede'*, p. 481.
79. Nicholas Ostler, *Empires of the Word: A Language History of the World* (London: HarperCollins, 2005), pp. 59, 79.
80. Harland, 'Vertical or Horizontal', p. 517.
81. E.g. Harland, 'Vertical or Horizontal', p. 528.
82. José Míguez-Bonino, 'Genesis 11:1-9—A Latin American Perspective', in Priscilla Pope-Levison and John R. Levison (eds.), *Return to Babel: Global Perspectives on the Bible* (Louisville, KY: Westminster/John Knox Press, 1999), pp. 13-16.
83. Brueggemann, *Genesis*, p. 98.

pax Americana experiences in practising self-critique.[84] In our day, it is arguable that religion in the United States has been captured for the buttressing of imperial ideologies and policies. While the tower is not in fact the focus of the Babel story—the city is—it is easy to see why it has reigned in collective memory and artistic representations as the visual symbol of this narrative. Towers symbolize imperial cities. It is no accident that the Twin Towers became the target for attack on the US empire, and that the sight of their destruction remains the lasting visual image of that assault.

Monolingualism and Empire
Babel is in part a story about linguistic power inappropriately exercized, about the social and political meaning of monolingualism and multilingualism. The modern European nation-state was created with the ideology that a nation should have one single language. That concept still haunts most twenty-first-century nations. Monolingualism is frequently imperial and coercive against other languages. For the people of Babel their imperial language was a means to unity and power just as empires throughout history have striven for monolingual domination whether through Aramaic, Latin, French, Chinese or English. But in the reading I am suggesting, Babel is a charter for linguistic diversity, a manifesto for multilingualism rather than a lament for lost monolingualism.[85] The post-Babel variegation of people and languages was, then, not only or even primarily a punishment, but an opportunity. Far from being a curse, Babel is a blessing in disguise.

The Centrality of New Listening
Finally, the issue of listenership: in the analysis above I discussed the reading of *shema'* as 'listening' as well as 'understanding', and the echoes which that has in the prophets. Brueggemann suggests that the issue at Babel may have been one of failure to listen rather than confusion in speaking.[86] There are clear intertextual links with the New Testament. The need to listen was emphasized in Jesus' teaching, especially in the frequent coda, 'Listen— if you have ears!' (e.g. Lk. 8.8). The account of Pentecost also stresses

---

84. Brueggemann, *Genesis*, p. 101.
85. Not that I want to be seen to claim that 'God is against monolingualism', including imperial lingua francas. Aramaic became the native language of Jesus. The New Testament was written in the lingua franca that was imposed by Alexander the Great. And while I have argued that the day of Pentecost affirms linguistic diversity, it also confirms the utility of 'world languages'. Peter's sermon (Acts 2.14ff) will have been in Aramaic (or perhaps Greek), otherwise his linguistically diverse audience could not have understood it. People have always taken and turned lingua francas to their own communicative and identity ends; so has God.
86. Brueggemann, *Genesis*, p. 103.

listenership. The repeated emphasis in Acts 2 was that people *heard* in their own languages rather than that diverse languages were *spoken*. Ricoeur's approach explicitly shares these principles of new 'listening'. He stresses the centrality of ownership to interpretation, and the centrality of fresh reading to ownership. We are to be open to the matter of a text, not to our preconceptions about it. Encounter with a text involves new knowing, which challenges both the given self and the given sociopolitical structures.

Conclusion

It seems clear that Ricoeur's thought, and the Interpretive Arc I have adapted from it, offers an approach that is congenial to theological interpretation of the Bible. I take as criterial to theological interpretation a concern not just to analyze biblical texts, but to set them loose in the life of the believer and the church. Murray Rae (this volume) stresses the centrality of listening to interpretation, and the essential merger between being a hearer of the word and being a doer and follower. Ricoeur's contention that interpretation is only completed in 'ownership' of the word—in transformation into a new self formed by the text—is valid for the biblical text beyond all others.

Ricoeur's insistence on sidelining author intention will seem a barrier to some scholars, but I believe it is less of an obstacle than it appears. What he is trying to achieve with his sometimes radical statements on this question is to uncouple interpretation from the deduction of author intent, and to dethrone intent as the arbiter of interpretation. Texts can mean something more, something less or something different from what their authors intended, and this applies to the biblical writers as much as anyone.

The sharper issue is whether this applies to God as the ultimate author of Scripture. Human writers may not be sovereign over their own texts and their potential readings, but surely God is sovereign over the interpretation of Scripture? Yes—but what does that mean? Not that a biblical text allows just one interpretation. God may intend multiple meanings. In fact, that is precisely what we should expect. A state of estrangement holds between readers and all human authors, making the text independent of the author's intention. But uniquely as the active author of the living word, God can intend fresh meanings for fresh audiences; the Spirit leads into all truth.

The meaning of the biblical text is thus neither determinate nor indeterminate. There is no one meaning, but nor are there unlimited meanings. Too often the imputation of divine intent can be an excuse for remaining with our pre-view of a text, for being bound by old readings, for not listening with fresh ears. We think God intends what we intend rather than vice versa, which is precisely the stance that Jesus attacked so forcefully among the religious leaders of his day. And this is why we approach every text with humility, especially the biblical. We owe courtesy to the text.[87] Texts have rights: we are answerable to what they say. Our readings must be warranted.

Babel is an instance of 'plurivocity' in interpretation. We have seen how clashing readings from the same text can be: Babel as negative or positive, as destructive or creative, as judgment or beneficence, as curse or blessing. And the variety of languages and cultures are, in my reading, aspects of being human which are not to be trammelled or overridden by the dominion of empire. The domination of the 'mono' is to be problematized, whether it is the monocultural, the mono-ethnic or the monolingual—or, as so often, all of those intertwined. Multiplicity and plurality are to be accepted as hallmarks of common human good, for all the challenge they bring, whether manifested in multiculturalism, multi-ethnicism, plurilingualism or plurivocity.

To close with a last word on Babel, Ricoeur's word. He delivered a lecture on 'The Paradigm of Translation' in 1998, when he was aged 85. It was published in French the year before his death in 2005, and in English the year after. In this paper Ricoeur offers a 'more benign' reading of Babel than that of 'irremediable linguistic catastrophe'.[88] He characterizes the Babel story as 'non-judgmental',[89] as lacking in either lamentation or accusation. He regards the outcome of Babel as matter-of-fact, even benevolent, rather than condemnatory. Ricoeur's congruent reading encourages me in the interpretation I have offered.

---

87. Craig Bartholomew, 'Before Babel and after Pentecost', in Bartholomew, Greene and Möller (eds.), *After Pentecost*, pp. 131-70.

88. Paul Ricoeur, *On Translation* (trans. Eileen Brennan; London: Routledge, 2006), p. 12.

89. Ricoeur, *On Translation*, p. 18.

5

THE ASCENT OF THEOLOGICAL READING: ICONOCLASM AND THE DIVINE EVENT OF MAKING READERS

John C. McDowell

A Prefatory Sign

The Bible has increasingly been read with divergent methods for proliferating purposes over recent centuries: historical, literary, liberationist-political and so on.[1] According to Augustine, however, 'anyone who thinks that he has understood the divine Scriptures or any part of them, but cannot by his understanding build up this double love of God and neighbour, has not yet succeeded in understanding them'.[2] This statement concerning the context and *telos* of the event of reading was normative for the medieval tradition, according to Grace Jantzen.[3] Consequently, she maintains, 'It is not primarily the acquisition of information that is important, not even information about God, let alone about the historical authors and their circumstances'.[4] Certainly these further matters are not incidental and avoidable, but they have their proper significance in informing or serving the 'religious use' of the text.[5] In such a scenario, and this is the preeminent or paradigmatic form of reading the text *as Scripture*, the Bible cannot be interpreted well if all things are left as they are. 'It was...the means whereby one could be soaked in the love of God, so that the divine would permeate all thought and

---

1. Gerard Loughlin, *Telling God's Story: Bible, Church and Narrative Theology* (Cambridge: Cambridge University Press, 1996), p. 107.
2. Augustine, *De doctrina christiana* (trans. R.P.H. Green; Oxford: Oxford University Press, 1995), 1.86.
3. Grace Jantzen, *Power, Gender and Christian Mysticism* (Cambridge: Cambridge University Press, 1995), p. 81.
4. Jantzen, *Power, Gender and Christian Mysticism*, p. 81.
5. Søren Kierkegaard 'warns against the error of coming to inspect the mirror instead of to see oneself in the mirror' (*For Self-Examination: Recommended for the Times* [trans. Edna Hong and Howard Hong; Minneapolis: Augsburg, 1940], p. 23).

activity'.[6] The theological reading of Scripture, then, is not merely a way of 'telling God's story', in Gerard Loughlin's telling phrase, that can otherwise distance storytellers from the demands of God's own storytelling. It equally involves readers in becoming those who are engaged in God's creative telling of the eschatological story of creation, and its retelling as the story of reconciliation and redemption.[7] Theological reading emerges in this double sense from the event of divine Self-giving as God Self-identifiably gives the abundance or flourishing of creatures made to be God's people. In that respect, a *theological reading* of the Bible is not an additional (one method among the methods), or even alternative (against the other methods), method for interpreting the text alongside others, but the very means of engaging with the *Sache* itself that draws the interpretative methods to the Bible's *telos* (uniting and transforming the methods).

In marked contrast, Maurice Wiles claims that the church has arbitrarily imposed an illegitimate unity on the biblical texts in order to accord them 'an authoritative status as Scripture'.[8] New critical discoveries about the nature of the text—such as the social conditioning of the texts, the diversity of opinions among them, and the unreliability of their historical witness, among other things—encourage him to yearn for the day when the Bible will be regarded instead as an 'indispensable resource rather than as a binding authority'.[9] If one responds with what Augustine calls the 'rules for interpreting the Scriptures',[10] Wiles's counter reveals an important political worry. For him, 'the grammatical rules for reading the Christian story...have served the cause of institutional control at least as much as the cause of religious truth'.[11] In its current form, however, Wiles's judgment is too loose. The phrase 'at least as much as' suggests a lazy decision to support a proposal for the 'descripturation' of biblical interpretation such as has been common among many modern biblical interpreters. One of this chapter's fundamental theological moves calls Wiles's political judgment about the biblical texts into question while continuing to read the texts as scriptural. There is 'little to be learned' from criticisms that simply target that which

---

6. Jantzen, *Power, Gender and Christian Mysticism*, p. 81.

7. This account develops the ambiguity of the term 'theological', referring to both 'the concept "god"...[and] "God"' (Alan Torrance, 'Can the Truth Be Learned? Redressing the "Theologistic Fallacy" in Modern Biblical Scholarship', in Markus Bockmuehl and Alan J. Torrance [eds.], *Scripture's Doctrine and Theology's Bible* [Grand Rapids: Baker, 2008], p. 144).

8. Maurice Wiles, 'Scriptural Authority and Theological Construction: The Limitations of Narrative Interpretation', in Garrett Green (ed.), *Scriptural Authority and Narrative Interpretation* (Philadelphia: Fortress Press, 1987), p. 46.

9. Wiles, 'Scriptural Authority and Theological Construction', p. 50.

10. Augustine, *De doctrina christiana*, Preface 1.

11. Wiles, 'Scriptural Authority and Theological Construction', p. 51.

even the tradition, at its best, would itself agree was a 'dreadful caricature'.[12] In order to sustain the allegation that Wiles's criticism is itself a 'dreadful caricature' of the shape of the tradition this chapter needs to deal with 'the grammatical rules for reading the Christian story' that he maintains 'have served the cause of institutional control at least as much as the cause of religious truth'. Admittedly, the rules will largely be addressed only in the background, however. The foreground space will be occupied instead by a theological reading of a particular biblical text, that found in Exodus 32. Within this decisive moment in the development of the biblical tradition is the kind of text that demands a theological reading that resists and subverts the theo-politics that Wiles is so concerned with.

The selection of this particular passage is not an arbitrary one. First, within the biblical collection of texts Exodus 32 is a significant narrative involving God's very *founding* of the community of the people of God, Israel. Exodus 32 somewhat fleshes out what is involved in the giving of God's 'name' to Moses. Moreover, even in the density of its own particularity this foundation story is extensively determinative for a typological reading of the larger depiction of God's ways with God's people. It prefigures the account of God's covenantal faithfulness and the judgment on the people's idolatrous behaviour that is prevalent in the trajectory of the 'Deuteronomistic History'. Idolatry, at least in this instance, is not the act of the pagan 'other', but the act of God's own people, and a tragically unwitting one to a considerable degree. Second, it provides an important set of resources for a *theological* reading of the Bible as Scripture, especially in relation to *God's making responsible readers* to be God's people through the dramatic engagement with the scriptural texts. Theological reading, then, is primarily that work of divine grace for creatures whereby God orders persons in covenant responsibility. As Oliver Davies claims with respect to Exodus 32, as paradigmatically real, the text 'redefines for us our own relation to the everyday real, and…does so from within the world of sensible reality'.[13] Third, the text reorders what is meant by 'the theological' by enabling consideration of its relation to iconoclasm. Idolatry has been understood as the most serious of disordered acts, the decisive manifestation of sinfulness in the biblical and rabbinic traditions, having to do with the very disorder of self-understanding and action.[14] If, as Eberhard Jüngel

---

12. Eberhard Jüngel, *God as the Mystery of the World: On the Foundation of the Theology of the Crucified One in the Debate between Theism and Atheism* (trans. Darrell L. Guder; Edinburgh: T. & T. Clark, 1983), p. 9.

13. Oliver Davies, 'Reading the Burning Bush: Voice, World and Holiness', *Modern Theology* 22 (2006), pp. 444-45.

14. See, e.g., Brian Rosner, *Greed as Idolatry: The Origin and Meaning of a Pauline Metaphor* (Grand Rapids: Eerdmans, 2007), p. 131.

maintains, theology has to do with following the demands of God's Self-identifying coming-to-speech, it equally and in substantial qualification demands thought be paid to the *unspeakability* of God, or the mystery of the incomprehensible ground of our existence, the One whom Pseudo-Dionysius praises as being 'beyond being...above and beyond speech, mind, or being itself'.[15] If this is not to slip into processes of reasoning about indeterminate reading by autonomous reading subjects, then the reflections must draw reading agents into theological reflection on the ground of their *given* subjectivity. This rich set of claims permits one to judge that even for a good determinate or ruled reading of the Bible as Scripture there is sense in Karl Barth's declaration that 'There can be no completed work. All human achievements are no more than Prolegomena; and this is especially the case in theology.'[16]

A further advance warning is needed. This chapter's reading of Exodus 32 is itself principally an indirect one, in fact largely three times removed from the text; the focus will be on two broadly theological readings of Arnold Schoenberg's opera *Moses und Aron*, those of the intellectual polymath George Steiner and the theological philosopher and ethicist Donald MacKinnon. On the one hand this procedure implies that readings have a history, and that the history of readings is ever-changing. Moreover, this trio of responses to Exodus 32 indicates something of the pluriformity of theological responses to biblical texts, without being hampered either by the banality of questions concerning the phenomena of the text, or by a certain kind of indeterminacy of reading (although, as we will see, Steiner's response is less able to resist indeterminacy than Mackinnon's). On the other hand, these particular readings are instructive for deep issues concerning God's speakability, enabling insight into what is involved in 'the kind of speakability' and unspeakability which is appropriate to God.[17] Or to refer the point to the theme of this book, they reveal much about what goes on, for good and ill, in practices of *theological reading of Scripture*. So Nicholas Lash argues that 'The function of theology...is to facilitate acquaintance [with God] by checking our propensity to go whoring after false gods'.[18] For someone like Wiles, or other more sophisticated ideology-critics, to suspiciously ask a question about the ideological function of religion, or the hegemony of the church, or even the texts turning terrible, is to find that he

---

15. Pseudo-Dionysius, 'The Divine Names', in *Pseudo-Dionysius: The Complete Works* (trans. Colm Luibheid and Paul Rorem; New York: Paulist Press, 1987), Chapter 1.1, 588A.
16. Karl Barth, *The Epistle to the Romans* (trans. Edwyn C. Hoskyns; Oxford: Oxford University Press, 6th edn, 1968), p. 3.
17. Jüngel, *God as the Mystery of the World*, p. 12.
18. Nicholas Lash, 'Considering the Trinity', *Modern Theology* 2 (1986), p. 187.

must take his place in a long tradition that includes theologians since, as Denys Turner observes, 'for the Christian, ideology and idolatry are synonyms'.[19]

Reintroducing the Reader as Theologian

Wiles's politically interested critique requires that an account be given of what constitutes an appropriate hermeneutics through articulating the approach of a *good reader*, or the traits that are necessary for a fitting approach to the text: characteristics or skills like attentiveness (to the particularity of the text), carefulness (in reading text in context), suspicion (of authors' ideological determinations), honesty (over one's own interpretative limitations) and so on. Even the types of reader-response criticism that contest the appeal to 'objectivity' that have dominated the various historical-critical approaches are not free from determinations of readers, so that readers can constructively play with the text in order for meaning to emerge in the event. What about a theological reading of the text? According to Kevin Vanhoozer, 'Theological hermeneutics…is the act of discerning the divine discourse in the work'.[20] However, this claim could potentially be made by a historical-critical reader, even if that would involve a slightly unusual act of paying more attention to the text itself than to what historically lies behind it. One might suggest that a Theological reading (capitalization of 'Theological' intended), conversely, is more demanding of the reader than that of theological reading, and something of the radicality of what this entails is suggested in Vanhoozer's talk of 'reforming the reader'.[21] This hermeneutical activity involves a consideration of 'interpretive virtue', and this has a twofold reference: first, the reader's responsibility to the activity of reading; and, secondly, the responsible life that is required to read the Bible as Scripture.

Gregory of Nazianzus's Theologian indicates something of what is at stake here. In his first *Theological Oration* (Oration 27), delivered in the Church of Anastasia while bishop of Constantinople, Gregory polemically announces that it does not belong to everyone to philosophize about God,

---

19. Denys Turner, *Marxism and Christianity* (Oxford: Blackwell, 1983), p. 227. The image of the terrible text is an allusion to Phyllis Trible, *Texts of Terror: Literary-Feminist Readings of Biblical Narratives* (Philadelphia: Fortress Press, 1984). On 'ideology' see Terry Eagleton, *Ideology: An Introduction* (London: Verso, 1991), p. 5.

20. Kevin J. Vanhoozer, 'Imprisoned or Free? Text, Status, and Theological Interpretation of the Master/Slave Discourse of Philemon', in A.K.M. Adam, Stephen E. Fowl, Kevin J. Vanhoozer and Francis Watson, *Reading Scripture with the Church: Toward a Hermeneutic for Theological Interpretation* (Grand Rapids: Baker, 2006), p. 66.

21. Kevin J. Vanhoozer, *Is There Meaning in This Text? The Bible, the Reader and the Morality of Literary Knowledge* (Leicester: Apollos, 1998), title of Chapter 7.

and not at all times and places. Is this an instance of the discriminatory theological discourse that expresses the emerging strategies of ecclesiastical power imposed on others in order to gain and then maintain control through the ideologically binding elitism that can be policed by ecclesiastical order? Certainly Gregory offers particularly harsh words for the neo-Arians, and his own rhetoric serves to legitimate his perspective. Yet there are important indications that something different is occurring here, something that opens up meaningful talk of the *theological* reading of the Bible as Scripture and offer broad suggestions of a way of reading beyond the determination of ideological hegemony. The particular discriminations he announces are immediately explained: with respect to the matter of *who* is worthy of the risk of legitimately undertaking the theologico-philosophical activity Gregory explains that it is only for those who have been examined, have meditated, and have been, or are at least being, purified in soul and body. As he argues in Oration 28, the Theologian ought to be, as far as may be, pure in order to know the light of God. This is sharply contrasted with the disposition of his theological opponents who are depicted in the previous oration as 'sophists', proud of their eloquence but who neglect the righteous path and therefore pay no attention to the proper approach to the Great Mystery. The God-talk of such people, Gregory is not slow to assert, is in danger of being made a thing of little consequence. In other words, those whom Gregory describes as the permitted persons are those for whom the subject is of real concern, and not those who reduce it to pleasant gossip befitting any other thing. The contrast is marked out between those who take the subject-matter seriously, and thereby approach it in ways appropriate to it, and those who engage it frivolously in ways that not only fall outside proper bounds but which distort the subject-matter. So in an earlier oration Gregory criticizes those who rely on 'hearsay' for their theological knowledge without attempting to undertake a diligent 'study' of the Scriptures.[22] If *God* is the subject of the Theologian's philosophizing, then the mode of engagement in reasoning must be appropriate to the knowing of God, a mode that involves the Pure purifying the impure Theologian.

John Webster argues,

> Reading Scripture is thus a moral matter, [which] requires that we become certain kinds of readers, whose reading is taken up into the history of reconciliation. The separation of reason from virtue in modernity has made this acutely difficult to grasp.[23]

---

22. Gregory of Nazianzus, *Oration* 2.49, in Philip Schaff (ed.), *Nicene and Post-Nicene Fathers*. II/7. *Cyril of Jerusalem, Gregory Nazianzen* (Edinburgh: T. & T. Clark, 1893), p. 215.

23. John Webster, *Holy Scripture: A Dogmatic Sketch* (CIT; Cambridge: Cambridge University Press, 2003), p. 87.

More of what is entailed in these observations regarding Gregory's Theologian, and particularly of the role of scriptural reading in the event of making and disciplining the Theologian, can be gleaned from attending to the image that comes to dominate Oration 28. The Theologian, Gregory implies, is a type of Moses who ascends the mountain of God. Is this too not potentially expressive of a hegemonic religious elitism? Moses, after all, is specifically called to *lead* the Israelites out of bondage, and *authoritatively* to announce the words and works of God; and Moses *alone* is called up the mountain, while Aaron, Nadab, Abihu and the seventy elders are directed to worship from a distance. How the theological type is handled is significant for comprehending the Theological task, and with it the task of the Theological reading of Scripture.

From the Sublime to the Particularist: Figuring, Disfiguring and Reconfiguring Moses' Speech

George Steiner's Kantian Sublimity

Commonly, readings of Exodus 32 suggest that the idolatry lies in the *materiality* of the image. This corrupt 'materialization of deity' is contrasted with the emphatic aniconism of Moses as faithful representative of covenanted Israel, and the former falls foul of the ban on visualisable images given in the Decalogue's second commandment when understood as having to do with directing *how* worship should occur. The antithesis becomes one of physical/ spiritual, with the latter being particularly associated with the rational and verbal.[24] To put it in terms of Augustine's eminent distinction in *On Christian Doctrine*, influencing as it did the standard medieval manual of Peter Lombard's *Sentences*, this aniconic reading would suggest that the idolatrous act has to do with the making of a *visible* sign (*signum*) that is mistaken for the *invisible* thing (*res*).[25] Steiner's reflections on Schoenberg's *Moses und Aron*, however, depict the issue between the titular characters quite differently from what this reading would suggest for two main reasons: first, Moses's very word-expressed faith is itself not free from idolatrous imaginings; and, second, there are forms of visibility in God's ways with Israel.

Although Steiner understands Moses's aniconic understanding of God to be 'much more authentic, much deeper', 'his is essentially mute or accessible

---

24. J.A. Motyer, 'Idolatry', in J.D. Douglas *et al.* (eds.), *New Bible Dictionary* (Leicester: Inter-Varsity Press, 2nd edn, 1982), pp. 503-505; E.M. Curtis, 'Idol, Idols', in *ABD*, III, p. 379; John Calvin, *Commentary on Deuteronomy* 4.12, cited in R.C. Zachman, *Image and Word in the Theology of John Calvin* (Notre Dame, IN: University of Notre Dame Press, 2007), p. 3. Cf. G.K. Beale, *We Become What We Worship: A Biblical Theology of Idolatry* (Downers Grove, IL: IVP Academic, 2008), p. 76.

25. Augustine, *De doctrina christiana*, 1.2.

only to the few' and therefore there is a grain of truth in Aaron's perspective.²⁶ Moses can only speak in a highly cadenced, formal discourse, a form of stylized song-speech (*Sprechstimme*), a discourse shockingly unable to give musical form to his vision. Aaron, on the other hand, is the eloquent one, the 'soaring tenor' who is able to express his God-talk through exuberant tones.²⁷

> Without Aaron, God's purpose cannot be accomplished; through Aaron it is perverted. That is the tragic paradox of the drama, the metaphysical scandal which springs from the fact that the categories of God are not parallel or commensurate to those of man.²⁸

Yet while Schoenberg's Moses imagines himself to represent a purer form of Yahwehism, it seems that he is unable to offer this since he is no less guilty of anthropomorphism than Aaron. Moses's concepts, his dialogue with God, his reception of revelation are themselves limitations of God, *images* of the unimaginable. After all, as Augustine articulates, words are preeminent *signs*, and the richest form of signification is the written verbal record.²⁹ They participate in the act of signification in a way that nonverbal signs do, only more intensively by the very nature of their communicability. Schoenberg's Aaron recognizes this and insists that the tablets of the Law are themselves an image, an expression of an imagistic idea. As Richard Viladesau observes, 'Aaron's insight implies that every conception of God's activity in history, or of human dialogue with God, including the most abstract, is involved in image making'.³⁰ Moses' ideas (Greek *eidos*) are as imagistic as the visible (Greek *eidō*, 'I see') material of the calf that becomes an idol (Greek *eidōlon*).³¹ The difficulty is that, in David Burrell's terms, 'Without a clear philosophical means of distinguishing God from the world, the tendency of all discourse about divinity is to deliver a God who is the "biggest thing around"'.³² For as Thomas argues in his *Summa contra gentiles*, God is not being in general, or reducible to being, but is rather

---

26. George Steiner, *Language and Silence: Essays 1958–1966* (Harmondsworth: Penguin Books, 1967), p. 178.
27. Steiner, *Language and Silence*, p. 176.
28. Steiner, *Language and Silence*, p. 178.
29. Augustine, *De doctrina christiana*, 2.6.
30. Richard Viladesau, *Theological Aesthetics: God in Imagination, Beauty and Art* (Oxford: Oxford University Press, 1999), p. 49.
31. See Bruce Ellis Benson, *Graven Ideologies: Nietzsche, Derrida and Marion on Modern Idolatry* (Downers Grove, IL: InterVarsity Press, 2002), pp. 19-24. Benson can legitimately speak, therefore, of 'Conceptual idolatry' (p. 19).
32. David B. Burrell, 'Distinguishing God from the World', in Brian Davies (ed.), *Language, Meaning and God: Essays in Honour of Herbert McCabe OP* (London: Geoffrey Chapman, 1987), p. 76.

particular and distinguishable from all other beings.[33] In fact, the Exodus narrative explains that Moses himself succumbed to a desire for the sight of God (Exod. 33.18). This glimpse is denied so that all Moses could see was the effect of the passing of the divine glory (Exod. 33.19-23). The opera turns on the fact that Moses begins to admit the incompleteness of his aniconism and seemingly recants somewhat, while Aaron nonetheless eventually dies untriumphant in the uncompleted Act III. Schoenberg depicts Moses, in an act of frustration, smashing the tablets and asking God to relieve him of his task.[34] Schoenberg's reading, in other words, cannot involve as simple an aniconism as is commonly advocated by Exodus 32's readers.

The question that the Exodus text poses, however, has to do with *what it is that is represented* by the golden calf image. What is idolatrous in the people's act? A clue can be found in Augustine's discussion of the relation between a sign (*signum*) and a thing (*res*) which focuses attention away from neat separations of spirit and matter, with service or *latreia* belonging properly to the former. The Bishop of Hippo speaks of things that are useful to our happiness, things to be enjoyed. However, we can be led astray from the true enjoyment and thus from our wellbeing by being led into lower gratifications, where by the 'lower' Augustine means those desired pursuits which direct us away from wellbeing. When our wellbeing is 'God' as *summum bonum*, God-alone-to-be-enjoyed not instrumentally for-the-sake-of-anything-else, then all else that is enjoyed in-and-for-itself ultimately deforms us. The problem for Augustine, then, is not so much a confusion of the *sign* with the *thing* as a misshapen desire no longer ordered towards its *telos* in the *summum bonum*. First, the desire for things which are instrumentally to aid us in true enjoyment is perverted when these things are enjoyed

---

33. Thomas Aquinas, *Summa contra gentiles* (trans. Joseph Rickaby; London: Burns & Oates, 1905), I.27.4.

34. Not only was God's word inscribed on the tablets of stone, but the Ark (God's throne) was subsequently constructed, the Tabernacle became the tent of meeting with God and God led the people by the visible pillars of cloud and fire. These *biblically legitimated* images are suggestive; God performs a Self-materialization, a communicative clothing in material form that John Calvin describes as visible words of divine 'accommodation': creation, the self with its *sensus divinitatis*, Christ, Scripture, church. In the terms of Thomas, the mind may be raised to God through corporeal and sensible things (*Summa contra gentiles*, III.121.1). On Calvin as aniconic, see Beale, *We Become What We Worship*, p. 19; cf. John Calvin, *Commentaries on the Last Four Books of Moses* (trans. Charles William Bingham; Grand Rapids: Eerdmans, 1964), II, pp. 116-17; David Vandrunen, 'Iconoclasm, Incarnation and Eschatology: Toward a Catholic Understanding of the Reformed Doctrine of the "Second" Commandment', *IJST* 6.2 (2004), pp. 130-31. Yet, on Calvin's pronounced iconicism and contrast between 'dead images' and 'living images', see Zachman, *Image and Word*, pp. 2, 7-9.

in and for themselves. Second, and concomitantly, idolatry has to do with desire's instrumentalization of that which should be enjoyed in-and-for-itself.

We might say, then, that the calf is not a thing-in-itself and therefore not an idol as such, but a sign of what becomes idolatrous desire and in that way an idol. After all, the *worship of it as God* does not seem to be what the people at the foot of Mount Sinai are guilty of, and MacKinnon's accusing Aaron of conscious idolatry in 'seeking to meet the religious needs of an ill-sorted horde of human beings' is difficult to sustain from the Exodus tradition.[35] Aaron attempts to encourage the people by inviting them to be patient, attempting to stall until Moses' return; he is then seized by fear as he sees their presumption grow; and finally, the people themselves throw the gold into the fire whence (we are not told how) the calf takes form (the rest is done by the fire). Moreover, Aaron announces a connection between the image and the divine liberation from Egyptian bondage (Exod. 32.3, 5). This is a restrained carnality, and crucially it is one in accord with Hebrew traditions that connected God, *El*, with the notion of a young bull representing power and fertility. The word used by the people in 32.1 to 'name' their liberator from Egypt, 'God', is *'elohim*. Even the diminutive translated as 'calf' seems to imply a contrast between the minuteness of this image and the God it signified. Moreover, according to Martin Noth, among others,

> As the ancient Near East (in contrast to Egypt) knows no theriomorphic deities but only the association of beasts with deities pictured in human form and whose companions and bearers they are, the 'golden calf' of the royal sanctuaries of Jeroboam [as reflections of the 'calf' at Sinai] are also surely as pedestals for the God who is imagined to be standing invisibly upon them.[36]

In that respect, the image even functions to retain something of a strong critical sense of God's transcendence in a way not entirely unlike the pillars of cloud and fire that move *ahead of* the people and *in which* God cannot be directly perceived. Therefore, Bori maintains that 'the people, through Aaron, do not give themselves other gods, but make for themselves an image of the Mosaic God, the God of the exodus'.[37]

If they are said to have come to *worship the image* it is because of something else, the nature of their distorted desire, and here, as Noth suggests in reflections on the reference at Dan and Bethel in 1 Kgs 12.28, 'an exaggeration of the original circumstances...has purposively been

---

35. D.M. MacKinnon, *Themes in Theology: The Three-Fold Cord: Essays in Philosophy, Politics and Theology* (Edinburgh: T. & T. Clark, 1987), p. 11.

36. Martin Noth, *Exodus: A Commentary* (London: SCM Press, 1962), p. 247.

37. Pier Cesare Bori, *The Golden Calf and the Origins of the Anti-Jewish Controversy* (Atlanta: Scholars Press, 1990), p. 9.

introduced with polemical intent'.[38] The text suggests that the writer uses a form of *tragic irony* to describe the people laying down their gold to celebrate a festival to God, but come to 'rise up' (Exod. 32.6, NRSV) to worship something other than God. The tragedy is not the one of linguistic communicability and representation that Steiner perceives, but rather of the fusion of religious horizons; the Liberator from Egypt is fused with the cultic Canaanite deities (in particular Baal) in a form of religious syncretism that the 'Deuteronomistic historian' came to characterize Israel as being prone to. The cattle image is itself an ambiguous one, and in its ambiguity the Israelites are depicted as having their spiritual feet back in the paganism of Egypt, the nation of their recent captivity, and on into Canaan. That would appear to be the reason for the ambiguous shift in the people's use of the plural in 32.4 ('gods') and Aaron's use of the singular in 32.5 ('the Lord'). Aaron's vision is seemingly itself misperformed by the paganizing people unaware of their error. Idolatry, at least in this instance, is not a simple substitution of something else for God, and thus the act of the pagan 'other'. It has to do with, to use Thomas's terms, the *undue* or improper use of sensible things that now fails to raise the mind to God and therefore fixes the mind on inferior things that are not God. So Viladesau claims that 'the problem is...[not] the use of images, but their misuse'.[39] To put it another way, this is Yahwehism lost in translation, so to speak, and it raises concretely the question of who *alone* is worthy of worship.

In the later parts of Schoenberg's opera it now seems to be taken for granted that it is possible for both words and images to serve and express the 'idea', if they remain grounded in the divine transcendence. But what does it mean to express the idea of divine transcendence? In her reflections on Schoenberg's opera Edith Wyschogrod suggests that Schoenberg understands the proper trajectory of a well-ordered iconoclasm to involve an imaginative indeterminacy. She argues that 'the golden calf is not an image but rather stanches the flow of runaway images and is an attestation of fixity'.[40] Here she makes a good point about the freezing of the divine event, or the impoverishment of the plenitudinous richness, involved in limiting attention to a singular image. As Randall Zachman claims, when referring to Calvin's perspective, making images out of creatures distracts 'our eyes from contemplating the living image of God in the whole creation, as well as the image and likeness of God in other human beings'.[41] In this regard, the

---

38. Noth, *Exodus*, p. 247.
39. Viladesau, *Theological Aesthetics*, p. 48.
40. Edith Wyschogrod, 'Eating the Text, Defiling the Hands: Specters in Arnold Schoenberg's Opera *Moses und Aron*', in John D. Caputo and Michael J. Scanlon (eds.), *God, the Gift and Postmodernism* (Bloomington: Indiana University Press, 1999), p. 248.
41. Zachman, *Image and Word*, p. 9.

calf figurally fetters the imagination, and it manifests a desperate attempt to check the polyphonic stream of images. Consequently, 'No principle is offered by means of which the genuine and spurious claimants can be distinguished because no principle applicable to sensual images could possibly determine which acts embody God's power'.[42]

MacKinnon's Apophatic Therapy
MacKinnon contrasts an anthropomorphism 'that ultimately reduces the divine to the status of a magnified human worldly reality', with 'an agnosticism which continually insists that where God is concerned, we may only confidently affirm that we do not know what we mean when we speak [or conceive] of him'.[43] In this vein he speaks of the primacy of the apophatic, and suggests that we 'we continually swing between…anthropomorphism… and…agnosticism'.[44] Yet without further theological qualification there is a difficulty with this form of negation. The so-called *negative way*, if that be grounded in the event of unspeakably determining one's own subjectivity or in reaching the limits of human reason, can be construed as equally a reflection (albeit as a negative reflection) of personal subjectivity of the God-imagist. Steiner is an example of this tendency. He warns that 'Those who would press language beyond its divinely ordained sphere, who would contract the *Logos* into the word, mistake both the genius of speech and the untranslatable immediacy of revelation'.[45] His concern is less with the honest and self-purificatory unnaming of God in every act of naming (and both are necessary tasks) than with protecting the mystical immediacy in silent contemplation. So Steiner speaks of the intolerable burden and inwardness of Moses' sense of the immediacy of revelation which Aaron betrays, crucially, in the very act of communicating it outwardly to others.

Theologies attuned to an iconoclastic apophaticism could agree that 'speech so precisely fails us'. Elie Wiesel, for instance, declares, 'There is healthy silence, Sinai, and an unhealthy silence, that of chaos'.[46] Yet Steiner's emphasis lies on the disjunction, or competitiveness of human and divine discourses rather than on the excessive plenitude of the covenantal God's being God, for example. 'The paradox' of the disjunction between idea and representation 'is resolved in defeat, in a great cry of necessary silence… [in order to appropriately] serve a Deity so intangible to human mimesis'.[47] As Graham Ward surmises from the Ockhamist de-ontologization

42. Wyschogrod, 'Eating the Text', p. 251.
43. MacKinnon, *Themes in Theology*, p. 12.
44. MacKinnon, *Themes in Theology*, p. 12.
45. Steiner, *Language and Silence*, p. 62.
46. Elie Wiesel, in Harry James Cargas and Elie Wiesel, *Harry James Cargas in Conversation with Elie Wiesel* (New York: Paulist Press, 1976), p. 46.
47. Steiner, *Language and Silence*, pp. 174, 177.

of words and metaphysics of linguistic atomism that underlies this account, 'God is now encountered on the far side of language and knowledge'.[48] What we seem to be left with is Schoenberg's post-Kantian inexpressibility of the noumenon (or 'thing-in-itself' that lies behind our knowledge of the phenomena, or 'things-as-they-appear-to-us').[49] When the reader is turned in on herself away from the window onto others, what she gazes at is a mirror of her own interiority, and this is a hermeneutical idolatry. Even in the poetic task, words distort; eloquent words distort absolutely.[50] However, Steiner's account of the acts of reading and translating will find it difficult to provide the momentum for a hope that is anything more than a *sheer act of will* or the arbitrary fiat of a Pascalian inspired *wager* on transcendence.

For MacKinnon, in contrast, not any kind of theological silence will do. Unlike this kind of 'bowdlerized apophaticism' in which God 'is but vaguely glimpsed through the clouds of metaphysical [and linguistic] distance', apophasis functions very much in terms of the theological purification or therapy of theological speech, and thus has a *determining* context, or set of conditions that shape our ability properly to perform theological *askesis* (or sanitizing self-denial).[51] As Denys Turner claims, 'That we cannot form any "concept" of God is due not to the divine vacuousness', or we could add of the predicable limitations of reason reaching its boundary position, 'but, on the contrary, to the excessiveness of divine plenitude'.[52] That means that the ways of negation and affirmation cannot be seen as sequential or independent. Thus when MacKinnon concludes with the comment that 'It is therefore only within the context of the most rigorous discipline of silence that we dare think of such a reality [of divine love]', the kind of silence he has in mind already moves beyond the empty silence of a Steiner. MacKinnon has in this context already mentioned 'the strange and perhaps hardly explored silence of Christ in his passion'. This speaks not of a release from the constraints of a proper sense of the divine inexpressibility, but provides the very site of, or rule for, its learning. MacKinnon's reading, in other words, begins implicitly to contest the possibility of an indeterminate reading.

---

48. Graham Ward, 'In the Daylight Forever? Language and Silence', in Oliver Davies and Denys Turner (eds.), *Silence and the Word: Negative Theology and Incarnation* (Cambridge: Cambridge University Press, 2002), p. 164.

49. Christopher Insole: 'The apophatic God can be as straightforward a projection of this intensely private romantic self as the Swinburnean model is of the Cartesian self' ('Anthropomorphism and the Apophatic God', *Modern Theology* 17 [2001], p. 482).

50. Steiner, *Language and Silence*, pp. 176-77; cf. pp. 61-62.

51. Citation from Robert W. Jenson, 'The Hidden and Triune God', *IJST* 2 (2000), p. 6.

52. Denys Turner, 'On Denying the Right God: Aquinas on Atheism and Idolatry', *Modern Theology* 20 (2004), p. 148.

MacKinnon detects a particular disturbing implication with the kind of procedural negativity he describes as a 'pitiless negation' of all theological discourse. The 'God' we approach in this way too easily becomes 'a God whose infinity renders him indifferent to the very distinction between good and evil on which Moses lays such weight'.[53] This 'God' becomes a morally absent space, an emptiness or void at the heart of human performance, a conceiving of divine *difference* that results in moral indifference. Again Steiner's account is instructive here. His understanding of language and silence can be depicted as involving a pronounced loss (loss of self-transcendence, loss of otherness before God), emptiness (emptying the self out of its being-in-mutual-covenantal-responsibility), and isolation (isolating the self from discursive formation and relations of *différence*). This Romantic strain of word-loss, enforced by his reading of the post-Shoah loss of trust in the word, is reiterated and highlighted in his articulation of Schoenberg's Schopenhauerian assessment that 'music is, in the final analysis, superior to language, that it says more or more immediately'.[54] This aesthetic form enables Steiner to construct an immediate private experience beyond the distortion of language, and this constitutes an aesthetic so *full* of, or secure in, itself that its subject needs no time for others. Moreover, it is a subjectivity that has little that can resist consumerism's fetishization of the privatized self or prevent silence from dissolving into a 'stillness' that speech with others can only but disrupt.[55] Steiner's Romanticism, which somewhat subverts Schoenberg's sense that Idea (*Vorstellung*) can indeed be mediated or give itself to Representation (*Darstellung*), constructs an *exitus* from and a *reditus* to a silence beyond the corruptions of language's materiality, and consequently leaves little responsibly to articulate in between. Given his concern to articulate the 'strange' place of the Jewish people in the world, Steiner's account serves to separate the covenanted Jewish people from the later prophetic witness of the people of God drawing the nations of the world into the creative agency of God. He is unable to play the role, in Wyschogrod's terms, of 'the heterological historian'. Wyschogrod's 'heterological historian' testifies from 'an ardour for the others in whose name there is a felt urgency to speak' in the stead of others who are disfigured by the

---

53. MacKinnon, *Themes in Theology*, p. 17.
54. Steiner, *Language and Silence*, p. 64. For Schopenhauer, music expresses the inmost essence of the world as 'will'. On the aesthetic of the sublime and the role of music in Romantic aesthetics see Andrew Bowie, *Aesthetics and Subjectivity: From Kant to Nietzsche* (Manchester: Manchester University Press, 2nd edn, 2003).
55. Steiner, *Language and Silence*, p. 13, certainly intends to resist what he calls the 'vulgarity, imprecision and greed...in a mass consumer society' characterized as having that use of language only for what he calls *kitsch*. And yet, as Ward argues, Steiner's sublime is an ambiguous silence that is a mirror of the kitsch ('In the Daylight Forever?', p. 169).

cataclysm of their death, 'binding oneself by a promise to the dead to tell the truth about the past'.[56]

MacKinnon asks whether Moses must 'not also accept for himself the discipline of silence, [and] even admit with a smile that the Aarons of this world help administer such discipline?'[57] For MacKinnon, in contrast to Steiner, the issue is not simply one of speech and silence, but one of the nature of human existence, and thus one of ontology with an ethical significance. In fact, the abandonment of the God of the commandments results in moral disintegration, as the people negate the proper shape of their being-as-responsible-agents. MacKinnon's Aaron, in marked contrast to Steiner's, is in error not in the attempt at public communication, but, despite his pastoral concerns for servicing the religious needs of the people, his mistake is in yielding to the pressure of the demand for a visible and comprehensible form of the restoration of 'the old gods'.[58] As Benson argues, 'The problem of idolatry is not simply *which* concepts and images we employ (though it is that also) but *how* we employ them'.[59] Aaron's god 'is wonderfully made to measure', 'accessible'.[60] A clue to what MacKinnon has in mind here can be found in his claim that Moses represents a religious 'austerity incomparably grander than the comforting, indulgent worship Aaron believed that human nature craved'.[61] Aaron's is 'comforting, indulgent worship'. MacKinnon does not suggest that the Truth is not comforting (Mt. 5.4), but his target is a disposition that pre-eminently requires comfort, since this is a self-indulgence that instrumentalizes the faith and ultimately trivializes it and distorts it by blunting its interrogative and transformative edge. Aaron's is a 'conforming, consoling, too humanly human idol' that 'trivializes the worship of God to the level of devotion to a godling who will condone every human weakness and indulgence'.[62]

It is not that Israel imagines that the image replaces divine ineffability or casts more than a faint shadow on the incomprehensible, but rather that she is able to control the contours of that ineffability in a way that does not fundamentally rupture her living, what Thomas calls service to the master

---

56. Edith Wyschogrod, *An Ethics of Remembering: History, Heterology, and the Nameless Others* (Chicago: University of Chicago Press, 1998), p. xi.

57. MacKinnon, *Themes in Theology*, p. 18.

58. MacKinnon, *Themes in Theology*, p. 11. The phrase in Exod. 32.6 'and rose up to play' suggests sexual orgiastic behaviour of the type important to Canaanite fertility cults.

59. Benson, *Graven Ideologies*, p. 26.

60. MacKinnon, *Themes in Theology*, p. 11; Jean-Luc Marion, *God without Being* (trans. Thomas A. Carlson; Chicago: University of Chicago Press, 1991), p. 15.

61. MacKinnon, *Themes in Theology*, p. 17.

62. MacKinnon, *Themes in Theology*, p. 18.

who disposes all things to their due actions.[63] The ineffable God does not theophanically pass before them as a guide. The notion of idolatry is of an image that acts as a mirror, reflecting back the worshippers' controlling desires and values rather than as a window that takes the worshippers' gaze through to transcendence, critical transcendence. As Jean-Luc Marion observes, 'the idol allows the divine to occur only in man's measure'.[64] In this way, according to Ephrem the Syrian, with the calf the people 'could worship openly what they had been worshipping in their hearts'.[65] That means that 'the god they embody...will indulge them in ways that will ultimately undermine and pervert their sensibility'.[66] So John Chrysostum proclaims that the people 'were committing disorder'.[67] It is noticeable in this regard how Aaron in Exod. 32.4 defensively pitches the story to Moses: he instructed the people to cast their gold into the fire 'and out came this calf!' Israel had *conjured* the figuration (or the people imaging-forth God), and a commodified one at that out of her own precious objects. Thereby she mummified her living Liberator, conjuring an inert God who could not lead by fire and smoke but could be led, and indeed required the work of the people to become mobile in the first place. The calf anthropomorphism, then, really is a construction of the people, an *object* of their revelry, and thereby rendered impotent in its potential for critical interrogation and transformation of its devotees (or God imaging-forth the people). Here the contrast with Moses is acute, so Augustine draws attention to Moses' 'maternal and paternal instincts' on behalf of the 'sacrilegious people' whom 'God threatened';[68] and Cassidorus observes that Moses put the nation's well-being ahead of his own by offering his life to the punitive judgment of God as a sacrifice in Israel's place.[69]

Probingly, MacKinnon's reflections conducted in apophatic mood enable a differentiation of silences. '[W]hat sort of silence,' he asks, 'what sort of repudiation of every image best conveys the ultimacy not of judgement but of love?'[70] This question is a significant one, an ethical one and one about

---

63. Thomas Aquinas, *Summa contra gentiles*, III.120.5.
64. Marion, *God without Being*, p. 15.
65. Ephrem the Syrian, *Homily on our Lord*, 17.3–18.1, in Joseph T. Lienhard (ed.), *Ancient Christian Commentary on Scripture, Old Testament*. III. *Exodus, Leviticus, Numbers, Deuteronomy* (Downers Grove, IL: InterVarsity Press, 2001), p. 140.
66. MacKinnon, *Themes in Theology*, p. 12. The idea here is not merely that idolatry is generated by idolaters, but that it, in turn, generates and reinforces idolatrous behaviour. So, according to Rabbi Levi b. Hama, 'If one worships idols he becomes like unto them' (cited in Beale, *We Become What We Worship*, p. 158).
67. John Chrysostum, *Homilies on Colossians* 4, in Lienhard (ed.), *Exodus*, p. 142.
68. Augustine, *Sermon* 88.24, in Lienhard (ed.), *Exodus*, p. 142.
69. Cassiodorus, *Exposition of the Psalms* 105.23, in Lienhard (ed.), *Exodus*, p. 142.
70. MacKinnon, *Themes in Theology*, p. 19.

hope. It is not merely (or even primarily perhaps) one about how to use concepts, but rather about how to convey the ultimacy of love. What kind of imagining does Steiner provide given his talk of the necessity of the God-distorting work of Aaron in the accomplishment of God's purposes, and of God's people as only being themselves in as far as they are *atopos*? For Steiner, language can always only come 'too late'.[71] His indeterminacy has all too little sense of Moses' role as a determinate prophetic witness, performing his obedient hearing modestly through the symbolic and the parabolic.

Conclusion

In a brief discussion explaining why it is useful to study ethics Herbert McCabe draws an analogy with the study of grammar, and suggests two reasons why the latter is a fitting topic for reflection. The first reason provided is that 'it is always satisfactory to see the reasons and principles and patterns behind what we do'.[72] This, we might term, 'practice-seeking-understanding'. The second reason involves a more critical mood concerning grammatical rules: 'even though we speak quite grammatically for the most part, there may be times when we make mistakes or are puzzled about some linguistic form. And a study of grammar will help us to avoid mistakes in these cases.' The metaphor is helpful in discerning what is going on in the practice of biblical hermeneutics. According to Benson, Smith and Vanhoozer, hermeneutics stands at the crossroads today.[73] The intersections they have in mind are threefold: those of different intellectual disciplines bearing on the interpretative process; the moods of premodernity, modernity and postmodernity; and the recognition of cultural-linguistic traditions. However, there is another intersection that is significant: that between determinate and indeterminate strategies for reading. If the former is often associated with modernity, the latter is invariably associated with postmodernity. To return to McCabe's metaphor, for deterministic reading strategies grammar is something stable and given, and consequently it becomes a way of determining hermeneutical activity through its stable specification of criteria for what is meaningful. The issue that is less well handled, however, is that

---

71. See John C. McDowell, 'Silenus' Wisdom and the "Crime of Being": The Problem of Hope in George Steiner's Tragic Vision', *Literature and Theology* 14 (2000), pp. 385-411.

72. Herbert McCabe, *The Good Life: Ethics and the Pursuit of Happiness* (London: Continuum, 2005), p. 3.

73. Bruce Ellis Benson, James K.A. Smith and Kevin J. Vanhoozer, 'Introduction', in Bruce Ellis Benson, James K.A. Smith, and Kevin J. Vanhoozer (eds.), *Hermeneutics at the Crossroads* (Bloomington: Indiana University Press, 2006), pp. xiii-xviii.

of how to cope with changes in grammar. For suspicion-ridden indeterminist reading strategies, in contrast, grammar is never stable and is always in flux. In this case, nonetheless, what is less well managed is how one accounts for meaningful communication across grammars, and how one differentiates between which grammatical changes constitute 'growth in our understanding and what is merely a decay, what…is a new and linguistic form, and what is mere slovenliness'.[74]

Theological readings of Scripture cannot naïvely imagine that they float free from the impact of these approaches. But given that theology has to do with the freedom of *God* and the understanding that is appropriate to this God theological readings cannot commit themselves uncritically to any specific cultural fashion and ideology, and therefore they have much to learn about the debates between these hermeneutical approaches and the conflict of interpretations they produce. Even so, by not being committed to any of them uncritically theology has the capacity for moving beyond these options.

Attention to Exodus 32 can gesture towards a set of reading skills that enables the theological reader to keep to McCabe's question of legitimately indicating or meaningfully determining what genuine development looks like in contrast to the decay of slovenliness. 'If…we are to read well', Webster argues, 'we have to be made into certain kinds of readers'.[75]

First, *reading is specific*. Theological readers could claim that a 'general hermeneutics' is inappropriate since it does not pay attention to the particularities of the theological. Put another way, not all readings have *God* as their focus. There is such a thing as idolatrous reading. Of course, these skills, or in more theological terms 'virtues', may overlap in many ways with the findings of more general accounts of hermeneutics, and it would be odd if there were not points of intersection given that it is the interpretation of *texts* that is being considered. At its best, historical-critical readings of the Bible can serve a theological reading by enabling attention to be paid to readers' responsibilities to the historic density or the concrete particularities of the texts and their contexts. Yet it is difficult to specify in advance where these conjunctions will lie, lest the specificities again be undermined.

Second, theological reading is specific and *takes place within givenness*. Most crucially, this refers to readers' receptivity of, and determining dependency on, the Self-specification of God. Even if the incomprehensible God cannot directly be described we can at least gesture towards theologically describing God's Self-manifesting actions. While there is a sense of

---

74. McCabe, *The Good Life*, p. 4.
75. John Webster, 'Reading Scripture Eschatologically', in David F. Ford and Graham Stanton (eds.), *Reading Texts, Seeking Wisdom: Scripture and Theology* (London: SCM Press, 2003), p. 249.

responsiveness of the reader in Steiner's account, what is lacking is a further sense of givenness—that of the generative contexts of the reading communities. All theological reading is bound up with learning within the midst of the theological readings by Christian communities of the past and present. '*Listening*', Ricoeur observes, '*excludes founding oneself*. The movement towards listening requires, therefore, a...letting go,...giving up (*dessaissement*) the human self in its will to mastery, sufficiency, and autonomy.'[76]

Third, reading is specific and takes place within givenness *by communities prone to idolatry*. Mention of the communities of readers and thus of readers' accountability not only reminds us that we are never alone as we approach texts, but it generates attention to the multiplicity of reading communities and therefore to the fact that there is an array of scriptural readings. This produces two further claims: readings are never stable, but change and develop; and readings are performed by people whose desires and ideological contexts can shape readings in all manner of complex ways. Here it is important to recall that the idolatrous behaviour at Sinai was an act not of pagan communities but tragically conducted by God's own covenanted people who confused the covenantal God of Israel with the other gods of the day by desiring a controllable deity. The confusion results in a 'theophanic conjuration', a constructive action of the community in order to master and control divine presence for their benefit without regard for the otherness of God and the demand for transformation into responsibility on the people's part.[77] There is a significant difference in readings conducted by charitable readers who are *followers* struggling with the text and those conducted by narcissistic readers who are *users* of texts.[78] Wiles misses the fact that someone like MacKinnon demands that critical interrogation be a necessary and perennial task in the service of purging theology.

Fourth, reading is specific and takes place within givenness by communities prone to idolatry that are embraced *by the covenant of God*. The otherness of the text is bound to the Otherness of the text's *Sache* which is God, and theological reading is a response to the life-giving claim of this covenanting God on readers. The reader is 'summoned', to adapt Ricoeur's description of the prophet.[79] To put this in dogmatic terms (which is appropriate given the kind of work a theological reading does), a theological reading involves not merely the ongoing event of response to the God these texts are claimed to witness to, but pre-eminently the purposive divine

---

76. Paul Ricoeur, *Figuring the Sacred: Religion, Narrative, and Imagination* (ed. Mark I. Wallace; trans. David Pellauer; Minneapolis: Fortress Press, 1995), p. 224 (emphasis original).
77. Citation from Wyschogrod, 'Eating the Text', p. 230.
78. See Vanhoozer, *Is There Meaning in This Text?* p. 374.
79. Ricoeur, *Figuring the Sacred*, p. 262.

activity of covenantally making a people that is shaped in virtue by scriptural reading together. Without this dogmatic description, the metaphysics of creative and recreative divine agency, the hermeneutical performance is problematically decoupled not only from its theological ground, but also from its eschatological *telos*, and consequently it can idolatrously slip into imagining that the *Sache* (God) is a thing that can be read off the text by the master reader.

Fifth, and finally, reading is specific and takes place within givenness by communities prone to idolatries that are embraced in the covenant of God *by the God who makes a people that is mutually responsible*. The incident at Sinai turns on a contrast between the self-promoting revelry of the people (that results in idolatry) and the concern for the people by Moses (in covenantal responsibility). According to McCabe, 'the Decalogue is precisely an *outline* of friendship. That is to say it draws a boundary around friendship to show where it stops: beyond these limits friendship does not exist.'[80] Persons are bound together in mutual responsibility generated by the regulative context of the covenant that manifests the commitment of God to the people. Spiritualist or aniconic accounts of Exodus 32 endanger crucial elements of this responsibility—the significant role of bodies in the well-being of God's people.

This activity of 'theological reading', then, cannot be either a sacrificial offering to the gods of hermeneutical fashion, or a method among methods. Instead, to be theologically formed as virtuous readers who theologically witness to the God of the Scriptures is to make sense of the role of this particular set of texts in the ongoing activity of God's healing of creatures. And yet a properly iconoclastically attentive theological reading, or more simply 'theologically vigilant reading', cannot *guarantee* that a theological interpretation will be a theological reading and not simply another ideological legitimation of power-interests. Rather than an admission of despair, this rule for a 'theologically vigilant reading' involves an interrogative and reparative task expressive of hope. Reading iconoclastically gives up the desire to 'master' and 'grasp' in order to live in self-dispossession as readers committed to God's purification and transformation of persons. Good theological reading, in the end, involves training 'in silence, watchfulness, and the Spirit's drastic appearance in judgement, recognition, conversion, for us and for the whole world'.[81]

---

80. Herbert McCabe, *God Still Matters* (London: Continuum, 2002), p. 192.
81. Rowan D. Williams, *On Christian Theology* (Oxford: Blackwell, 2000), p. 43. Williams here is speaking of 'good doctrine', but what he says is relevant to good theological reading.

6

LEX ORANDI, LEX VIVENDI:
A THEOLOGICAL INTERPRETATION OF DISCIPLESHIP IN THE GOSPEL OF MATTHEW

Marianne Meye Thompson

In the Gospel of Matthew, Jesus begins his public ministry by proclaiming that the kingdom of heaven has come near and calling Simon and Andrew to follow him (4.17-18). Throughout the Gospel, Jesus continues to call disciples to follow him (8.22; 9.9; 10.38; 16.24; 19.21), and teaches them in a series of discourses about the kingdom, mission, and life together in the church, among other topics. The Gospel sets the bar high for Jesus' would-be disciples. Jesus warns them that their righteousness must exceed that of the scribes and Pharisees (5.20), calls them to imitate the perfect and generous love of God (5.48), and exhorts them to live out their commitments by doing the will of Jesus' heavenly Father (7.21; 21.31-32). Not without reason, Jesus has been characterized in Matthew as the teacher *par excellence*, even a new Moses. This Moses instructs his disciples that the heart of the law is to be found in the commands to love God and love neighbor (22.34-40). In brief, Jesus is presented as a teacher of the will and way of God, and his disciples are able learners who understand all that he tells them (13.51).

Discipleship is surely not less than understanding Jesus' instruction in Matthew. But it is also more. The purpose of this paper is to explore what that 'more' might look like. Just what does it mean to learn discipleship from Jesus? In this paper, I wish to investigate that question not so much by turning to the past, to ask what Jesus' call to discipleship might have meant at one point in time, but to read the Gospel with attention to its continuing capacity to form the communal life of the people of God. This reading, therefore, (1) grounds the teachings about discipleship in practices of the community, including baptism, the Lord's supper, communal living (forgiveness), prayer, and the daily exercise of trust in God; (2) shows how Jesus embodies and models the kind of life to which he calls others, so that 'following' Jesus is simultaneously a following after the Messiah, an obedience to his commands, and an imitation of his life of doing the will of God; and (3) reveals ultimately that the disciple's life is not one of performance to attain the favor of God, but rather constant receptivity to the gifts of God, especially the initial status or welcome into the family of God and the continued blessing of unmerited forgiveness. The primary question of this paper, then, is how Matthew's Gospel serves to form the faith and practice of disciples of Jesus—that is, not only how it *describes* discipleship, but how it *forms* the faith and practice of disciples of Jesus wherever and whenever they live.

My starting point is the Lord's Prayer (6.9-15). Since Matthew links the prayer to Jesus' instructions not to pray 'as the Gentiles do', it has often been assumed that the 'Lord's Prayer' provides instruction on 'how to pray', that is, on what one should say in prayer and what constitutes genuine prayer. Here we encounter Jesus not only as one who teaches the disciples, but teaches them to pray. Not surprisingly, this prayer was an important part of early church liturgy. Outside the Gospels of Matthew and Luke, the prayer is found in the *Didache* (8.2-3), an early Christian letter or manual providing instruction in matters of Christian faith, morals, and ecclesiastical order and practice. The Lord's Prayer has continued to serve as a template for prayer, and in Christian worship, and additionally become part of numerous catechisms across the years, instructing the people of God how to pray. The disciples need to learn from Jesus, and the disciples need to learn to pray from Jesus.

But they need more than a 'template' of prayer. The fact that Jesus teaches his disciples to pray underscores the point that discipleship involves the cultivation of habits and disciplines such as prayer, forgiveness, receptivity, and trust. It is worth noting that the Lord's Prayer is found in Matthew within the context of the so-called Sermon on the Mount (chs. 5–7). In its structure the sermon leads from Jesus' teaching regarding the demand of the 'higher righteousness' (5.20) and the 'perfection' that mirrors God's perfection (5.43-48) into instructions on piety, praying and the Lord's Prayer, and then back again to further instruction regarding doing the will of the Father, as taught by Jesus. It is a path from practices that mirror the perfection of the Father, to prayer to the Father, and back to the practices of the 'good works' that Jesus calls for. The very structure of these chapters shows that prayer, in which one places oneself before and in relationship to God, stands at the heart of what Jesus calls people to be and to do. As Ulrich Luz writes, 'Matthew knows of the depth of the connection of practice and grace in prayer'.[1]

---

1. For this whole discussion, see here Ulrich Luz, *Matthew 1–7* (trans. Wilhelm C. Linss; Minneapolis: Fortress Press, 1989), p. 388.

In many ways the prayer also summarizes key aspects of Jesus' teaching. Jesus' disciples understand God as their Father in heaven, who now brings his kingdom near, whose will is to be done, and who calls together a people who should cultivate the habit and virtue of forgiveness. Tertullian famously labeled the prayer 'a breviary of the whole Gospel'.[2] In other words, the prayer instructs: *lex orandi, lex credendi*. But it is a prayer, and it instructs precisely as prayer.

The disciples need to learn to pray that they may live as Jesus taught them, and that they may follow the example of his life given to them. For ultimately the obedience and the posture before God to which Jesus calls his disciples are most fully visible in Jesus' own life, death, and resurrection. What it means, then, to learn discipleship from Jesus is to learn not only as he instructed others to live, but to live as he lived. And, as we shall see, to an amazing degree, Matthew's narrative shows Jesus at every turn obediently living out the words of this prayer that he gives to his disciples. They need to learn to pray in order to learn how to live: *lex orandi, lex vivendi*.

Finally, then, in Matthew's Gospel, Jesus' faithful embodiment of the petitions of the prayer he teaches comes to its climactic expression in his prayer in Gethsemane and his death on the cross, where his obedient doing of the will of the Father forms the basis for the forgiveness of sins that is offered to the disciples who do not live as he lives. While Jesus calls his disciples to do the will of the Father, at the end of the day the disciples will need the forgiveness of sins that they have prayed for and that comes through Jesus' death on the cross. In short, Matthew presents discipleship as rooted in the practices of community, lived out in following Jesus' own example, and finally dependent on the death of Jesus for the sealing of the covenant of the forgiveness of sin. We turn, then, to an analysis of the individual petitions of the prayer, in their context in the Gospel of Matthew.

'Our Father in Heaven'

The Lord's Prayer opens with an invocation of 'our Father' (Mt. 6.9).[3] In instructing his disciples to invoke God as 'our Father', Jesus assumes and explicates a relationship between God and his disciples. First, among the many ways of understanding God, such as king, judge, master or Lord, Jesus' disciples are to pray to God as Father. The term comes from the realm of family and kinship, rather than from the political or legal sphere. It also comes from the Scriptures that Jesus interprets and teaches. Second, then, Jesus' disciples are to address God as '*our* Father', acknowledging that God

---

2. Tertullian, *De Oratione*, CSEL 20:181:19, calls the prayer *breviarium totius evangelii*.

3. All translations are taken from the NRSV unless otherwise noted.

is the Father of others and that in invoking God as Father, they do so in company with others. Jesus calls God 'my Father', but when the disciples turn to God as Father, they acknowledge that they do so in company with others. Third, this Father is 'in heaven', that is, neither absent nor distant, but transcendent with respect to this earth. And because this is the case, this God can be trusted to deal with the matters of this earth. The 'Lord *of* heaven and earth' (11.25) is the God who has sovereignty over them,[4] and who therefore has the power to shape events and circumstances on the earth as in heaven.

The disciples do not, however, call upon 'our God in heaven' or 'our Lord in heaven' but upon 'our Father in heaven'. The address to God as Father, or the understanding of God as 'our Father', can be found in both the Old Testament and subsequent Jewish literature. On the one hand, God is portrayed as the father of the king of Israel. Those kings who were to sit on David's throne after him would be as sons to God, who would be as a father to them (2 Sam. 7.14; 1 Chron. 17.13; 22.10). God may therefore address the king as 'my son' (Ps. 2.7; Mt. 3.17; 17.5). Thus the king of Israel has a distinctive relationship to God, and this relationship requires faithfulness, obedience, and integrity. On the other hand, God is a father to Israel, calling it into existence, loving, caring and providing for them, and disciplining them as a father cares for his own children.[5] Not only does Matthew use 'Father' in address to God or in Jesus' speech about God more often than Mark and Luke combined, but Matthew definitely prefers possessive formulations, in which Jesus—and Jesus alone—speaks of God as 'my Father' and, with reference to the disciples, of God as 'your Father'.[6] Matthew's frequent personal references highlight both Jesus' particular relationship to God ('my Father') and his stress that God is a Father who knows and provides for the needs of his children ('your Father', 'your heavenly Father').[7]

---

4. For God of heaven, or God of heaven and earth, see Gen. 24.3, 7; 2 Chron. 36.23; Ps. 136.26, and elsewhere in the Old Testament in Ezra, Nehemiah, and Daniel; for 'Lord of heaven and earth', see Mt. 11.25 (par. Lk. 10.21); Acts 17.24; Tob. 10.13; Jdt. 9.12.

5. Thus Matthew has some form of 'my Father' about fifteen times (compared to four times in Luke, never in Mark), and 'your Father' about fifteen times as well (three times in Luke, once in Mark).

6. For God as the father of the king, see 2 Sam. 7.12-14; and for God as the father of Israel, see Deut. 32.6; Isa. 63.16; 64.8; Jer. 3.4-5, 19; 31.9; Sir. 23.1, 4; Tob. 13.4; *Jub.* 1.23-25; *3 Macc.* 6.2-3; and the discussion in Marianne Meye Thompson, *The Promise of the Father* (Louisville, KY: Westminster/John Knox Press, 2000).

7. Note that the creeds begin with the acknowledgment of God as 'the Father', and go on to speak of 'Jesus Christ, his only Son'. The creeds thus mirror the structure found throughout the New Testament; the God whom the church confesses as 'the Father Almighty' is the God who is the 'Father of our Lord Jesus Christ'.

Jesus' instruction to pray to God as 'our Father in heaven' is not the first time that Jesus has spoken of God as the Father of his disciples. Earlier they had been told to let their good works give glory to 'your Father in heaven' (5.16) and that their actions show them to be 'children of your Father in heaven' (5.45); exhorted to be perfect as 'your heavenly Father' is (5.48); and instructed to await reward only from 'your Father in heaven' who sees and rewards in secret (6.1, 4, 6, 8). In their relationship to their 'heavenly Father', the disciples are instructed that God expects certain conduct of them. While the bar is set high, it is neither a king nor a judge who sets the standard of conduct, but the God who is Father of the disciples. To be sure, this Father has authority and expects obedience, as is clear from biblical precedent and other material in Matthew. But those who come to read Matthew having read the Scriptures that Matthew frequently cites will also know that they may approach this Father knowing that their frailty is taken into account and that God maintains his steadfast love for them (e.g., Ps. 103.13-18). Not surprisingly, Jesus does not appeal to his hearers to believe *that* God is their heavenly Father, but rather calls on them to trust in the one whom they, in contrast to 'Gentiles', acknowledge as Father:

> Look at the birds of the air; they neither sow nor reap nor gather into barns, and yet your heavenly Father feeds them…. Therefore do not worry, saying, 'What will we eat?' or 'What will we drink?' or 'What will we wear?' For it is the Gentiles who strive for all these things; and indeed your heavenly Father knows that you need all these things (Mt. 6.25-26, 31-32).

If they are not to worry and strive as the Gentiles do, neither are they to pray as the Gentiles do, since God is their heavenly Father who may be trusted to provide for the needs of his children. Throughout the Gospel, Jesus instructs his disciples to call and rely on God as Father, to adopt a posture towards God of trust and receptivity. They learn such a disposition by *doing* Jesus' words, and by *praying* to the Father of whom Jesus speaks. That is, learning to be a disciple of Jesus is not simply a matter of understanding words, or following commands, but of being formed so as to rely on and trust in God. Such habits may be learned in many ways, but the witness of the Gospel of Matthew is that such a disposition arises out of and is manifested above all in prayer. That, at least, is what is modeled by Jesus himself.

Thus, following Jesus' pronouncement of judgment upon Chorazin, Bethsaida, and Capernaum, Jesus turns to God in prayer, giving thanks to the Father, 'Lord of heaven and earth', that he has 'hidden these things from the wise and intelligent' and has instead 'revealed them to infants; yes, Father, for such was your gracious will' (11.25-26). Jesus here muses on the mystery of his Father's will; while is it a gracious will—gracious to the least among the people—it nevertheless apparently comes with judgment as well. God's will is expressed in both the judgment that is pronounced over the towns that did not welcome Jesus and in the repentance of those that did (11.20). Jesus himself, as the Son of the Father, is the one through whom such judgment is pronounced and such revelation, leading to repentance, is made. Jesus thus participates in the realities of which he speaks: the manifestation of the will of the Father. As he is part of those, Jesus manifests a posture of receptivity, gratitude, and praise. His understanding of the Father's will arises, at least in part, out of his participation in the performance of God's will.

In the passion narrative of Matthew's Gospel, Jesus frequently calls on or refers to God as Father, in all cases with the possessive pronoun (26.29, 39, 42, 53). He speaks of 'my Father's kingdom' (26.29); and, as we shall see later, he twice calls upon God as 'my Father' in his prayers in Gethsemane (26.39, 42), and stays the sword of his would be defenders in referring to the angels whom 'my Father' would send if asked (26.53). Jesus thus demonstrates his own trust, even in his most agonizing moments, in the one whom he had commended to his disciples as trustworthy.

But can this Father be trusted? It is not apparent that Jesus' prayer in Gethsemane is even acknowledged, let alone answered. Jesus wrestles alone, bereft of human companionship and without visible signs from heaven that he has been heard. The narrative drives the reader forward to discover whether Jesus' trust has been vindicated. Not only does the resurrection provide an affirmative answer to that question, but the final words of Jesus in the Gospel spell out the nature of the relationship of the Father and Son: 'All authority, on heaven and on earth' has now been given to the Risen One. Therefore, it is appropriate to make disciples in the name of 'the Father, the Son, and the Holy Spirit' (28.18-20). The one who had taught his disciples to call God 'our Father', who had demonstrated his unswerving trust in his Father, now speaks with ultimate authority granted to him by that Father.

Here, then, one discovers the difference between Jesus' relationship and that of his disciples to God as Father. Jesus is the one who has been given 'all authority' by his Father and, hence, may both commission his disciples to go forth and promise his constant presence with them. Those who acknowledge Jesus' particular authority as teacher and as the agent of the one who has granted him all authority are those who not only heed Jesus' exhortations and commands, but who also enter into the family that is constituted by Jesus and who call on God as 'our Father'. Then they will surely discover the ways in which God works through their mission both to hide and to reveal, to lead both to judgment and to repentance, in hidden and visible ways even as he seemed to be both hidden and visible in the life and ministry of Jesus himself. This experience should lead them, as it led Jesus, to pray, to give thanks, to trust in the God who is not only 'Lord of heaven and earth', but the Father whose gracious will is worked out through the Son and his followers.

'Your Kingdom Come'

The proclamation of the kingdom of God begins in the Gospel of Matthew with John the Baptist, whose message is identical to that of Jesus: 'Repent, for the kingdom of heaven has come near' (3.2; 4.17). Jesus in turn commands his disciples to preach precisely the same thing (10.7). The proclamation of this kingdom also stands alongside Jesus' healing ministry (4.23; 9.35), in fulfillment of the promises of Isaiah (11.4-5). Jesus promises the kingdom to the 'poor in spirit' (5.3), and to those who are persecuted for the sake of righteousness (5.10), and urges his disciples to 'seek first the kingdom of God' (6.33). The parables of ch. 13 are decidedly parables of the kingdom. The sower sows 'the word of the kingdom' (13.19; cf. Mk 4.14; Lk. 8.11). The apparently mixed crop of weeds and wheat in the present will someday be harvested and separated (Mt. 13.24-30), illustrating how it will be 'at the close of the age', when the Son of man 'will send his angels, and they will gather out of his kingdom all causes of sin and all evildoers' (13.36-43). Similarly, the kingdom can be compared to a net that gathers fish 'of every kind', until the day when they are sorted out, and the bad are discarded and destroyed (13.47-50). The kingdom is valuable, like a pearl of great price, or a treasure hidden in a field (13.44-46). These (peculiarly Matthean) parables accentuate the present hiddenness and final manifestation in the 'glory' of the kingdom. When this kingdom is revealed, the authority and power of the 'Son of man' will be revealed as well. Through his agency, the kingdom will be established in righteousness. Thus the Gospel moves inexorably forward toward the glorious and final manifestation of God's kingdom and God's righteousness.

When the disciples pray, 'your kingdom come', they are praying for the final arrival of this kingdom. They do not do so as spectators, but rather from the perspective of those who are 'involved in the great redemptive drama that is beginning to unfold'.[8] That is to say, those who pray for God's kingdom to come pray not as outsiders, but as recipients of and participants in the unfolding narrative of the kingdom's arrival. They are among those who proclaim the kingdom, as Jesus instructed (10.7), who are among the crops that are being harvested and separated, who have found the pearl of great price, who await the glorious coming of the Son of man, and so on. Prayer is one way in which disciples place themselves at the service of the Father whom they petition now to bring the kingdom that they proclaim and of which they are the grateful recipients.

---

8. Donald A. Hagner, *Matthew* (2 vols.; WBC, 33A-33B; Dallas, TX: Word Books, 1993), I, p. 152.

Within this kingdom of the Father, Jesus has a distinctive role; he is in many ways the king in that kingdom. First acknowledged as king of the Jews in connection with his birth (2.3), Jesus is later hailed as king when he rides into Jerusalem in fulfillment of Zechariah's prophecy (21.5); and is mocked, condemned, and crucified as 'king of the Jews' (27.11, 29, 37; 'king of Israel', 27. 42). Virtually every acknowledgment or identification of Jesus as king leads not to acclamation, but rather to offense and rejection. Like the kings of Israel, Jesus is anointed, appropriately with 'very costly ointment' (26.7). But this act does not pave the way for Jesus to ascend the throne. Rather it prepares him for death (26.12), and induces Judas to consult with the authorities about handing Jesus over to them. Jesus' tacit acknowledgment that he is the Messiah, the anointed one of God, and his promise that the Son of Man will be seated in power at God's right hand, lead again not to public acclamation, but rather to the passing of his death sentence (26.66). Pilate puts the question to him most sharply, 'Are you the king of the Jews?' (27.11), to which Jesus gives an implicitly affirmative reply. There are subsequently two responses: the crowds ask for the release of Barabbas and Jesus' crucifixion, and the Roman soldiers mock his claims prior to crucifying him. Every admission or acknowledgment of Jesus' kingship leads him nearer to his death.

While at first glance it seems that Matthew underscores both the misunderstanding and rejection of Jesus, it is precisely in the juxtaposition of Jesus' identification as king and his impending death that we see the nature of Jesus' kingship. This is graphically portrayed in the narrative of the Roman mockery of Jesus:

> Then the soldiers of the governor took Jesus into the governor's headquarters, and they gathered the whole cohort around him. They stripped him and put a scarlet robe on him, and after twisting some thorns into a crown, they put it on his head. They put a reed in his right hand and knelt before him and mocked him, saying, 'Hail, King of the Jews!' They spat on him, and took the reed and struck him on the head (27.27-30).

The scene is heavy with irony. Here a whole cohort of Roman soldiers honors the 'king of the Jews', the powerful oppressor in mock homage of the helpless and oppressed. The mockery will be repeated in the formal charge which is nailed on the cross, 'This is Jesus, the King of the Jews' (27.37) and echoed by religious authorities in their sarcastic reference to the 'King of Israel' (27.42). And here is that king dressed in the robe and crown of royalty, eventually to be stripped not only of that robe but also of his own clothes, as he hangs on the cross (27.36).

Here then is the final demonstration of the nature of the kingdom and its presence in the world in the depiction of the king as rejected, scorned, weak, and dying. Like the treasure in the field, the kingdom lies hidden, to be discerned only with the eyes of faith. Yet it is not that glory and power are hidden under the disguise of humiliation and weakness, so that if the disguise were to be torn off, the true kingdom would be revealed. Rather, Jesus assumes his kingship precisely as the one who goes to his death, as one who is meek, humble, and lowly in heart. Through and in such humility the kingdom of God comes to expression. While the disciple who prays 'your kingdom come' today does so after Jesus' vindication, and thus in the hope of the final revelation of God's kingdom, in Matthew's Gospel Jesus teaches his disciples this prayer prior to his crucifixion. Jesus essentially teaches his disciples to petition God to bring the kingdom that will come through Jesus' death and resurrection.

Nowhere is that more evident than in the way that Matthew links Jesus' predictions of his impending death with instructions about the shape of discipleship. If he is one who will take up his cross, and be killed, so too his disciples will take up their crosses (16.24). Like Jesus, they will 'lose their life', but now for Jesus' sake (16.25). What, then, does that mean? In the chapters that follow Jesus' first passion prediction and lead up to his eventual death on the cross, the disciples learn some of what this kingdom that is coming is all about. To be 'greatest in the kingdom' is to be like a child, humbly welcoming other such humble persons, and being careful not to cause them to stumble (18.1-6; 19.13-15). The kingdom can be compared to a king who generously forgives a servant who owes him an enormous sum of money; to live in this kingdom is to cease to keep track of wrongs and to be overflowing with forgiveness (18.21-35), and not to begrudge the generosity of God (20.1-16). The kingdom of heaven is more easily entered by those who have nothing to lose than by those who grasp tightly to the material stuff of this world (19.21-26).

The prayer, 'your kingdom come', entails the suffering and death of Jesus—his cross—and so calls on the disciples likewise to take up their crosses. The prayer thus shapes the communal identity of those who would be Jesus' disciples, who follow him as the king who is humble on his royal entrance into the holy city (21.5)—even as the children he welcomes are characterized as 'humble'. In praying 'your kingdom come', they not only entrust the kingdom's coming to the Father, but also entrust their own lives into his hands. They are called to give of themselves, as Jesus did; to be humble, as he was; and this is not only expressed, but also learned, in prayer. Even if the coming of the kingdom lies finally in the hands of the Father, its coming brings both blessing and judgment, demand and promise, and calls for humility, thanksgiving, and receptivity. To pray 'your kingdom come' is to be shaped into and by these dispositions.

'Your Will Be Done'

The rigor of Jesus' command in Matthew can be summarized under the petition 'your will be done'. The phrases 'the will of my Father' and 'the will of your Father' are unique to Matthew (7.21; 12.50; 18.14; 21.31; 26.42), and the phrase 'the one who does the will of my Father' is a virtual description of a disciple. In warning about future judgment, Jesus asserts, 'Not everyone who says to me, "Lord, Lord," shall enter the kingdom of heaven, but the one who does the will of my Father who is in heaven' (7.21). Jesus' parable about two sons—one who said he would go to work in the vineyard, but did not, and one who said he would not, but in the end did—raises the question, 'which of the two did the will of his father' and followed in 'the way of righteousness' (21.32)? The 'way of righteousness' consists of conduct that reflects God's will, and, hence, is both the goal and way of life of those who would follow the Messiah.

In the passion narrative, Jesus is the obedient Son of God, who does the will of the Father. This petition also constitutes the essence of Jesus' prayer in the garden. More than the other Synoptics, Matthew emphasizes the specific wording of Jesus' prayer, twice recounting it in vivid direct discourse, each time with the address to 'my Father', and each time with a variation of the petition, 'your will be done' (26.39, 'not as I will, but as you will'; 26.42, 'your will be done'). Matthew renders Jesus' prayer in exact replication of the Lord's Prayer, 'your will be done' (6.10, *genēthētō to thelēma sou*). Jesus himself prays what he teaches his disciples to pray; and Jesus obediently does the will of his Father. What he taught his disciples to pray, he prays at the end of his life. What he taught them to do, he does even though it leads him to his death.

Much in the way that the petition 'your kingdom come' is answered in part through the death of Jesus, so the petition 'your will be done' is explicitly voiced and carried out by Jesus in approaching his death. The Messiah lives, and dies, according to his own teaching, namely, the requirement to 'do the will' of the Father. The effect of this portrayal is twofold. First, it underscores the mystery of doing the will of God. Nowhere is there an explanation for why Jesus' path must lead to the cross, although Matthew repeatedly, if somewhat vaguely, affirms that 'it must happen this way' so that the 'scriptures of the prophets may be fulfilled' (26.54, 56). Matthew lays the accent on Jesus' own understanding of the necessity of the pathway that leads to his death as part of his obedience to God. Matthew casts the spotlight on Jesus, the obedient Son, who understands the will of God and does it.

Second, Jesus' prayer and death allow no glib praying of the Lord's Prayer. People who complacently pray, 'your will be done', may find the cost of doing the will of God far exceeds what they had expected. Those who read the Gospel for the first time would undoubtedly be caught up short when they come to realize that when Jesus prays the very words he had taught them to say, they result in his death. And those who already know that at the end of his life Jesus prayed, 'your will be done', and that this will included his death, must pray this petition of the Lord's Prayer with some fear and trembling. Such realization surely emphasizes the gravity of some of the other words of Jesus, 'Whoever does not take up the cross and follow me is not worthy of me' (10.38), and 'If any want to become my followers, let them deny themselves and take up their cross and follow me' (16.24). Those who think that such commands are lighter than Jesus' words, 'If you wish to be perfect, go, sell your possessions, and give the money to the poor, and you will have treasure in heaven; then come, follow me' (19.21) might now find themselves thinking that selling all one's possessions would be preferable to taking up a cross. If it is only through doing the will of the Father that one enters the kingdom of heaven, it is through doing the will of the Father that Jesus establishes the kingdom of heaven.

The prayer that Jesus teaches his disciples is thus not only a demonstration of how to pray 'not like the Gentiles' but rather as the children of the heavenly Father do, but it reveals that doing the Father's will leads into engagement in the world and not protection from it. Jesus prayed alone, but he died at the hands of Roman imperial power in a public crucifixion. Those who learn to pray as Jesus prayed must also learn to live as Jesus lived: *lex orandi, lex vivendi*.

'Give Us This Day our Daily Bread'

In the time of his testing in the wilderness, Jesus was confronted by the tempter who said to him, 'If you are the Son of God, command these stones to become loaves of bread'. Jesus responded by quoting from Deut. 8.2: 'One does not live by bread alone, but by every word that comes from the mouth of God'. Jesus himself is the quintessential sojourner in the wilderness, who does not repeat Israel's pattern of faithless murmuring, but rather manifests his faithfulness in reliance on God. Jesus does not deny the need for daily bread, but he does voice his full reliance on God's provision, a generous Father who will not give a stone to a child who asks for bread (Mt. 7.9-11).

Those who are given the prayer with the petition 'give us this day our daily bread' ought to understand, then, that while bread is necessary and is given by God, it nevertheless points to God as the source and sustainer of all life. Ringing in the ears of those who pray this prayer is Jesus' reminder, in example and word, that 'we do not live by bread alone'. Three subsequent narratives in the Gospels demonstrate the need for bread for the body and bread for the spirit. Again, in the desert, Jesus is confronted with a lack of bread—this time, not his own lack, but that of the crowds who have come to hear him. Alone in the wilderness with an enormous, hungry crowd, Jesus' disciples have only a little bread and a few fish, but Jesus provides for them (14.13-21). Later, in similar circumstances, they come to him with only seven loaves. Jesus took them, 'and after giving thanks he broke them and gave them to the disciples, and the disciples gave them to the crowds. And all of them ate and were filled; and they took up the broken pieces left over, seven baskets full' (15.33-37). Jesus himself now grants the petition 'give us this day our daily bread'.

And at the last supper, Jesus offered them another sort of bread: 'While they were eating, Jesus took a loaf of bread, and after blessing it he broke it, gave it to the disciples, and said, "Take, eat; this is my body"' (26.26). The parallels with the feeding narrative are palpable; in each Jesus took the bread, blessed it, broke it, and distributed it. The accounts of Jesus' wilderness feedings present Jesus as offering one sort of daily bread, and the account of Jesus' last supper presents him as offering another. Jesus' body, his very life, is given to sustain the disciples.

How this works is more fully spelled out through the sharing of the cup, 'my blood of the covenant, which is poured out for many for the forgiveness of sins'. When disciples pray, 'Give us this day our daily bread', they not only express trust in their heavenly Father, but they are reminded that they do not live by bread alone. They need the bread that Jesus gives, in life and in death. Matthew's version of Jesus' words at the Last Supper lacks the injunctions, 'Do this, in remembrance of me' (Lk. 22.19; 1 Cor. 11.24-25). But it is difficult to doubt that those who read the Gospel of Matthew celebrated the Lord's Supper. To be sure, the only New Testament document outside the Gospels that repeats the words of institution is Paul's letter to the Corinthians. But other early Christian documents reflect the keeping of the Eucharist even when the form of the words pronounced differs (see *Did.* 9.1-5; Ignatius, *Phld.* 4.1; Ignatius, *Smyrn.* 7.1, 8.1). The account of Jesus' 'last supper' and the words of his institution of the 'lord's supper' were repeated not just because they were thought to have happened once, but because the Father, who gives bread to the hungry, continues to feed his people, then and now, through the work of Jesus, his Son.

Those who pray this prayer place themselves in the position of the hungry, the needy, those who lack, and who depend on God for sustenance. To be sure, such a posture can be dangerous; when those who have in abundance falsely parade as those who are in need, they denigrate the real needs of those who suffer constantly from hunger and privation. But it is important that disciples of Jesus learn to pray 'give us this day our daily bread', because this puts them always in the posture of receptivity.

But the story does not end there. While Jesus promises his people that his heavenly Father feeds those who are hungry, he later tells a parable in which the hungry were fed through the hands and deeds of those who saw Jesus in the poor and needy. In the parable of the sheep and the goats, the sheep are separated from the goats on the basis of their care and feeding of the poor, the hungry, the naked, and the imprisoned (Mt. 25.31-46). Apparently, this is how God feeds the hungry, clothes the naked, and takes care of the imprisoned and poor. The point is clear: those who have learned to receive from the Father's graciousness, those who have been fed by Jesus, who himself was hungry and relied on God, now see in the poor and hungry those who also rely on God. Those who have received, give; those who have been fed, feed others; those who have been clothed like the lilies of the field, clothe the naked. Such generosity is learned through practice, in community, and in prayer.

'Forgive Us our Debts'

In Matthew, Jesus speaks uncompromisingly of the need to forgive. The perfection that Jesus requires includes forgiving others. Even as Jesus instructed his disciples to petition God for their own forgiveness, so he exhorted them to forgive others and warned them of the consequences of failing to do so (6.14-15). It is Matthew's Gospel which includes Peter's query about how many times he must forgive another, and Jesus' response that forgiveness must neither be limited nor reckoned on a tally sheet (18.21-22). Again peculiar to Matthew is the somewhat paradoxical parable about a servant who is forgiven an enormous debt, but cannot forgive a fellow servant a small sum owed (18.23-35).

From the beginning of the Gospel of Matthew, Jesus is presented as one who 'saves his people from their sins' (1.21). His public ministry begins by associating with John's call for baptism 'for repentance', and John's protest of Jesus' coming to him for baptism (3.14). But from the outset, Jesus identifies with sinners. He offers forgiveness to a paralytic who comes for healing, thus providing the fullness of God's blessings to him (9.2-5). He ate with 'many tax collectors and sinners' (9.10) so that he was derided as their friend (11.29). He came to call sinners (9.13). He was betrayed into the hands of sinners (26.45). Prior to that, at the last supper, Jesus spoke of his blood of the covenant that was to be poured out for the forgiveness of sins. While prayer for forgiveness of sin is important and necessary, as is the willingness to forgive others, in the end neither is enough. Jesus' covenant blood must be poured out 'for the forgiveness of sins' (26.28). The petition for forgiveness, the acts of forgiving a brother or sister as many as seventy times seven, must be sealed through the blood of the covenant.

And this 'blood' through which forgiveness is offered is 'innocent blood' (*haima athōon*; 27.4). Though Pilate washes his hands of the whole matter, pronouncing himself innocent of Jesus' 'blood', he thus seeks more to excuse himself than to render the appropriate verdict that Jesus is innocent (27.24). Similarly, the crowd that accepts the legal responsibility for Jesus' death with the cry, 'His blood be on us and our children!' fails to acknowledge Jesus' innocence (27.25). It is as though they say to Pilate, 'You let him go! We cannot, for we deem him guilty of the charges brought against him.' Pilate fails to render a legal verdict, but his indifference scarcely makes him more innocent of Jesus' death. In the end, those judged guilty are innocent, and those who parade as innocent are guilty. The innocent one, and only he, can forgive those who are guilty.

The disciples learn of the need to forgive through the instruction of Jesus and example of Jesus: he taught them to forgive; he forgave sins; he died for the forgiveness of sins. But the disciples learn to forgive sins through doing it in the community that follows the one who offers forgiveness. Thus, in being baptized, as Jesus was, they receive the forgiveness of sins; in celebrating the Lord's Supper together, they again receive that forgiveness; in praying, they are reminded to forgive as they have been forgiven. In the practice of forgiveness they will learn what it costs; and then they will need to pray, 'Forgive us our debts, as we forgive our debtors'.

'Lead Us Not into Temptation'

This petition also looks back to Jesus' own time of testing in the wilderness. When he teaches his disciples to pray 'lead us not into temptation',[9] he does so as one who has faced the temptation to turn away from trusting God and to make his own way (4.1-11). Later Jesus faces the same temptation to turn from God's ways when Peter recoils in horror at the thought of Jesus' path leading to a cross (16.21-22); Jesus rebukes Peter, who tempts him to turn from 'the things of God' to 'the things of human beings' (16.23). While Jesus wrestles in prayer in Gethsemane, the inner circle of three disciples cannot even stay awake to pray with Jesus, as he had instructed them to do, so he reminds them, 'Pray that you may not enter into temptation' (26.41). The temptation from which they must pray to be delivered is the lure of following the easy way through the wide gate, thus avoiding the hard way that leads to life (7.13-14). Precisely because of the disciples' weakness, they must pray for deliverance from temptation, that is, that temptation to abandon that trust in God that Jesus himself manifests; but precisely because

---

9. The NRSV renders *eis peirasmon* as 'do not bring us to the time of trial'.

of their weakness, they are unable to do even that. In sharp contrast, Jesus labors and agonizes in prayer, asking that God's will be done. At the end of his life, Jesus prays the very prayer that he had taught his disciples, a prayer born out of and tested by experience. Not only does he pray that prayer, but he lives out that prayer. The disciples can neither pray, nor live out the substance of what they pray for.

Yet that is not the end of the story. In spite of their weakness and inability in the moment, the disciples do not fall away. Although at the end of the Gospel the response to Jesus is mixed ('and they worshiped him, but some doubted'; 28.17), nevertheless, the disciples are still following Jesus. They still need to learn to pray; they continue to need to learn what it means to follow Jesus. They will do so as they participate in the community to which he called them, learning what it means to do the will of the Father, eat the Lord's Supper together, receive forgiveness and anticipate the coming kingdom which they in turn proclaim to others, welcoming them into the family by means of baptism (26.28-29).

Summary Reflections

What makes such a reading a 'theological interpretation' of discipleship in Matthew? One goal of the theological interpretation of Scripture is to read with attentiveness to its capacity to form the faith of communities and individuals. On such readings, the role of Scripture is not simply to inform its readers about the past, about what discipleship and faith might have meant to some persons in a different time and place, but to continue to form its readers in the present. Such readings arise from the twin assumptions that the church is one church, and that those addressed in Scripture are the one people of God.

This interpretation also assumes that the Gospels' affirmations about Jesus are true: not only did his actions during his lifetime demonstrate the amazing authority that God had given to him (9.8), but he has indeed been given 'all authority' by God (28.19). The primary questions here are not those of historical or tradition criticism, that is, whether Jesus actually uttered the famous 'great commission' attributed to him (28.19-20), but whether Jesus indeed has the authority to commission his own disciples to go and make disciples. If indeed Jesus has such authority, then his call to follow becomes not simply the challenge from a figure of the past, but contemporary address to follow the one who lives. Such address, if heard and obeyed, is tested, deepened, and shaped by the practices of the community that include mutual forgiveness, prayer, generous giving, baptism, and celebration of the Lord's Supper.

Because Jesus is living, and has authority given to him by God, he continues to call people to follow him 'to the end of the age' and continues to teach them to pray. The interpretation offered here assumes that the Gospel does not merely intend to report what Jesus once taught his disciples to pray, but how he continues to teach them to pray and, in so doing, how he continues to shape the practices and habits of those who follow him. And the Gospel accomplishes this in part by narrating the life of the one who not only taught the disciples to pray, but lived out, from beginning to end, that which he taught them to do. One cannot learn from Jesus without learning from the Gospel. The Gospel, the interpreted narrative of Jesus' life, grounds the practices and commitments of disciples for all time in the very life of Jesus. And here we see that he taught them to pray what he lived: *lex orandi, lex vivendi.*

7

'HE ASCENDED INTO HEAVEN':
JESUS' ASCENSION IN LUKAN PERSPECTIVE, AND BEYOND

Joel B. Green

anelthonta eis tous ouranous
ascendit in cœlos

[He] ascended into heaven...

—The Nicene–Constantinople Creed[1]

According to John's Gospel, Jesus anticipated his ascension in his first conversation in the garden of the empty tomb, when he advised Mary Magdalene, 'Don't hold on to me, for I haven't yet gone up to my Father. Go to my brothers and sisters and tell them, "I'm going up to my Father and your Father, to my God and your God"' (20.17).[2] The writer of Ephesians apparently presupposes Jesus' ascension when he writes, 'God has given his grace to each one of us measured out by the gift that is given by Christ. That's why scripture says, *When he climbed up to the heights, he captured prisoners, and he gave gifts to people*' (4.7-8). In fact, numerous New Testament texts presuppose something like an ascension as they bear witness to and celebrate Jesus' exaltation to the place of honor at God's side.[3]

---

1. Greek and Latin texts from *The Creeds of Christendom* (ed. Philip Schaff; rev. David Schaff; 3 vols.; Grand Rapids: Baker, 6th edn, 1983 [1889]), II, p. 60; the Latin Version of Dionysus reads *ascendit in cœlum* [*cœlos*] (p. 57), and the Received Text of the Roman Catholic Church reads *ascendit in cœlum* (p. 59). Affirmations of the ascension of Jesus Christ are found already in the old (fourth-century) Roman form of the Apostles' Creed (I, p. 21; *ascendit in cœlos*—II, p. 49) and the Athanasian Creed (*ascendit ad* [*in*] *cœlos*—II, p. 69).

2. Unless otherwise noted, translations of biblical texts follow the Common English Bible.

3. Representative texts are noted, e.g., by Bruce M. Metzger, 'The Meaning of Christ's Ascension', in J.M. Myers, O. Reimherr and H.N. Bream (eds.), *Search the Scriptures: New Testament Studies in Honor of Raymond T. Stamm* (Gettysburg Theological Studies, 3; Leiden: Brill, 1969), pp. 118-23; Douglas Farrow, *Ascension and Ecclesia: On the Significance of the Doctrine of the Ascension for Ecclesiology and*

However, the ascension itself is described only twice in the New Testament, both in Luke's writings: at the end of Luke's Gospel (24.51) and the beginning of the Acts of the Apostles (1.9-11).[4] As with the virginal conception of Jesus, so with his ascension, what might seem from the perspective of the New Testament as a whole to be a minor point has itself been exalted so as to occupy a signature place in the Rule of Faith, that 'divine economy by which God has put together the mosaic of scripture'.[5] Of all the things that could be said of Jesus, how did these words, 'he ascended into heaven', propel themselves from a few lines taken from the entirety of Scripture into a place of prominence within the church's précis of its own faith?

The starring role of Jesus' ascension is especially startling from the perspective of Lukan scholarship in the modern period. This is because the single most-discussed question regarding Luke's testimony has to do not so much with its theological ramifications but with its historical veracity. The first obstacle is timing, since Acts 1 envisions a 40-day period between Jesus' resurrection and his ascension, whereas many scholars think that Luke 24 portrays the ascension as having occurred on resurrection day.[6]

Cosmology (Grand Rapids: Eerdmans, 1999), pp. 275-77. None, however, describe the ascension per se (cf. Gerhard Lohfink, *Die Himmelfahrt Jesu: Untersuchungen zu den Himmelfahrts- und Erhöhungstexten bei Lukas* [SANT, 26; Munich: Kösel, 1971], pp. 81-98). Douglas Farrow urges that Jesus' ascension is woven into the warp and woof of Scripture itself (*Ascension Theology* [London: T. & T. Clark, 2011], pp. 1-14).

4. See also Mk 16.19, which belongs to the inauthentic 'Long Ending' of Mark's Gospel.

5. This description of the Rule of Faith is taken from John J. O'Keefe and R.R. Reno, *Sanctified Vision: An Introduction to Early Christian Interpretation of the Bible* (Baltimore, MD: The Johns Hopkins University Press, 2005), p. 37.

6. E.g., Joseph A. Fitzmyer, *The Gospel according to Luke: Introduction, Translation, and Notes* (AB, 28–28a; 2 vols.; Garden City, NY: Doubleday, 1981/85), II, p. 1588; Hans Klein, *Das Lukasevangelium* (KEK; Göttingen: Vandenhoeck & Ruprecht, 2006), p. 742; Richard I. Pervo, *Acts: A Commentary* (Hermeneia; Minneapolis: Fortress Press, 2009), p. 37. Elsewhere in Lk. 24, Luke is careful to mark the chronology of his account (see vv. 1, 13, 21, 33, 36), but the connective in v. 50 (*de*) lacks this specificity; hence, the ascension may not be located temporally as firmly in the Gospel of Luke as scholars have tended to conclude.

'Forty days' designates the interval prior to the ascensions of Ezra (*4 Ezra* 14.23, 40) and Baruch (*2 Bar.* 76.4). With regard to Jesus' ascension, other intervals appear in the developing tradition—e.g., *Gos. Pet.* 5.19: from the cross; *Barn.* 15.9: resurrection day (literally, 'the eight day', *tēn hēmeran tēn ogdoēs*); *Ep. apost.* 51: 3 days; *Ap. Jas* 2: 550 days; the Valentinians, according to Irenaeus, *Adv. haer.* 1.3.2: 18 months; *Pistis sophia* 1.1: 11 years (cf. Kirsopp Lake, 'The Ascension', in F.J. Foakes-Jackson and Kirsopp Lake [eds.], *The Acts of the Apostles. V. Additional Notes to the Commentary* [Beginnings of Christianity, 1; London: Macmillan, 1933], pp. 19-20; Morton S. Enslin, 'The Ascension Story', *JBL* 47 [1928], pp. 60-73).

This issue pales into insignificance, however, when compared with the embarrassment registered over the cosmology of the ascension. Writing in the first half of the nineteenth century, David Friedrich Strauss identified the problem with characteristic scorn:

> [A]ccording to a just idea of the world, the seat of God and of the blessed, to which Jesus is supposed to have been exalted, is not to be sought for in the upper regions of the air, nor, in general, in any determinate place;—such a locality could only be assigned to it in the childish, limited conceptions of antiquity.... Thus there would be no other recourse than to suppose a divine accommodation to the idea of the world in that age, and to say: God in order to convince the disciples of the return of Jesus into the higher world, although this world is in reality by no means to be sought for in the upper air, nevertheless prepared the spectacle of such an exaltation. But this is to represent God as theatrically arranging an illusion.[7]

It is perhaps for this reason that biblical studies, disconcerted by the historical problems Luke presents, has generally moved away from historical criticism in its examination of Jesus' ascension.

This essay is concerned particularly with the account of Jesus' ascension in Acts 1.9-11, though not with demonstrating its historical veracity. As with almost every line of the Creed, Jesus' ascension stands outside the realm of the scientifically demonstrable, the *sine qua non* of modern historical criticism. If Jesus' ascension is to be studied, then, it will be in terms of its contribution to Luke's narrative representation of historical events—in this case, Luke's account of a visionary experience on the part of Jesus' followers within its narrative co-text.[8] First, I will summarize some recent

---

The apparent tension between Lk. 24.50 and Acts 1.3 is neither overcome by source theories like that of C.F.D. Moule (who postulates that Luke came across the tradition of 40 days after having completed the Gospel ['The Ascension—Acts i.9', *ExpTim* 68 (1956–57), pp. 205-209]; cf., already, Enslin, 'Ascension Story', p. 72), nor helped by theories of Luke's ineptness like that of Stephen G. Wilson (who conjectures that Luke had simply forgotten what he had previously written ['The Ascension: A Critique and an Interpretation', *ZNW* 59 (1968), p. 271]).

7. David Friedrich Strauss, *The Life of Jesus Critically Examined* (ed. Peter C. Hodgson; trans. George Eliot; Life of Jesus Series; 1840 repr.; Philadelphia: Fortress Press, 1972), pp. 750-51.

8. I refer to the ascension as a visionary experience because it is told from the perspective of Jesus' followers. See the brief treatment in John B.F. Miller, *Convinced That God Had Called Us: Dreams, Visions and the Perception of God's Will in Luke–Acts* (BIS, 85; Leiden: Brill, 2007), pp. 168-70. In fact, largely missing from the itinerary adopted by biblical scholars in their assessment of Jesus' ascension are perspectives from the study of the phenomenology of religious experience, an area of study that, if taken seriously, would raise a cautionary flag against indictments against the historical value of Luke's account. Initial forays into this area of research in biblical studies are collected in

emphases among Lukan scholars attempting to take seriously the theological ramifications of Jesus' ascension. This will allow me, second, to examine the significance of Jesus' ascension among selected second-century writings, and thus to show the apparent gap between the recent assessment of Luke's ascension-theology when compared with its reception in the second century. Finally, I will show that, reading backward, from the perspective of the second century, aspects of the Lukan narrative largely thrust into the shadows by New Testament study are brought into sharp relief. Accordingly, this essay exemplifies one way of conceiving the relationship between Scripture and the Rule of Faith within a theological hermeneutic, which we can formulate as a question: What do we see as we read Scripture through the prism of the creeds that we would not otherwise see?

From Cosmology to Theology

The Limits of Form Criticism
Generally, biblical scholarship in recent decades has drifted away from an interest in the historicity of Jesus' ascension, initially in favor of a form-critical assessment of Luke's accounts. This has allowed for a de-emphasis on the problematic cosmology of the Lukan narrative in favor of reflection on the ascension in literary and mythological terms. Indeed, form-critical study has led to the view among some that Acts 1.9-11 represents a kind of baptism of parallel accounts in Jewish and/or Greco-Roman literature, and thus to the conclusion that Luke has generated a report from traditional themes drawn from the wider literature of antiquity in order to describe how Jesus came to occupy his place at God's right side.[9] Luke's account has points of contact with Old Testament and Jewish as well as Greco-Roman accounts of 'heavenly journeys' and 'raptures', though its closest kin are to be found among Jewish traditions.[10] None follow the particular sequence of

---

Frances Flannery *et al.* (eds.), *Experientia*. I. *Inquiry into Religious Experience in Early Judaism and Early Christianity* (SBLSymS, 40; Atlanta: Society of Biblical Literature, 2008).

9. E.g., Leslie Houlden, 'Beyond Belief: Preaching the Ascension', *Theology* 94 (1991), pp. 177-78. On form-critical and source-critical grounds, Lohfink argued that Luke was the originator of the ascension (*Himmelfahrt*).

10. For this material, see, e.g., Lohfink, *Himmelfahrt*; Alan F. Segal, 'Heavenly Ascent in Hellenistic Judaism, Early Christianity and their Environment', *ANRW* 2.23.2 (1980), pp. 1333-94; Mary Dean-Otting, *Heavenly Journeys: A Study of the Motif in Hellenistic Jewish Literature* (JU, 8; Frankfurt am Main: Peter Lang, 1984); D.W. Palmer, 'The Literary Background of Acts 1.1-14', *NTS* 33 (1987), pp. 432-34; Martha Himmelfarb, *Ascent to Heaven in Jewish and Christian Apocalypses* (Oxford: Oxford University Press, 1993); James D. Tabor, 'Heaven, Ascent to', in *ABD*, III, pp. 91-94; A.W. Zwiep, *The Ascension of the Messiah in Lukan Christology* (NovTSup, 87; Leiden:

the Lukan account (death → resurrection → earthly interlude → ascension), however, with the result that its significance can be determined on the basis of literary precedents only in general terms.[11] Painting with broad strokes, such accounts bear witness to the exalted status of the one taken up and address the crisis of divine presence, serving to reaffirm the relationship of God to his people. Additionally, in a number of accounts of 'ascent' in Jewish apocalypses, ascent signifies investiture and enthronement as a royal priest, sometimes with the character of a scribe and prophet, sometimes in order to share God's reign.[12] These motifs invite further exploration with reference to Luke's narrative. For example, even though Jesus' ascension breaks the pattern of the ascended one who typically returns to earth to communicate a divine revelation, this emphasis on divine presence remains important to Luke. This is because Jesus' relationship to the Spirit in Acts is such that it is through the Spirit that Jesus is present with his followers; although enthroned in heaven, Jesus is actively present in the life and mission of the church.[13] Beyond these general considerations, form criticism is of limited assistance in our reading of Luke's account. Mary Dean-Otting, for example, has identified eleven elements that she regards as constitutive of the form of a Jewish heavenly journey, but only two of these are possibly shared with the ascension account in Acts.[14]

Brill, 1997), esp. pp. 36-79; Zwiep, 'Assumptus est in caelum: Rapture and Heavenly Exaltation in Early Judaism and Luke–Acts', in Friedrich Avemarie and Hermann Lichtenberger (eds.), *Auferstehung — Resurrection* (WUNT, 135; Tübingen: Mohr Siebeck, 2001), pp. 323-49.

11. Contra Zwiep (*Ascension of the Messiah*; 'Rapture'), who allows his form-critical conclusions (which are themselves problematic, since Luke's account is both like and unlike those with which he pairs it) to determine what the ascension cannot mean for Luke–Acts.

12. See Himmelfarb, *Ascent to Heaven*.

13. Cf., e.g., William J. Larkin, Jr, 'The Spirit and Jesus "on Mission" in the Post-resurrection and Postascension Stages of Salvation History: The Impact of the Pneumatology of Acts on its Christology', in Amy M. Donaldson and Timothy B. Sailors (eds.), *New Testament Greek and Exegesis: Essays in Honor of Gerald F. Hawthorne* (Grand Rapids: Eerdmans, 2003), pp. 121-39; H. Douglas Buckwalter, *The Character and Purpose of Luke's Christology* (SNTMS, 89; Cambridge: Cambridge University Press, 1996); Buckwalter, 'The Divine Saviour', in I. Howard Marshall and David Peterson (eds.), *Witness to the Gospel: The Theology of Acts* (Grand Rapids: Eerdmans, 1998), pp. 107-23. Contra, e.g., Zwiep, *Ascension of the Messiah*, for whom 'Luke advocates an "absentee christology", i.e. a christology that is dominated by the (physical) absence *and present inactivity* of the exalted Lord' (p. 182; emphasis original).

14. Dean-Otting, *Heavenly Journeys*, pp. 4-5. The two points of overlap are that the ascent is initiated by God rather than by the visionary and that the journey ends with the visionary returning to earth.

In fact, we find Luke's ascension account embedded in a far more impressive list of parallels within the Lukan narrative itself, tying together the closing of Luke's Gospel and the opening of Acts. Both record:
- appearances of Jesus to his followers
- Jesus eating in front of/with his followers
- demonstrations that Jesus is really alive
- the directive to remain in Jerusalem
- references to the fulfillment of the Father's promise (of the Holy Spirit)
- the appointment of Jesus' followers as 'witnesses'
- references to the universal scope of the impending mission
- the ascension
- the disciples' return to Jerusalem in obedience to Jesus' directive

That is, almost every detail in Acts 1.1-14 finds its antecedent in Luke 24, strongly indicating that, rather than isolating Acts 1.9-11 from its narrative co-text, the path forward is one that takes seriously the contribution of Luke's narrative. In the immediate co-text of this episode, this is signaled by the opening of v. 9, 'After Jesus said these things....'

Again, far from being an isolated incident reported at the beginning of Acts, Jesus' ascension has been anticipated as far back as the scene of transfiguration and the onset of Jesus' journey to Jerusalem in Luke 9, at which points the third evangelist speaks of Jesus' impending 'departure [*exodos*], which he would achieve in Jerusalem' (v. 31), and of the approaching time when 'Jesus was to be taken up into heaven' (v. 51). In fact, there is a host of ways in which Luke ties his account of Jesus' ascension back into the transfiguration story—e.g.:

Luke 9.28-36	Acts 1.9-11
Location on a mountain (*eis to oros*, v. 28)	Location on a mountain (*apo orous*, v. 12)
'After Jesus said these things' (*meta tous logous toutous*, v. 28)	'After Jesus said these things' (*tauta eipōn*, v. 9)
'He...went up' (*anabainō*, v. 28)	'He was lifted up' (*epairō*, v. 9)
'His clothes flashed white [*leukos*]' (v. 29)	'In white [*leukos*] robes' (v. 10)
'Two men...' (*kai idou andres duo*, v. 30)	'Two men...' (*kai idou andres duo*, v. 10)
'Departure' (*exodos*, v. 31)	'Go into heaven' (*poreuomonon eis ton ouranon*, v. 11)
'Cloud' (*nephelē*, v. 34)	'Cloud' (*nephelē*, v. 9)
Visual emphasis (vv. 29, 30, 31, 32)	Visual emphasis (vv. 9 [2×], 10, 11 [2×])[15]

15. See the comparable chart in J.G. Davies, *He Ascended into Heaven: A Study in the History of Doctrine* (Bampton Lectures, 1958; London: Lutterworth Press, 1958), p. 186.

Of course, there are obvious differences in emphasis, perhaps the most important being that, in the transfiguration, the revelatory word is spoken from heaven regarding Jesus on earth, whereas, in the ascension, the revelatory word is spoken on earth regarding Jesus in heaven. If Luke's account of the transfiguration discloses in unassailable terms the divine honor accorded Jesus in anticipation of human rejection, so the ascension reveals an unimpeachable, heavenly endorsement of the now-crucified-and-resurrected Jesus. Here is the first of many hints in our investigation that Acts 1.9-11 not only marks the literary hinge of Luke's two volumes but constitutes a theological pivot-point as well.

On the Making of Maps (and History)
Recognition of the limits of form criticism notwithstanding, historical questions have not altogether disappeared.[16] Instead, the veracity of Luke's account has found its champions among some theologians and philosophers seeking to take seriously the portrait Luke has given us divorced from its literalism. For example, Peter Brunner writes, 'It is simply so that if the Bible told us that the Lord Jesus flew into heaven like a balloon, on and on until he reached his heavenly palace, that would indeed be only a fairy tale'[17]—this before urging that the reality of Jesus' ascension is God's exalting the Crucified to divine power and honor. More interesting, perhaps, is Stephen Davis's argument that Luke speaks in metaphor, that Jesus' ascension is simply a way of saying that Jesus passed from the presence of his followers to the presence of God.

> The Ascension of Jesus was primarily a change of state rather than a change of location. Jesus changed in the Ascension from being present in the realm of space and time to being present in the realm of eternity, in the transcendent heavenly realm.[18]

---

16. See James D.G. Dunn, 'The Ascension of Jesus: A Test Case for Hermeneutics', in Avemarie and Lichtenberger (eds.), *Auferstehung—Resurrection*, pp. 301-22; as well as the earlier exchange between Dunn and D.W. Gooding: Dunn, 'Demythologizing—The Problem of Myth in the New Testament', in I. Howard Marshall (ed.), *New Testament Interpretation: Essays on Principles and Methods* (Grand Rapids: Eerdmans, 1977), pp. 285-307; Gooding, 'Demythologizing Old and New, and Luke's Description of the Ascension: A Layman's Appraisal', *IBS* 2 (1980), pp. 95-119; Dunn, 'Demythologizing the Ascension—A Reply to Professor Gooding', *IBS* 3 (1981), pp. 15-27; Gooding, 'Demythologizing the Ascension—A Reply', *IBS* 3 (1981), pp. 46-54.

17. Peter Brunner, 'The Ascension of Christ: Myth or Reality?', *Dialog* 1.2 (1962), p. 38.

18. Stephen T. Davis, 'The Meaning of Ascension for Christian Scholars', *Perspectives* 22.4 (2007), p. 16. Metzger had sketched an analogous understanding in his 1969 essay ('Christ's Ascension', pp. 123-25).

For his part, Robert Jenson wonders, '[C]an one really—and even if one be the Christ—get to God by space travel?' He then goes on briefly to sketch Calvin's view of 'heaven above' as outside the universe—a view Jenson critiques for its failure to take seriously the embodied nature of the risen Christ and its problematic reading of biblical portraits of heaven.[19]

What these attempts have in common is their concern to validate Luke's account in the courtroom of scientific exegesis, and especially in terms appropriate to a historical-critical interest in 'what really happened'. For those of us concerned with the theological interpretation of Scripture, this will not do. This is because we are concerned with theological reflection *with Scripture*, not with theological reflection on the basis of an account reconstructed by even our best historians. N.T. Wright is closer to the mark when he resists reading Luke's narrative within the framework of a two-decker or a three-decker cosmology and insists that we take note of the theological sophistication of the biblical writers, Luke among them, in their references to *earth* and *heaven* as 'parallel and interlocking universes inhabited by the creator god on the one hand and humans on the other'.[20] This seems to be close to Jenson's preferred explanation, that heaven describes not so much a reality 'up there' as '"the place in the world from which" God's inner worldly movement begins'.[21] The point is, puzzling over Luke's scientific knowledge has masked the way his account underscores Jesus' heavenly destination, which is itself set within a narrative co-text manifestly concerned with rewriting the disciples' notions of space (and time).

My first claim, regarding Luke's interest in Jesus' heavenly destination, is easy enough to document. In Acts 1.9-11, the term *heaven* (*ouranos*) is found four times—once in v. 10: 'as they were staring *toward heaven*' (v. 10); and three times in v. 11: 'Galileans, why are you standing here, looking *toward heaven*? This Jesus, who was taken up from you *into heaven*, will come in the same way that you saw him go *into heaven*.' This is congruent with Luke's earlier note about the cessation of Jesus' earthly career 'when he was taken up *into heaven*' (1.2; cf. Lk. 9.51: 'when Jesus was to be taken up *into heaven*'). But Luke's readers have already been put on notice regarding issues of space-time in the immediately preceding exchange between Jesus and his followers. 'Lord, are you going to restore the kingdom of Israel now?' they want to know. Jesus responds, 'It isn't for you to know the times or seasons that the Father has set by his own

---

19. Robert W. Jenson, 'On the Ascension', in Michael Welker and Cynthia A. Jarvis (eds.), *Loving God with our Minds: The Pastor as Theologian: Essays in Honor of Wallace M. Alston* (Grand Rapids: Eerdmans, 2004), p. 334.

20. N.T. Wright, *The Resurrection of the Son of God* (Christian Origins and the Question of God, 3; Minneapolis: Fortress Press, 2003), p. 655.

21. Jenson, 'Ascension', p. 337.

authority. Rather, you will receive power when the Holy Spirit has come upon you, and you will be my witnesses in Jerusalem, in all Judea and Samaria, and to the end of the earth' (1.6-8). From the disciples' question regarding what will happen *now*, Jesus underscores their agnosticism regarding the Father's timetable, and the two angels go on to speak of an indeterminate future time when Jesus will return from his heavenly abode. From a concern with Israel, Jesus goes on to chart the world in terms of the divine plan. But the map he provides cannot be read in terms of so many degrees latitude and longitude, as though Jerusalem or Samaria or the end of the earth might be reduced to places on a cartographer's map bound at the back of modern Bibles. Geography is not a naive container but a social—and, for Luke, theological—construct that both reflects and configures particular ways of construing the world. Just as *Jerusalem* calls to mind important social, political, economic, and religious considerations, so Judea ('land of the Jews'), Samaria ('land of the Samaritans'), and 'the end of the earth' reflect the structuring of socio-religious relations—indeed, entire lifeworlds. The result is centrifugal rather than centripetal, less a focus on Jerusalem as the earth's center and more on the blurring of distant, outer boundaries. Luke has chosen a wide-angle lens rather than a telescopic one, and adopted a distal rather than proximate position from which to view the world. With the immediately adjacent account of Jesus' ascension, the shift in Luke's geographical perspective is only compounded. The divine plan and its actualization within Luke's narration are not determined by earth-bound views but by a heavenly perspective. Indeed, the dominion regarding which Jesus' followers had questioned him in v. 6 is not earthbound but heavenly. It is, after all, God's kingdom, and God's throne is heaven itself (7.49; citing Isa. 66.1). Earth and heaven are distinguished, so that Jesus' ascension removes him from their sight (1.9), but this emphasis on Jesus' heavenly journey now opens the way for earthly history to be grasped in terms of heavenly space and heavenly time. Indeed, the Holy Spirit promised them is none other than '*heavenly* power' (*ex hypos dynamis*, Lk. 24.49); the coming of the Spirit is accompanied by 'a sound *from heaven*' (Acts 2.2); and this Spirit empowers them to serve as Jesus' witnesses (1.8) beginning on the day of Pentecost, in Jerusalem, where 'pious Jews from every nation *under heaven*' were living (2.5). Jesus remains in heaven (3.21), where he is seen in Stephen's visionary experience (7.55-56), and from where he can provide empowerment and direction (e.g., 9.3; 10.11).[22]

22. For heaven as source of disclosure, cf. Lk. 3.21; 10.21; 20.4-5; Acts 2.2; 9.3; 10.11, 16; 11.5, 9, 10; 22.6; as source of judgment, cf. Lk. 9.54; 17.29; and as divine residence, cf. Lk. 3.21; 9.16; (10.15); 11.13, 16; 15.7, 18, 21; 18.13; 20.4-5; Acts 1.10, 11; 2.2; 3.21 (Jesus' abode); 7.49 (God's abode), 55-56 (Jesus' and God's abode). For the notion of heavenly perspective, cf. Lk. 15.7; 18.22.

In other words, heaven now becomes the reality that structures and maps the life of Jesus' followers.[23] Whatever else this entails, this means that any attempt to analyze Luke's account of Jesus' ascension and its sequelae in ways that reduce Luke's narrative to what can be scientifically verified or validated on historical-critical grounds is essentially wrongheaded as a reading of Luke's narrative. For Luke, the ascension undercuts any reductive historicism that assumes that the story of Acts is played out on a human-made map of the cosmos. The terrain on which our understanding of Acts 1.9-11 within the historical narrative of Luke–Acts might be mapped is essentially *theological*.

Ascension Theology in Lukan Studies
How has Lukan scholarship articulated the theological significance of the ascension for Luke? In his 1985 Tyndale New Testament Lecture, John Maile focused on the ascension, devoting 25 pages to a range of critical issues before turning to a three-and-a-half-page assessment of 'The Significance of the Ascension Narratives in Luke–Acts'. He lists six motifs. The ascension: (1) confirms Christ's exaltation and present lordship; (2) explains the continuity between Jesus' ministry and the church's ministry; (3) brings to a close the resurrection appearances; (4) introduces the sending of the Holy Spirit; (5) sets the groundwork for Christian mission; and (6) serves as the pledge of Christ's return.[24] How each of these interpretations can be attributed to Luke's narrative is not always clear, undoubtedly due to the cursory nature of the theological contribution of Maile's discussion—itself testimony to the backseat generally reserved for theological reflection in biblical studies even with the onset of redaction criticism. Moreover, one of Maile's points—that the ascension brings to a close the resurrection appearances—assumes what is not in evidence, namely, that Jesus' typical abode during the forty days after the resurrection was heaven, with the result that we must assume that Jesus came and went, came and went, prior to the ascension.

More recent discussion has brought with it different emphases. Consider, for example, an alternative list of theological implications from Steve Walton, for whom the ascension marks Jesus' transition from earth to heaven. This heavenly position (1) implies that Jesus now reigns in heaven alongside God; (2) anticipates Jesus' return to earth from heaven; (3) identifies Jesus

23. See now the sophisticated analysis of Matthew Sleeman, *Geography and the Ascension Narrative in Acts* (SNTSMS, 146; Cambridge: Cambridge University Press, 2009).
24. John F. Maile, 'The Ascension in Luke–Acts', *TynBul* 37 (1986), pp. 29-59; similarly, Paul Palatty, 'The Ascension of Christ in Luke–Acts', *Bible Bhashyam* 12 (1986), pp. 166-81.

as the Lord of the Spirit, who now pours out the Spirit; (4) implies that Jesus has universal authority, so that he welcomes believers, like Stephen, to heaven; (5) means that Jesus can appear and act from heaven; (6) signifies that the barrier between heaven and earth has been pierced, allowing two-way traffic—e.g., angelic activity and the coming of the Spirit; and (7) means that believers may approach God through Jesus with confidence.[25] What is interesting about the shift in perspective between these two mile-markers in the discussion is, first, Walton's renewed emphasis on 'heaven', which takes its cue from the fact that 'heaven' is mentioned four times in Acts 1.9-11; and second, the heightened emphasis on Christology in contemporary discussion of Jesus' ascension among New Testament scholars.

In fact, it is not too much to say that a renewal of interest in the possibility of a divine Christology in Luke–Acts finds its center in Luke's interpretation of Jesus' ascension.[26] On the one hand, a major current of Luke's soteriology is grounded in Jesus' exaltation, a term that summarizes theologically the significance of Jesus' resurrection and ascension.[27] It is on the basis of Jesus' exaltation to God's right side, for example, that Jesus is 'leader and savior', enabling Israel's repentance and forgiveness of sins (Acts 5.31).[28] This is especially interesting in that, for Israel, divine forgiveness is an act of covenant renewal marking the restoration of God's people.[29] This restoration theme is likewise in view with the outpouring of the Spirit at Pentecost.[30] Thus, we learn from Peter's Pentecost address not only that the outpouring of the Spirit actualizes Joel's prophecy regarding Israel's restoration, but also that the outpouring of the Spirit is the consequence of Jesus' exaltation to God's right side and concomitant reception from the Father of the promised Holy Spirit (Acts 2.16-21, 33). In short, both Lukan pneumatology

---

25. Steve Walton, 'Ascension of Jesus', in Joel B. Green (ed.), *Dictionary of Jesus and the Gospels* (Downers Grove, IL: InterVarsity Press, 2nd edn, in press).

26. This is not meant to be an exclusive claim, as some studies have ranged across other evidence in the Lukan narrative; cf., e.g., Buckwalter, *Luke's Christology*; C. Kavin Rowe, *Early Narrative Christology: The Lord in the Gospel of Luke* (BZNW, 139; Berlin: W. de Gruyter, 2006).

27. The relationship among these three—exaltation, ascension, and resurrection—is debated. See the critical assessment in Kevin L. Anderson, *'But God Raised Him from the Dead': The Theology of Jesus' Resurrection in Luke–Acts* (Paternoster Biblical Monographs; Milton Keyes: Paternoster Press, 2006), pp. 41-47.

28. On the exaltation as salvific event, see, e.g., Joel B. Green, '"Salvation to the End of the Earth" (Acts 13.47): God as Saviour in the Acts of the Apostles', in Marshall and Peterson (eds.), *Witness to the Gospel*, pp. 83-106.

29. Cf. Jer. 4.14; 31.31-34; 2 Macc. 7.1-42; 8.27-29; *1 En.* 5.6.

30. This is a major emphasis in Max Turner, *Power from on High: The Spirit in Israel's Restoration and Witness in Luke–Acts* (JPTSup, 9; Sheffield: Sheffield Academic Press, 1996).

and soteriology are grounded in Lukan Christology, and Luke's divine Christology turns on Jesus' ascension.

The significance of Jesus' ascension for Luke's Christology is the focus of a number of essays by Max Turner in which he puts forward a sophisticated argument that takes seriously the historical-theological milieu within which Luke writes, the character of Luke's interpretation of Jesus' exaltation, and a range of possible counter-proposals.[31] The primary contours of his thesis are easily traced. (1) God resurrected Jesus and exalted Jesus to God's right side (Acts 2.24-36). Jesus, then, shares with the Father the divine throne itself.[32] (2) Even though Luke has it that Peter emphasizes in his Pentecostal address that it is *God* who says that he will 'pour out my Spirit' (2.17), Peter goes on to claim that, at his exaltation, Jesus 'received from the Father the promised Holy Spirit' and that it is Jesus who 'poured out this Spirit' (2.33). This actualizes Jesus' earlier promise that he himself would send 'what my Father promised' (Lk. 24.49). Accordingly, 'Jesus is identified as one with Yahweh as the "Lord" (2.36) upon whose name one is to call for salvation, and in whose name one is baptized (2.38-40)'.[33]

Andy Johnson has taken a different route to reach a similar conclusion.[34] First, he observes with others before him the intertextual relationship between the accounts of Jesus' ascension in Acts 1.9-11 and Elijah's ascension in 2 Kgs 2.1-18, particularly with respect to the parallel emphases on 'seeing' and the connection of 'seeing' with the reception of the spirit (or Spirit) of the one ascending. We read in 2 Kgs 2.9-10:

31. See especially M.M.B. Turner, 'The Spirit of Christ and Christology', in H.H. Rawdon (ed.), *Christ the Lord: Studies in Christology Presented to Donald Guthrie* (Leicester: Inter-Varsity Press, 1982), pp. 168-90; Max Turner, 'The Spirit of Christ and "Divine" Christology', in Joel B. Green and Max Turner (eds.), *Jesus of Nazareth: Lord and Christ: Essays on the Historical Jesus and New Testament Christology* (Grand Rapids: Eerdmans, 1994), pp. 413-36; '"Trinitarian" Pneumatology in the New Testament? Towards an Explanation of the Worship of Jesus', *AsTJ* 57-58 (2002–2003), pp. 167-86.

32. On this point, Turner is dependent on Richard Bauckham, *God Crucified: Monotheism and Christology in the New Testament* (Grand Rapids: Eerdmans, 1998), especially Chapter 1; 'The Throne of God and the Worship of Jesus', in *Jesus and the God of Israel:* God Crucified *and Other Studies on the New Testament's Christology of Divine Identity* (Grand Rapids: Eerdmans, 2008), pp. 152-81. Cf. Metzger, 'Christ's Ascension', pp. 127-28.

33. Turner, 'Trinitarian Pneumatology', p. 178. Whether *hypsoō* in v. 33 identifies Jesus' 'exaltation' with his resurrection or with his ascension is debated. In v. 33, Jesus' exaltation appears to be the consequence of his resurrection (*oun*, 'therefore'), while in v. 34 Jesus' exaltation is contrasted with David's failure to ascend into the heavens (*gar*, 'for') which by implication urges an identification of Jesus' ascension with his exaltation.

34. Andy Johnson, 'Resurrection, Ascension and the Developing Portrait of the God of Israel in Acts', *SJT* 57 (2004), pp. 149-52.

> When they had crossed, Elijah said to Elisha, 'What do you want me to do for you before I'm taken away from you?' Elisha said, 'Let me have twice your spirit.' Elijah said, 'You've made a difficult request. If you can see me when I'm taken from you, then it will be yours. If you don't see me, it won't happen.'

Then, as Elijah is taken up into heaven in a windstorm, 'Elisha was watching' until 'he could no longer see him' (v. 12). Subsequently, the group of prophets recognizes that 'Elijah's spirit has settled on Elisha!' (v. 15), while also distinguishing Elijah's spirit from the LORD's spirit (v. 16). Johnson goes on to observe that, like the account in 2 Kings 2, Luke's narration of the ascension is bracketed by promises of receiving the Spirit (Acts 1.4, 5, 8) and a report of the reception of the Spirit (2.1-13). Likewise, Luke emphatically documents that Jesus' ascension was for the disciples a manifestly visual experience (mentioning sight five times in three verses).[35] After a delay of ten days, at Pentecost, we learn in Acts 2, Jesus did pour out a spirit on his followers; indeed, they received the promised Holy Spirit of the Father. That is, even though, on the basis of the story of Elijah and Elisha, we might expect *Jesus'* spirit to empower his disciples, according to Luke's narrative, the identity of the promised spirit who is coming is none other than the Holy Spirit (1.4-5). Moving beyond any parallels with 2 Kings 2, then, the spirit of the ascended one is the Spirit of the LORD, who is subsequently known to us as 'the Spirit of Jesus' (Acts 16.7).

Biblical scholarship on Jesus' ascension according to Acts, then, has largely moved away from issues related to the historical veracity of Luke's account, its potential sources, and its literary form, underscoring more and more its theological significance. In contemporary study, this significance has been parsed above all in christological terms, including examination of the ramifications of Jesus' exalted status as Lord and Christ for Luke's pneumatology and soteriology, set within the overarching narrative of God's engagement with Israel.

Ascension Theology:
Reading Luke–Acts from the Second Century

Writing in the last quarter of the second century, Irenaeus locates Jesus' ascension in his précis of the faith received by the whole church from the apostles and their disciples:

---

35. The parallel is weakened by our recognition that the condition for their reception of the Holy Spirit was not that they see Jesus' ascension, but that they wait in Jerusalem (Lk. 24.49; Acts 1.4).

in one God the Father Almighty, the Creator of heaven and earth and the seas and all things that are in them; and in the one Jesus Christ, the Son of God, who was infleshed for our salvation; and in the Holy Spirit, who through the prophets preached the Economies, the coming, the birth from a Virgin, the passion, the resurrection from the dead, and the bodily ascension into heaven of the beloved Son, Christ Jesus our lord, and His coming from heaven in the glory of the Father to recapitulate all things, and to raise up all flesh of the whole human race, in order that to Christ Jesus, our Lord and God, Savior and King, according to the invisible Father's good pleasure, *Every knee should bow [of those] in heaven and on earth and under the earth, and every tongue confess Him*, and he would exercise just judgment toward all... (*Against Heresies* 1.10.1).[36]

This suggests the secure place the ascension occupied in the church's kerygma from early on and invites reflection on its significance theologically. I will mention three milestones in the reception of Jesus' ascension: the writings of Justin Martyr from the mid-second century, the apocryphal *Acts of Peter* from the second half of the second century, and the work of Irenaeus.

Ascension Theology in the Second Century

Justin Martyr's primary contribution to the conversation appears to have been his efforts to secure the ascension within the church's confession. We find in his work two interrelated strategies. The first is his appeal to Scripture—particularly Psalms 19; 24; 47; 68; 110[37]—to prove Jesus' ascension: 'we prove that all things which have already happened had been predicted by the prophets before they came to pass...' (*First Apology* 52 [*ANF*, I, p. 176]). Scripture is recruited as testimony regarding the truth of the christological kerygma, in which Jesus' ascension figures (*First Apology* 21), over against pagan myths uttered by 'the poets' under the influence of 'wicked demons' concerning those whose careers were mere imitations of Christ (*First Apology* 54 [*ANF*, I, p. 181]). These imitations included not only the virginal conception of Jesus but also his ascension:

> For you know how many sons your esteemed writers ascribed to Jupiter; Mercury, the interpreting word and teacher of all; Aesculapius, who, though he was a great physician, was struck by a thunderbolt, and so ascended to heaven; and Bacchus too, after he had been torn limb from limb; and Hercules, when he had committed himself to the flames to escape his toils; and the sons of Leda, and Dioscuri; and Perseus, son of Danae; and Bellerophon, who, though sprung from mortals, rose to heaven on the horse Pegasus. For what shall I say

---

36. ET: Irenaeus, *Against Heresies* (trans. and ed. Dominic J. Unger; rev. John J. Dillon; Ancient Christian Writers, 55; Mahwah, NJ: Paulist Press, 1992), p. 49 (emphasis original).

37. See Davies, *He Ascended*, pp. 71-73.

of Ariane, and those who, like her, have been declared to be set among the stars? And what of the emperors who die among yourselves, whom you deem worthy of deification, and in whose behalf you produce some one who swears he has seen the burning Caesar rise to heaven from the funeral pyre?

But, Justin goes on to say, 'wicked devils perpetrated these things' (*First Apology* 21 [*ANF*, I, p. 170]). The logic at work here has two steps: Ascension marks one as a god, but the only true ascension is the one predicted beforehand, namely, that of Jesus Christ. Indeed, for Justin Jesus' ascension evidences his divinity (e.g., *Dialogue with Trypho* 64).

We find in the *Acts of Peter* a similar interest in ascension as the mark of divine legitimation.[38] This document narrates an encounter between Peter and the sorcerer Simon known to us from Acts 8.5-25. Simon claims that he is 'the great power of God, and that without God he does nothing', with the result that people wonder if he might be the Christ. When Simon is acclaimed in Rome as 'God in Italy', 'saviour of the Romans', he responds with an aerial display by which he arrives at the city gate in a dust cloud (*Acts Pet.* 4). The ensuing narrative prepares us for a final showdown between Peter and Simon. Simon promises that he will 'fly up to God' (*Acts Pet.* 31[2]), and challenges Peter with these words:

> Peter, now of all times, when I am making my ascent before all these onlookers, I tell you: If your god has power enough—he whom the Jews destroyed, and they stoned you who were chosen by him—let him show that faith in him is of God; let it be shown at this time whether it be worthy of God. For I by ascending will show to all this crowd what manner of being I am.

The story continues, 'And lo and behold, he was carried up in to the air, and everyone saw him all over Rome, passing over its temple and hills' (*Acts Pet.* 32[3]). Peter reacts by crying out to his God, the Lord Jesus Christ, that Simon might fall and be crippled but not die—and this is what transpired, so that the Christian community was rescued from deception and actually increased in number.

The collocation of ascension with divine legitimation in Justin and the *Acts of Peter* is interesting because of the different audiences these writings serve. That is, with regard to discourse both within the church and between the church and its wider world, ascension is a mark of divine sanction. This suggests the ease with which we might consider early readings of Luke's account of Jesus' ascension as a means of undermining imperial Rome, with its tales of heavenly assumption or deification on the occasion of death.[39]

---

38. ET: Wilhelm Schneemelcher, 'The Acts of Peter', in Wilhelm Schneemelcher (ed.), *New Testament Apocrypha* (rev. Edgar Hennecke; 2 vols.; Louisville, KY: Westminster/John Knox Press, 1992), II, pp. 271-321.

39. Cf. Wright, *Resurrection*, e.g., pp. 76-77, 656.

This is true irrespective of the reality that Luke's narrative is more similar to Jewish than to Greco-Roman accounts of heavenly journey and that Luke himself seems not to have explicitly developed the significance of Jesus' ascension in anti-imperial terms.

What, then, of Irenaeus? The Rule of Truth cited above appears in Book 1, Chapter 10, of *Against Heresies*. In the preceding chapters, Irenaeus has explicated the Valentinian Gnosticism known to him (chs. 1–8) and critiqued it (ch. 9), accusing his opponents primarily for their bad exegesis. In doing so, he offers this analogy: Someone might glean from Homer phrases and names, recasting them in a poem that the naive might regard as Homeric. In the same way, Gnostics collect expressions and names scattered throughout Scripture, then place them in a narrative of their own construction—but a narrative that could never be confused with the *hypothesis* (or narrative sense) of Scripture. Their 'system' derives not from the words of the prophets, not from the teaching of the Lord Jesus, and not from the traditions delivered by the apostles, but from sources outside the Scriptures; indeed, they disregard 'the order and the connection of the Scriptures' (1.8.1).[40] Those who retain the Rule of Truth received at their baptism will recognize immediately the proper order and position of scriptural expression and so understand Scripture rightly (1.9.4). It is in this context, then, that Irenaeus goes on to articulate the unity of the church's faith, the Rule of Truth, derived from the apostles and their disciples. His argument, then, is an exegetical one, but one that is ruled in relation to Scripture's *hypothesis*.[41]

Among the issues Irenaeus discusses, anthropology is pivotal, with the human being understood by the Gnostics as comprising three classes: the psychic, the somatic, and the pneumatic. This division of humanity into classes has its counterpart in what we might refer to as their Christology. For them, the Savior had a psychic body, so that, in their formulation, the ascension would have been the return of the spiritual to the spiritual; for Irenaeus, however, this flies in the face of John's Gospel, which declares that the Word became flesh. As this discussion relates to Jesus' ascension, then, we can identify three related emphases. First, just as Irenaeus marks the beginning of Jesus' career with his having been 'infleshed for our salvation', so he marks its end with Jesus' 'bodily ascension'. Irenaeus devotes much of the fifth book of *Against Heresies* to this claim—arguing, for example,

---

40. Irenaeus, *Against Heresies* (trans. and ed. Dominic J. Unger), p. 41.
41. Cf. his own exegesis of Ps. 68.17-18 in *Proof of the Apostolic Preaching* 83; *Against Heresies* 2.20.3. See the helpful discussion of Irenaeus' view of the ascension in Douglas B. Farrow, 'The Doctrine of the Ascension in Irenaeus and Origen', *Arc: The Journal of the Faculty of Religious Studies, McGill University* 26 (1998), pp. 31-50; Farrow, however, conceptualizes the issue in systematic rather than exegetical terms.

> For, in what way could we be partakers of the adoption of sons, unless we had received from Him through the Son that fellowship which refers to Himself, unless His Word, having been made flesh, had entered into communion with us? Wherefore also He has passed through every stage of life, restoring to all communion with God (5.18.7, *ANF*, I, p. 448).

Second, to reiterate, for Irenaeus Jesus' ascension was 'bodily'. As he notes, 'But if the Word of the Father, who descended, is the one who also ascended, namely the Only-begotten Son of the one God, who according to the Father's good pleasure became flesh for the sake of men, then John is not speaking of anyone else…, but of the Lord Jesus Christ' (1.9.3).[42] Third, as Jesus recapitulates the life of human beings in his own career, so now humanity, *embodied* humanity, may likewise be raised up. That is, the effect of Jesus' ascension for humanity, in all its physicality, is life in God's presence, reflecting God's image and likeness (cf. 5.31.2). Pivotal to this argument is the non-negotiable emphasis on human embodiment, an emphasis that would come to be stated negatively in the Fifteen Anathemas of the sixth century: 'If anyone shall say that after the resurrection the body of the Lord was ethereal…: let him be anathema' (§10 [*NPNF*^{2}, XIV, p. 319]).

Luke–Acts, Divine Legitimation, and Human Embodiment
An emphasis on human embodiment such as Irenaeus has articulated may seem strange to readers of Luke's account, and more at home in the work of systematic theologians. In fact, as we have seen, recent work on Jesus' ascension in Acts by New Testament scholars has been concerned to demonstrate Luke's divine Christology, not Jesus' humanity; and affirmations that the ascended Christ challenges docetic tendencies and affirms the enduring consequences of the incarnation have come from systematic theologians. Noting that 'the Incarnation is no "thirty-three-year experiment"', Cynthia Rigby speaks for many when she concludes that 'the ascended Christ exalts us, *via* our humanity with him, to participation in the very life of the triune God'.[43] New Testament scholar Leslie Houlden has criticized just this sort of theologizing, however, referring to it as an attempt 'to slot "the Ascension"

---

42. Irenaeus, *Against Heresies* (trans. and ed. Dominic J. Unger), p. 47.
43. Cynthia L. Rigby, 'Divine Sovereignty, Human Agency, and the Ascension of Christ', *QR* 22 (2002), pp. 157, 163. Cf., e.g., Nick Needham, 'Christ Ascended for Us— Jesus' Ascended Humanity and Ours', *Evangel* 25.2 (2007), pp. 42-46; Brian K. Donne, 'The Significance of the Ascension of Jesus Christ in the New Testament', *SJT* 30 (1977), pp. 564-65 (though without reference to this motif in Luke–Acts); Joseph Haroutunian, 'The Doctrine of the Ascension: A Study of the New Testament Teaching', *Int* 10 (1956), pp. 278-79; Gerrit Scott Dawson, *Jesus Ascended: The Meaning of Christ's Continuing Incarnation* (London: T. & T. Clark, 2004).

as a topic into the systems of theology', an attempt, he claims, that does not have much to do with Luke's story.[44]

My question is not whether these theological emphases might find a foundation in Luke's account, but whether second-century reflection on the ascension might lead to our reading Luke–Acts in a new light. Of course, whatever else it does, this concern with Jesus' embodied humanity calls attention to the kinship of Luke's account with Jewish rapture stories, which typically speak to the somatic nature of the experience—as opposed to those in the Hellenistic tradition, which trace the journey of the disencumbered soul. What more can be said of reading the Lukan account of Jesus' ascension from the second-century perspective of the developing credal tradition? Do we observe emphases we might not otherwise have noticed?

Luke's account of Jesus' ascension is no stranger to an interpretation that emphasizes Jesus' elevated status, and the fact that 'he was lifted up' (passive of *epairō*) certifies that his exalted status was God's doing. In fact, images of upward and downward movement dot the landscape of Luke's narrative, so much so that we can speak of a Lukan *verticality schema*. Working only with data from Luke's Gospel, we see how honor and shame are measured in terms of verticality. For example,

- Honor is associated with the head of the table, so that guests of lower status are seated at the lowest seats and guests of higher status are told, 'Move up higher' (14.7-10; cf. 20.46).
- Attitudes of deference and dispositions of submissiveness are embodied through kneeling or sitting at one's feet—as in the cases of Simon Peter (5.8), a Gerasene man from whom demons had gone (8.35), Mary (10.39), or the one leper who had seen that he had been healed (17.15). On the Mount of Olives, Jesus knelt to pray (22.41).
- Reflecting the polarity present already in Mary's Song (cf. 1.52-53), on two different occasions Luke reports Jesus' words, 'All who lift themselves up will be brought low, and those who make themselves low will be lifted up' (14.11; 18.14).

For our purposes, another strand of evidence is even more telling:
- Heaven is up, so Jesus looks up (*anablepō*) when he blesses the loaves and fish (9.16), Jesus anticipates his ascension (*analēmpsis*, 9.51), and at the end of the Gospel Jesus is carried up (*anapherō*) into heaven (24.51). The God known as Most High (1.32, 35, 76; 6.35; 8.28) speaks from above (3.22; 9.35). In his humility, the toll collector would not even lift his eyes toward heaven (18.13).

---

44. Houlden, 'Beyond Belief', p. 179.

Contrariwise, *hadēs*, the place of the dead, is the underworld—as in Jesus' pronouncement of judgment: 'And you, Capernaum, will you be lifted up to heaven? No, you will be thrown down to Hades' (10.15, my translation).

Luke's verticality schema illustrates conceptual metaphor theory, which operates from the basic premise that semantic structure mirrors conceptual structure, as we conceive the world around us by projecting patterns from one domain of experience in order to structure another domain. The one is a source domain, the other a target domain, and studies have shown that where these two domains are active simultaneously, the two areas of the brain for each are active.[45] Borrowing a principle from the neuropsychologist Donald Hebb, known as Hebb's Rule, we know that *neurons that fire together wire together*—with the result that conceptual metaphor theory is actually grounded in the embodiment of the conceptual patterns by which we conceive the world, which we share with people across cultures, and which drive our responses to the world around us.[46] Essentially all of our abstract and theoretical concepts draw their meaning by mapping to embodied, experiential concepts hardwired in our brains. Cognitive scientist Jerome Feldman puts it like this:

> In a general way, the embodied basis for abstract meanings can be seen as inevitable. A child starts life with certain basic abilities and builds on these through experience. Everything the child learns must be based on what she or he already understands.[47]

In this case, a child observes the rise and fall of levels of piles or fluids as more of a given substance is added or some is subtracted. That part of her brain concerned with vertical orientation is activated, and is correlated with the subjective experience of changing quantities. In this way, her experience provides a physical basis for an abstract understanding of quantity. Returning to our reading of Luke's account, then, questions of cosmology aside, at a preconscious level we understand Jesus' heavenly ascension in terms of God's granting him the highest status.

---

45. E.g., Michael I. Posner and Marcus E. Raichle, *Images of Mind* (New York: Freeman, 1997), p. 115; V.S. Ramachandran, *A Brief Tour of Human Consciousness* (New York: Pi, 2004), Chapter 4; Jerome A. Feldman, *From Molecule to Metaphor: A Neural Theory of Language* (Cambridge, MA: The MIT Press, 2006); Raymond W. Gibbs, Jr, *Embodiment and Cognitive Science* (Cambridge: Cambridge University Press, 2006), pp. 158-207.

46. Cf. Ning Yu, 'Metaphor from Body and Culture', in Raymond W. Gibbs, Jr (ed.), *The Cambridge Handbook of Metaphor and Thought* (Cambridge: Cambridge University Press, 2010), p. 248.

47. Feldman, *Metaphor*, p. 199.

Whether Jesus' status is correlated in Acts with an anti-imperial challenge is another matter. One possibility for reflecting on Luke's interest in this question is raised in Acts 4, where Peter has it that Jesus' having been chosen by God as the cornerstone opens the way for this claim: 'Salvation can be found in no one else. There is no other name under heaven given among humans through which we must be saved' (v. 12, my translation). Given Jesus' abode *in heaven* and Luke's phrase 'no other name *under heaven*', would these words not counter claims about salvation having come through the emperor,[48] as well as claims regarding the heavenly assumption of past emperors upon their deaths?

What, then, of the humanity of the one who ascends? We begin with Luke's portrait of the post-resurrection existence of Jesus in Luke 24, where the evangelist demonstrates Jesus' corporeality without allowing his physicality to determine exhaustively the nature of his existence. On the one hand, Jesus' post-resurrection, bodily existence was extraordinary. He disappears and appears suddenly (24.31, 36), as though he were an angel.[49] His appearance is elusive to the two disciples on the Emmaus road (24.15-16); his gathered followers in Jerusalem 'thought they were seeing a ghost' (24.37), the disembodied residue of the dead. On the other hand, Jesus goes to great lengths to establish his physicality. He grounds the continuity of his identity ('It's really me!' [24.39]), first, in his physicality—in the constitution of flesh and density of bones: 'Touch me and see, for a ghost doesn't have flesh and bones like you see I have' (24.39). Here is no phantom, no spirit-being. Jesus presses further, requesting something to eat, then consuming broiled fish in the presence of his disciples (24.41-43), proving that he is no angel (cf. Tob. 12.15, 19). In Luke's report, Jesus' post-resurrection existence is one of transformed embodiment. And it is this embodied Jesus of whom Luke reports, 'He was lifted up' (Acts 1.9).

Two seemingly minor details within the ascension account itself are also suggestive. The first is the angels' address to Jesus' followers in Acts 1.11: 'Galileans'. Manifestly, Jesus' followers are not at home, though paradoxically they are where they should be as members of Jesus' reconstructed family (cf. Lk. 8.21)—and this calls to mind both the long journey they have undertaken from Galilee to Jerusalem (where 'Jesus was to be taken up into

---

48. See, e.g., *OGIS*, II, p. 458 (which has it that, in Augustus, Providence sent a savior); more broadly, Georg Fohrer and Werner Foester, '*sōtēr*', in *TDNT*, VII, pp. 1004-12); MM, p. 621.

49. Cf. Acts 10.30. On the connections of this material with angelophanies, see Crispin H.T. Fletcher-Louis, *Luke–Acts: Angels, Christology and Soteriology* (WUNT, 2.94; Tübingen: Mohr Siebeck, 1997), pp. 62-70. Fletcher-Louis helpfully analyzes Luke's presentation of Jesus in these scenes as both more divine than angels and more human.

heaven', Lk. 9.51; cf. Acts 13.31) and the way Luke has designated Galilee as the point of beginning of Jesus' mission (see Lk. 22.59; 23.5, 49, 55; 24.6). The second detail is the angels' reference to 'this Jesus' (Acts 1.11), which inexorably identifies the Jesus of the Galilean ministry, the Jesus of the journey to Jerusalem, the Jesus who was executed and resurrected, the Jesus with whom the disciples had spent the previous forty days after his resurrection—the Jesus of whom Luke had written in his first volume concerning everything he 'did and taught from the beginning' (1.1)—'*this* Jesus', as the same Jesus whose ascension they had witnessed and the Jesus who could come again.[50] These observations, taken together with Luke's repeated references to the disciples' having seen Jesus taken from their sight, bring us close to Irenaeus' emphases on the ascension as the culmination of Jesus' earthly, bodily career and on the essential physicality of the ascension itself. The Jesus who reigns from heaven may share in God's own identity, as some Lukan scholars have recently urged, but Luke also has it that, in his ascension, Jesus brings humanity, embodied humanity, to his heavenly place.

Conclusion

In the past half-century, New Testament scholarship on the Lukan accounts of Jesus' ascension has centered on a range of critical concerns, some historical, some literary, some intertextual, and some theological. On the whole, though, there has been a basic disconnect between the concerns and interests of Lukan scholars and the concerns and interests of those early Christians for whom Jesus' ascension was a core affirmation of faith. Returning to the Lukan narrative with interests more characteristic of second-century reflection than contemporary scholarship, however, we find emphases very much at home in Luke–Acts. This is interesting, first, because of recent complaints about the creed, that it neglects the ministry of Jesus as it moves from his virginal conception to his crucifixion under Pontius Pilate. To the contrary, we have seen that interest in Jesus' ascension is profoundly grounded in the embodied life of Jesus of Nazareth, even if this interest is registered differently when comparing Irenaeus and Luke–Acts. It is interesting, second, because we see how the second-century reception of Jesus' ascension highlights Lukan emphases, even emphases latent from the perspective of contemporary study of Luke–Acts.

---

50. Cf. Acts 2: The Jesus whom the Jerusalemites, 'with the help of wicked men... killed by nailing him to a cross' (v. 23), '*this* Jesus (*touton ton Iēsoun*), God raised up' (v. 32).

8

THE ANABAPTIST VISION OF THE CHURCH AND FAITH IN THE EPISTLE TO THE HEBREWS

Matthew C. Easter

Introduction

Over seventy years ago, Ernst Käsemann described the 'wandering people of God' in Hebrews, and applied this corporate dimension to faith itself: 'we may deny to Hebrews any "private Christianity," and describe faith as well as obedience as the true attitude of the community'.[1] However, Käsemann does not address the connection between this corporate faith and the faith through suffering that Jesus exemplifies (nor has any subsequent reader of Hebrews, for that matter). In this essay I argue that the christological and ecclesiological dimensions of faith in Hebrews are inseparable: faith entails enduring through suffering like Jesus, and we exercise this faith most clearly by remaining faithful with the people of God who are 'going to Jesus outside the camp, bearing his reproach' (13.13).[2] This essay proceeds in three broad stages. First, I address briefly the depiction of Jesus' faith in Hebrews. Second, we explore at length the way in which faith in Hebrews is a corporate reality. Finally, I bring this reading of faith in Hebrews into conversation with the vision of the church in the Anabaptist tradition. This last step will help sharpen what we find in Hebrews.

Hebrews and the Faith of Jesus

Interpreters have long noticed the theme of *imitatio Christi* in the Epistle to the Hebrews. Within the New Testament canon, the call to follow the example of Christ is perhaps no clearer than in Heb. 12.1-3, where the author enjoins us to cast off our encumbrances of sin and look to Jesus, the pioneer and perfecter of faith.

---

1. Ernst Käsemann, *The Wandering People of God* (trans. Roy A. Harrisville and Irving L. Sandberg; Eugene, OR: Wipf & Stock, 1984), p. 22.
2. Unless otherwise noted, all translations are mine.

The faith Jesus models in Hebrews is consistently one of endurance through suffering to death, in hope of eschatological life to follow. In 12.2, the author depicts Jesus as one who 'endured the cross' (*hupemeinen stauron*). The language of Jesus' 'enduring the cross' is unique. This is the only place in the New Testament where Jesus' crucifixion is depicted in such an active manner. In Hebrews, Jesus is not passively crucified, but he actively endures the cross. Speaking of Jesus' crucifixion in this manner would be tantamount to someone saying, 'The death row inmate *endured* the lethal injection needle'. However, we do not typically speak this way. Instead, we depict the inmate in passive terms, like: 'The death row inmate *was executed by* lethal injection'. The author of Hebrews, by describing the execution of Jesus as his 'enduring the cross', gives Jesus the active role of endurance rather than the passive role of being crucified.[3]

The author of Hebrews expects us to endure in the same way as Jesus. In 12.1, the author describes our 'running with endurance' (*di' hupomonēs trechōmen*) in similar terms to Jesus' endurance of the cross (*hupemeinen stauron*). This connection is strengthened by the author's exhortation that the runners 'look to Jesus'. By looking to Jesus, we see the one who has already completed the race, has received his reward, and is now waiting at the finish line for those who would join him. By depicting us as runners in the same race as Jesus, the author of Hebrews imagines us as running a race constituted by enduring suffering in the face of death.

Like Jesus, the race we are to endure is a race of persecution that may in fact involve death. The author depicts his hearers as a group of people who have either actually experienced persecution or who at least perceive themselves to be experiencing persecution.[4] The author recalls their former days,

---

3. See also Craig R. Koester, *Hebrews* (AB, 36; New York: Doubleday, 2001), p. 536.

4. On perceived persecution, see William L. Lane: 'And while they may not have been under actual persecution at the time, the perception of persecution can be just as shaking to a community as persecution itself' ('Living a Life of Faith in the Face of Death: The Witness of Hebrews', in Richard N. Longenecker [ed.], *Life in the Face of Death: The Resurrection Message of the New Testament* [Grand Rapids: Eerdmans, 1998], p. 248). That the hearers of Hebrews were a group of people who endured persecution is widely acknowledged in the secondary literature. See, e.g., P.C.B. Andriessen, 'La communauté des "Hébreux": Etait-elle tombée dans le relâchement?', *NRTh* 96 (1974), pp. 1054-66; Herbert Braun, *An die Hebräer* (HNT, 14; Tübingen: Mohr Siebeck, 1984), pp. 408-409; John Dunnill, *Covenant and Sacrifice in the Letter to the Hebrews* (SNTSMS, 75; Cambridge: Cambridge University Press, 1992), p. 37; Patrick Gray, *Godly Fear: The Epistle to the Hebrews and Greco-Roman Critiques of Superstition* (AcBib, 16; Atlanta: SBL, 2003), pp. 155-86; Elisabeth Schüssler Fiorenza, 'Der Anführer und Vollender unseres Glaubens: Zum theologischen Verständnis des Hebräerbriefes', in J. Schreiner (ed.), *Gestalt und Anspruch des Neuen Testaments* (Würzburg: Echter Verlag, 1969), pp. 262-81; Hans-Josef Klauck, 'Moving in and Moving Out: Ethics and

when after 'being enlightened' they 'endured a great conflict of sufferings, partly by being made a public spectacle through reproaches and tribulations, and partly by becoming sharers with those so treated'. The author praises them for previously 'showing sympathy to the prisoners and accepting joyfully the seizure of their property' (10.32-34). He encourages them to 'remember those in prison, as though in prison with them, and those who are mistreated, since you yourselves also are in the body' (13.3). Those in prison could very well be members of the community or perhaps even the author himself.[5] In 13.7, the author encourages the hearers to remember their former leaders and to consider the outcome of their conduct (*tēn ekbasin tēs anastrophēs*) and imitate their faith. This 'outcome' (*ekbasis*) may well have been their deaths.[6] Similarly, immediately following the depiction of Jesus' endurance of suffering, the author in 12.4 ominously says that we have not *yet* resisted to the point of bloodshed in our struggle against sin. The 'sin' against which we struggle is likely a periphrasis for the 'sinners' from whom Jesus experienced hostility (12.3).[7] 'Not yet' (*oupō*) appears emphatically as the first word in the sentence. In view of the other references to the hearers'

Ethos in Hebrews', in Jan G. van der Watt (ed.), *Identity, Ethics, and Ethos in the New Testament* (BZNW, 141; Berlin: W. de Gruyter, 2006), p. 436; Koester, *Hebrews*, pp. 67-71; 'Conversion, Persecution, and Malaise: Life in the Community for Which Hebrews Was Written', *HvTSt* 61 (2005), pp. 231-51; William L. Lane, *Hebrews 1–8* (WBC, 47A; Nashville: Thomas Nelson, 1991), pp. lvii, c; Harold M. Parker, 'Domitian and the Epistle to the Hebrews', *Iliff Review* 36 (1979), pp. 38-41; Iutisone Salevao, *Legitimation in the Letter to the Hebrews: The Construction and Maintenance of a Symbolic Universe* (JSNTSup, 219; London: Sheffield Academic Press, 2002), pp. 133-40; C. Adrian Thomas, *A Case for Mixed-Audience with Reference to the Warning Passages in the Book of Hebrews* (New York: Peter Lang, 2008), pp. 118-20; Ian G. Wallis, *The Faith of Jesus Christ in Early Christian Traditions* (SNTSMS, 84; Cambridge: Cambridge University Press, 1995), p. 152; and Norman H. Young, 'Suffering: A Key to the Epistle to the Hebrews,' *ABR* 51 (2003), pp. 47-59.

5. We cannot be sure on this point, but the author may have been imprisoned. At the end of the book, he bemoans his delay to meet with them personally, and asks for their prayers. He claims, 'We are sure that we have a clear conscience, desiring to act honorably in all things' (13.18), and believes that his ability to return to them is somehow contingent on their diligent prayers (13.19). Furthermore, both the author and the hearers know a common Timothy, 'our brother', who has been 'released (*apoluō*)' perhaps from prison, and the author hopes to visit them with this Timothy (13.23).

6. See also Harold W. Attridge, *The Epistle to the Hebrews* (Hermeneia; Philadelphia: Fortress Press, 1989), p. 392; Erich Grässer, 'Die Gemeindevorsteher im Hebräerbrief', in Gerhard Müller and Henning Schröer (eds.), *Vom Amt des Laien in Kirche und Theologie* (Festschrift Gerhard Krause; Berlin: W. de Gruyter, 1982), p. 75; Luke Timothy Johnson, *Hebrews: A Commentary* (NTL; Louisville, KY: Westminster/John Knox Press, 2006), pp. 345-46; Koester, *Hebrews*, p. 567.

7. Andriessen, 'La communauté,' p. 1062; Braun, *Hebräer*, p. 409; Lane, 'Living a Life of Faith', pp. 250-51.

persecution elsewhere in Hebrews, the author in 12.4 is likely anticipating bloody persecution for the community. The race which we must run with endurance, therefore, is precisely the race of endurance unto death that Jesus already ran.

Nevertheless, the author of Hebrews is clear that the death of Jesus is not the end of the story: he endured 'for the joy set before him' (*anti tēs prokeimenēs autō*), and he realized this joy by being seated at the right hand of God's throne after death (12.2). Jesus' experience of postmortem blessing should motivate us who stand at the brink of death, as we 'consider him who endured from sinners such hostility against themselves,[8] and so not grow weary or fainthearted' (12.3). In summary, Jesus' faith in 12.1-3 is one of enduring suffering in the face of death, in hope of eschatological life to follow.

We see this same pattern in 2.13. Here, the author puts Isa. 8.17 on the lips of Jesus directed to God: 'I will put my trust in him'.[9] Jesus' confession of trust in God comes within the discussion of his camaraderie with humanity in Hebrews 2.[10] Jesus, who is called the pioneer and perfecter of

---

8. Or, 'against himself'. The manuscript evidence favors the plural reading, attested as early as $\mathfrak{p}^{13}$ and $\mathfrak{p}^{46}$, in the first hand of D, and in the first and second hands of ℵ. Further, the plural is also the more difficult reading. Probably for this reason translations typically opt for the singular (ESV, NRSV, NASB, NET, RSV, KJV) or leave it out altogether (NIV, NJB). For commentators preferring the singular translation, see Attridge, *Hebrews*, pp. 353-54 n. 10; F.F. Bruce, *The Epistle to the Hebrews* (NICNT; Grand Rapids: Eerdmans, rev. edn, 1990), pp. 340-41; David deSilva, *Perseverance in Gratitude: A Socio-Rhetorical Commentary on the Epistle 'to the Hebrews'* (Grand Rapids: Eerdmans, 2000), p. 426 n. 111; Johnson, *Hebrews*, p. 313; and Koester, *Hebrews*, p. 525. See also Bruce M. Metzger, *A Textual Commentary on the Greek New Testament* (Stuttgart: Deutsche Bibelgesellschaft, 2nd edn, 2002), pp. 604-605, who notes that the majority of the UBS committee preferred the singular reading, despite the external evidence strongly favoring the plural. He attributes this decision to 'the difficulty of making sense of the plural' (p. 605). For commentators preferring the plural, see Paul Ellingworth, *The Epistle to the Hebrews* (NIGTC; Grand Rapids: Eerdmans, 1993), pp. 643-44; William L. Lane, *Hebrews 9–13* (WBC, 47B; Dallas, TX: Word Books, 1991), pp. 397, 400 n. u, 416. Given the stronger manuscript evidence for the plural reading and the difficulty of 'against themselves' (and thus the reading more likely to be altered), the plural reading is to be preferred. As such, with 'biting irony' the author of Hebrews depicts those showing hostility to Jesus as in fact harming themselves (Lane, *Hebrews 9–13*, p. 416).

9. This phrase appears in 2 Sam. 22.3; Isa. 8.17; 12.2. Given that the latter half of Heb. 2.13 ('behold, I and the children God has given me') is from Isa. 8.18, the author is most likely quoting Isa. 8.17 with *egō esomai pepoithōs ep' autō*. See also Attridge, *Hebrews*, p. 90.

10. DeSilva suggests that Jesus here confesses trust not in God, but in human beings, his brothers and sisters: 'this verse is now being offered as proof that Christ is not ashamed to associate himself closely with those whom he receives into his protection (2.11). I would suggest, therefore, that the author would have the believer see himself or

faith in 12.2, is here put forward as the Son of God, the 'pioneer of salvation' through whom God is bringing many sons and daughters to glory (2.10). Jesus is a brother with God's children (2.11-17), who directs his trust toward God (2.13). Jesus, who shared in blood and flesh with his human siblings (2.14), exhibits the trust that all humans should embody.[11]

Just as Jesus' faith in 12.2 is one of suffering, so also Jesus' confession of trust in 2.13 is one of trust through suffering. The context in Hebrews 2 is inundated with references to suffering. Jesus, who for a short time was made lower than the angels, received the crown of glory and honor on account of his *suffering of death*, whereby he *tasted death* for everyone (2.9). God made Jesus perfect through *sufferings* (2.10). Jesus became like his human siblings in every way so that *'through death* he might destroy the one who has the power of death' (2.14), thereby freeing humanity from their slavery to the fear of death (2.15). Jesus made atonement for the sins of the people (2.17), and on account of his *testing in suffering*, he can offer help to those being tested (2.18). Jesus' trust in 2.13, therefore, is a trust in the midst of suffering.[12]

There is a hint of hope associated with Jesus' confession of trust amid suffering. In 2.12, the author puts the words of Ps. 21.23 LXX on the lips of Jesus: 'I will announce your name among my brothers and sisters; in the midst of the congregation I will praise you'. Psalm 21 LXX (22 MT) is a plea for help in a time of suffering.[13] Jesus' cry of dereliction in Mt. 27.46 and Mk 15.34 alludes to Ps. 21.2: 'My God, my God, why have you forsaken me?'[14] The psalmist laments his feelings of abandonment (vv. 2-3) and his ill treatment from others (vv. 7-19). In images repeated in the passion traditions

---

herself as the object of Jesus' declared trust' (*Perseverance in Gratitude*, p. 116). This suggestion is unlikely. In 2.13, Jesus confesses trust in the singular 'him' (*ep' autō*). Throughout the context in 2.10-18, the author speaks of human beings in the plural (*pollous huious* in 2.10; *hoi hagiazomenoi* and *adelphous* in 2.11; *adelphois* in 2.12; *paidia* in 2.14; *toutous* in 2.15; *adelphois* in 2.17; and *tois peirazomenois* in 2.18). God is the only singular figure in the context (*autō* in 2.10; *ho...hagiazōn* in 2.11; and *se* in 2.12). The author uses the singular with reference to humans only in 2.16, where they are described as *spermatos Abraam*. Nevertheless, this likely carries a plural sense, as the NRSV translates it: 'descendants of Abraham'. Therefore, when Jesus confesses trust *ep autō* in 2.13, this refers to the singular figure in the context: God.

11. See also Attridge, *Hebrews*, p. 91; Johnson, *Hebrews*, p. 99; Koester, *Hebrews*, p. 239; Todd Still, 'Christos as Pistos: The Faith(fulness) of Jesus in the Epistle to the Hebrews', *CBQ* 69 (2007), p. 748.

12. Also noted in Lane, 'Living a Life of Faith', p. 263.

13. So John Goldingay on Ps. 22 [MT]: 'The Psalter presents it as a model for the prayer of ordinary Israelites or Christians when they experience affliction' (*Psalms. I. Psalms 1–41* [BCOTWP; Grand Rapids: Baker Academic, 2006], p. 340).

14. *ho theos mou ho theos mou, eis ti enkatelipes me* (Mk 15.34); *ho theos ho theos mou prosches moi hina ti enkatelipes me* (Ps. 21.2 LXX).

in the Gospels, the psalmist is poured out like water (Ps. 21.15 LXX; Jn 19.34), experiences extreme thirst (Ps. 21.16 LXX; Jn 19.28), and others cast lots for his clothing (Ps. 21.19 LXX; Mt. 27.35; Mk 15.24; Lk. 23.34; Jn 19.24). In Ps. 21.21-22 LXX (the verses immediately prior to the one quoted in Hebrews), the psalmist begs God: 'Rescue my soul from the sword, and from a dog's claw my only life! Save me from a lion's mouth, and my lowliness from the horns of unicorns' (NETS). The tone of Ps. 21 LXX shifts at v. 23, the verse quoted in Hebrews. With the promise to 'tell of your name to my kindred' is a shift in the psalm, as the psalmist moves from lament and pleas for help to jubilant confidence. The psalmist exhorts everyone to praise the Lord because he has heard the petition of the poor (vv. 24-27). As Lane notes, this latter half of the psalm 'is appropriate to an experience of vindication and exaltation after suffering and affliction'.[15] By putting these words on the lips of Jesus, the author of Hebrews depicts Jesus as one who has endured suffering, and now rejoices in vindication.[16]

Therefore, Jesus' confession of trust in 2.13 is a faith in the face of suffering that realizes reward following this suffering. Given that he makes this confession as a Son among God's children, Jesus exemplifies the type of faith that all sons and daughters of God are called to exercise: trusting God, enduring suffering, hoping for vindication.[17]

But how do we participate in this suffering-faith of Jesus? The answer for Hebrews, I propose, is ecclesiological.

Hebrews and Ecclesiological Faith

Faith for Hebrews is corporate. To be sure, drawing too sharp a distinction between individual and corporate faith can lead to false dichotomies. Groups are composed of individuals; Greco-Roman and Jewish society understood the category of 'individual',[18] and, as we will see, the author of Hebrews

---

15. Lane, *Hebrews 1–8*, p. 59.
16. See also George H. Guthrie, 'Hebrews', in G.K. Beale and D.A. Carson (eds.), *Commentary on the New Testament Use of the Old Testament* (Grand Rapids: Baker Academic, 2007), p. 949.
17. For more on Jesus' experience of eschatological life and our hope of the same, see Matthew C. Easter, '"Let Us Go to Him": The Story of Faith and the Faithfulness of Jesus in Hebrews' (PhD thesis, University of Otago, 2011), pp. 192-220.
18. Gary W. Burnett, *Paul and the Salvation of the Individual* (BIS, 57; Leiden: Brill, 2001), pp. 23-87. Within the New Testament, the Gospel of John is probably the best representative of individual faith. C.F.D. Moule explains: 'This is the Gospel, par excellence, of the approach of the single soul to God: this is the part of Scripture to which one turns first when trying to direct an enquirer to his own, personal appropriation of salvation' ('The Individualism of the Fourth Gospel', *NovT* 5 [1962], p. 185; see also John F. O'Grady, 'Individualism and Johannine Ecclesiology', *BTB* 5 [1975], pp. 227-61).

shows a definite concern for the wellbeing of individuals within the group.[19] I am not, therefore, suggesting that faith in Hebrews lacks any individual component. Rather, I am arguing that an individual's faith is demonstrated most clearly by being faithful as part of the corporate travelling people of God. In other words, the author insists that faith is impossible apart from the community, and faith is demonstrated most clearly by remaining with the community. To fall away from the community is to fall away from faith.

This corporate construal of faith aligns with the group-oriented mindset in the ancient world, where people typically operated with a strong perception of the group. Generally speaking, individuals in strong group societies understand themselves as embedded in a group, and their identity is defined in great part by the group.[20]

To demonstrate the ecclesiological dimension of faith in Hebrews, I will first establish the corporate nature of thought in Hebrews, then show how the individual fits within this corporate exhortation, and finally show how corporate faith is associated with the suffering of Christ. In doing so, we will see that faith for Hebrews cannot be divorced from the community: an individual demonstrates faith most clearly by enduring Christ's suffering with the people of God.

The 'Church' in Hebrews
Hebrews is written to a specific group of people who meet together (10.25).[21] The author knows his audience,[22] and he often writes with first-person plural

---

19. It is worth noting that someone can recognize the unique identity of an 'individual' without being 'individualistic', a term which often connotes a system whereby the 'individual person is above the group and is free to do what he or she feels right and necessary, normally using other persons, objects in the environment, and groups of people in the society to facilitate individually oriented personal goals and objectives' (Bruce J. Malina, *Christian Origins and Cultural Anthropology: Practical Models for Biblical Interpretation* [Atlanta: John Knox Press, 1986], p. 19).

20. See Malina, *Christian Origins*, pp. 19-20. See also Malina, 'The Individual and the Community-Personality in the Social World of Early Christianity', *BTB* 9 (1979), pp. 126-38; Matthew J. Marohl, *Faithfulness and the Purpose of Hebrews: A Social Identity Approach* (PTMS; Eugene, OR: Pickwick, 2008), pp. 81-97; Jerome H. Neyrey, 'Dyadism', in John J. Pilch and Bruce J. Malina (eds.), *Biblical Social Values and their Meanings: A Handbook* (Peabody, MA: Hendrickson, 1993), p. 51; Jerome H. Neyrey, 'Group Orientation', in Pilch and Malina (eds.), *Biblical Social Values*, p. 88.

21. On the hearers of Hebrews as a distinct social group, see Marohl, *Faithfulness*, pp. 101-105.

22. As Norman R. Petersen highlights, every letter presupposes a relationship between the sender and the receiver (*Rediscovering Paul: Philemon and the Sociology of Paul's Narrative World* [Philadelphia: Fortress Press, 1985], pp. 63-64). While Hebrews reads like a sermon, it appears to have been sent from a distance as a letter (13.22-25).

pronouns.[23] Although the author does not name individual members, he is aware of leaders within their community (13.7, 17, 24). He hopes to be reunited with them (13.19) and to visit them with their common acquaintance, Timothy (13.23). He knows of their previous experiences, of how they endured persecution and were compassionate toward those in prison (10.32-34). Given that as far as we know not all Christ-followers experienced the plundering of property, the fact that the hearers of Hebrews did experience such persecution indicates their membership in a distinct group.[24]

Therefore, while admittedly 'Hebrews does not have a developed theology of the church',[25] the author is clearly addressing people who understand themselves as a group.[26] This is further evidenced by the nature of his exhortations.

Corporate Exhortation
The author describes Hebrews as 'a word of exhortation' (13.22), and his exhortations are consistently directed to a group. In fact, the author exhorts *individuals* only in 6.11-12: 'And we desire *each of you* (*hekaston humōn*) to show the same earnestness....' Nevertheless, it is worth noting that this exhortation to individuals is still corporate in effect, as the author expects *every* member of the community to heed his words and for the whole community not to be sluggish (6.12). Beyond this possible exception, the rest of the exhortations in Hebrews are directed specifically to the group with plural verbs (usually first-person plural subjunctive or second-person plural imperative).

Exhortations in Hebrews	
Exhortation to Forward Movement[27]	
4.11	Let us strive (*spoudasōmen*) to enter the rest
6.1	Let us press on (*pherōmetha*) to maturity
12.12	Strengthen (*anorthōsate*) weakened hands and knees
12.13	Make (*poiete*) straight paths for your feet

23. Heb. 1.2; 2.1, 3; 3.1, 6; 4.13, 15; 5.11; 6.20; 7.14, 26; 9.14, 24; 10.15, 20, 26, 39; 11.40; 12.1, 9, 25, 29; 13.6, 20, 21, 23. Noted also by Marohl, *Faithfulness*, pp. 101, 105.
24. Marohl, *Faithfulness*, p. 105.
25. Barnabas Lindars, *The Theology of the Letter to the Hebrews* (Cambridge: Cambridge University Press, 1991), p. 127.
26. See also Thomas Söding: 'Der Hebräerbrief entwickelt keine eigentliche Lehre von der Kirche. Aber er ist ekklesiologisch äußerst relevant' ('Gemeinde auf dem Weg: Christsein nach dem Hebräerbrief', *BK* 48 [1991], p. 187).
27. None of these subcategories are mutually exclusive, but I divide them as such to highlight the key themes.

	Exhortation to Endurance
3.6	Let us hold fast (*kataschōmen*) boldness and boasting of hope
3.14	Let us hold fast (*kataschōmen*) the beginning of the reality
4.14	Let us hold fast (*kratōmen*) the confession
10.23	Let us hold fast (*katechōmen*) the confession of hope
10.35	Do not throw away (*apobalēte*) your boldness
12.1	Let us run (*trechōmen*) with endurance
12.7	Endure (*hupomenete*) [suffering] as discipline[28]
	Exhortation to Corporate Attendance and Accountability
3.12	Watch out (*blepete*) lest there be in anyone among you an evil unbelieving heart
3.13	Exhort (*parakaleite*) one another
4.1	Let us fear (*phobēthōmen*) lest any of you fail to reach God's rest
10.24	Let us consider (*katanoōmen*) how to provoke one another to love and good works
12.14-15	Pursue (*diōkete*) peace with everyone and holiness…seeing to it (*episkopountes*) that no one fails to obtain the grace of God
13.2	Do not neglect (*epilanthanesthe*) hospitality
13.16	Do not neglect (*epilanthanesthe*) doing good and sharing
	Exhortation to Attend to a Theological Truth or God's Voice
2.1	We must pay closer attention (*prosechein*) lest we drift away (*pararuōmen*)
12.25	See that (*blepete*) you do not refuse (*paraitēsēsthe*) the one who is speaking
13.9	Do not be carried away (*parapheresthe*) by diverse and strange teachings
	Exhortation to Look to Jesus or Follow Jesus
3.1	Consider (*katanoēsate*) Jesus
12.1-2	Let us run (*trechōmen*)…looking to (*aphorōntes*) Jesus
12.3	Consider (*analogisasthe*) the one who endured hostility
13.13	Let us go (*exerchōmetha*) to him outside the camp
	Exhortation to Draw Near to God in Worship
4.16	Let us draw near (*proserchōmetha*) to the throne of grace with confidence so that we might receive (*labōmen*) mercy and find (*heurōmen*) grace
10.22	Let us draw near (*proserchōmetha*) with a true heart
12.28	Let us show gratitude (*echōmen charin*) and offer worship (*latreuōmen*) to God
13.15	Let us offer (*anapherōmen*) a sacrifice of praise continually
	Exhortation to Obey or Imitate Local Leaders
13.7	Remember (*mnēmoneuete*) your leaders…considering (*anatheōrountes*) the outcome of their way of life, imitate (*mimeisthe*) their faith
13.17	Obey (*peithesthe*) your leaders and submit (*hupeikete*) to them

28. Or, if *hupomenete* is second person plural indicative: 'you endure (*hupomenete*) [suffering] as discipline'.

As the table demonstrates, with the possible exception of 6.11-12 (as I have noted), the author of Hebrews never exhorts an individual, but only the group.

Corporate Concern for the Individual

Nevertheless, while the author of Hebrews exhorts communities, he also shows a definite concern for the individual. The individual must stay in step with the travelling people of God. The maintenance of this continued participation, however, is the group's responsibility.

The hearers of Hebrews are responsible for one another. The author encourages his hearers to care for one another physically (13.2-3) and spiritually. He acknowledges the presence of leaders in the community (13.7, 17, 24), but the call in Hebrews is nevertheless directed to the entire group.[29] The author values their intercessory prayer (13.18).[30] Each member of the community is a kind of priest, as the author calls on everyone to 'offer up continually a sacrifice of praise to God' by acknowledging God's name, doing good, and sharing possessions (13.15-16).[31] The author entrusts the

29. See also Markus Bockmuehl, 'The Church in Hebrews', in Markus Bockmuehl and Michael B. Thompson (eds.), *A Vision for the Church* (Festschrift J.P.M. Sweet; Edinburgh: T. & T. Clark, 1997), p. 138.

30. Christopher D. Marshall, 'One for All and All for One: The High Priesthood of Christ, the Church, and the Priesthood of Believers in Hebrews', *Journal of the Christian Brethren Research Fellowship* 129 (1992), p. 9.

31. As Víctor M. Fernández explains, the author of Hebrews depicts the Christian life in priestly terms: 'la novedad de la vida cristiana está descrita como una capacidad sacerdotal: Podemos entrar en el santuario (10,19; 6,19; 9,8), tenemos un altar (13,10), salimos fuera del campamento (como el sumo sacerdote: 13,13 = Lv 16,27; 4,12), ofrecemos un culto agradable a Dios (12,28; 9,14), que es un verdadero *sacrificio* (13,15-16)' ('the novelty of the Christian life is described as a priestly capacity: We enter the sanctuary [10.19; 6.19; 9.8], we have an altar [13.10], we went outside the camp [like the high priest: 13.13 = Lev 16.27; 4.12], offer worship acceptable to God [12.28; 9.14], which is a true *sacrifice* [13.15-16]') ('La vida sacerdotal de los cristianos según la carta a los Hebreos', *RevistB* 52 [1990], p. 146 [italics original]). On the priesthood of the hearers of Hebrews, see also John M. Scholer, who understands the hearers as members of a 'proleptic priesthood' who 'are already enjoying access to God and offering sacrifices of praise, worship, and thanksgiving since the end-time days are here (e.g. 1.2; 9.26), and all the while they are anticipating the eschatological future when full and direct access will be enjoyed' (*Proleptic Priests: Priesthood in the Epistle to the Hebrews* [JSNTSup, 49; Sheffield: Sheffield Academic Press, 1991], p. 205). See also Peter J. Leithart, who argues that baptism in 10.22 is a rite of priestly ordination ('Womb of the World: Baptism and the Priesthood of the New Covenant in Hebrews 10.19-22', *JSNT* 78 [2000], pp. 49-65). Still, as Fernández notes, we owe our priesthood to Jesus' high priestly sacrifice: 'nuestra acción sacerdotal es totalmente dependiente del Sacerdocio de Cristo' ('our priestly action is totally dependent on the Priesthood of Christ') ('La vida sacerdotal,' pp. 146-52 [p. 146]).

task of overseeing (*episkopountes*) to everyone: 'See to it (*episkopountes*) that no one comes short of the grace of God' (12.15a).³² The wellbeing of individuals within the group has a definite impact on the community, as 'a root of bitterness' can 'defile many' (12.15b).³³

The 'church' in Hebrews, therefore, is a group of people who must care for one another. The wellbeing of individuals within the group affects the group, and so the members of the group must look out for one another.³⁴ This corporate dimension of faith becomes clearer upon further investigation into how the author expects the individual to relate to the group.

Corporate Faith

The author of Hebrews insists that the whole community move forward in faith, and this is most evident in his image of the church as a travelling people of God. In 3.7–4.11, the author recalls the story of the wilderness generation at Kadesh. In this story (which appears in Num. 13–14), the Israelites were situated at the brink of the Promised Land, but did not trust that God would deliver the land to them, and so in fear they refused to enter 'God's rest'. Two of the twelve leaders³⁵ wished to enter the land, but their voices were not sufficient—the whole community disobeyed God by refusing to trust God and so enter.

The author of Hebrews recalls this story of corporate disobedience in 4.1-2, where he urges the community to be united in faith instead of following the negative example of the wilderness generation: 'Let us fear, therefore, while the promise of entering God's rest still stands, lest any of you (*tis ex humōn*) might be deemed (*dokē*)³⁶ to have failed to reach it. For good news came to us (*esmen euēngelismenoi*) just as to them, but the message they heard did not profit them, since *they were not united in faith* (*mē sunkekerasmenous tē pistei*) with those who listened.'³⁷ Here faith is clearly a corporate

---

32. Bockmuehl, 'Church in Hebrews', p. 138.
33. See Lane, *Hebrews 9–13*, p. 454.
34. Therefore, Verlyn D. Verbrugge overstates his case when he suggests that 'the writer [of Hebrews] is not so much interested in each separate individual as he is in the congregation as a whole' ('Towards a New Interpretation of Hebrews 6:4-6', *CTJ* 15.1 [1980], p. 67).
35. *Archēgoi* in Numbers; cf. Jesus in Heb. 2.10 and 12.2 as *archēgos*.
36. On this translation of *dokē*, see Attridge, *Hebrews*, p. 124.
37. The understanding of this verse is compounded by the textual variant in 4.2, where the plural accusative *sunkekerasmenous* also appears as the singular nominative *sunkekerasmenos*. If the singular nominative *sunkekerasmenos* is followed, then the subject of the participle would shift from the plural group ('they') to a singular 'it' (most likely the 'message they heard; *ho logos tēs akoēs*'). The resulting translation, then, would be: 'but the message they heard did not profit them, since *it was not united in faith* in those who heard' (see RSV, NASB, NIV). However, the manuscript evidence strongly

reality. God's message to enter God's rest did not profit the wilderness generation because they failed to *unite in faith* and so enter the land.[38]

This image harkens back to 3.12-13, where the author urges the community to watch out for one another: 'Watch out, brothers and sisters, lest there be in anyone among you (*estai en tini humōn*) an evil unbelieving heart that falls away from the living God. But exhort one another every day, as long as it is called "today", so that no one among you (*tis ex humōn*)[39] may be hardened by the deceitfulness of sin.' The author speaks similarly in 4.11, where the community's striving helps keep the individual from failing to enter God's rest: 'Let us therefore strive to enter that rest, *so that* (*hina*) no one may fall by the same kind of disobedience.' The author shows a definite concern that individuals continually move forward with the group, because it is in remaining with the group that an individual remains faithful; and it is by being united in faith that the group can realize the eschatological hope.[40]

Human faith, therefore, is ecclesiological. A person cannot be faithful without being part of the travelling people of God.

'Getting in' and 'Getting out'?

The author of Hebrews gives no specific indication of how a person can 'get in' to the Christian movement. He may have explained his understanding of how one 'gets in' at another time, but our present text does not address this

---

supports the plural accusative *sunkekerasmenous*, attested in $\mathfrak{p}^{13vid}$, $\mathfrak{p}^{46}$, Codex Vaticanus, and a number of other uncial and minuscule manuscripts. The nominative singular *sunkekerasmenos* appears in Codex Sinaiticus, but in no other uncial or minuscule manuscripts. Therefore, the verse is rightly translated 'since they were not united in faith' (see NRSV, ESV, NJB). See also Metzger, *Textual Commentary*, p. 595.

38. Contra Attridge: 'The author is not saying that the ancient Israelites were not united to the faithful remnant, Caleb and Joshua, who heard the message. Rather, he says that they were not united to "us" who do, he hopes, listen to the message' (*Hebrews*, pp. 125-26). However, the author does not say that 'we' (in the present) have listened to the message, but that the good news came to 'us' just as to 'them'. The ones who heard the message appear with the aorist participle *tois akousasin*. The author never says that 'we' are *tois akousasin*. The clear context of the Kadesh narrative suggests that *tois akousasin* are in fact the people in the wilderness generation who did not unite in faith with Joshua and Caleb, the faithful *archēgoi* in the story

39. For *tis ex humōn* as 'one among you', see Lane, *Hebrews 1–8*, p. 86.

40. See also Grant R. Osborne: 'In Hebrews, in fact, there are two antidotes to apostasy: the vertical side, the confession of our hope before God; and the horizontal side, the involvement of the community in the life of the individual believer' ('A Classical Arminian View', in Herbert W. Bateman IV [ed.], *Four Views on the Warning Passages in Hebrews* [Grand Rapids: Kregel, 2007], p. 99). See also Koester: 'Deteriorating community life (10:25) increased the threat of apostasy, because it is through community members speaking the word to each other—as the author is doing in written form—that the community's faith is maintained' (*Hebrews*, p. 265).

question directly.⁴¹ Therefore, insofar as we can answer this question of how one 'gets in', the answer must be derived from our understanding of how the author of Hebrews wishes for us to exercise faith *after* 'getting in'.

On the basis of the account of faith I have developed, it appears that a person first 'gets in' by joining with the community of faith and with the community enduring suffering like Christ. Therefore, 'getting in' (or 'conversion') is contingent upon a person's identification with the travelling people of God and subsequently moving forward with this community of faith. Put another way, I suspect that if a person asked the author of Hebrews, 'what must I do to inherit eternal life' (Mt. 19.16; Mk 10.17; Lk. 18.18), he would likely respond, 'do not neglect to meet together; let us go to Jesus outside the camp and bear his reproach, for here we have no lasting city, but we seek the city that is to come' (Heb. 10.25; 13.13-14). A person '*gets in*' by joining the group of people who are '*going out* to Jesus'.

This group-oriented account of 'getting in' aligns with sociologists' findings with respect to religious conversion.⁴² John Lofland and Rodney Stark

---

41. He refers to 'the elementary teaching of Christ', and names a number of foundational concepts: repentance from dead works, faith toward God, instructions about washings, the laying on of hands, the resurrection of the dead, and eternal judgment (6.1-2). The author never suggests, however, that assent to these teachings or participation in these practices is what secures a person's place in the Christian movement. After this, the author of Hebrews describes a number of marks of a Christian: having been enlightened, having tasted the heavenly gift, having shared in the Holy Spirit, and having tasted of the goodness of the word of God and the powers of the age to come (6.4-5). Whether these descriptors refer to a full Christian or one who has only made a profession is debated in some circles. For a 'false profession' reading, see Wayne A. Grudem, 'Perseverance of the Saints: A Case Study from Hebrews 6:4-6 and the Other Warning Passages in Hebrews', in Thomas R. Schreiner and Bruce A. Ware (eds.), *Still Sovereign: Contemporary Perspectives on Election, Foreknowledge, and Grace* (Grand Rapids: Baker Academic, 2000), pp. 133-82; Dave Mathewson, 'Reading Heb. 6:4-6 in Light of the Old Testament', *WTJ* 61 (1999), pp. 209-25; Roger R. Nicole, 'Some Comments on Hebrews 6:4-6 and the Doctrine of the Perseverance of God with the Saints', in Gerald F. Hawthorne (ed.), *Current Issues in Biblical and Patristic Interpretation* (Festschrift Merrill C. Tenney; Grand Rapids: Eerdmans, 1975), pp. 355-64; and Thomas, *Mixed-Audience*, pp. 260-65. The vast majority of interpreters, however, acknowledge that the type of person described in Heb. 6.4-6 is Christian. For a strong argument for this reading, see Scot McKnight, 'The Warning Passages of Hebrews: A Formal Analysis and Theological Conclusions', *TJ* 13 (1992), pp. 43-55. Nevertheless, the author never suggests *how* a person is first enlightened, first shares in the Holy Spirit, or first tastes the powers of the age to come.

42. I am not suggesting that the sociological discoveries arising out of studies in twentieth- and twenty-first century Western contexts give meaning to how the author of Hebrews understood conversion. Instead, I am suggesting that these later sociological studies have demonstrated that such a group-oriented conversion is a conceivable possibility.

observed converts to the 'Moonie' religious group and noted that those people who did not identify with the group were the ones who did not convert.[43] This conclusion was reaffirmed later by other researchers with respect to adolescent conversion.[44] A person's association with the group is the determining factor in conversion, as Stark later summarizes:

> Although several other factors are also involved in the conversion process, the central sociological proposition about conversion is this: *Conversion to new, deviant religious groups occurs when, other things being equal, people have or develop stronger attachments to members of the group than they have to nonmembers.*[45]

It is conceivable, therefore, that the author of Hebrews expects us to 'get in' by joining with the people of God.

---

43. They explain: 'thus, verbal conversion and even a resolution to reorganize one's life for the D.P. [Divine Precepts] is not automatically translated into total conversion. One must be intensively exposed to the group supporting these new standards of conduct.... Persons who accepted the truth of the doctrine, but lacked intensive interaction with the core group, remained partisan spectators, who played no active part in the battle to usher in God's kingdom' (John Lofland and Rodney Stark, 'Becoming a World-Saver: A Theory of Conversion to a Deviant Perspective', in Charles Y. Glock [ed.], *Religion in Sociological Perspective: Essays in the Empirical Study of Religion* [Belmont, CA: Wadsworth, 1973], p. 47 [reprint of an article with the same name published in *American Sociological Review* 30 (1965)]). For an example of an interpreter within New Testament studies following Lofland and Stark's conclusions, see Douglas A. Campbell, *The Deliverance of God: An Apocalyptic Rereading of Justification in Paul* (Grand Rapids: Eerdmans, 2009), pp. 128-36; see also Alan F. Segal, *Paul the Convert: The Apostolate and Apostasy of Saul the Pharisee* (New Haven, CT: Yale University Press, 1990), p. 74.

44. Willem Kox, Wim Meeus, and Harm't Hart find: 'Eighty percent of the converts establish affective bonds with other members of the group. This is very meaningful to people who experience little support from parents and peers. It seems justified to suppose that religious groups have a twofold appeal: ideological, by offering a new perspective on life, and social, by providing a satisfactory social network' ('Religious Conversion of Adolescents: Testing the Lofland and Stark Model of Religious Conversion', *Sociological Analysis* 52 [1991], p. 238). See also Eugene V. Gallagher, who studied *Acts of John*, *Joseph and Aseneth*, and *Metamorphoses* (or *The Golden Ass*) and found: 'Each of the texts considered portrays conversion as a continuing process, which involves entering a new community, adopting specific forms of behavior, and participating in ongoing ritual life. The texts emphasize the continuity between "personal" and "institutional" religious experience. ... Conversion narratives become community stories as much as individual stories because in their telling they reflect the continuing integration of the convert into the community' ('Conversion and Community in Late Antiquity', *JR* 73 [1993], p. 14).

45. Rodney Stark, *The Rise of Christianity: A Sociologist Reconsiders History* (Princeton, NJ: Princeton University Press, 1996), p. 18 (italics original).

Given this account of conversion and the ecclesiological nature of faith, the problem of 'falling away' (or 'getting out') is redefined. Apostasy for Hebrews is not simply intellectual doubt or a failing to believe certain tenants of Christian doctrine, but an individual's abandoning of the community. When an individual abandons the community, this person abandons hope of realizing the promise, as Käsemann notes: 'Only in union with Christ's companions is there life, faith, and progress on the individual's way of wandering. As soon as a person is no longer fully conscious of membership and begins to be isolated from the people of God, that person must also have left the promise behind and abandoned the goal.'[46] Abandoning the group is abandoning faith.

Corporate and Christological Faith
The final dimension to note with respect to ecclesiological faith is the community's identity as Christ-sufferers.

Unlike Paul, Hebrews has no explicit language of being baptized into Christ's death or of being crucified with Christ. Instead, the sense in Hebrews is ecclesiological. The author of Hebrews envisions us as part of the traveling community running the race Christ ran (12.1-3), and so invites us to 'go outside the camp, bearing Christ's reproach' (13.13).

The author's exhortation in 13.13 is wholly corporate: 'let *us* go (*exerchōmetha*) to him outside the camp, bearing (*pherontes*) his reproach'. The invitation to bear Christ's reproach (*oneidismos*) recalls the author's images of persecution elsewhere.[47] The community has exemplified endurance through persecution in the past (they were 'publicly exposed to reproach [*oneidismois*]', 10.33), and in 13.13 the author invites his hearers to continue enduring such reproach. The image of going to Jesus, then, is 'a distinctive understanding of discipleship', whereby the 'task of the community is to emulate Jesus, leaving behind the security, congeniality, and respectability of the sacred enclosure, risking the reproach that fell upon him'.[48] Those

46. Käsemann, *Wandering*, p. 21.
47. Some interpreters have read 13.13 as the author's exhortation to leave the physical city of Jerusalem. See, e.g., Carl Mosser, 'Rahab outside the Camp', in Richard Bauckham *et al.* (eds.), *The Epistle to the Hebrews and Christian Theology* (Grand Rapids: Eerdmans, 2009), pp. 383-404; and Peter Walker, *Jesus and the Holy City: New Testament Perspectives on Jerusalem* (Grand Rapids: Eerdmans, 1996), pp. 217-20. Even if this is true, the call to endure suffering with Christ is still clear.
48. Lane, *Hebrews 9–13*, p. 543. Although the author of Hebrews does not speak of 'taking up the cross' as Jesus does in the Synoptic Gospels (Mt. 10.38; 16.24; Mk 8.34-38; Lk. 9.23-25; 14.27), the image of going to Jesus outside the camp is a parallel concept. So Attridge: 'In this equivalent of the call to take up the cross, Hebrews suggests where it is that true participation in the Christian altar is to be found—in accepting the "reproach of Christ"' (*Hebrews*, p. 399).

who 'go to Jesus outside the camp' do so anticipating the enduring city to come (13.14), an image of the eschatological hope that Jesus himself realized.

Summary: Faith in Hebrews
In summary, then, faith in Hebrews entails, among other things (such as hope and obedience), enduring suffering in the face of death. This suffering follows the model of Jesus, the pioneer and perfecter of faith who 'endured the cross for the joy set before him' (12.2), and realized a blessed future following his death. Human beings demonstrate such faith most clearly by aligning with the people of God, and with this people 'going to Jesus outside the camp, bearing his reproach' (13.13).

Anabaptist Believers' Church and Faith in Hebrews

One of the more difficult challenges to this reading of Hebrews is how to say that faith is one of corporate suffering like Christ, while at the same time acknowledging that many people who seem to be faithful do not suffer persecution. To be clear, the suffering I am proposing here is the specific dimension of suffering persecution on account of being associated with Jesus, and not suffering in general. Surely the answer cannot be to tell these people to seek suffering for suffering's own sake. Here is where the Anabaptist vision of the church has an answer for us.

By 'Anabaptist' I refer generally to various groups that we could include as members of the radical reformation, such as the Swiss Brethren, South German Anabaptists, Mennonites, Hutterites, Philipites, and Moravians. To be sure, these groups had their own distinguishing marks, but they shared a number of ecclesiological convictions. The Schleitheim Confession, formulated predominately by Swiss and South German Anabaptists, names seven points on which they are united in unanimous agreement: (1) believers' baptism; (2) the ban as church discipline; (3) the Lord's Supper as remembrance, reserved for those baptized as believers; (4) separation from the world; (5) local pastoral leadership; (6) renunciation of violence and political involvement; and (7) refusal to make oaths. The Anabaptists' ecclesiology is their most distinctive characteristic. Anabaptists understood the church as, among other things, a gathering of believers who are suffering on account of their association with Christ. For our purposes in this essay, I narrow our discussion to only three Anabaptists (two from the early Anabaptist era, and one Mennonite from the twentieth century): Dirk Philips, Menno Simons, and John Howard Yoder.

Dirk Philips lists suffering among the seven ordinances of the church.[49] Philips insists, 'All that will live godly in Christ Jesus shall suffer persecution.... [T]he entire Holy Scripture testifies that the righteous must suffer and possess his soul through suffering'.[50] Therefore, for Philips, suffering is not a nuisance that some followers of Jesus may experience, but an ordinance of the church. Without suffering, the church is not fully church, just as the church would be lacking without other ordinances Philips lists, such as believers' baptism, the Lord's Supper, foot washing, or the ban.

Similarly, Menno Simons names communal cross-bearing as a sign of the church:

> This very cross is a sure indicater [sic] of the church of Christ, and has been testified not only in olden times by the Scriptures, but also by the example of Jesus Christ, of the holy apostles and prophets, the first and unfalsified church, and also by the present pious, faithful children.[51]

Menno names Heb. 12.2 among others as proof of this sign of the church. He is convinced that godly obedience leads assuredly to persecution, and he sees this theme running throughout the Scriptures, seen in figures such as Abel, David, and Stephen.[52] Given that the church is a gathering of obedient disciples, and obedience leads to persecution, the church will consequently be marked by suffering. Menno's vision of the Christian life bears a certain resemblance to Hebrews' exhortation to 'go outside the camp and bear Christ's reproach', when he writes:

---

49. These seven ordinances are: (1) right doctrine of Scripture and ministerial leadership; (2) believers' baptism and the Supper; (3) foot washing; (4) the ban; (5) loving one another; (6) living a godly life; and (7) suffering (Dietrich Philips, 'The Church of God, c. 1560', in George Huntston Williams and Angel M. Mergal [eds.], *Spiritual and Anabaptist Writers* [LCC, 25; London: SCM Press, 1957], pp. 240-55).

50. Philips, 'Church of God', p. 252. Philips further insists that the ban is the Christian community's only tool for spiritual discipline, and must not resort to violence. Insofar as a community of Christians persecutes others, it is no longer the church: 'Hence they can nevermore stand nor be counted as a congregation of the Lord who persecute others on account of their faith' (p. 252).

51. Menno Simons, 'Reply to Gellius Faber, 1554', in John Christian Wenger (ed.), *The Complete Writings of Menno Simons* (Scottdale, PA: Herald, 1956), pp. 741-42 (here 742). Menno names six marks of the church: (1) salutary and unadulterated doctrine of God's holy and divine Word; (2) believers' baptism and the Lord's Supper for the penitent; (3) obedience to the holy Word and living a pious life; (4) love of neighbor; (5) confession of Christ in the face of struggle; and (6) the cross of Christ, which is borne for the sake of his testimony and Word (pp. 739-41).

52. Menno Simons, 'The Cross of the Saints, c. 1554', in Wenger (ed.), *The Complete Writings of Menno Simons*, pp. 587-98.

> [A]ll those who believe the Word of the Lord with true hearts, who have become partakers of the Holy Ghost, who are clothed with power from on high, and out of whose mouths pour grace and wisdom, who rebuke the world's shame and sin...must with Stephen be cast *out of the city* and get a taste of flying stones.[53]

Finally, John Howard Yoder also names 'the cross' as one of the four 'nota' of the church.[54] The church, for Yoder, does not view suffering as a random unexpected divergence from normalcy, but as precisely what it means to be church. He explains, 'The suffering of the church is not a passing tight spot after which there can be hope of return to normalcy; it is according to both Scripture and experience the continuing destiny of any faithful Christian community'.[55] Like Dirk Philips and Menno Simons before him, Yoder also emphasizes that the suffering in view

> is not the resigned acceptance of limitations or injustice in an imperfect world but the meaningful assuming of the cost of nonconformed obedience.... [It] is to be understood much more narrowly as that kind of suffering that comes upon one because of loyalty to Jesus and nonconformity to the world.[56]

The Anabaptist vision of the church as a suffering community helps answer the question of how faith can be understood as 'suffering' without at the same time urging people to seek out suffering for suffering's own sake. For the Anabaptists, suffering was certainly more than a philosophical idea, but a reality.[57] For example, Michael Sattler, who was influential in the formation of the Schleitheim Confession,[58] was brutally tortured and subsequently executed for heresy, along with his wife and other companions.[59] It is important to note, however, that the Anabaptists never view suffering as

---

53. Simons, 'Cross of the Saints', p. 594 (italics mine).

54. John Howard Yoder names four notae of the church: (1) holy living; (2) brotherly and sisterly love; (3) witness; and (4) the cross (*The Royal Priesthood: Essays Ecclesiological and Ecumenical* [Grand Rapids: Eerdmans, 1994], pp. 79-89).

55. Yoder, *Royal Priesthood*, p. 86.

56. Yoder, *Royal Priesthood*, pp. 86-87. The 'world' for Yoder 'is neither all nature nor all humanity nor all "culture"; it is *structured unbelief*, rebellion taking with it a fragment of what should have been the Order of the Kingdom' (p. 62, italics his).

57. To be sure, this was also the case for others in the same day, but a significant percentage of Anabaptists experienced persecution. See Brad S. Gregory, 'Anabaptist Martyrdom: Imperatives, Experience, and Memorialization', in John D. Roth and James M. Stayer (eds.), *A Companion to Anabaptism and Spiritualism, 1521–1700* (Brill's Companions to the Christian Tradition, 6; Leiden: Brill, 2007), pp. 467-506.

58. On Sattler's role at Schleitheim, see John Howard Yoder, *The Legacy of Michael Sattler* (Scottdale, PA: Herald, 1973), pp. 30-34.

59. See G.H. Williams (trans.), 'Trial and Martyrdom of Michael Sattler', in Williams and Mergal (eds.), *Spiritual and Anabaptist Writers*, pp. 138-44, esp. the description on pp. 143-44.

an end in itself. Instead, suffering is an expected product of a life of discipleship. The Anabaptists never extol suffering for suffering's own sake; suffering is not something we seek. Indeed, many of Menno's works are addressed in whole or in part to magistrates or other outsiders, appealing for the cessation of persecution.[60] Instead, for the Anabaptists, suffering is a natural consequence of a life of obedience, and given that the church is comprised of followers of Jesus, suffering will naturally be a mark of the church.

If the church itself is defined as followers of Jesus who are suffering for this discipleship (which I suggested is expressed in Hebrews as 'going out to Jesus, bearing his reproach'), then suffering is not something we seek for its own sake. Instead, suffering is an expected consequence of following Jesus, the one whose faith is marked by enduring suffering in the face of death. Insofar as the church suffers, it receives this suffering as a natural corollary of its identity. Yoder explains, 'one does not seek [suffering], but when it comes neither does one consider it simply as a matter of having been providentially chosen for a hard time'.[61]

Faith as corporate suffering is about the community's *willingness* and *readiness* to suffer. (To be sure, a community that is *not* suffering may need to check itself to see if it is truly following Jesus in such a manner that could see suffering as a viable consequence for its present discipleship.) Again, Yoder writes:

> Thus willingness to bear the cross means simply the readiness to let the form of the church's obedience to Christ be dictated by Christ rather than by how much the population or the authorities are ready to accept. When stated in this way it is then clear that the readiness of the church to face suffering thus understood is precisely the only way in which it is possible to communicate to that society and to its authorities that it is Christ who is Lord and not they.[62]

In short, if the church is not suffering physical persecution in the present, it need not actively seek such suffering for suffering's own sake. At the same time, the church needs to be ever ready to accept suffering and follow Jesus in such a way that would expect suffering, given that suffering is what defines it. On this vision of faith and the church, the Anabaptists and the author of Hebrews are in perfect agreement.

---

60. See (page numbers from Wenger [ed.], *The Complete Writings of Menno Simons* are given in parentheses) 'Foundation of Christian Doctrine' (pp. 105-226, esp. pp. 190-221); 'Christian Baptism' (pp. 229-87, esp. pp. 284-87); 'Why I Do Not Cease Teaching and Writing' (pp. 292-320); 'Confession of the Distressed Christians' (pp. 501-22); 'A Pathetic Supplication to All Magistrates' (pp. 525-31); 'Reply to False Accusations' (pp. 543-77).
61. Yoder, *Royal Priesthood*, p. 88.
62. Yoder, *Royal Priesthood*, pp. 88-89.

9

1 TIMOTHY 3.16 AS A PROTO-RULE OF FAITH

Paul Trebilco

Introduction

The theological interpretation of Scripture involves a wide range of practices, one of which is 'ruled reading', that is, being guided in our interpretative practices by a 'rule of faith'.[1] The rule of faith was developed in the early Christian communities and came to be expressed in creeds such as the Apostles' Creed or the Nicene Creed. Such rules summarized the significance of what Jesus said and did, functioned as a guide in the reading of Scripture, and provided what has been called 'theological boundary markers for Christian identity'.[2]

The rule of faith is closely related to Scripture. As Billings notes,

> the rule of faith emerges from Scripture, and yet it provides extrabiblical guidance about the center and periphery of God's story of salvation accessed through Scripture. In light of the rule of faith, Christian scriptural interpretation takes place on the path of Jesus Christ, empowered by the Spirit to transform God's people into Christ's image, anticipating a transformative vision of the triune God.[3]

Irenaeus shows the value of such a rule. In writing about how the Valentinians misuse Scripture to support their own views, he writes:

> they endeavour to adapt with an air of probability to their own peculiar assertions the parables of the Lord, the sayings of the prophets, and the words of the apostles, in order that their scheme may not seem altogether without support. In doing so, however, they disregard the order and the connection of

---

1. J.T. Billings, *The Word of God for the People of God: An Entryway to the Theological Interpretation of Scripture* (Grand Rapids: Eerdmans, 2010), p. xiv, refers to 'reading Scripture within a "rule of faith"'.
2. R.W. Wall, 'Reading the Bible from within our Traditions: The "Rule of Faith" in Theological Hermeneutics', in J.B. Green and M. Turner (eds.), *Between Two Horizons: Spanning New Testament Studies and Systematic Theology* (Grand Rapids: Eerdmans, 2000), p. 89.
3. Billings, *Word of God*, p. xiv.

the Scriptures, and so far as in them lies, dismember and destroy the truth. By transferring passages, and dressing them up anew, and making one thing out of another, they succeed in deluding many through their wicked art in adapting the oracles of the Lord to their opinions. Their manner of acting is just as if one, when a beautiful image of a king has been constructed by some skilful artist out of precious jewels, should then take this likeness of the man all to pieces, should rearrange the gems, and so fit them together as to make them into the form of a dog or of a fox, and even that but poorly executed; and should then maintain and declare that *this* was the beautiful image of the king which the skilful artist constructed, pointing to the jewels which had been admirably fitted together by the first artist to form the image of the king, but have been with bad effect transferred by the latter one to the shape of a dog, and by thus exhibiting the jewels, should deceive the ignorant who had no conception what a king's form was like, and persuade them that that miserable likeness of the fox was, in fact, the beautiful image of the king.[4]

Irenaeus' image of the mosaic is a powerful one. If the patterns in Scripture are properly discerned, then the pieces which make up the mosaic can be fitted together to form the 'beautiful image' of the king, who is clearly Christ. But the most appropriate connections can be broken and the pieces can be put together in the wrong way, resulting in a portrait of a dog or a fox. Thus, Scripture can be interpreted in many ways that distort the truth. As Billings notes: 'By distorting the inherent pattern (the rule of faith) that holds Scripture together, false (Gnostic) interpretations of Scripture miss what Scripture itself points to: Jesus Christ, as witnessed to by the Old and New Testaments.'[5]

In this paper I will suggest that 1 Tim. 3.16 can function as a 'proto-rule of faith' for us with regard to the Scriptures. I am not suggesting that 1 Tim. 3.16 replaces the Apostles' Creed, or the rule of faith as it took shape in the early church. However, I am suggesting that 1 Tim. 3.16 can assist us in our reading of Scripture in the church and that it legitimates and encourages the development of such rules in the post-New Testament era.

1 Timothy 3.16 as a Proto-Rule of Faith

Embedded in 1 Timothy 3 is v. 16, which is introduced in 1 Tim. 3.14-15 (NRSV, slightly modified):

> [14]I hope to come to you soon, but I am writing these instructions to you so that, [15]if I am delayed, you may know how one ought to behave in the household of God, which is the church of the living God, the pillar and foundation of the truth. [16]Without any doubt, the mystery of our religion is great:

---

4. Irenaeus, *Against Heresies* (trans. and ed. Dominic J. Unger; rev. John J. Dillon; ACW, 55; Mahwah, NJ: Paulist Press, 1992), 1.8.1.
5. Billings, *Word of God*, p. 21.

> He was revealed in flesh (*hos ephanerōthē en sarki*),
> vindicated in spirit (*edikaiōthē en pneumati*),
> seen by angels (*ōphthē angelois*),
> proclaimed among nations (*ekēruchthē en ethnesin*),
> believed in throughout the world (*episteuthē en kosmō*),
> taken up in glory (*anelēmphthē en doxē*).

The form of 1 Tim. 3.16 has often led to the conclusion that it is a very early creed or hymn—or a part of a creed or hymn[6]—that the author quotes at this point. For the argument of this paper, we need not decide whether it functioned as a creed or as a hymn, but a number of points suggest that here the author quotes a preformed liturgical tradition that would be known to the readers.[7] First, the creed begins abruptly with the masculine relative pronoun *hos* ('who'),[8] which has no antecedent and so is not related to what precedes it, although it clearly must refer to Christ. Bassler suggests the first line of the creed or hymn was 'Blessed be our Lord and Savior Jesus Christ who...', but that this line was dropped when the creed was quoted here.[9]

Second, the creed is introduced by the author with these words: 'without any doubt (*homologoumenōs*)'. This word 'combines ideas of confession and common agreement in matters under dispute',[10] and so seems to indicate that a quotation or separate saying will follow.[11]

Third, the six lines of the verse are almost identical in form and rhythm. In each case we have a third person verb in the aorist passive indicative,

---

6. S.E. Fowl, *The Story of Christ in the Ethics of Paul: An Analysis of the Function of the Hymnic Material in the Pauline Corpus* (JSNTSup, 36; Sheffield: Sheffield Academic Press, 1990), p. 45, notes that 'hymns' are to be understood 'in the very general sense of poetic accounts of the nature and/or activity of a divine figure'.

7. See M. Dibelius and H. Conzelmann, *The Pastoral Epistles* (Hermeneia; Philadelphia: Fortress Press, 1972), p. 61; H.A. Blair, *A Creed before the Creeds* (London: Longmans, Green & Co, 1955), pp. 4-5. E.K. Simpson, *The Pastoral Epistles: The Greek Text with Introduction and Commentary* (London: Tyndale, 1954), pp. 60-61, suggests it 'reads like a citation from canticle or catechism. We seem to be listening to a primitive epitome of Christological instruction, half divulged, half concealed.'

8. On the textual issue here, see I.H. Marshall, *The Pastoral Epistles* (ICC; Edinburgh: T. & T. Clark, 1999), p. 505; it is certain that *hos* is original.

9. J.M. Bassler, *1 Timothy, 2 Timothy, Titus* (AbNTC; Nashville: Abingdon Press, 1996), p. 75. P.H. Towner, *The Letters to Timothy and Titus* (NICNT; Grand Rapids: Eerdmans, 2006), p. 278 n. 33, notes: 'The relative pronoun was used to insert traditional pieces into New Testament letters (Tit. 2.14; Rom. 8.32; Phil. 2.6; 1 Pet. 2.22-24; 3.22).'

10. A.J. Hultgren and R. Aus, *I–II Timothy, Titus, II Thessalonians* (Augsburg Commentary on the New Testament; Minneapolis: Augsburg, 1984), p. 77.

11. This is also suggested by Marshall, *Pastoral Epistles*, p. 522, who notes that *homologoumenōs* 'is designed to elicit from the readers a corporate acknowledgement that what is about to be said is accepted truth'.

generally followed by *en* and then a noun (in the dative, following *en*).[12] This regularity of form and rhythm suggests it is a hymn or creed of some sort.

Fourth, the content of the six clauses goes well beyond the theological issues raised in the immediate context and is different from what precedes and follows.

It seems likely then that v. 16b is a quotation from a creed or a hymn, probably one that was known to the readers.[13] We should think of a community gathered for worship reciting this creed, and through it reciting the story of salvation as it is expressed in this verse.[14]

Accordingly, I will call this verse a creed. My interest here is in its function as a 'proto-rule of faith', that is, a creed which is very similar to the post-New Testament 'rules of faith'. Clearly a distinction is to be made between 1 Tim. 3.16 and later rules of faith, which are longer and more comprehensive. Hence, my suggestion that this is a *proto*-rule. But my argument here is that the creed in 1 Tim. 3.16 can function *for us* in the same way as did later rules of faith: to guide our reading of Scripture and to form a framework within which to read. This is *not* an *historical* argument; I am not claiming that the creed in 1 Tim. 3.16 functioned as a rule for the author of the Pastorals or for the readers, or that it functioned in this way as regards the New Testament corpus. It *could* well have done this—particularly if it was a well-known creed or hymn which was recited when they gathered in assembly. But we have insufficient evidence for early Christian worship, or for the circulation and use of 1 Tim. 3.16, to actually claim this.[15]

---

12. The one exception is line 3, where *en* is lacking: ōphthē angelois.

13. In the conclusion I will note that it is best seen as a proto-creed or proto-rule of faith, but I will mainly simply call it a 'creed' in this paper. Marshall, *Pastoral Epistles*, p. 499, notes that the fact that v. 16 is clearly 'a structured piece...does not settle the question whether it has been taken over or composed by the author'. He notes that to classify it as a confession or hymn (p. 499 n. 3) 'does not necessarily mean that it is a piece of tradition used by the author rather than his own composition. The view that it is a pre-formed tradition is held almost universally...but Hasler, 30, has revived the view of Klöpper, 360, that the hymn was composed by the writer of the letter. The similarities to the theology expressed elsewhere in the [Pastoral Epistles] are so strong that this possibility is preferable.' It does not really alter my argument if 3.16 was written by the author, since I am looking at how 3.16 might function *for us* as a proto-rule. Further, the similarities of 3.16 to the rest of the letter might well be due to the influence of such credal material on the Pastor's theology.

14. On the importance of hymns or songs in worship, see 1 Cor. 14.26; Eph. 5.18-20; Col. 3.16-17.

15. However, *Diognetus* 11.3 is probably based on 1 Tim. 3.16; see Marshall, *Pastoral Epistles*, p. 500 n. 6.

Rather my argument here is a *theological* one relating to *our* practice of interpretation: that 1 Tim. 3.16 can function *for us* as a rule, as a framework to guide our reading of the New Testament, and so in our theological engagement with Scripture. But firstly, I need to discuss some matters relating to 1 Tim. 3.16 in its context in 1 Timothy.

1 Timothy 3.16 in the Context of 1 Timothy 3.14-16

Along with many interpreters, I consider the Pastorals to be pseudonymous, written by a Pauline disciple who sees himself as within the Pauline tradition.[16] In this context, 1 Tim. 3.14-15 indicates that 'these instructions' are given so that the readers 'may know how one ought to behave in the household of God' (3.15), that is, how to conduct themselves in the ongoing life of the church.[17]

The instructions relate to conduct in the 'house of God' (*oikos theou*), the church. The church is spoken of as an *oikos* eight times in the Pastorals.[18] It can be translated either as a house (the building) or a household (the community who live in the building). However, *oikos* certainly means household in 1 Tim. 3.4, 5, 12 and this seems the most appropriate meaning here since the conduct in view in the previous sections relates to members of God's family, and thus can be understood to relate to God's 'household'.[19] The reference is to 'a divinely ordered social structure',[20] with the church being seen as an extended family living life together. What is involved in v. 15 then is not just the question of behaviour in 'God's household' (which might be understood as meaning 'when the church gathers'), but rather what kind of conduct or life style is appropriate for Christians (all the time and

---

16. See P.R. Trebilco, *The Early Christians in Ephesus from Paul to Ignatius* (WUNT, 166; Tübingen: Mohr Siebeck, 2004), pp. 197-202. M. Davies, *The Pastoral Epistles* (NTG; Sheffield: Sheffield Academic Press, 1996), p. 18, notes differences between 1 Tim. 3.16 and other epistles attributed to Paul.

17. Given the similar statement in 1 Tim. 1.18, 'these instructions' referred to in 3.14 are the charges in 1 Tim. 2-3, particularly since the material in 1 Tim. 2.1-3.13 all refers to conduct in God's house. But the instructions given in the whole letter may be in view too. The instructions are presented as addressed to Timothy ('*you*' is singular in v. 14), but he is to teach them in the church (4.11; 6.2), so in effect the instructions are to the whole church.

18. See 1 Tim. 3.4, 5, 12, 15; 5.4; 2 Tim. 1.16; 4.19; Tit. 1.11.

19. The translation of *oikos* as 'house' might be possible, given the building terms (pillar and foundation) that follow. The church would then be depicted as the sacred place, or the temple, where the living God dwells with his people (cf. 1 Cor. 3.16; Eph. 2.21, 22). However, the use of *oikos* in 1 Tim. 3.4, 5, 12 seems determinative for its meaning in 3.15.

20. Bassler, *1 Timothy, 2 Timothy, Titus*, p. 73.

wherever they are), who are members of God's household. The instructions about conduct given in the letter are standards for a household that is none other than God's, and the teaching given here, including 1 Tim. 3.16, provides directions for relationships amongst God's people.

The church is 'the church of the living God'. What is said of the *ekklēsia* here suggests the word is being used in the sense of the church at large (1 Cor. 12.28; Col. 1.18, 24) rather than to refer to the local congregation (Gal. 1.22; 1 Cor. 14.19).[21] As the church of the living God, the church belongs to God, and is 'a sacred space in which the living God dwells'.[22] '*Living* God' here emphasizes that God is the only God and is the source of life. Further, that the church is 'the church of the living God' implies that God is present in and with the church, working through the community.[23] Right conduct and responsiveness to God is also needed in the church precisely because God is present in the community.

The author goes on to speak of components of a house in order to say more about the nature of the church, with the idea of the church as God's temple coming to the fore.[24] As God dwelt in the temple of Israel, so now by the Spirit, God dwells in the new temple, the church. Architectural words are used. *Stulos*—'pillar'—is used of pillars in Solomon's temple. *Hedraiōma* is best translated as 'foundation',[25] particularly in view of the *Rule of the Community* 5.6 at Qumran which speaks of members laying 'a foundation of truth for Israel'. The church then is called to uphold and protect the truth, for it is founded and established on the basis of the truth.[26] Part of this is the role of the church in safeguarding true teaching.[27] As Hultgren notes: 'The truth does not rest upon the church, as though the church can never err, but the church is ever seeking to uphold the truth.'[28] The church is seen as the servant of God's truth, with a clear role and responsibility with regard to upholding the truth of the gospel.

---

21. See Marshall, *Pastoral Epistles*, p. 509.
22. R. Saarinen, *The Pastoral Epistles with Philemon and Jude* (BTCB; Grand Rapids: Brazos, 2008), p. 68.
23. See Bassler, *1 Timothy, 2 Timothy, Titus*, p. 74; Marshall, *Pastoral Epistles*, p. 508.
24. See 1 Cor. 3.16-17; 2 Cor. 6.16; see also G.D. Fee, *1 and 2 Timothy, Titus* (NIBC; Peabody, MA: Hendrickson, 1988), p. 92.
25. See Marshall, *Pastoral Epistles*, p. 510; 'mainstay, fortress' are other options.
26. Marshall, *Pastoral Epistles*, p. 511.
27. Probably in view in the verse are the false teachers who will be spoken of in 1 Tim. 4.1-5, and who have abandoned the truth (1 Tim. 6.5; 2 Tim. 2.18; 3.8; 4.4). The church should be a strong and stable structure supporting the truth of the gospel, standing firm in the midst of conflicting claims and in the face of assaults by false teachers.
28. Hultgren, *I–II Timothy, Titus*, p. 77.

1 Timothy 3.16 then elaborates on the greatness of the 'truth', of which the church of the living God is to be 'the pillar and foundation'. The verse makes it clear that the truth is manifested in the revelation of Christ. The creed is introduced with the phrase 'without any doubt, the mystery of our religion is great' (3.16a). 'Without any doubt' (*homologoumenōs*) means 'by common consent'[29] or 'demonstrably'.[30]

The creed elaborates on 'the mystery of our religion (*to tēs eusebeias mustērion*)', so clearly this phrase refers to Christ, the subject of the creed. As Montague writes, 'After the mention of mystery, we would expect the next clause to begin with "which," but it begins with *who*. The mystery, then, is not a thing but a person, Jesus Christ.'[31] 'Mystery' is used because God's plan for salvation had been kept secret and so was inaccessible, but now has been revealed in the appearance of Jesus Christ.[32] Normally *eusebeia* refers to 'the duty which people owe to God', but here it is 'thought of in a more objective way as the content or basis of Christianity'.[33] 'Religion' or 'piety' then is an appropriate translation.[34] The true 'religion' that has been revealed is the person of Jesus Christ. The mystery of our religion is 'great' in the sense that it is sublime or important.[35] By introducing the rest of v. 16 in this way, the author recognizes the importance of the creed, which Montague calls 'the theological center of the letter'.[36]

The Structure of 1 Timothy 3.16

The content of 'the mystery of our religion' is given in six clauses that describe key moments in Christ's ministry as well as the continuing impact

---

29. J.N.D. Kelly, *A Commentary on the Pastoral Epistles* (BNTC; London: A. & C. Black, 1963), p. 88.

30. A.T. Hanson, *The Pastoral Epistles* (NCB; Grand Rapids: Eerdmans, 1982), p. 84.

31. G.T. Montague, *First and Second Timothy, Titus* (CCSS; Grand Rapids: Baker Academic, 2008), p. 88, emphasis original.

32. On *mustērion* here see G.S. Magee, 'Uncovering the "Mystery" in 1 Timothy 3', *TJ* NS 29 (2008), pp. 247-65.

33. Fee, *1 and 2 Timothy, Titus*, p. 92.

34. Note also 1 Tim. 3.9 where it is said that deacons 'must hold fast to the mystery of the faith (*to mustērion tēs pisteōs*) with a clear conscience'. The similar use of *mustērion* in 1 Tim. 3.9, 16 indicates that 'faith' and *eusebeia* are seen as equivalents.

35. Towner, *Timothy and Titus*, p. 277, sees in the use of 'great' here 'a subversive echo of the city's bold claim, "Great is Artemis of the Ephesians" (Acts 19.28, 34; cf. 19.27, 35)'.

36. Montague, *First and Second Timothy, Titus*, p. 90; see also Towner, *Timothy and Titus*, p. 271, who calls it 'the rhetorical and theological high point of the letter'. 1 Tim. 3.16, particularly its implicit affirmation of the value of the 'earthly' and so the goodness of creation, is also built on in 1 Tim. 4.1-5, where the false teachers' ascetic views are attacked; see Fowl, *Story of Christ*, pp. 183-92.

of that ministry. There have been many suggestions about the structure of the creed, and since discerning the structure provides assistance to exegesis, it will be considered first, although exegetical considerations will also be drawn on here.

First, it has been suggested that the clauses are arranged chronologically,[37] but this is unlikely since 'taken up in glory', which almost certainly refers to the ascension,[38] is given after 'proclaimed among nations'.[39]

Second, others have seen the hymn's structure as two sets of three lines:
 (1) revealed in flesh, vindicated in spirit, seen by angels;
 (2) proclaimed among nations, believed in throughout the world, taken up in glory.[40]

Here the first triplet would refer to the earthly life of the incarnate One while the second would refer to the exalted Lord and the reception of his work. However, this view overlooks the alternation between earth and heaven which is at the heart of the next view.

Third, the most widely accepted view is that the creed is divided into three contrasting couplets.[41] This view builds on the contrast between pairs of lines, which is the most obvious structural feature of the creed:

 (1a) (Earth)   revealed in *flesh*
 (1b) (Heaven) vindicated in *spirit*

 (2a) (Heaven) seen by *angels*
 (2b) (Earth)   proclaimed among *nations*

---

37. See C.K. Barrett, *The Pastoral Epistles in the New English Bible, with Introduction and Commentary* (New Clarendon Bible; Oxford: Clarendon Press, 1963), p. 66; he takes clause 6 to refer to 'the final victory of Christ'; see also D.J. MacLeod, 'Christology in Six Lines: An Exposition of 1 Timothy 3:16', *BSac* 159 (2002), pp. 338-48.

38. A chronological view would see the last clause as referring to the parousia, but this seems very unlikely.

39. See Dibelius and Conzelmann, *Pastoral Epistles*, p. 61.

40. See Fee, *1 and 2 Timothy, Titus*, pp. 93-96; W. Mounce, *The Pastoral Epistles* (WBC, 46; Nashville: Thomas Nelson, 2000), pp. 216-18.

41. See, e.g., R.H. Gundry, 'The Form, Meaning and Background of the Hymn Quoted in 1 Timothy 3:16', in W.W. Gasque and R.P. Martin (eds.), *Apostolic History and the Gospel: Biblical and Historical Essays Presented to F.F. Bruce on his 60th Birthday* (Exeter: Paternoster Press, 1970), pp. 206-209; Dibelius and Conzelmann, *Pastoral Epistles*, pp. 61-62; A.Y. Lau, *Manifest in Flesh: The Epiphany Christology of the Pastoral Epistles* (WUNT, 2.86; Tübingen: Mohr Siebeck, 1996), p. 91; Marshall, *Pastoral Epistles*, p. 501; G. Strecker, *Theology of the New Testament* (New York: W. de Gruyter, 2000), p. 580; cf. J. Murphy-O'Connor, 'Redactional Angels in 1 Tim 3:16', *RB* 91 (1984), pp. 179-80.

(3a) (Earth) believed in throughout the *world*
(3b) (Heaven) taken up in *glory*.⁴²

As shown here, the contrasts are between flesh and spirit, angels and nations, world and glory. We see the repetition of the one antithesis between earthly and heavenly, although in the second couplet the order is reversed and becomes heavenly—earthly. The structure then is *a/b, b/a, a/b*. The creed presents Christ 'at the two contrasting and complementary levels of "flesh" and "spirit", heaven and earth'.⁴³ The creed can then be thought of as structured spatially rather than chronologically.

Exegetical Discussion of 1 Timothy 3.16

Before discussing how we might read with this rule of faith, I will exegete each of the clauses of the creed in turn.

'He was revealed in flesh' (hos ephanerōthē en sarki)
Phaneroō here means 'to cause to become visible, reveal'.⁴⁴ As noted above, this refers to Christ and so speaks of his being made manifest on earth.

Christ became visible *'en sarki'*. Here *sarx* means 'the physical body as functioning entity...physical body',⁴⁵ and indicates that Christ became a real human being. The manifestation or revelation of Christ thus happened by

---

42. This structure is from Marshall, *Pastoral Epistles*, p. 501. Gundry also points to the synthetic parallelism in the creed. There is parallelism between (2) 'vindicated in spirit' which leads to (3) 'seen by angels' and (4) 'proclaimed among nations' which results in (5) 'believed in throughout the world'. Then it can be seen that (1) and (6) 'form a couplet which appropriately frames the whole verse—again with synthetic parallelism: the appearance in flesh culminates in the ascension to heaven.... In other words, the recognition of the parallelism, between lines 1 and 6, 2 and 3, and 4 and 5 takes advantage of the synthetic pairs of datival nouns flesh/glory, spirit/angels, and nations/world—and the synthetic pairs of verbs—manifested/taken up, vindicated/seen, and proclaimed/believed on—which receive no attention when our gaze fixes exclusively on the antithetic pairs of datival nouns' (Gundry, 'Form, Meaning and Background', pp. 208-209). This is an additional structural feature, although it is made somewhat less compelling by the fact that the 'flesh/glory' pair is better seen as antithetic rather than synthetic.

43. J.L. Houlden, *The Pastoral Epistles* (PNTC; Harmondsworth: Penguin Books, 1976), p. 85; compare Marshall, *Pastoral Epistles*, p. 502: 'This explanation of the structure is attractive but not finally compelling. The proposed pattern of contrasts is certainly odd and no convincing rationale for it has really been offered (cf. Fee, 96).'

44. BDAG, 1048; see also Fowl, *Story of Christ*, p. 158.

45. BDAG, 915; *sarx* is used with reference to Christ in a range of passages; see, e.g., Rom. 1.3; 8.3; 9.5; Eph. 2.14; Col. 1.22; cf. Jn 1.14; 6.63; Heb. 2.14; 5.7; 10.20; 1 Pet. 3.18; 4.1; 1 Jn 4.2; 2 Jn 7. There is no necessary connotation of sinfulness in the use of *sarx*, as is shown by the *addition* of *hamartia* in Rom. 8.3: 'by sending his own Son in the likeness of sinful flesh (*en homoiōmati sarkos hamartias*)'.

way of incarnation. Given that *sarx* is used in some passages to refer to human life in general (Gal. 2.20; Phil. 1.22, 24; Heb. 5.7), and that *phaneroō* is used rather than, for example, the passive of *gennaō* ('to be born'), the reference can be seen to be to the entire human life of Jesus, not simply his birth.[46] The emphasis can be seen to be on his identification with humanity and his full participation in the earthly sphere and in human experience.[47] The passive form of *phaneroō* means he was *revealed* by another, that is, by God. Accordingly, the incarnation is rooted in the will and activity of God. Since it is said that Christ was revealed, it is implied that he previously existed but was unknown. Therefore this clause presupposes Christ's preexistence.[48] As Fee notes: 'In Christ, God himself has appeared "in flesh"'.[49]

'Vindicated in spirit' (edikaiōthē en pneumati)

Dikaioō here means to 'prove to be right',[50] so the reference to Jesus' earthly life is followed by a reference to vindication or validation.[51] Christ's vindication takes place *en pneumati*. This could be translated as 'in Spirit',[52] or 'in spirit', but the contrast between *en sarki* and *en pneumati* makes it more likely that 'in spirit' is meant, since this meaning preserves the antithesis which forms the structuring device of the creed. 'In spirit' is a reference

46. See Gundry, 'Form, Meaning and Background', p. 209.
47. Marshall, *Pastoral Epistles*, pp. 524-25, notes that it is more difficult to be sure about the exact nuance of *en sarki*: 'There is considerable uncertainty whether the prepositional phrase *en sarki* is intended to express the *mode* of Jesus' manifestation, i.e. as a human being, or the *sphere* of his manifestation, i.e. either the world as the place where salvation-historical events occur (Roloff, 203) or the sphere of human existence in which Jesus participates (Gundry, 210; Kelly, 90). The most that can be said is that the historical event of the incarnation is in mind; the stress is similar to that in 1 Tim 2.5, and the thought of Jesus' participation in human experience is therefore probably uppermost in mind. The statement is sufficiently general to be capable of suggesting a number of concepts by which Jesus' redemptive participation among people was interpreted, including his suffering and death for sin which the early church understood to be the climax and goal of the incarnation (Rom 8.3; Phil 2.7f.).'
48. See, e.g., Strecker, *Theology of the New Testament*, pp. 580-81; B. Fiore, *The Pastoral Epistles: First Timothy, Second Timothy, Titus* (SP; Collegeville, MN: Liturgical Press, 2007), p. 85; see also Lau, *Manifest in Flesh*, pp. 96-99. 1 Tim. 1.15 and 2 Tim. 1.9 also speak of Christ's pre-existence.
49. Fee, *1 and 2 Timothy, Titus*, p. 93. There is no emphasis on the humiliation or weakness of Christ; see Marshall, *Pastoral Epistles*, p. 524. *Phaneroō* is used with reference to the incarnation in 1 Pet. 1.20; Heb. 9.26; 1 Jn 3.5, 8.
50. BDAG, 249. *Dikaioō* is also found with this sense in Ps. 50.6 (LXX); Mt. 11.19; Lk. 7.29, 35; 10.29; Rom. 3.4; see also Ign. *Phld.* 8.2; *Pss. Sol.* 2.16; 3.5; 4.9; 8.7.
51. See P.H. Towner, *The Goal of our Instruction: The Structure of Theology and Ethics in the Pastoral Epistles* (JSNTSup, 34; Sheffield: JSOT Press, 1989), p. 90.
52. This would be to take *en* in an instrumental sense: 'through the Spirit'.

to the spiritual sphere in which Jesus' vindication occurred, in contrast to his life 'in flesh' on earth.[53]

This suggests that the vindication occurred at the point when Christ entered the spiritual or heavenly realm;[54] Christ's vindication in resurrection and exaltation (cf. Acts 2.23-24; 10.39-40) is in view.[55] Again the passive form of the verb shows that the clause speaks of God's activity, and so of God's affirmation and vindication of Jesus. This shows that the cross was not the end and that God was faithful to Jesus by raising him from the dead. Further, the clause speaks of the vindication by God of all that Jesus said and did in his ministry, including that Jesus was Messiah and Son of God despite appearances to the contrary,[56] as well as Christ's victory over evil powers.

Although I have argued that *en pneumati* means 'in spirit', this does not mean that all reference to the Holy Spirit is excluded. As Marshall notes, 'resurrection allowed access to this realm in which the operative agent is the Holy Spirit'.[57]

'Seen by angels' (ōphthē angelois)

The meaning of this clause depends on the referent of *angeloi*. It could refer to human messengers, and thus be a reference to the apostolic witnesses of the resurrection.[58] In connection with this, it has been suggested that *ōphthē* is used here with a technical sense in reference to resurrection appearances (see Lk. 24.34; Acts 1.2; 9.17; 13.31; 26.16; 1 Cor. 15.5-8), but the verb *oraō* is not limited to this meaning in the New Testament, and can often

---

53. See I.H. Marshall, '1 Timothy, Book of', in K.J. Vanhoozer (ed.), *Dictionary for Theological Interpretation of the Bible* (Grand Rapids: Baker Academic, 2005), p. 802. Dibelius and Conzelmann, *Pastoral Epistles*, p. 62, note: 'The phrases [5.1 and 5.2] speak about realms of being'.

54. Dibelius and Conzelmann, *Pastoral Epistles*, p. 62, note that *dikaioō* refers 'to the entrance into the divine realm, the realm of righteousness (*dikaiosunē*).... Therefore "vindicated" refers to the exaltation of Jesus.'

55. Many New Testament texts associate Jesus' vindication with his resurrection from the dead and exaltation to God's right hand; see Rom. 1.4; 1 Cor. 2.1-9; Phil. 2.5-11; Col. 2.8-15; Eph. 1.20-21; Acts 2.23-24; 3.11-15; 4.10-12; 10.39-40; 20.34-43; 1 Pet. 3.21.

56. See G.W. Knight, *The Pastoral Epistles: A Commentary on the Greek Text* (NIGTC; Grand Rapids: Eerdmans, 1992), p. 184; also Fowl, *Story of Christ*, pp. 162-64.

57. Marshall, *Pastoral Epistles*, p. 526. Towner, *Goal of our Instruction*, p. 91, notes of the supernatural or spiritual sphere: 'the sphere and its operative Agent (the Holy Spirit) are difficult to separate in *en pneumati*'.

58. See Murphy-O'Connor, 'Redactional Angels', pp. 186-87; L.T. Johnson, *The First and Second Letters to Timothy: A New Translation with Introduction and Commentary* (AB, 35A; New York: Doubleday, 2001), pp. 233-34.

simply mean 'become visible'.[59] In addition, *angelos* is rarely used of people in the New Testament.[60]

Most scholars therefore argue that *angelois* refers to angels here. As we have noted, *oraō*, along with the person to whom Christ appeared, is the regular way for the New Testament to speak of Jesus' resurrection appearances,[61] so this is probably in view here, with the clause recalling that angels were often messengers of the resurrection. Reference to the ascension is probably also included, as well as the appearance of the risen Christ before heavenly angelic powers in the spiritual realm, which can involve both their subjection and their worship.[62] The reference to angels underlines the cosmic nature of Christ's work and triumph and hence of God's vindication of Christ. The universality of this event is such that it affects all cosmic regions.

'Proclaimed among nations' (ekēruchthē en ethnesin)
The next clause speaks of an activity on earth. *Kērussō* has the sense of 'preach, proclaim' with the content of the proclamation clearly being Jesus, the implied subject of all six clauses.

En ethnesin could mean 'Gentiles' or 'nations'; the latter would include Israel, the former would not. But we should note what we might call the 'maximalist' framework of the creed, which is most obvious in the fifth clause: *episteuthē en kosmō*. Although *kosmos* here means 'world', it does have 'cosmic' overtones and can be seen to include at least the *angeloi* of the previous clause. In addition, *sarx* in clause one clearly implies that Jesus was manifested in the form that is universal for *all* humanity, and the mention of angels in clause three suggests the implied contrast between clauses three and four is between superhuman and human beings, not between angels and Gentiles. In this context, it is best then to see *en ethnesin* as a reference to all nations, and not just Gentiles.[63]

Christ is thus said to be 'proclaimed among nations'. The preaching is done by the church, and its scope is universal. The Christ who has been vindicated in both heaven and earth is the subject of this proclamation. As Marshall notes, implicit in the creed 'is the church's task of participating in that vindication by preaching Christ' to the world.[64]

---

59. See BDAG, 719-20; Fowl, *Story of Christ*, p. 165; see, e.g., Acts 7.2; Rev. 11.19; 12.1, 3.

60. It is used of humans in Mt. 11.10; Mk 1.2; Lk. 7.24; 9.52; Jas 2.25.

61. Lk. 24.23; Acts 9.17; 13.31; 1 Cor. 15.5-8.

62. See Eph. 1.21; Col. 2.15; Heb. 1.3-4; 1 Pet. 3.22; Rev. 5.8-14; see also Marshall, *Pastoral Epistles*, p. 567.

63. See Gundry, 'Form, Meaning and Background', pp. 215-16; Marshall, *Pastoral Epistles*, p. 528; see also 1 Tim. 2.7.

64. Marshall, '1 Timothy', p. 802. Towner, *Timothy and Titus*, p. 283, notes: 'Together, lines 4-5 create the missiological necessity emerging from the Christ-event'.

Accordingly, these two clauses present a contrast between the heavenly revelation to angels after the resurrection and the earthly proclamation to the nations.

'Believed in throughout the world' (episteuthē en kosmō)
Having begun the salvation story by speaking of Christ's identification with humanity, and going on to his exaltation, the creed now refers to the response to the proclamation of Christ on earth.

This clause continues the emphasis on mission from clause four. The successful outcome of proclamation is faith, which is again understood as universal in scope. The worldwide proclamation of clause four is paralleled to the response *en kosmō* presented here. As in other texts, we see an emphasis on the 'world-wide' nature of the gospel and its impact.[65]

Clearly the importance of Christian proclamation is emphasized. Marshall also notes: 'It is significant that the object of belief is not the gospel but the actual person to whom it testifies'.[66]

'Taken up in glory' (anelēmphthē en doxē)
Having presented the response to Christ in the world in clause five, the creed speaks of Christ being *taken up in glory*. Glory indicates 'brightness, splendor, or radiance and denotes in particular the glory, majesty and sublimity of God'.[67] To enter glory is thus to enter God's presence. The emphasis is on Christ's triumph and that he comes to share in the heavenly glory of God.

The clause is most likely to be a reference to the ascension, as is also indicated by the fact that *analambanō* is used elsewhere of Christ's ascension (Acts 1.2, 11, 22; Lk. 9.51). Hence, this clause shows that the creed is not structured chronologically.[68] But the phrase implies, not just that Christ ascended, but 'that he has been taken up into the realm of divine glory, there to reign with the Father'.[69] The emphasis then is on the result of the ascension: the exaltation of Christ to the realm of glory and hence of triumph. Clause six is the glorious climax of the story, which began in clause one with the enfleshment of the incarnation. It can be seen as a doxological conclusion.

---

65. See, e.g., Col. 1.5-6; 1 Tim. 1.15; 2.4-6.
66. Marshall, *Pastoral Epistles*, p. 528.
67. Knight, *Pastoral Epistles*, p. 186; see also D.C. Arichea, 'Translating Hymnic Materials: Theology and Translation in 1 Timothy 3.16', *BT* 58 (2007), p. 182.
68. But note that the instruction to preach the gospel and the implied promise that people will come to believe is given *between* the resurrection and the ascension in Lk. 24.47, and before Jesus' presumed departure in Mt. 28.16-20; see R.W. Micou, 'On ὤφθη ἀγγέλοις, I Tim. iii. 16', *JBL* 11 (1892), p. 202; Davies, *Pastoral Epistles*, p. 18.
69. Kelly, *Pastoral Epistles*, p. 92.

Reading with This Rule of Faith

How might this passage guide and shape our reading of the Scriptures in helpful ways? For as Billings notes, a rule of faith 'provides guidance for our functional theology: it provides a general theological framework in which the Bible is read.... it is a distillation of core Christian teaching that can help unveil the inherent patterns of Scripture'.[70] A rule can also function negatively by providing telling 'theological boundary markers' that guide and warn us. Here I will present how 1 Tim. 3.16 might function as such a rule for us.

Trinitarian

Although the creed is not overtly trinitarian, it can be seen to speak of the activity of the triune God. The use of the divine passive in clause one—*hos ephanerōthē en sarki*—reminds us that the action of the verb was undertaken by God the Father.[71] This is a clear and unequivocal statement of incarnation. The incarnation is rooted in the will and activity of the Father; he was the originator of the story told by the creed, and hence of the way of revelation and salvation. The pre-existence of the incarnate One is also spoken of, since the enfleshed One is said to have been 'manifested', and so was once hidden but now revealed. The creed does not underline the obedience of the One who was manifested in flesh, but this can be seen to be an implication of what is said, for Jesus was in fact manifested.

We have noted that the most likely meaning of *edikaiōthē en pneumati* is 'vindicated in spirit' with the reference being to the spiritual realm. But even so, this is the realm of the Spirit, for the spiritual realm is precisely to be understood as 'characterized by the presence and power of the Spirit'.[72] Hence, the Spirit is to be thought of as involved and active in the vindication of Jesus.

The creed as a 'rule' then speaks of the triune God. It establishes this framework for our reading. To fully understand the Scriptures involves understanding the God who is spoken of here and throughout Scripture as triune. For example, the creed proclaims that to comprehend the identity of the Jesus of the Gospels, we are to see him as the pre-existent one who was manifested in flesh by the Father. The Jesus of the Gospels cannot be fully understood without seeing him as the one who is manifested by and manifests another, that all the other actions proclaimed in the creed—vindication, seeing, preaching, believing, ascending—might also come to fruition.

---

70. Billings, *Word of God*, p. 22.
71. Clauses two and six also have divine passives, which speak of the activity of God the Father.
72. Towner, *Timothy and Titus*, p. 280; see, e.g., Mt. 26.41; Jn 3.6; Rom. 8.4-6, 13; Gal. 3.3; 4.29; Col. 2.5; 1 Pet. 3.18.

Story
The creed tells a story, a story of what God has done in God's world. This reminds us of the importance of narrative or story as a category as we interpret Scripture, although of course Scripture itself governs the meaning that we give to 'story', rather than this being an external category that we impose on Scripture. First and foremost, Scripture presents us with a narrative of God's activity for the salvation of the world. This strongly affirms the current trend of a narrative approach to interpretation, whilst of course not ruling out other approaches.

It is also a story in which those reciting the creed have a place. As we too recite it, we are reminded that we are actors, participants in the story that is told. It is the contemporary world of flesh, inhabited by the creed's readers, in which Jesus was manifested. Jesus' vindication in the spiritual realm has affected and affects the readers' lives deeply through the in-breaking of resurrection life. The gospel has been preached to us as those who recite the creed, and we have come to believe. Jesus has been taken up in glory, and the glorified Lord is present with the community by the Spirit. So this is a story in which those who recite the creed are involved, the story in which 'the church of the living God' finds its own story. In fact, this *gives* us our story. It is not a distant, 'intellectual' creed, but rather engages *us*. It quite simply tells *our* story.

Anti-dualistic
The creed was written and first read in a world where many lived within a worldview that was fundamentally dualistic. The material world was conceived of as a world of bondage, and salvation could be thought of as an escape from materiality. By contrast, the real world was the world of ideas, or the realm of spiritual reality. Of course, the impact of such dualism led to Docetism and to Gnostic thought.

Our creed is fundamentally anti-dualistic. It does not define precisely how the realms of 'earth' and 'heaven', or 'flesh' and 'spirit' are to be related. Rather it intimately ties earth and heaven together, but does so through the person of Jesus, the incarnate One. It is because he has been 'manifested in *flesh*' and then 'vindicated in *spirit*'—in the realm of the spirit—that he has tied these two potential antinomies together into one overarching unity. The potential dualism has not been overcome intellectually through brilliant reasoning or such like, but rather *personally* by the en-flesh-ment of the pre-existent one. As Schweizer notes, Christ's dominion 'is so all-embracing that it has welded heaven and earth together again'.[73] Categories that the

---

73. E. Schweizer, *Lordship and Discipleship* (London: SCM Press, 1960), p. 66; see also Fowl, *Story of Christ*, p. 193: 'in the Christ-event God overcame the barrier between material existence and heavenly status'. See also E. Schweizer, 'Two New Testament

world considers opposites—heaven and earth—have been united by Christ, who has come to share in both spheres.

This provides a significant lens through which to read the New Testament. Essentially, it functions negatively; as a 'rule of faith' it undermines and prohibits any reading that would fundamentally divorce earth and heaven. For example, parts of the New Testament can be read as dualistic; thus it might be possible to read Revelation in such a way that the physical 'stuff' of earth was thought to be unimportant, or totally dispensable. 2 Pet. 3.10-13 is similar. For some interpreters, the new life of the Spirit has been understood to be purely 'spiritual'. The creed undermines such anti-materialism, and proclaims the importance of the earthly and of the material.[74]

In so doing, the creed also proclaims the unity of reality, again not through philosophical argument but by proclaiming that in the person of the incarnate One heaven and earth—all reality—has been unified and has been determined to be the realm of his self-disclosure. As Strecker notes, 'the universality of the Christ event...embraces earth and heaven.... The reality and claim of the preexistent, earthly and exalted Christ are all-embracing. There is nothing that can withdraw itself from his mysterious presence (3.16a).'[75]

Universal
There is another sense in which the creed is universal. As noted above, *ekēruchthē en ethnesin* here means preached among all nations, not simply among 'Gentiles'. Similarly *episteuthē en kosmō*—'believed on in the world'—is all-encompassing. So the creed functions negatively at this point too. The Christ-event is not simply for Israel, but nor does it exclude Israel. The horizon of the creed is universal, and it denies any attempts to limit the significance of the Christ-event. Of course, it affirms the significance of believing, but it does not limit such believing ethnically, nor in any other way.

Creeds Compared: 1 Corinthians 15.3-5 and 1 Timothy 3.16', in W. Klassen and G.F. Snyder (eds.), *Current Issues in New Testament Interpretation: Essays in Honor of Otto A. Piper* (New York: Harper & Brothers, 1962), p. 171.

74. L.W. Donelson, *Colossians, Ephesians, First and Second Timothy, and Titus* (WestBC; Louisville, KY: Westminster/John Knox Press, 1996), p. 136, writes: 'Jesus' appearance in the flesh, coupled with God's vindication and glorification of him, validates and accentuates our own life in the flesh. Once again, Christology leads to ethics; the story of Jesus shows us how to live this life here.' See also Fowl, *Story of Christ*, p. 192, who notes how the content of 1 Tim. 3.16, with its vindication of Christ's appearance in the flesh, is the basis for the rejection of the false teachers' asceticism in 1 Tim. 4.1-5.

75. Strecker, *Theology of the New Testament*, p. 581.

Mystery

The hymn is introduced with this clause: 'without any doubt, the mystery of our religion is great'. This introduction provides the overall framework that the author wants us to bear in mind as we read the creed.

The use of *mustērion* serves to underline the importance of revelation. The creed reveals the story of the incarnate One and so in a crucial sense it is a revelation of a former secret, a manifestation of the *mustērion*. What was once unimaginable and unknown has now been revealed in the world, in flesh. In context, the 'mystery of our religion' is in fact Christ, and so the relative pronoun is given in its masculine form, *hos*. As Marshall notes, 'the mystery is at one and the same time the message about Christ and the Christ-event'.[76] The radical particularity and specificity of the life of the incarnate One is where the mystery has been concretely unveiled.

The mystery then is revealed and received. In this context, the proper perspective from which we are to approach our reading is one of faith, faith in the one who has manifested the incarnate One and so revealed the unimaginable, faith in Christ's vindication and exaltation which has happened in heaven. We seek not a neutral perspective from which to critique the Scriptures (as if there was such a position), but a perspective of believing from which we can receive the gift of the unveiling of the *mustērion*, as well as a perspective from which we can acknowledge that there still remains much which is beyond our knowing and understanding. Accordingly, it is the church, the community of those who have believed in Christ throughout the world in response to the proclamation of the story, and who are gathered in worship to recite creeds such as this one, which is the primary locus of theological interpretation.

The Church's Place in the Creed

The church does not simply proclaim this creed from a spectator's vantage point. As already noted, it is the worshipping community's story. But it is *also* significant that the ongoing activity of the church—in proclamation and in seeking to be the vehicle of saving faith—is *part* of the creed. Gospel proclamation and response is actually embedded as a part of the mystery of God's saving work,[77] and as a dimension of salvation history, since 'proclaimed among nations, believed in throughout the world' are clauses which are *part of* the creed. As Dibelius and Conzelmann note: 'proclamation and

---

76. Marshall, *Pastoral Epistles*, p. 523. Note also L.T. Johnson, *Letters to Paul's Delegates: 1 Timothy, 2 Timothy, Titus* (The New Testament in Context; Valley Forge, PA: Trinity Press International, 1996), p. 157: 'The "mystery of godliness" for this community is a living person, the resurrected Lord Jesus'. On *mustērion* see Towner, *Goal of our Instruction*, pp. 87-89.

77. See D. Krause, *1 Timothy* (Readings; London: T. & T. Clark, 2004), p. 82.

faith itself are included in the salvation event'.[78] This is to impart a huge significance to the ongoing mission of the church.[79] The outcome of salvation history is such that it can be proclaimed in aorists, but *part* of that story is the ongoing work of proclamation that is the church's calling.

This could be seen as a vote of confidence in the ability of the church to proclaim the gospel. But this would be to misread the theological thrust of the creed. The creed is about the triumph of God in the world; it is about the unveiling of God's mysterious actions to achieve God's overarching purposes through Christ. The emphasis then is on God's work through, with and in God's people. The confidence reverberating through the creed is this confidence in God's ability to transform and to sovereignly achieve God's purposes. The activity of proclamation and of being a vehicle for faith is in the end seen as God's activity and the work of God in which the church participates.

This is a powerful perspective to bring to *our* reading of Scripture. From God's eschatological perspective, we can see that God's work *will* be accomplished through our reading, and through our proclamation of the Living Word. Our all-too-human activity of reading, studying and proclaiming is to be perceived as part of God's overarching work, and a participation in God's saving story in the world.

Victory

As well as telling a story, we see a progression, or a theological *direction* in the six clauses: the first couplet concentrates on Christ's work accomplished, the second on Christ's work made known, and the third on Christ's work acknowledged.[80] Overall the emphasis is on the triumph of Christ and the effects of that triumph.

Thus, the hymn concludes with the triumph or victory of Christ being 'taken up in glory'. This underlines the total vindication of the incarnate One, and the demonstration of that vindication in the cosmos. But the

---

78. Dibelius and Conzelmann, *Pastoral Epistles*, p. 63. Simpson, *Pastoral Epistles*, p. 62, comments on the clause 'preached among nations': 'Was this fact worthy to be chronicled among divine marvels?' See also Barrett, *Pastoral Epistles*, p. 66; Krause, *1 Timothy*, pp. 80-81.

79. The emphasis on the believing community in 1 Tim. 3.16 is in keeping with what is said about the church in 3.15: the church is 'the household of God, which is the church of the living God, the pillar and bulwark of the truth'. The church is not an added extra, but plays a crucial role.

80. See Knight, *Pastoral Epistles*, p. 186. Gundry, 'Form, Meaning and Background', p. 208, writes of 'roughly synonymous couplets' which concern revelation, proclamation and reception; Marshall, *Pastoral Epistles*, p. 504, speaks of appearance, proclamation and recognition; see also Lau, *Manifest in Flesh*, p. 91.

confidence of the creed is also evident in *edikaiōthē en pneumati*; the one whose life ended on a cross was then vindicated in the triumph of resurrection, raised to the spiritual realm and seen by angels. Overall then, the creed proclaims the triumph of God in the work of Christ.[81]

As we have noted, all the verbs used in the creed are aorist passives. This is understandable with regard to clauses one to three and for clause six, since they refer to past events. However, as the Christian assemblies recite the creed, clauses four and five cannot on any reckoning be regarded as completed past events: 'proclaimed among nations' (*ekēruchthē en ethnesin*), 'believed in throughout the world' (*episteuthē en kosmō*).[82] Other New Testament passages reflect something of this same sense of completeness; note Col. 1.5-6: 'You have heard of this hope before in the word of the truth, the gospel that has come to you. Just as it is bearing fruit and growing in the whole world, so it has been bearing fruit among yourselves from the day you heard it and truly comprehended the grace of God.'[83] But still the use of the aorists in clauses four and five is remarkable.

What is happening here? The perspective of the creed is thoroughly eschatological.[84] This is how things will be—and they are so certain that even ongoing processes with significant future elements (for clearly as the author writes, the gospel proclamation is ongoing, and people will continue to believe) can be spoken of as if they were completed. These matters are so certain that they are proclaimed as completed events.

The creed then proclaims the certainty of the future for it is being seen from God's point of view. It also reveals that in which the element of triumph is founded. It is not a confidence in the church's ability in proclamation, or its power to convince the world. Rather, confidence is squarely

---

81. Krause, *1 Timothy*, p. 79, sums this up well: 'In a sense the rhetorical effect of the passive verbs with dative objects places Jesus in the centre of both God's saving actions in him and the Gentiles and "world's" belief in him. In other words, this aspect of the hymn makes plain the way in which Christ is the meeting point between God and God's people.'

82. Towner, *Timothy and Titus*, p. 285: 'The aorist tenses are not to be read as signalling completion, but rather fact. In God's salvation drama, Paul (and the church) has proclaimed the gospel and the mission has produced results. But the ministry and the results are characteristic of the church's present age—as the age continues toward the end, so must the activity.' However, the last sentence does not give sufficient emphasis to the eschatological perspective of the two clauses.

83. The sense of the gospel 'for the world' is also found, for example, in Rom. 1.8; 1 Pet. 5.9; see also Mt. 5.14; 8.11; 24.14; Mk 13.27; Jn 1.29; 3.16-17; 4.42; 12.47; Acts 1.8; 13.47; Rom. 9.17; 10.18; 11.15; 2 Cor. 2.14; 3.2; 5.19; Col. 1.23; 1 Thess. 1.8; 1 John 4.14.

84. Marshall, *Pastoral Epistles*, pp. 527-28, writes on clause four: 'The clause is clearly written from the church's post-resurrection perspective; the aorist *ekēruchthē* sums up an ongoing process which in principle has already decisively taken place'.

based in God's actions and God's nature. God is the one who, having begun the story will bring it to completion. All of history is seen here from its end, even though the community lives at a time before the reality that the creed proclaims is fully accomplished. From God's perspective the future is certain, and so can be proclaimed in the creed. This is not misplaced human triumphalism—but rather a conscious awareness of the Lordship of Christ over the future.

As we undertake our interpretative task, this perspective on 'the whole story' is helpful. For example, in our detailed debates on ethics, and on the polity of the church in the present, this proclamation of the *surety* of the conclusion of the story should remain in view. As we read Scripture 'between the times' the testimony of these aorists about the certainty of events from God's perspective reminds us of what is ultimate, and what is merely transitory. This overarching perspective of the conclusion of the story, and of the reality of God's triumph in Christ should inform our reading of Scripture.

Doxological and Celebratory
The creed emphasizes and underlines the importance of worship. This is not a text that *simply* tells a story. Rather its home in the early Christian communities was almost certainly as part of the worshipping life of the assemblies. It is thus to be entered into in a spirit of praise and worship, rejoicing that this is who God is for the world. This is particularly highlighted by the way the creed finishes; the believers are in some sense to themselves be 'taken up in glory' as they recite or sing it. We are reminded that the incarnate One is now in glory, in the presence of the Father, and our contemporary worship is to enter into the ongoing worship of heaven. As Saarinen notes: 'the believers' confession of their faith, expressed in this christological hymn, let[s] them be partakers of the eschatological glory. In this way the liturgical hymn connects the believers' reality with life in the spirit and in glory.'[85] The creed also emphasizes that the true goal of our reading of Scripture is worship, to the glory to God.

Conclusion

It is not my intention to argue that the creed given in 1 Tim. 3.16 is sufficient as a 'rule of faith' for us. It clearly leaves too much unsaid for this.[86] Hence, it is best to call it a 'proto-creed'. But I hope to have shown that this proto-

---

85. Saarinen, *Pastoral Epistles*, p. 73.
86. For example, the death of Christ is not emphasized here, although clearly it is implied. Hultgren, *1–11 Timothy, Titus*, p. 80, comments: 'The hymn reflects a theological outlook, but it does not intend to be comprehensive'. Further, it is possible that only a part of the creed is quoted here; see Gundry, 'Form, Meaning and Background', p. 219.

creed has multiple functions in a 'ruled reading' of Scripture. Further, the presence of such a proto-creed encourages us—as perhaps it encouraged the early Christians—to further develop such creeds and to further develop the practice of reading Scripture using a rule of faith. The presence in Scripture itself of such a proto-rule, that can be seen to function in rich and positive ways in the reading of the New Testament, legitimates, encourages and stimulates our activity of ruled reading.

10

'EXEGESIS AS LOVE':
ENCOUNTERING TRUTH IN JOHN 14.15-26

Tim Meadowcroft

I was first alerted to the possibility of 'exegesis as love' by an article by Clifton Black in which he considers 'exegesis as prayer'.[1] In the context of a wide-ranging reflection on prayer in the Bible, Black notes that 'exegesis, like prayer, is not cold conjecture but relationship with a God so madly in love with us and the world that only the foolishness of the cross makes sense (1 Cor. 1.18-31)'.[2] Although the comment is made with respect to prayer as a response of gratitude to God that pervades all that the believer does, at this point Black notes the love both of God and for God that undergirds this response. In doing so he thereby points, intentionally or not, toward the deeper possibility that any interaction with the word of God on the part of humanity is an act of love—hence, 'exegesis as love'.

In the matter of the human encounter with the word of God, this is in tune with the words of Jesus in his final discourse (Jn 14.15-26), which suggest that, in the Johannine perspective, the word of God becomes most audible in the dynamic of love activated by the Holy Spirit.[3] This emerges in that the word of God as Scripture and the Word of God as Jesus, the incarnate one, comes to humanity as and by means of love. As a result, I will argue, the reading and interpretation of Scripture, which for the purposes of this essay are assumed under the rubric 'exegesis', are also, or ought to be, participation in an act of love. And interwoven with the theme of love is the emergence of truth, as a result of which also, it is argued, this loving participation in the reading and interpretation of Scripture entails an encounter

---

1. C.C. Black, 'Exegesis as Prayer', *Princeton Seminary Bulletin* 23 NS (2002), pp. 131-45.
2. Black, 'Exegesis as Prayer', p. 143. The article is based on a lecture on his inauguration into the Otto A. Piper chair of Biblical Theology at Princeton Seminary.
3. See also T.J. Meadowcroft, *The Message of the Word of God: The Glory of God Made Known* (BSTBT; Leicester: Inter-Varsity Press, 2011), pp. 244-55.

with truth. In that context I suggest that 'truth' in Jesus' final discourse may fruitfully be thought of in wider terms as 'knowing'.

This essay is primarily an exposition of the biblical passage in question, and takes its lead from the form and content of Jesus' discourse as remembered in the Johannine tradition, albeit from the selective perspective of an exploration into the interpretation of Scripture. This is informed from time to time by allusion to more systematic treatments of such themes as love, participation, hospitality and the relational nature of knowing.

On Love: A Theological Background

Before beginning, a word on love itself is in order. The Bible itself nowhere defines love, and perhaps this is why theologians generally have themselves wisely desisted from trying to do so. The trouble is, though, that there has also been a corresponding decentralization of love, at least in the Western theological tradition.[4] Or, to shift the metaphor, it has not generally been seen as a starting point. This is partly attributable to the fact that love, by its nature, is not something to be talked about so much as to be experienced. It is possible to define something without experiencing it, but to do so in the case of love is somewhat beside the point.[5] When I write of the encounter with the Bible as 'love' I am then speaking of encountering the Bible as part of entering into an experience, and the experience, for the purposes of this essay, is that which is conveyed through the Gospel of John.

When I speak of love, then, I refer to what happens when love is present. A programmatic verse in that respect is Jn 3.16. Although that verse suffers from having become a cliché it is still profoundly true that the great defining act of love is the identification of God with the *kosmos* by means of Jesus. The self-giving of Jesus shows us love. A response of love to that love is marked by keeping the word of Jesus (14.23), and the word is kept because a response of love also entails belief that Jesus is who he says he is (16.27). But this is not merely a cerebral response; it entails the same giving of oneself to the other that the life of Jesus exhibited. For 'no one has greater love than this, to lay down one's life for one's friends' (15.13). Love thereby entails both a commitment to truth as discovered in knowing Jesus, and a corresponding life lived for others that reflects the life of Jesus.[6] By 'exegesis

---

4. T.J. Oord, *The Nature of Love: A Theology* (St Louis, MO: Chalice Press, 2010), pp. 7-15. Contra my comments here, Oord then attempts to define love, rather unwisely and not particularly satisfactorily, in my view.

5. A similar case of the value of experience over description is that of the comedic. I have never read a treatment of the nature of comedy that comes close to capturing the experience of well done comedy.

6. D.M. Smith, *The Theology of the Gospel of John* (Cambridge: Cambridge University Press, 1995), p. 135: 'These Christians, and especially the members of the Johannine

as love', therefore, I mean the reading and interpretation of Scripture as an important aspect of participation in a life and way of knowing that is modeled and formed by Jesus.[7]

The work of trinitarian theologians gives a systematic expression of this notion in respect both of the relational and of the interpretive aspects. Jürgen Moltmann, for example, explores what it means to say that 'God is love'.[8] For him the very nature of God is that the persons of the Trinity respond to one another in love. Indeed, for Moltmann, to speak of a person with respect to the trinitarian conception of God is to speak of 'existing-in-relationship'.[9] Inherent in his thought is the possibility that this love flows out to affect all else that may be spoken of as in relationship with this God who is 'existing-in-relationship'.[10]

If key elements in this overflow of Godhead love towards those whom God has created and redeemed are Scripture and Christ the Word, then the reading and interpretation of those words must surely be soaked in love. This leads N.T. Wright to speak, albeit tentatively, of a 'hermeneutic of love' in reading the words of Scripture.[11] Whether he is right that the best way to express this methodologically is by means of what he calls a 'critical realism', he is surely right that the whole process of reading Scripture entails love in the sense of 'attention' to the other in our reading. The reading process is therefore a 'conversation'.[12] Or, to reprise the term used by Fiddes, it is 'participation' in an exchange.

The intermingling of truth with love in the passage that we are about to examine also alerts us to the epistemological significance of a loving encounter with Scripture and the Word to whom Scripture bears witness. Somehow the love of God into which we are drawn and which we express in the reading of Scripture works itself out in the manner in which we know. In one comprehensive exploration of the possibilities, Esther Lightcap Meek sets out a covenantally based epistemology which she entitles

---

community, saw in Jesus' perfect fulfillment of the commission and love of God in his ministry and death the model for their own lives and relationships'.

7. P.S. Fiddes, *Participating in God: A Pastoral Doctrine of the Trinity* (London: Darton, Longman & Todd, 2000), pp. 33-34, 37, speaks of this loving engagement with a God who loves as 'participation'.

8. J. Moltmann, *The Trinity and the Kingdom of God: The Doctrine of God* (trans. M. Kohl; London: SCM Press, 1981), p. 58.

9. Moltmann, *The Trinity and the Kingdom of God*, p. 171.

10. Moltmann, *The Trinity and the Kingdom of God*, p. 59: 'That is why we have indeed to see the history of creation as *the tragedy of the divine love*, but must view the history of redemption as *the feast of the divine joy*' (emphasis original).

11. N.T. Wright, *The New Testament and the People of God* (Minneapolis: Fortress Press, 1992), p. 63.

12. Wright, *The New Testament and the People of God*, p. 64.

Loving to Know.[13] There may be other starting and organizing points around which an epistemology of love might be organized, but Meek is surely right to remind us that 'human knowing is fraught with covenantally constituted interpersoned relationship'.[14] Jesus would have called this 'love' and in doing so spoken of the accompanying encounter with truth in relationship.

This theological background—of participation in the love of God as a hermeneutical and epistemological key to the reading and interpretation of Scripture—is that against which I now turn to the reading of Jn 14.15-26.

Love

During his final discourse, as recorded in John's Gospel, Jesus' promise of the Spirit is interlaced by the theme of love. The opening sentence of the passage under examination calls for the disciples to love Jesus (v. 15). They in turn are 'loved by my Father' and by Jesus (v. 21).[15] Somehow we sense also as we read vv. 23-24 that this love into which the disciples are caught up is the very love enjoyed within the Godhead between the father and the son. This becomes more explicit at 15.10: 'If you keep my commandments, you will abide in my love, just as I have kept my Father's commandments and abide in his love'. A little further on in the discourse it also becomes evident that this Godhead love into which the disciples are incorporated emanates out to characterize relationships between the disciples themselves: 'I am giving you these commands so that you may love one another' (15.17).[16] Of course, this dynamic of love is not always a guarantee of peace; Jesus was clear on that a little later in his discourse when he warns the disciples that this very love is capable of attracting hatred and opposition (15.18-25).

On the evidence of Jesus' final discourse, an important aspect of the ongoing communication between God and humanity is that it is soaked in love. The words of Scripture are a central part of that communication, and so therefore is their interpretation. That means that the process of reading and interpretation is also imbued with love.

The Paraclete

It is not possible to derive an accurate technical description of the Godhead from these verses, if in fact it is possible or desirable to do so at all, but it is clear that this process of love is fuelled by the work of the 'Advocate' (v. 16;

---

13. E. Lightcap Meek, *Loving to Know: Introducing Covenant Epistemology* (Eugene, OR: Cascade, 2011).
14. Meek, *Loving to Know*, p. 402.
15. Unless otherwise indicated, biblical quotations in English are from NRSV.
16. For a theological exposition of this principle, see M. Volf, *After our Likeness: The Church as the Image of the Trinity* (Grand Rapids: Eerdmans, 1998), pp. 192-98.

Greek: *paraklētos*). This is a term whose meaning is subject to much debate.[17] Etymologically, the sense of the word is of one who is called to be alongside another one. The English translation 'advocate' is in that respect a good one, as it contains the idea of somebody who takes the part of another and is present with him or her. In another respect, however, the translation is problematic in that 'advocate' in English has also acquired connotations of a protagonist in a formal court room setting, one perhaps more interested in the advancement of an argument than the care of a person. The Greek word being translated is more inclusive of the notion of 'compassion' within its meaning.[18] The Spirit, as one who is called alongside to take the part of another, also cares deeply and compassionately about the one for whom the Spirit advocates.

Note that in v. 16 the promise from Jesus is that 'another' advocate will be given to the disciples, one with no expiry date who will extend beyond the time frame of the earthly life of Jesus. This implies that the love between Jesus and his followers will be sustained 'forever' (v. 16) by the agency of the advocate, also known as 'the Spirit of truth' (v. 17).

The significance of the relationship and its continuity with Jesus is emphasized by the vocabulary employed in v. 17b. This Spirit is one who will 'abide with' and 'be in' the disciples. The Greek phrase translated as 'abide with', *menō para*, foreshadows Jesus' comments on the vine in the next chapter in that the verb *menō*, translated in the NRSV as 'abide with' and referring to the relationship of Jesus himself with his disciples (15.4-10), is the same as the one used here of the paraclete. As for the paraclete, the outworking of the words of Jesus 'abiding in' the disciples is love (15.12-14). There is a difference, however, in that the preposition governing the indirect object of the verb is *para* ('with') in ch. 14 rather than *en* ('in') as it is later in the discourse. Prepositions are notoriously unstable in most languages, including New Testament Greek, so care must be taken in drawing too well defined a distinction of meaning based on their occurrence. Nevertheless, it does seem that the choice of *para* here is a deliberate play on words with the term *para-klētos*, and implies a relationship between two beings. As one who draws alongside, the paraclete draws alongside the disciple. This is slightly different from the idea of incorporation into Christ implied by the vine imagery of John 15. However, that image and the idea of incorporation is then implied in the final phrase of v. 17 regarding the paraclete, who, as well as drawing alongside, 'will be in' the disciples. By means of this portmanteau foreshadowing of John 15—abiding with and being in—the writer indicates that the 'Spirit of truth', the paraclete, both

---

17. A.J. Köstenberger, *John* (Grand Rapids: Baker Academic, 2004), p. 435.
18. Max Turner, 'Holy Spirit', in J.B. Green and S. McKnight (eds.), *Dictionary of Jesus and the Gospels* (Downers Grove, IL: InterVarsity Press, 1992), p. 349.

incorporates the believer and is in relationship with the believer. The two ideas remain in creative tension with each other.

If the reading and interpretation of Scripture flow from and reflect the love of God, this tension between relationship and incorporation that characterizes the disciple's relationship with God is also a feature of reading and interpreting Scripture. On the one hand, we encounter the Scriptures as autonomous responsible beings meeting an entity other than and different from ourselves. We bring all that we are to the task: our context, abilities, learning and experience. We initiate a conversation with the text such that the potential meaning of the text is drawn out by the particular reader/interpreter in a way that would not be possible for any other reader/interpreter. This does not mean that the text can be made to say anything the reader wants it to say, but it does mean that the reader has a responsibility to 'make' meaning as he or she reads, to hear the voice of the text in all its particularity and relevance. On the other hand, the reader/interpreter is in some way incorporated into God and reads as one indwelt by the Spirit.[19] This means that the words of Scripture are able to be perceived as God's words with all the possibilities that flow from that.

This tension is relevant to how a Spirit-dwelt exegesis of love relates to postmodern understandings of reader responses to the text. The respect for the personality of the reader implicit in Jesus' promise does seem to place a responsibility on the reader to bring him or herself into the reading. To that extent, a careful listening to people like Jacques Derrida with his emphasis on deconstruction,[20] and Elizabeth Schussler Fiorenza with her hermeneutic of suspicion,[21] is important. For they challenge us to know well what we bring to the conversation with Scripture, and to acknowledge that we do not read in a vacuum but out of a context and a set of assumptions. A hermeneutic of suspicion, for example, teaches us at the very least to deconstruct and suspect the assumptions and distortions that beset our own readings, but also to understand that our own experience and context may enrich our readings.

At the same time incorporation into the love of God leads to a reading that identifies closely with the text itself, because in the Spirit we dwell in

---

19. W. Olhausen, 'A "Polite" Response to Anthony Thiselton', in C. Bartholomew, C. Greene and K. Möller (eds.), *After Pentecost: Language and Biblical Interpretation* (Carlisle: Paternoster Press, 2001), pp. 127-28.

20. The issues raised by the work of Jacques Derrida are neatly summarized by J. Barton, 'Beliebigkeit', in Y. Sherwood (ed.), *Derrida's Bible (Reading a Page of Scripture with a Little Help from Derrida)* (New York: Palgrave MacMillan, 2004), pp. 301-303.

21. E. Schüssler Fiorenza, *In Memory of Her: A Feminist Theological Reconstruction of Christian Origins* (New York: Crossroad, 1983), especially her introductory material (pp. 1-96).

the God whose story is told by the text. This engenders in the Christian reader an ethic of reading that takes seriously the intentions of the text, as far as they may be discerned.[22] To this extent, a reading that is tuned by the indwelling presence of the Spirit allows the text to speak with its own voice. Somehow both an appreciation of the independence of the reader from the text and an indwelling respect for the text itself must feature in an exegesis of love. After all, that is the nature of participation.

The Spirit of Truth

This paraclete, who draws alongside the follower of Jesus, is also 'the Spirit of truth' (v. 17). This implies that the dynamic of love of which Jesus speaks has also to do with knowing and understanding. The first hint in that direction is that the people of God have not been '[left]... orphaned' (v. 18). The coming of the paraclete as the Spirit of truth encapsulates God's commitment in Christ to maintaining a conversation with humanity. The quest for truth is not one that we undertake alone; it is one that takes place within the context of knowing God. It is something that has been made possible by the incarnation of God in Christ and remains possible through the ongoing work of the Spirit who draws alongside.[23]

This has implications for Christian knowing, not least that any quest for truth is undertaken in conversation with the great story of God's involvement with humankind that is contained in the pages of Scripture. This does not mean that all that needs to be known resides within the pages of the Bible; I may be led in aspects of the exploration of the good earth that God has made by those whom the writer of John's Gospel might categorize as in 'the world'. It does mean, however, that all knowledge is best received and understood against the backdrop of God's ongoing involvement in the creation and redemption of the world that he has made and its inhabitants.

John somewhat complicates this by his insistence that there are those who do not have this relationship with the truth that comes through knowing God. He is at his most blunt at v. 19: 'the world will no longer see me, but you will see me'. This is reinforced in v. 24: 'Whoever does not love me does not keep my words'. If, as I am suggesting, the notion of truth in the discourse of Jesus has to do with the nature of knowing as well as with the content of knowing God in Christ, does this mean that only Christians can achieve competence in various skills and knowledge? This appears to be at

---

22. Note the reference to the 'morality' of reading in the subtitle to the influential volume by K.J. Vanhoozer, *Is There a Meaning in This Text? The Bible, the Reader and the Morality of Literary Knowledge* (Leicester: Apollos, 1998).

23. In that respect this exegesis and epistemology of love is a thoroughly trinitarian enterprise.

odds with the understanding indicated above that God's truth is not confined to the religious dimension of life, and it is certainly at odds with experience. Part of the resolution to this lies in an appreciation of the use in John's Gospel of the word *kosmos* or 'world'.[24] This word sometimes simply refers to the created order, all of which is loved by the creator; at other times it refers to that part of the created order that chooses not to acknowledge the creator. It is the latter understanding that is in play here. So the gospel writer is not saying that comprehension and even a measure of enlightenment in its broadest sense is only available to Christians. He is saying that understanding in the light of God's story in Christ and through the Holy Spirit gives a unique—and we can say even a particularly true—appreciation of the way the world works and is.[25] Christians ought then to bring a value added contribution to the task of exegesis and to the wider enterprise of epistemology—of the very nature of our knowing—because of our participation in the love of the Godhead. That is one of the consequences of the promise of Jesus here recorded.

But a caveat: this does not eliminate the need for humility on the part of Christian readers and interpreters of Scripture. For creation also springs from the love of God, and creation, flawed and broken as it may be, still in some measure reflects that love. There is plenty of truth in the world that God has made that may come in surprising ways and from surprising sources.

The Teaching

There are several points at which the link between the love of the Father, Jesus, and the paraclete are explicitly linked with some expression of God's speaking. Our passage opens with Jesus' own directive, 'If you love me, you will keep my commandments' (v. 15). This sentiment is repeated in v. 21. The same point is made using slightly different vocabulary in v. 23: 'Those who love me will keep my word'.

Jesus then draws the same continuity link between himself and the paraclete with respect to his commandments or teaching that we have already noted with respect to love. The baton of teaching represented by 'these things [which I have said] to you while I am still with you' (v. 25) will be grasped by the 'Holy Spirit', who will 'will remind [the disciples] of everything that [Jesus has] said to [them]' (v. 26). The Spirit will also 'teach [them] everything' (v. 26). There are two categories of instruction here—

---

24. J. Painter, 'World', in Green and McKnight (eds.), *Dictionary of Jesus and the Gospels*, pp. 889-90.
25. N. Wolterstorff, *Art in Action: Toward a Christian Aesthetic* (Carlisle: Solway, 1980), pp. 67-78.

everything which Jesus has conveyed to his disciples and 'everything' *per se*—with just the hint that the instruction of Jesus is a subset of a wider field of knowledge that the Holy Spirit will convey to believers. The teaching of Jesus does not end with his death, resurrection and ascension; it continues, and perhaps is even enhanced, through the agency of the Sprit drawing alongside and indwelling followers of Jesus. This enhancement of knowing in the wake of Jesus' death is foreshadowed by the dynamic of memory described in 2.22 (and treated further below); we might now suppose that this dynamic is enhanced by the ongoing activity of the Spirit.

An important question to consider is what Jesus may have meant in referring to his commandments and to what he has taught. In particular, was he referring only to the content of his spoken communications with the disciples or was there something wider in mind? The evidence of the Gospel itself is mixed. More often than not, reference to Jesus' 'words' or 'word' is to his particular utterances. However there are hints that these are gradually forming into something that transcends the immediate context. A technical word for that is the *kerugma*, the proclamation of the gospel witnessed to by the earliest believers and now encapsulated in Scripture.[26] Jn 12.47-49 suggests that possibility, as does 17.6. In the latter context, Jesus is commending his disciples into the future without him and a recurrent theme therein is that they will take his 'words' with them into that future. For the first generation, that may well have been the orally shared memory of Jesus' words, but we know that that 'word' was subsequently formed into a text bearing witness to the 'word' and the Word.

Correspondingly, 'commandments' in this context should not be thought of merely as a prescriptive list of instructions.[27] The Greek *entolē* is overwhelmingly the term of choice by the Septuagint to translate *mitzvah*, commandment. In the Old Testament usage, most evident in Ps. 119, this is virtually synonymous with *torah*, a term that implies a body of teaching. So it is that reference to Jesus' 'commandments' may also be understood as a reference to a body of teaching rather than merely to particular utterances in the imperative mood.

There is a tantalizing glimpse of the interaction between the word as *kerugma* and the Word, Jesus, at Jn 2.22, alluded to above. The context is Jesus' cleansing of the temple which culminates in Jesus' cryptic identification of himself with the temple building. Only at the end of his earthly life were the disciples able to discern what he was talking about. They did so by reflection on 'the scripture and the word that Jesus had spoken'. We also

---

26. D.S. Ferguson, 'Kerygma', in W. Elwell (ed.), *Evangelical Dictionary of Theology* (Grand Rapids: Baker Academic, 2nd edn, 2001), pp. 653-54.

27. D.A. Carson, *The Gospel according to John* (Leicester: Inter-Varsity Press, 1991), p. 498.

glimpse elsewhere that the notion of Scripture, while having its most obvious referent to the Old Testament, also gradually came to include certain writings from the apostolic age (2 Pet. 1.19-21; 3.16). Together these writings—the Old Testament and the apostolic—along with the spoken words of Jesus bring understanding to the disciples.[28] By the end of the book of Revelation, the author of that book expects that the text created by the spoken word contains the words of God (22.7).

With respect to the context of John 14, it is unlikely that the disciples understood the paraclete as one who would deliver texts to them. If they understood at all at that pre-resurrection point, they would probably have assumed some kind of continuation of the oral interaction with their existing Scriptures and traditions that were the hallmark of Jesus' teaching with them. The wider *kerugma*, however, shows the gradual formation of a testimony to the things bequeathed to the disciples by Jesus.[29] Furthermore, the work of the Spirit of truth was seen to be a crucial element in the formation of the textual witness to this testimony (1 Pet. 2.1-19).[30] By the time of the formation of the Gospel of John, one or two generations after the discourse recorded in John 14,[31] it would have been clear to the followers of Jesus that part of the role of the advocate was the scriptural preservation of Jesus' words. These themselves become part of the spreading circle of witness envisaged by John's Gospel (e.g., 15.26-27).[32]

From this distance we may then see that one of the outcomes of the formation and preservation of Scripture is a continuation of the dynamic of love and truth with which Jesus is concerned in his final discourse. The truth encapsulated in the Scriptures springs from the loving heart of the Godhead, and is discerned by the disciples who themselves are caught up into this love and truth and bear witness to it in the formation of the Scriptures. The Scriptures themselves, breathed as they are by the Spirit, continue to bear the

---

28. Smith, *Theology of the Gospel of John*, p. 79: 'Johannine theology presupposes God, scripture, Jesus, tradition about him, and a distinctly Christian understanding of who he was'. In the same context, Smith speaks of this at work in the church as a community of the Spirit.

29. For further, see G.E. Ladd, *A Theology of the New Testament* (Grand Rapids: Eerdmans, 1993), pp. 364-78.

30. See also Rev. 22.7. The work of prophecy was assumed to be the work of the Spirit, so the binding of the words of prophecy into a scroll implies the preservation in text of the witness of the Spirit.

31. On the dating of the Johannine literature, see F.J. Moloney, *The Gospel of John* (Collegeville, MN: Liturgical Press, 1989), pp. 2-3.

32. On the extension of the mission of Jesus on the part of the disciples, see A.J. Köstenberger, *The Mission of Jesus and the Disciples according to the Fourth Gospel: With Implications for the Fourth Gospel's Purpose and the Mission of the Contemporary Church* (Grand Rapids: Eerdmans, 1998), pp. 141-69.

love and truth of God's word. They become the very means by which the words of God the truth and the acts of God who is love speak and act in the lives and communities of those who preserve and interpret them. Their reading and interpretation are thereby participation in the love between God and the followers of Jesus.

'Keeping' the w / Word

By focusing on knowing with respect to love in my consideration of John 14, I have thus far omitted to acknowledge an important aspect of this experience, namely, the requirement to 'keep' the teaching and commands of Jesus. This aspect peppers the final discourse of Jesus. Verses 15, 21, 23 and 24 all speak of 'keeping' the commands, while the latter two references draw a line between those who 'keep' and those who do not. In each case, the Greek word is *tēreō*. While *tēreō* may in certain contexts include the idea of obedience (as implied by the NIV translation of vv. 23-24, for example, with 'obey'), it primarily entails guarding or preserving or protecting something. It contains the idea of taking responsibility for the well being of something. And that something, as we have seen, is the teaching and commands of Jesus.

Since there is a Greek verb available to the writer which more explicitly means 'to obey' (*hupakouō*), presumably the more allusive term has been used here for a reason. We have been gradually uncovering a dynamic of love and reception of truth which reflects the word of God made visible in Christ and sustained through the Spirit. Participation in this dynamic is made possible by the text of Scripture which has come to embody the words and commands of God. Therefore, the attitude which is adopted towards this text is critical. That is why Jesus calls for his disciples to 'keep' his commands and words. This may include obedience to the text but it entails much more than that. It also asks the follower of Jesus to take on a responsibility for the words of Jesus as encountered in the Scriptures: to care for them, to foster them, to guard them, to preserve them and to read and interpret them. Love for God is expressed as the reader/interpreter undertakes this care for God's word, and in doing so participates in the exegetical conversation.

Christ Shows Himself

The outcome of the process uncovered above is that Jesus may be made known to his disciples. The train of thought goes like this. On the day that the earthly presence of Jesus is no longer available, anyone who loves Jesus is also loved by the Father and will be loved by Jesus in return. Moreover, to such people, despite his physical absence, Jesus will show himself. One of the disciples, Judas, then asks about this promise of Jesus to show himself with the question, 'how is it that you will reveal yourself?' (v. 22). The phrase translated as 'how is it that' (*ti gegonen*) is difficult to capture exactly. The sense is more 'what has happened' or 'how can it be' that you are about to show yourself to us.[33] The expression implies that Jesus has somehow cut across the assumptions of his listeners, as he was often wont to do. Most commentators assume at this point that the problem is that Judas and his colleagues were expecting a more visible and politicized manifestation of the presence of Jesus, hence his use of the phrase 'and not to the world' (v. 22).[34]

But it is also possible that Judas' puzzlement arises from the notion that Jesus will continue to reveal himself to those who had not known him in the flesh but somehow do still see him and hence know him. These are certainly the terms in which Jesus responds, whether because he is deliberately adding a new dimension to the question or because that was how he too understood the question. In a sense, it does not matter which. What is important is that what follows in the answer is an explanation, albeit still somewhat cryptic, which picks up on the two aspects of the question posed by Judas. The first is clarification as to why this manifestation of himself is 'not to the world'. We have discussed something of this above and will not revisit it now. The second is an explanation as to how Jesus will continue to make himself known. In brief, he does so through both the word and the love contained in that word that he has spoken and that will continue to be available through the ministration of 'the Advocate, the Holy Spirit' (v. 26). The logic of this train of thought is that the love of the Father and the Son for each other and for the disciples, and which is returned by the disciples, the truth that is generated out of this love, and the teachings and the text that bear witness to this truth and love, all reveal Jesus.

The verb that contains this notion of revelation is *emphanizō*, which Jesus uses to express that he will 'reveal' himself to future disciples (v. 21) and which Judas then echoes in his clarificatory question (v. 22). It occurs only here in John's Gospel and eight other times in the New Testament. There are similarly ten uses in the Greek Old Testament (the LXX including apocryphal books), only four of which are not in the apocryphal material and hence with a Hebrew equivalent available to us. At one level the word simply concerns passing on information, although there is a sense of it being information that could not otherwise have been known by the recipient.[35] It

---

33. B.F. Westcott, *The Gospel according to St John* (1880 repr.; London: James Clark, 1958), p. 207, suggests: 'how is it that?'

34. See, e.g., R.E. Brown, *The Gospel according to John (XIII–XXI): Introduction, Translation, and Notes* (AB, 29A; Garden City, NY: Doubleday, 1970), p. 647.

35. E.g., Acts 23.15, 22; 24.1; 25.2, 15; 2 Macc. 3.7; 11.29.

can contain a hint of mystery and otherworldly communication.[36] And on at least one occasion it speaks of the appearing of the heavenly Christ (Heb. 9.24). There is nothing too portentous about the word when it translates from Hebrew except at Exod. 33.13. However, what is interesting is that on two of the three occasions in the Septuagint that it translates the Hebrew (Isa. 3.9; Esth. 2.22), it translates a word (*ngd*) which has a similar range of meaning—from fairly every day to quite revelatory—as that contained within the Greek *emphanizō*.

The consequence of all this is that when Jesus speaks of 'revealing' himself to those who love him and obey his teaching he could be understood in more than one way. For those who have ears to hear, there is a hint of revelation about the term. This is all the more the case given the context of the final discourse set by the Prologue to the Gospel, which speaks of light and darkness and of the *logos* coming into the world as light (Jn 1.4, 5, 9). When the light 'shines' in the darkness the word is *phainō* (1.5), a verb from the same stem as *emphanizō*. At one level of meaning in John 14, when Jesus talks of showing himself to his followers he is speaking of their enlightenment. This enlightenment emerges from the trinitarian activity of the Godhead, by which the believer is drawn into the love that characterizes the Godhead, and the truth that emerges thence. An indispensible part of this process is the teaching both of Jesus the Word and the Spirit of truth who continues that teaching. And an essential part of that teaching is its formation and preservation in the texts of Scripture and their subsequent interpretation or 'exegesis'.

These verses themselves only hint at the importance of the text itself, but in doing so they reflect other contexts where the place of Scripture in the encounter with the risen Christ and the Holy Spirit is more explicit. At the same time, they leave no doubt as to the enlightening resource—the text of Scripture—available to those whom Jesus loves and who themselves seek to express that love in a sometimes hostile world.

---

36. E.g., Wis. 17.4; 18.18; Mt. 27.53.

11

THEOLOGICAL INTERPRETATION AND THE BOOK OF LAMENTATIONS: A POLYPHONIC RECONSIDERATION[*]

Miriam J. Bier

Theology and Lamentations

It was Norman Gottwald who first put theological matters on the agenda in modern study of Lamentations. His 1954 study identifies Deuteronomic theology as the primary theological *influence* on Lamentations.[1] According to Gottwald, there was an inconsistency between Deuteronomic understandings of punishment and retribution, and the suffering experienced after Josiah's reforms. If the people had indeed corrected their behaviour, why were they now suffering and exiled? There seemed, to Gottwald, to be a 'discrepancy between the historical optimism of the Deuteronomic reform and the cynicism and despondency evoked by these reversals of national fortune'.[2] Consequently, he proposed that 'the theological significance of Lamentations consists in its bold and forthright statement of the problem of national disaster: what is the meaning of the terrible historical adversities that have overtaken us between 608 and 586 BC?'[3] It was this discrepancy, argued Gottwald, that Lamentations sought to address, theologically.[4]

Bertil Albrektson then took up the question of theology in relation to Lamentations. He agreed broadly with Gottwald that the book addressed a clash between history as it was being experienced, and theological tradition as it was understood.[5] He disagreed, however, on the theological influence

---

[*] This paper was developed and adapted from Chapters 1, 3, and 8 of my PhD thesis, 'Perhaps There Is Hope: Reading Lamentations as a Polyphony of Pain, Penitence, and Protest' (University of Otago, 2012).

1. Norman Gottwald, *Studies in the Book of Lamentations* (SBT, 14; London: SCM Press, 1954), p. 66.
2. Gottwald, *Lamentations*, p. 51.
3. Gottwald, *Lamentations*, p. 48.
4. Gottwald, *Lamentations*, p. 49.
5. Bertil Albrektson, *Studies in the Text and Theology of Lamentations* (STL, 21; Lund: Gleerup, 1963), p. 215.

causing the dissonance. The tension was not because of any perceived unjust punishment after Josiah's reforms. For Albrektson, the internal witness of Lamentations and the historical books confirmed that punishment was entirely appropriate.[6] Rather, the tension to be resolved revolved around theological understandings of the inviolability of Zion.[7] The promise that there would always be a king in the Davidic line, and the belief that YHWH dwells in Zion forever, combined such that the holy city, Jerusalem, and her temple, were assumed to be inviolable (cf. Jer. 7). For Albrektson, then, 'it is this theological tradition of the inviolability of Zion which stands in unbearable contrast to the harsh historical reality after the fall of Jerusalem'.[8] The theological issue Lamentations sought to address, for Albrektson, was how Zion could possibly have been violated.

Both Gottwald and Albrektson initially read Lamentations as an exercise in theological meaning-making, an assumption that is itself problematic.[9] Further, quite aside from the questionable ethics of demanding that suffering have meaning, both Gottwald and Albrektson identify a *single* theological tension that they suppose Lamentations sought to address. But as Michael S. Moore points out,

> The problem with both of these hypotheses is that both put forward the conviction, *a priori*, that a single theological focus point can not only be found in this mini-collection of laments over Jerusalem, but also that such a postulated focal point might then serve as *the* major theological trust [*sic*] of the book; all else is secondary.[10]

Positing such 'a single theological focus tends, in the final analysis, to reduce and constrict the variegated impact of Lamentations' broad theological thrust'.[11] Multiple theological traditions participate in the backdrop to Lamentations, and since Gottwald and Albrektson commentators have increasingly recognized this. Indeed, Gottwald himself later acknowledged that his early work 'too one-sidedly connected the book with Deuteronomic

---

6. Albrektson, *Lamentations*, pp. 218-19.
7. Albrektson, *Lamentations*, p. 223.
8. Albrektson, *Lamentations*, p. 223.
9. As Claus Westermann contended in his landmark commentary (*Lamentations: Issues and Interpretation* [trans. Charles Muenchow; Minneapolis: Fortress Press, 1994], p. 81). For the morality, or otherwise, of imposing meaning on suffering, see further Emmanuel Levinas, 'Useless Suffering', in Steven T. Katz, Schlomo Biderman and Gershon Greenberg (eds.), *Wrestling with God: Jewish Theological Responses during and after the Holocaust* (Oxford: Oxford University Press, 2008), pp. 451-54. Levinas is adamant that attempting to make suffering meaningful by subjugating pain to theodicy is the worst kind of immorality (p. 452).
10. Michael S. Moore, 'Human Suffering in Lamentations', *RB* 90 (1983), pp. 535-36 (emphasis original).
11. Moore, 'Human Suffering', p. 538.

theology and morality'.[12] He identifies a variety of theological traditions influencing Lamentations, including Deuteronomic understandings of retribution in covenant context, popular Davidic or Zion theology of the temple's inviolability, priestly purity paradigms, prophetic motifs and wisdom discourse.[13] Of course, none of these theological influences are entirely independent of the others. In the interconnected expanse of the Hebrew Bible, theologies are never discrete, separate ideological systems, but are mutually implicating.[14] Even so, scholars agree that specific nuances of these theological traditions participate in the theological backdrop to Lamentations. The theology of Lamentations, if determined by observing the various strands of theological tradition that appear therein, is plural.

But the theological *significance* or *message* of Lamentations for today is not so widely agreed to be plural. Rather, commentators tend to monologize the text—reading either a clear acknowledgement of sin with a concomitant theological message of required penitence, or a clear indictment of YHWH and a corresponding theological imperative to voice protest. Assessments of the ongoing theological significance of Lamentations can thus be loosely divided into two streams of thought: those who tend toward a theodic reading of Lamentations, and those who tend toward an antitheodic reading of Lamentations.[15] While interpreters often recognize that both theodic and

---

12. Norman K. Gottwald, 'The Book of Lamentations Reconsidered', in *The Hebrew Bible in its Social World and in Ours* (Atlanta: Scholars Press, 1993), p. 171. Gottwald, moreover, critiques Albrektson for having 'just as one-sidedly identified Lamentations with the Davidic–Zion theology' (p. 171).

13. Gottwald, 'Lamentations Reconsidered', p. 171. Cf. F.W. Dobbs-Allsopp, who identifies 'at least four traditions that were bearers of the ethical vision [in Lamentations]: the Deuteronomistic theology, the prophetic concept of sin, the wisdom tradition and the Zion tradition' ('Tragedy, Tradition, and Theology in the Book of Lamentations', *JSOT* 74 [1997], p. 46). Elizabeth C. Boase similarly observes within Lamentations 'expressions which draw on the Deuteronomic school of thought, linking sin and consequences', as well as 'explicit links with the prophetic literature', 'wisdom traditions' (Lam. 3), and 'Zion theology concerning the inviolability of Jerusalem' ('The Many Voices of Lament: An Exploration of the Book of Lamentations', *AJL* 10 [2005], p. 9). Boase also provides a helpful overview of studies engaging these various theological traditions as they appear in Lamentations in *The Fulfilment of Doom? The Dialogic Interaction between the Book of Lamentations and the Pre-Exilic/Early Exilic Prophetic Literature* (LHB/OTS, 437; New York: T. & T. Clark, 2006), pp. 9-12.

14. For interaction between the prophets and Lamentations, see especially Boase, *Fulfilment of Doom*; Patricia Tull Willey, *Remember the Former Things: The Recollection of Previous Texts in Second Isaiah* (SBLDS, 161; Atlanta: Scholars Press, 1997); and Carleen R. Mandolfo, *Daughter Zion Talks Back to the Prophets: A Dialogic Theology of the Book of Lamentations* (SemeiaSt, 58: Atlanta: SBL, 2007).

15. Note that 'theodicy' and 'antitheodicy' are not terms known in the Old Testament itself. Indeed, the classical sense of theodicy as a (failed) moral, philosophical enterprise,

antitheodic sentiments appear in Lamentations,[16] they usually demonstrate a theological preference for reading one way or the other. That is, interpreters read Lamentations either as *primarily* theodic, in defence of YHWH, or as *primarily* antitheodic, in defence of Zion.

In this paper I demonstrate the rhetorical strategies interpreters employ to construe Lamentations as theodic or antitheodic, with reference to Lamentations 1 and in particular Lam. 1.18. I suggest that both straightforwardly theodic and straightforwardly antitheodic readings are ultimately dissatisfying, given that both monologize a work that is better understood as a polyphonic text. A theological reading approach appropriate to Lamentations should attempt to keep both theodic *and* antitheodic poles in tension. I offer one such strategy based on Mikhail Bakhtin's conception of the dialogism of the idea, reading Lamentations as a polyphonic text.

Reading Lamentations as Theodicy:
Interpretations in Which Suffering Is the Measure of Sin

Theodicy is defined most simply as 'the justification of God'.[17] Zachary Braiterman extends this definition to include as theodic 'any attempt to justify, explain, or find acceptable meaning to the relationship that subsists between God…evil, and suffering'.[18] A theodic reading of Lamentations thus sets out to defend the justice, rightness and goodness of God, even in the face of the immense suffering Lamentations depicts. Theodic readings focus on any note of hope and affirmation of God's goodness, diminishing the more violent portrayals of God in Lamentations. Such readings emphasize sin and the covenant context, with suffering construed as just punishment for sin (cf. Deut. 28). They appeal to the centrality of Lamentations 3,

---

deriving from Leibniz' response to the 1755 Lisbon earthquake attempting to explain evil/suffering in light of God, is completely foreign to the Old Testament. Rather than any moral reflection on the nature of God and suffering, Israel's concern is to negotiate ongoing relationship with YHWH (Walter Brueggemann, 'Some Aspects of Theodicy in Old Testament Faith', *PRSt* 26 [1999], p. 265). I am interested, however, not in whether the writer/s of Lamentations imagined themselves to be 'doing' theodicy or anti-theodicy, but in the way that interpreters now determine that particular utterances—and hence Lamentations as a whole—either defend or accuse God. It is in this sense that I characterize interpretations as theodic or antitheodic.

16. Indeed, Boase notes that even the most theodic and antitheodic readers cannot help but recognize elements of the other perspective within the text (*Fulfilment of Doom*, p. 17).

17. Zachary Braiterman *(God) after Auschwitz: Tradition and Change in Post-Holocaust Jewish Thought* (Princeton, NJ: Princeton University Press, 1999), p. 19.

18. Braiterman, *(God) after Auschwitz*, p. 4.

and highlight that chapter's male *geber*[19] (3.1, 27, 39) as the epitome of faithful penitence. This figure affirms the ongoing faithfulness and goodness of YHWH (3.22-25) and advocates sitting quietly in the dust, accepting suffering as just punishment of the Lord (3.26-30). The suffering figure of female Zion in Lamentations 1–2 may be noted and observed, but in theodic readings it is primarily statements conceding her sin that are highlighted— for example, when she asserts, 'The Lord is in the right, for I have rebelled against his word' (1.18). A theodic reading of Lamentations will take such statements at face value, as proof that Zion recognizes and accepts her

---

19. The term *geber*, most simply translated 'man', takes on a number of different nuances. Some commentators identify this *geber* with an historical figure, for example Jeremiah (Nancy Lee, *The Singers of Lamentations* [Leiden: Brill, 2002], p. 168); Philip Graham Ryken, *Jeremiah and Lamentations: From Sorrow to Hope* [Preaching the Word; Wheaton, IL: Crossway, 2001], p. 752); Jehoiachin (S.B. Gurewicz, 'The Problem of Lamentations 3', *ABR* 8 [1960], p. 22); Zedekiah (Magne Sæbø, 'Who Is "The Man" in Lamentations 3? A Fresh Approach to the Interpretation of the Book of Lamentations', in Graeme Auld [ed.], *Understanding Poets and Prophets* [JSOTSup, 152; Sheffield: Sheffield Academic Press, 1993], p. 304); or a defeated soldier, a 'strongman' (Kathleen M. O'Connor, *Lamentations and the Tears of the World* [Maryknoll, NY: Orbis Books, 2002], p. 44; William F. Lanahan, 'The Speaking Voice in the Book of Lamentations', *JBL* 93 [1974], p. 45). Hillers, on the other hand, designates the *geber* as an 'everyman', a universal representative sufferer (Delbert Hillers, *Lamentations: A New Translation with Introduction and Commentary* [AB, 7A; New York: Doubleday, 2nd edn, 1992], p. 122; cf. F.W. Dobbs-Allsopp, *Lamentations* [Interpretation; Louisville, KY: John Knox Press, 2002], p. 109). The *geber* is also sometimes identified as a communal representation of the people, indeed a continuation of Daughter Zion herself, now taking on an individual male perspective (e.g., Otto Eissfeldt, *The Old Testament: An Introduction* [trans. Peter R. Ackroyd; Oxford: Basil Blackwell, 1965], p. 503; Robert B. Salters, *Jonah and Lamentations* [OTG; Sheffield: Sheffield Academic Press, 1994], p. 186; Gottwald, *Lamentations*, pp. 39-41; Albrektson, *Lamentations*, pp. 126-28). Adele Berlin also takes the communal aspect, but as a communal representation of the exiles (*Lamentations* [OTL; Louisville, KY: Westminster/John Knox Press, 2002], p. 84). While a precise identity cannot be determined, there are a range of associations that inhere in the term. A *geber* is male, as distinct from women and children (cf. Exod. 10.11; 12.37; Num. 24.3, 15; Deut. 22.5; 2 Sam. 23.1; Isa. 22.17; Jer. 22.30, 30.6, 31.22, 43.6, 44.20; Ps. 127.5; Job 3.3; 38.3; 40.7; Prov. 6.34, 30.1, 19; Dan. 8.15; 1 Chron. 23.3; 24.4; 26.12). He is almost always an adult male, with the only exception in Job 3.3, where Job refers to himself in his infancy as a *geber* (NRSV, 'man-child'). He is a 'strong' man, perhaps even a warrior or a soldier (cf. Josh 7.14, 17, 18; Judg. 5.30; Jer. 41.16; Prov. 24.5; 28.3). In Psalms and Job the connotation of physical strength in the term is taken over to imply spiritual strength, such that a *geber* is a man in right standing with YHWH (cf. Job 3.3, 23; 4.17; 10.5; 14.10,14; 16.21; 22.2; 33.17, 29; 34.7, 9, 34; 38.3; 40.7; Pss. 18.26; 34.9, 37.23; 40.5; 94.12; 127.5; 128.4). This provides further irony, if the *geber* in Lamentations has, in fact, been guilty of sin (3.39, 42). Given the range of associations that inhere in the term, then, I avoid the simple translation 'man' and refer to him throughout as the *geber*.

primary role in the city's downfall. Utterances that could be construed as protesting her suffering, however, are downplayed or overlooked.

The conviction that 'the bitch had it coming to her'[20] is thus a hallmark of theodic readings of Lamentations, enabling interpreters to claim that 'Jerusalem deserved her desolation',[21] that 'the Lord's anger is "beyond measure"... with good cause, given the sin of Judah',[22] and that all the suffering that Zion experiences 'has happened as a result of Israel's guilt both past and present'.[23] In theodic readings '[i]t is a theological matter of principle that the Ruler of the whole world always does right, so even the tragedy of Jerusalem cannot seriously bring into question the correctness of God's actions'.[24] Lamentations becomes 'a confession of sin' that operates theologically to defend the justice of God, and to call people to repentance. In this understanding, the relationship between the people's suffering and their sin is construed as one of just punishment.

Recent commentators challenge this orthodoxy, resisting the impulse to make Lamentations 3 a message of required penitence determinative for

20. An apt phrase borrowed from the title of Peggy L. Day's article on Ezek. 16 ('The Bitch Had It Coming to Her: Rhetoric and Interpretation in Ezekiel 16', *BI* 8 [2000], pp. 231-54). Day uses the phrase ironically.

21. Ryken, *Jeremiah and Lamentations*, p. 739.

22. John Bracke, *Jeremiah 30–52 and Lamentations* (WestBC; Louisville, KY: Westminster/John Knox Press, 2000), p. 239.

23. Jože Krašovec, 'The Source of Hope in the Book of Lamentations', *VT* 42 (1992), p. 223.

24. Krašovec, 'Source of Hope', p. 225. Similar sentiments may be observed in, e.g., Homer Heater, 'Structure and Meaning in Lamentations', in Roy Zuck (ed.), *Vital Old Testament Issues: Examining Textual and Topical Questions* (Grand Rapids: Kregel, 1996), pp. 150-59; Michael D. Guinan, 'Lamentations', in R.E. Brown, J.A. Fitzmyer and Roland E. Murphy (eds.), *The New Jerome Biblical Commentary* (Englewood Cliffs, NJ: Prentice–Hall, 1990), pp. 558-62; F.B. Huey, *Jeremiah and Lamentations* (NABC, 16; Nashville: Broadman, 1993); S. Paul Re'emi, 'The Theology of Hope: A Commentary on the Book of Lamentations', in George A.F. Knight and Frederick Carlson Holmgren (eds.), *Amos and Lamentations: God's People in Crisis* (ITC; Edinburgh: Handsel, 1984), pp. 73-184. Robin A. Parry's recent theological reading gives much greater due to the depth of pain expressed in Lamentations, but continues to set the theological framework for Lamentations firmly as sin and punishment in covenant context, arguing that the *fact* of sin and punishment is never questioned in Lamentations, because 'the "why" is already known—Israel has broken the covenant law. Rather, the anguished questions behind Lamentations are, "Why punish *so severely*?" and "*How long* until you save?"' (*Lamentations* [THOTC; Grand Rapids: Eerdmans, 2010], p. 29, emphases original). Similarly, Paul R. House observes the pain expressed in Lamentations but insists that the prevailing sense is that 'the Lord is righteous, just, powerful, kind, severe, compassionate, faithful, and willing to hear and answer prayer' (*Lamentations* [WBC, 23B; Nashville: Thomas Nelson, 2004], p. 329). House is unequivocal in insisting that Zion's suffering is deserved punishment for sin.

theology in Lamentations. Tod Linafelt identifies three biases in interpretation that have allowed the 'central' message of penitence to dominate in assessments of theology and Lamentations: first, a male bias toward the man of Lamentations 3 over female Zion in Lamentations 1–2; secondly, a Christian bias toward reading the suffering man as analogous to Christ; and thirdly, a bias toward reconciliation over confrontation.[25] Linafelt finds the third of these to be especially pervasive, and demonstrates how, by focusing on guilt and sin, any question of the appropriateness of YHWH's actions falls away.[26] His analysis thus pinpoints the way in which '[t]he concept of guilt functions for interpreters as a way of retaining the notion of God as the author of the destruction...while nevertheless relieving God of any ultimate responsibility for the disturbing results'.[27] Linafelt contends with such interpretations, arguing that while they might convince as long as Lamentations 3 remains in focus, they are not so persuasive when Lamentations 1–2 are brought to light. He shifts the spotlight to attend to Zion in Lamentations 1–2, highlighting her presentation of pain and protest over the impulse to interpret pain and advocate penitence.[28] This provides him with an alternative model for 'surviving' the horror of Lamentations, a model of protest, rather than capitulation and submission,[29] which is tied, not to the male *geber*, but to female Zion.

Much of the impetus for this shift in focus is derived from Westermann's critique of two trends in reading Lamentations for theology after Gottwald and Albrektson, namely, reading so that 'either these laments offer some sort of explanation', or 'they point to a way out of a crisis'.[30] Both these stances sought to make meaning out of suffering, devaluing the role of the lament as

25. Tod Linafelt, *Surviving Lamentations: Catastrophe, Lament, and Protest in the Afterlife of a Biblical Book* (Chicago: University of Chicago Press, 2000), p. 5. Cf. Archie Chi Chung Lee, 'Mothers Bewailing: Reading Lamentations', in Caroline Vander Stichele and Todd C. Penner (eds.), *Her Master's Tools? Feminist and Postcolonial Engagements of Historical-Critical Discourse* (GPBS, 9; Atlanta: SBL, 2005), pp. 195-210.
26. Linafelt, *Surviving Lamentations*, pp. 9-10; cf. Lee, 'Mothers Bewailing', p. 195. See further Tod Linafelt, 'Zion's Cause: The Presentation of Pain in the Book of Lamentations', in *Strange Fire: Reading the Bible after the Holocaust* (New York: New York University Press, 2000), pp. 267–79.
27. Linafelt, *Surviving Lamentations*, p. 10; cf. Boase (*Fulfilment of Doom*, p. 13), who also observes the way in which 'making this connection between the confession of sin and the penitential hope of ch. 3, the theology of Lamentations becomes an orthodox expression of human culpability in the face of a righteous God'.
28. Linafelt, 'Zion's Cause', p. 268. Note, though, that while Linafelt tends to equate Zion with protest and the *geber* with penitence, both speakers express aspects of both perspectives.
29. Linafelt, *Surviving Lamentations*, p. 17; cf. Linafelt, 'Zion's Cause', p. 279.
30. Westermann, *Lamentations*, p. 76.

an expression of pure pain. Westermann rejected this impulse toward meaning-making, maintaining instead that '[t]he "meaning" of these laments is to be found in their very expression'.[31] This set the stage for Linafelt and others to think about Lamentations in terms of presentation of pain and protest, and to value lament *qua* lament rather than as an exercise in theological meaning-making.[32]

But Westermann still assumes the sin and guilt of Zion, not as a theological issue to be worked out in relation to suffering, perhaps, but as an underlying assumption, taken as given.[33] Boase and Linafelt both question this assumption, seeing it as a threat to Westermann's positive gains in valuing lament as lament.[34] They, and others like them, continue to champion valuing lament as expression of pain, while critiquing Westermann's unquestioned acceptance that Zion's suffering is deserved punishment for sin. These interpreters resist reifying Lamentations 3 and bring the protesting figure of daughter Zion in Lamentations 1–2 into the light. Their alternative readings challenge the assumption that 'the' theological message of the book revolves around the submissive penitence of the *geber*, and the acceptance of suffering as deserved punishment for sin from which one must repent. The conversation shifts from the central male *geber* to the marginal female Zion, attending to her protesting countervoice in the text. These counter readings can loosely be termed antitheodic.

Reading Lamentations as Antitheodicy:
Interpretations of Lamentations in Which Suffering
Is Not the Measure of Sin

Antitheodicy, then, is 'any religious response to the problem of evil whose proponents refuse to justify, explain, or accept as somehow meaningful the relationship between God and suffering'.[35] Antitheodicy undoes any

---

31. Westermann, *Lamentations*, p. 81; cf. Linafelt, 'Zion's Cause', p. 279; contra House, who contends that '[w]hile it is wrong to treat laments as merely "a way to fix things," it is also wrong to treat them as a way to shout about pain with no further intentions' (*Lamentations*, p. 409).

32. See also Dobbs-Allsopp, *Lamentations*, p. 2 and elsewhere; Berlin, *Lamentations*, p. 18 and elsewhere; Lee, 'Mothers Bewailing', p. 209; and Carleen R. Mandolfo, 'Lamentations', in Gail R. O'Day and David L. Petersen (eds.), *Theological Bible Commentary* (Louisville, KY: Westminster/John Knox Press, 2009), pp. 237-39.

33. E.g., Westermann, *Lamentations*, p. 79: '[I]n Lamentations we hear the voices of those who…have already come to the awareness that Israel itself was to blame for this collapse. No one first needed to be brought to this awareness, in order thereby to awaken a sense of guilt.' Cf. Hillers, *Lamentations*, p. 4; Parry, *Lamentations*, p. 29.

34. See Boase, *Fulfilment of Doom*, p. 17; Linafelt, *Surviving Lamentations*, p. 14.

35. Braiterman, *(God) after Auschwitz*, p. 31.

sense of measure as an appropriate index of God's work with humanity, insisting that some suffering is *never* justified, regardless of its precursors or origins in human sin. Rather than attempting to defend YHWH in the light of suffering, antitheodic readings refuse 'to justify, explain, or accept that relationship'.[36]

Antitheodic readings of Lamentations highlight statements in which God's actions are implicitly or explicitly questioned in the text, suggesting that these actions are beyond the required or just punishment of the people. Zion has received 'double' for her sins (cf. Isa. 40.1-3). They draw a negative portrayal of God in Lamentations, maintaining that God 'is sinister and brutal, executing his punishment upon Jerusalem with violent abandon', in an unjustifiable abuse of divine power.[37] While these readings may acknowledge the statements of hope and trust in Lamentations 3, they still reckon that 'the predominant opinion among [the testimonies heard within Lamentations] is that God is cruel and violently abusive'.[38] Antitheodic readings thus mitigate confessions of sin contextually, by drawing attention to the surrounding suffering and allowing this to take precedence over statements that could lend themselves to theodic interpretation. Further, regardless of sin, they argue that nothing is deserving of suffering in this extremity, appealing to accusations of God in Lamentations to call for a 'reassessment of both the logic and justness of God's actions'.[39] While conceding that '[t]here is genuine acknowledgement of sin in Lamentations', the point is that this 'is not the whole story, or even the most important part of the story. Whatever Judah's sin may have been—in light of the catastrophe, its exact nature is no longer important, it in no way can justify the extent and degree of suffering she has experienced'.[40] Antitheodic counter-readings thus assert that 'the sin of Judah was not equal to her suffering'[41] and so the theological *message* of Lamentations becomes something akin to: 'extreme suffering is never justified, and is properly raged against'.[42]

---

36. Braiterman, *(God) after Auschwitz*, p. 4.
37. Johanna Stiebert, 'Human Suffering and Divine Abuse of Power in Lamentations', *Pacifica* 16 (2003), p. 195.
38. O'Connor, *Tears of the World*, p. 110.
39. Mandolfo, *Daughter Zion*, p. 101.
40. Dobbs-Allsopp, 'Tragedy, Tradition, and Theology', p. 37.
41. Dobbs-Allsopp, 'Tragedy, Tradition, and Theology', p. 36.
42. Mandolfo, 'Lamentations', p. 239. For Dobbs-Allsopp, '[e]vil is not to be accepted passively but to be resisted actively. This resistance in Lamentations is modeled rhetorically in and through the various speaking voices' ('Tragedy, Tradition, and Theology', p. 55).

A Case Study: Lamentations 1.18

Lamentations 1.18: Reading for Theodicy

To demonstrate some of the rhetorical manoeuvres of both theodic and antitheodic interpreters of Lamentations in relation to a specific example I now focus on Lam. 1.18. Chapter 1 of Lamentations is spoken by two voices. A third person Lamenter begins by detailing the sorry situation of Zion's downfall (1.1-9b, 10-11b, 17), and he is interrupted by Zion herself (1.9c), who continues in the first person by drawing attention to her pain and lack of a comforter (1.12c-16, 18-22). Coming as the chapter draws to a close, Lam 1.18 can be read as the climax of both the Lamenter's accusations against Zion (1.5b, 8a, 9b), and Zion's own confessions of sin (1.14, 20b, 22b). Zion declares YHWH just (1.18a) and states that she has rebelled (1.18a; cf. 1.20b; 3.42) against his word (literally, 'his mouth', 1.18a). She entreats all the peoples to hear (1.18b; cf. 1.21) and see (1.18b; cf.1.12c) her suffering (1.18b; cf. 1.12b). A specific sorrow follows. Her young women and young men have gone into captivity (1.18c; cf. 1.5c).

At first blush, this is a clear confession of sin: 'The Lord himself is just; I rebelled against his word' (1.18a); followed by obvious consequences: 'My young women and young men have gone into captivity' (1.18c). Zion concedes that she has rebelled, or sinned, against YHWH. And indeed, explicit connections between suffering and sin appear more frequently in Lamentations 1 than in any other chapter of Lamentations. The Lamenter attributes sin to Zion twice in the first half of the poem (1.5b, 8a), and she herself admits transgression and rebellion (1.14a, 22b; 1.18a, 20b). In 1.5b, 18a, 20b and 22b, moreover, sin is causally connected to her suffering.

Prioritizing and privileging this network of mutually reinforcing sin and rebellion language within Lamentations 1 allows the chapter to be read theodically, so that 1.18 becomes a statement indicting Zion and exonerating YHWH. This reading strategy can be seen, for example, in Tremper Longman's reading of Lamentations 1. Longman argues emphatically that the prevailing perspective of the chapter, indeed the book, is that the people themselves are to blame for bringing about their predicament:

> The poet states clearly that 'The LORD has brought her grief because of her many sins' (1:5b) and 'Jerusalem has sinned greatly and so has become unclean' (1:8a). Personified Jerusalem herself proclaims, 'My sins have been bound into a yoke; by his hands they were woven together' (1:14a). As opposed to Linafelt, she exonerates God in 1:18a, 'The LORD is righteous, yet I rebelled against his command.'[43]

---

43. Tremper Longman III, *Jeremiah, Lamentations* (NIBC, 14; Peabody, MA: Hendricksen, 2008), p. 340. Similarly, Robert Gordis reads such that Lam. 1 confirms that 'Zion has deserved her fate because she has sinned and defied her God' (*The Song of*

In this understanding, not only does Zion confess, she also clears YHWH of any wrongdoing.[44] Zion concurs with her accusers that her punishment is deserved.[45]

Even when the severity of Zion's pain is recognized, theodic-leaning commentators are reluctant to waver from asserting that her suffering is just desserts for sin. Westermann, for example, observes motifs of both 'agony' and 'guilt' at play in Lamentations.[46] In his discussion of 1.18, he draws out both of these motifs:

> Those voicing the lament here clearly know that the terrible fate which has befallen them has been inflicted upon them because of their own guilt. Yet they do not stop with confirming that their punishment was deserved. Instead, they lay their bitter agony before God. They do so in order that, despite their guilt, God might graciously turn toward them once again.[47]

While Westermann's reading does acknowledge the extent of Zion's suffering, paying due regard to valuing her presentation of pain, he still asserts

---

Songs and Lamentations: A Study, Modern Translation and Commentary [New York: Ktav, 1974], p. 129). Lanahan claims that 'Jerusalem willingly admits the folly of her past behavior towards God in her making of futile alliances with the gentiles' ('Speaking Voice', p. 44). Heater rejects any 'effort to claim unjust punishment' insisting that 'Jerusalem freely admitted her culpability' and 'attributed the calamity to Yahweh as just punishment' ('Structure and Meaning', p. 152). House also insists that '[t]heir wounds are their own fault. God has not forsaken them for no reason. The whole chapter seeks to describe how God afflicts and forsakes the people who have rejected his word and have forsaken their covenant commitments' (*Lamentations*, p. 365; cf. Salters, *Jonah and Lamentations*, p. 73).

44. For example, Xuan Huong Thi Pham reads the chapter such that in 1.18 'Jerusalem acknowledges her sins. She deserves to be punished, to be deserted, forlorn and humiliated. She submits to Yahweh's judgment' (*Mourning in the Ancient Near East and the Hebrew Bible* [JSOTSup, 302; Sheffield: Sheffield Academic Press, 1999], p. 88). Similarly, Knut M. Heim finds that by this stage of the chapter, 'Lady Jerusalem's perspective has changed. She explicitly vindicates the Lord's dealings with her and acknowledges her guilt' ('The Personification of Jerusalem and the Drama of her Bereavement in Lamentations', in Richard Hess and Gordon J. Wenham [eds.], *Zion: City of our God* [Grand Rapids: Eerdmans, 1999], p. 150). For House, 1.18 is 'an emphatic declaration of God's righteousness in the matter of her punishment' (*Lamentations*, p. 361). While these interpreters acknowledge that this is *Zion's* perspective, they appear to agree with her theological evaluation of her situation in 1.18.

45. This insistence that Zion 'deserves to be punished, to be deserted, forlorn and humiliated' takes on sinister proportions in light of the ongoing power of the metaphor. Are the female victims of sexual violence, physical assault, and emotional manipulation similarly held to blame for the atrocities carried out against them?

46. Westermann, *Lamentations*, p. 140.

47. Westermann, *Lamentations*, p. 140. While Westermann identifies both pain and penitence, then, he does not dwell over much on protest.

that 'their punishment was deserved'. According to this kind of interpretation, even 'in the anguish of her victimage Zion is not held to be entirely innocent of complicity in her fate'.[48] Zion's suffering, while admittedly severe in its duration and intensity, is deemed to be equal to her sin.[49]

Lamentations 1.18: Reading for Antitheodicy
While theodic readers point to the preponderance of sin statements in Lamentations 1 to 'prove' Zion's complicity in her fate, Linafelt finds fewer references to sin therein than commentators usually observe. He maintains that 1.12-16 contains no reference to sin, that Zion herself 'mentions "sin" or "guilt" only twice (1:18, 22) and that her only statement of "repentance" (1:20) is textually very uncertain'.[50] For Linafelt, '[i]nstead of explanations for suffering, one finds in the [sic] Zion's speech an accusation against God combined with a terrifying description of misery'.[51] Reading antitheodically, any suggestion of confession is overwhelmed by Zion's agony and accusation. Even when Linafelt concedes that 'Zion does indeed admit her sins or disobedience', he suggests she does so 'flatly and not altogether wholeheartedly'.[52]

This perceived lack of wholeheartedness, for antitheodic readers, 'at the very least...appears to call into question the appropriateness of YHWH's response'.[53] Dobbs-Allsopp explains, 'The concern is not about the appropriateness of Yahweh's punishment, which is assumed from the start, but about what Exum most fittingly calls the "uneasy awareness" that Yahweh's punishment far exceeds the community's guilt'.[54] The extent of Zion's

---

48. Alan Mintz, *Hurban: Responses to Catastrophe in Hebrew Literature* (New York: Columbia University Press, 1984), p. 25.

49. Dobbs-Allsopp, 'Tragedy, Tradition, and Theology', p. 36, an assessment that Dobbs-Allsopp ascribes to Gottwald, *Lamentations*. Note, though, that while Gottwald does state that Yhwh's anger and Zion's suffering are 'commensurable' to her sin (p. 72), he later acknowledges that Lamentations 'senses an excess of punishment amounting to injustice' (Gottwald, *Lamentations*, p. 117). The inherent polyphony of the text thus draws competing assessments of the commensurability, or otherwise, of Zion's suffering and her sin, even within a single commentator's work.

50. Linafelt, *Surviving Lamentations*, p. 10. Dobbs-Allsopp notes the accusations in 1.5b and 8a, and the admissions in 1.18a and 22b, but is similarly suspicious of reference to sin in 1.14a and 20b (*Lamentations*, pp. 60-61).

51. Linafelt, 'Zion's Cause', p. 275.

52. Linafelt, *Surviving Lamentations*, p. 48. Linafelt does acknowledge that 'the character of Zion, for all her challenging of Yhwh, never claims complete innocence' (p. 46).

53. Charles William Miller, 'Reading Voices: Personification, Dialogism, and the Reader of Lamentations 1', *BI* 9 (2004), p. 401.

54. Dobbs-Allsopp, 'Tragedy, Tradition, and Theology', p. 45.

suffering suggests to antitheodic readers that YHWH's punishing response is far too extreme.[55] Instead of prioritizing her confessions of sin, allowing them to determine the theological stance of the chapter, these are understood to be 'subordinate to the focus of her speech, namely, a description of her suffering'.[56]

Dobbs-Allsopp and Linafelt, for example, encapsulate the antitheodic inclination in their jointly authored article exploring rape imagery in Lamentations 1. From their analysis of 1.8b-c, 10b-c, 12b, 13c and 22b, they find in Lamentations 1 a 'a network of mutually reinforcing images of rape'.[57] They summarize the chapter thus:

> The poet's figuration of Zion as rape victim personalizes the city's destruction in a way that is not easily ignored. We are compelled to compassion by these images of victimization, and in so far as Yhwh is envisioned as the perpetrator of this crime (Thr 1,12b. 13c. 22b) we are led by the poet to question the ethics of Yhwh's actions. Is there anything that can justify such an abhorrent crime? Our answer, and we believe the poet's answer as well, must be an emphatic no![58]

By prioritizing the network of rape imagery rather than the network of sin language in Lamentations 1, Dobbs-Allsopp and Linafelt prioritize Zion's expression of pain and the need for protest over any sense of penitence.

The cry directly following Zion's confession also causes pause for thought. Zion very quickly tempers her admission of sin (1.18a) by drawing attention to tremendous suffering (1.18b-19).[59] Further, by explaining that she has been deceived by her 'lovers' (1.19a; erstwhile political allies, cf. Jer. 22.20, 22; 30.14; Ezek. 16.33, 36, 37; 23.5, 9, 22), Zion shifts the focus of blame to those who did the deceiving. Highlighting her suffering and pointing out that it is not entirely her fault, Zion thus concedes that she has done wrong—but that regardless of the seriousness of her wrongdoing, nothing is deserving of the severity of her present situation.[60] This turns responsibility back over to YHWH.

---

55. See Miller, 'Reading Voices', p. 402; Dobbs-Allsopp, *Lamentations*, p. 61; Mandolfo, 'Lamentations', p. 238.
56. Miller, 'Reading Voices', pp. 400-401; cf. Boase, *Fulfilment of Doom*, p. 174.
57. F.W. Dobbs-Allsopp and Tod Linafelt, 'The Rape of Zion in Thr 1,10', *ZAW* 113 (2001), p. 81.
58. Dobbs-Allsopp and Linafelt, 'Rape of Zion', p. 81.
59. Cf. Dobbs-Allsopp, *Lamentations*, p. 71; Berlin, *Lamentations*, p. 59; Boase, *Fulfilment of Doom*, p. 179; Dobbs-Allsopp and Linafelt, 'Rape of Zion', p. 81; Johan Renkema, 'Theodicy in Lamentations?', in Antti Laato and Johannes C. de Moor (eds.), *Theodicy in the World of the Bible* (Leiden: Brill, 2003), p. 418.
60. Cf. Dobbs-Allsopp and Linafelt, 'Rape of Zion', p. 80.

Indeed, for Mandolfo, YHWH's actions in the greater context of Lamentations mean that 1.18a cannot possibly be taken at face value. She suspects Zion's confession is 'coerced', a double-voiced statement of the dominant discourse—'YHWH is just'—that Zion has recontextualized ironically.⁶¹ For Mandolfo, 'whether she has sinned or not seems nearly beside the point from where she is standing. YHWH's indiscriminate brutality takes center stage and thus mitigates the gravity of the charges against her'.⁶²

Even if not double voiced, given the hellish treatment Zion has received at the hands of YHWH, 1.18a must be recognized for the sinister statement that it is. It is entirely possible (*pace* Mandolfo) that Zion speaks 1.18a sincerely. But this itself is troubling, given what is known from sociology and psychology of battered women's incorrect perceptions that they are to blame for their partners' violent behaviours.⁶³ Even if Zion is sincere in her confession and desire to vindicate YHWH, then, there are grounds for challenging her own perception of the situation in light of the atrocities YHWH is depicted carrying out against her.

And so Stiebert admits of

> no evidence to substantiate the claim of 1.18: 'YHWH is righteous.' We see him only as brute: there is no indication of his capacity for pity (see also 2:2, 17, 21; 3:43), forgiveness, or mercy; there is no indication of his even hearing, let alone listening to Jerusalem's pleas (3:8, 44).⁶⁴

Rather than taking Lam. 1.18 as the climax governing the interpretation of the rest of the chapter, she finds that the rest of the chapter and the book cast a shadow on the veracity of the verse's claims.

This single verse, then, is found to be consistent with reading Lamentations either for theodicy or for antitheodicy, according to the interpretive stance of a particular reading.

Theodicy or Antitheodicy? The Problem with Trying to Choose

A problem with both theodic readings and antitheodic readings, however, is that both assume Lamentations has a single, identifiable, dominant theological significance. Both reading positions attest to an expectation that there is a central theology, a single controlling theological stance. Is there such a monologic message? Or is Lamentations better understood as presenting a

---

61. Carleen R. Mandolfo, 'Dialogic Form Criticism: An Intertextual Reading of Lamentations and Psalms of Lament', in Roland Boer (ed.), *Bakhtin and Genre Theory* (SemeiaSt, 63; Atlanta: SBL, 2007), pp. 87-88; cf. Mandolfo, *Daughter Zion*, pp. 92-98.
62. Mandolfo, 'Dialogic Form Criticism', p. 88.
63. Cf. O'Connor, *Tears of the World*, pp. 27, 29.
64. Stiebert, 'Human Suffering and Divine Abuse', p. 198.

multiplicity of theological perspectives?[65] If there are multiple views, can one of these be selected as the right or correct stance to take, and how might that be determined?

In the discussion above it becomes apparent that the sticking point is sin, and its relationship to suffering. Dobbs-Allsopp explains:

> For most commentators, the significance of these two themes and their relationship to each other seems quite straightforward: the poet has taken over the prophetic concept of sin that attributes the catastrophe to Yahweh's righteous judgment, and thus understands the ensuing suffering as deserved.[66]

This straightforward acceptance of a relationship between sin and suffering as deserved is evident in theodic readings outlined above. But as I have shown, antitheodic readings challenge accepting suffering as just punishment, equal to Zion's sin, asking whether, in fact, her suffering goes above and beyond what is warranted.[67]

Theodic or antitheodic leanings thus lead interpreters to read the relationship between sin and suffering in Lamentations in particular ways. While many readings do acknowledge, on the one hand, the culpability of Zion, and on the other, the extreme punishing action of YHWH, each tends to side with one as the real theological understanding of Lamentations. More recent acknowledgement of the value of the pain and protest elements ascribed to Zion has led to a recognition of potentially antitheodic content, even (grudgingly) among those who would prefer to read theodically. There is still reluctance, however, to allow these possibilities to gain a full hearing. But it is clear that selecting some central verses to define a theology for Lamentations can no longer go uncontested. Turning to attend to minority voices in Lamentations, and so redressing the balance of focus from Lamentations 3, to Lamentations 1–2, has thus been a crucial contribution to scholarship on Lamentations. At the same time, however, there is a sense in which readings that raise the register of Daughter Zion's discourse diminish the effect of hearing multiple voices in chorus. As Heath Thomas observes,

> If there has been an over-emphasis upon Lamentations 3—and the concomitant theodicy assumed in it for the theology of the book—to the neglect of the figure of Zion in Lamentations 1 and 2, then recently there has been an

---

65. So Boase, 'Many Voices of Lament', p. 4; Dobbs-Allsopp, *Lamentations*, p. 23; O'Connor, *Tears of the World*, p. 14. Contra House (*Lamentations*, p. 323) and Longman (*Jeremiah, Lamentations*, p. 339), who reject the possibility that multiple theological perspectives are present, maintaining that all voices are in agreement that Zion's suffering is due punishment for her sins.

66. Dobbs-Allsopp, 'Tragedy, Tradition, and Theology', p. 36.

67. *Can* suffering be measured, however? The Lamenter seems to think not (2.13).

overemphasis upon the poems of Lamentations 1 and 2 from Linafelt to the present—and the concomitant 'anti-theodicy' assumed with these chapters for the theology of the book—to the neglect of Lamentations 3.[68]

This is not to say that I want to see a return to reading Lamentations under the interpretive control of selected portions of Lamentations 3. Rather, I pursue an interpretation that, at least initially, allows all the voices in Lamentations to sound, reserving judgement as to which voice may be presenting the truth of the matter, indeed, contesting the possibility of determining one truth altogether. I seek an interpretation that allows plurality in Lamentations to be held in tension, an interpretation that allows all its voices to sound, and, at least initially, reserves judgement as to which voice may be presenting the 'truth' of the matter.

As such, I seek a reading approach that allows both theodic and antitheodic possibilities in the text to be identified and explicated, without having to resolve them immediately into a single, consistent theological stance. My approach to the multiplicity of theological expression is to read Lamentations as a polyphony, based on Mikhail Bakhtin's dialogism of the idea.[69]

Reading Dialogically: Lamentations as a Polyphony of Pain, Penitence and Protest

According to Bakhtin, a polyphonic text consists of multiple voices representing integral points of view in dialogic interaction.[70] Polyphonic works cannot be summed up with a monologic statement of meaning or significance, but instead exhibit a plurality of consciousnesses.[71] They represent embodied points of view in dialogue.[72] Polyphonic works resist system[73] and are 'unfinalizable'.[74] They leave the ends frayed at the edges, inviting response. Ultimately, polyphonic works represent dialogic truth, truth that cannot be pinned down to a single, controlling discourse.

---

68. Heath Thomas, 'Poetry and Theology in Lamentations: An Investigation of Lamentations 1–3 Using the Aesthetic Analysis of Umberto Eco' (PhD thesis, University of Gloucester, 2007), p. 22; cf. Longman, *Jeremiah, Lamentations*, p. 331; Parry, *Lamentations*, pp. 167-68. Thomas himself seeks to address this by reading chs. 1, 2, and 3 'in concert, synthetically' (p. 22).
69. Primarily as explicated in Mikhail Bakhtin, *Problems of Dostoevsky's Poetics* (trans. Caryl Emerson; Minneapolis: University of Minnesota Press, 1984).
70. Bakhtin, *Problems of Dostoevsky's Poetics*, p. 93.
71. Bakhtin, *Problems of Dostoevsky's Poetics*, p. 81.
72. Bakhtin, *Problems of Dostoevsky's Poetics*, p. 93.
73. Bakhtin, *Problems of Dostoevsky's Poetics*, p. 93.
74. Bakhtin, *Problems of Dostoevsky's Poetics*, p. 63.

Lamentations can be read as though it were such a polyphonic text. Lamentations' voices can be understood as plural consciousnesses each brought to bear on the happenings around 587 BCE. These voices are not disembodied propositions, but strongly visceral (e.g., 1.20-22; 2.11; 3.11-17). Even the traditional theological discourses that appear in Lamentations are mediated by being couched within lament language, so that these too are given personality (e.g., 3.25-39). While there is strong structural, poetic, and thematic unity, Lamentations does not display any systematic enunciation of theology. Further, the ambiguous ending of Lamentations 5, and the many survivals of Lamentations in ongoing literature,[75] demonstrate that the conversation is by no means closed.

Lamentations, then, can be read as a polyphony, a text that embodies dialogic truth. Reading Lamentations as polyphonic text 'suggests a model in which the "truth" about a difficult issue can only be established by a community of unmerged perspectives, not by a single voice, not even that of God',[76] or further, of the text claimed to be 'word of God'. Thus 'the rich interrelationships among utterances will need to take over from the tendency (so richly indulged by many) to extract and abstract quotes and think one has thereby made a free-standing statement or buttressed a point'.[77]

Conceptualizing Lamentations as a polyphony has implications for theological reading and interpretation. Murray Rae sets out the task of theological interpretation as seeking 'a hermeneutical framework within which the reading of biblical texts must take place if it is to be faithful to the distinctive theological character of the texts themselves'.[78] Polyphonic texts call for response, inducing future generations of readers and hearers to participate in the dialogue. Reading Lamentations as a polyphony thus has some major ramifications when teamed with this insistence that reading be faithful to the 'distinctive theological character of the texts themselves'. The polyphonic text as a medium invites participation in *both* penitence *and* protest, and further, participation in the very theological debate in which Lamentations takes part.

Reading according to the text of Lamentations itself, then, is to read dialogically, taking part in the ongoing dispute over the nature of YHWH, and the appropriateness, or otherwise, of imposing devastating suffering as punishment for sin.[79] Reading Lamentations as a polyphony means

75. See Linafelt, *Surviving Lamentations*.
76. Carol A. Newsom, 'Bakhtin, the Bible, and Dialogic Truth', *JR* 76 (1996), p. 298.
77. Barbara Green, *How Are the Mighty Fallen? A Dialogical Study of King Saul in 1 Samuel* (JSOTSup, 365; London: Sheffield Academic Press, 2003), p. 78.
78. Murray Rae, 'Texts in Context: Scripture and the Divine Economy', *JTI* 1 (2007), p. 45.
79. Cf. O'Connor, *Tears of the World*, pp. 121-22; Mandolfo, *Daughter Zion*, pp. 19-23.

recognizing, ideologically, that according to the responding and responsive nature of the text itself, further voices are compelled to participate.

Rather than asking which voice dominates, then, the question becomes: which voice do I choose to privilege? Whose theological evaluation of Zion's situation do I find persuasive? Do I side with the third person Lamenter, assuming his objectivity? What happens when he changes his mind and sides with Zion? Do I side with Zion, who, though she admits fault, protests her treatment bitterly? Do I sit with the *geber* in quiet penitence, figuring my troubles must somehow stem from sin? What about when he, too, lashes out in vehement accusation?

Further, might some of the voices in Lamentations actually need to be assessed, evaluated and critiqued, even rejected? On what grounds? I might wish, in a world with a penchant for weapons and revenge, to critique the imprecatory strands of Lamentations (1.20-22; 3.60-66; 4.21-22). I may wish, instead, to highlight and focus on aspects of Lamentations that demonstrate concern at the fate of women and children, and their rape and starvation as the tragic by-products of other people's wars. I might find myself, with the Lamenter, urging the community of God to repentance and faithfulness. But how do I decide? Do I privilege the voice of the victim, or of the penitent, or of the prestige languages that participate in the text? *Must* I align myself with one or other perspective—as both theodic and anti-theodic interpreters have done—or may I hold multiple, even contradictory, theological stances in tension?

Whatever stance I take, let me not be deceived that this is determined and demanded solely by the 'text itself'. There are myriad pre-existing theological, moral and ethical stances I bring to the text—and this makes a theological interpretation of Lamentations just as much a moral and ethical enterprise as it is a theological one.

This recognition takes me beyond the scope of this paper, but, appropriately, leaves the way open for further interaction and response. If I am going to assess, critique and argue with some or all of these voices, by which standards do I do so? What criteria will be used to determine which voices are privileged and prioritized? How might these moral and ethical stances be derived?

Lamentations expresses something of penitence and something of protest. Further, the burden of Lamentations throughout is to express pure pain. Both theodic and antitheodic possibilities within Lamentations are found by different interpreters to be persuasive, which in and of itself suggests that neither should be allowed to predominate. Neither the *geber*, who promotes penitence in the face of God's punishment, nor the figure of Zion, who protests God's severity, can be taken at face value as a dominant figure to whom to adhere when seeking a theology of Lamentations. The *geber*'s statements of faith—and his negations of them—and Zion's voicing of protest—and her admissions of sin—coexist. In its representation of dialogic truth, Lamentations presents a polyphony of pain, penitence and protest.

12

HISTORY, HERMENEUTICS, AND THEODICY IN LIGHT OF ISRAEL'S TRADITION OF PROTEST

James E. Harding

Die großen Prozesse oder Ereignisse einer Zeit dienen oft als Meilensteine der Geschichte. Auf sie beziehen wir, was 'vorher' und 'nachher' geschah.[1]

À la bonne heure, il ne faut envier à personne la consolation de raisonner comme il peut sur le déluge de maux qui nous inonde. Il est juste d'accorder aux malades désespérés de manger de ce qu'ils veulent. On a été jusqu'à prétendre que ce système est consolant.[2]

How does the tradition of protest in the Hebrew Bible help us to get to grips with what it might mean to interpret the Bible theologically, that is, not simply as a collection of ancient texts, but as a fundamental resource for speaking thoughtfully and faithfully of God? And what might it mean to pose such a question now? What I intend to do in this essay is to look back at the Hebrew Bible from a vantage point on the far side of the intellectual and ethical shifts created by two 'milestones of history', the Lisbon earthquake of 1755 and the Nazi death camps of the 1940s, and to argue that it is in relation to analogous events in the history and memory of ancient Israel that the writings of the Hebrew Bible are found to be most creative. It is in relation to implicit questions such as 'Where was YHWH when Shiloh, Samaria and Jerusalem were overthrown?' that the Hebrew Bible puts the theological resources of ancient Israel and Judah most fully to the test. What comes out of this is not a single, unassailable answer to such questions, but

---

1. Wolfgang Breidert (ed.), *Die Erschütterung der vollkommenen Welt: Die Wirkung des Erdbebens von Lissabon im Spiegel europäischer Zeitgenossen* (Darmstadt: Wissenschaftliche Buchgesellschaft, 1994), p. 1: 'The great processes [or, 'trials'] and events of an era often serve as milestones of history. We refer to them what happened "before" and "after".'

2. Voltaire, 'Bien, tout est bien', in *Oeuvres complètes de Voltaire: Dictionnaire philosophique, I* (Paris: Furne, 1835), p. 260: 'Please yourself, then—we should not begrudge anyone the consolation of reasoning as best they can about the flood of evils that overwhelms us. It is fair to let those who are incurably ill eat what they want. It has even been maintained that this system is consoling.'

rather a variety of different attitudes toward, and responses to, Israel's God. The result, for us, is that the faithful theological interpretation of the Hebrew Bible should not begin by assuming that there exists a single, univocal message behind the books of which this collection is composed, whether individually or as a collection: there is no reason to think that the biblical texts must contain an identifiable *message* that it is the interpreter's task to decipher. Instead, we need to pay attention to the various modes of speech in relation to God that the Hebrew Bible offers us, asking how they might shape the way we, too, might respond to God in situations that force our resources of faith to the limit.

Lisbon and Auschwitz

In her book *Evil in Modern Thought*,[3] Susan Neiman offers a revisionist history of modern philosophy, structured not in relation to questions of epistemology, ontology, and metaphysics, but rather in relation to the problem of evil. The core of Neiman's case is that the beginning and end of the modern can be identified in the way that the Lisbon earthquake of 1755,[4] and the Nazi atrocities emblematized and immortalized by the name Auschwitz, created forms of conceptual devastation that led to paradigm shifts in the ways in which natural and moral 'evil' could be addressed.[5] For reasons not attributable to some supposed quality inherent in the events themselves, but rather entangled in the complex strands that make up the development of modern thought—at least as rooted in the intellectual life of Western Europe during and in the aftermath of the Enlightenment[6]—Lisbon

---

3. Susan Neiman, *Evil in Modern Thought: An Alternative History of Philosophy* (Princeton, NJ: Princeton University Press, 2002).
4. Neiman, *Evil in Modern Thought*, esp. pp. 240-50.
5. This modern distinction, which implies that Lisbon and Auschwitz belong to two different categories of thing, i.e., 'human' and 'natural' disasters, albeit with the common denominator that in each case there is a perpetrator and a victim (cf. Breidert, *Erschütterung*, pp. 1-2), would have baffled the authors of the Hebrew Bible, for whom *ra'ah* could stand for both, and for whom the idea that a natural disaster could have been caused by human moral failings, which was still very much live in the eighteenth century of the common era, was normal and only rarely challenged (e.g., in Qoheleth). This very point highlights the arbitrariness of focusing on particular events as somehow epoch-making, yet this does seem to be how some of us at least organize our sense of how we fit into the flood of history, and, as will become clearer below, the Hebrew Bible has its own categories for doing this.
6. In addition to Neiman, see on the intellectual context of the mid-eighteenth century, and the effects of Lisbon on European thought and literature in its aftermath, the introduction to Breidert, *Erschütterung*, pp. 1-17, and the works collected in this anthology.

and Auschwitz have come to stand for the limits of the human ability to comprehend human suffering in relation to an ultimately trustworthy underlying order, whether that order be constituted in terms of an identifiable connection between natural disaster and underlying moral causes (overturned by Lisbon), or whether it be constituted in terms of a clear link between moral evil and underlying human intentions (undone by Auschwitz).[7]

There is, of course, nothing inevitable or universal about this perception of the significance of Lisbon and Auschwitz.[8] The natural world has never

---

7. Neiman identifies the rupture caused by Auschwitz as grounded in the inadequacies of an understanding of moral evil as linked with underlying individual evil intentions on the part of those who contributed to the atrocities of the Shoah (*Evil in Modern Thought*, pp. 267-81; cf. also Kenneth R. Surin's response to Dorothee Sölle in *Theology and the Problem of Evil* [Signposts in Theology; Oxford: Blackwell, 1986], pp. 119-22). The failure to recognize these inadequacies accounts, for Neiman, for misunderstandings of Hannah Arendt's response to the trial of Adolf Eichmann; however, the problem of the nature of the relationship between individual intention and evil act has a longer pedigree, arguably traceable in the traditions of Judaism and Christianity to Scripture, but in more recent literature perhaps most clearly identifiable in the figure of Ivan Karamazov, in the extent to which he is morally culpable for his father's death.

8. The issue here is the way Auschwitz has come to function as a paradigm of moral evil, not whether the event in and of itself is in some sense unique. The latter question is fraught and controversial, and while I cannot treat it adequately here, it must at least be acknowledged. Emil Fackenheim at one point criticized particularly 'non-Jews, who... maintain, affrontingly enough, that unless Jews universalize the Holocaust, thus robbing the Jews of Auschwitz of their identity, they are guilty of disregard for humanity' ('The Commanding Voice of Auschwitz', in S.T. Katz, S. Biderman, and G. Greenberg [eds.], *Wrestling with God: Jewish Theological Responses during and after the Holocaust* [Oxford: Oxford University Press, 2008], p. 435; repr. from *God's Presence in History: Jewish Affirmation and Philosophical Reflections* [Deems Lectures, 18; New York: New York University Press, 1970]). This highlights a serious risk, for when the Holocaust is abstracted in such a way, the identity of particular Jews murdered by the Nazis vanishes—and no one who has stood at Auschwitz and read the names of the murdered on the suitcases they came with, or seen the carefully woven braids of a young girl in a ghastly pile of hair cut from the condemned, could dare to indulge in such dehumanizing abstractions. But Fackenheim's is a *moral* claim, not an empirical one (cf. Michael Wyschogrod, 'Faith and the Holocaust', in Katz, Biderman, and Greenberg (eds.), *Wrestling with God*, p. 460; repr. from *Judaism* 20 [1971], pp. 286-94). Also in response to Fackenheim, see Eliezer Schweid's incisive critique, 'Is the Shoah a Unique Event?' in Katz, Biderman, and Greenberg (eds.), *Wrestling with God*, pp. 219-29 (trans. S. Biderman); originally published in *Iyyun* (1988), pp. 271-85 [Hebrew]. Perhaps the risk of universalizing the Holocaust could be avoided without diminishing the reality of the horror of other atrocities by saying that *all* suffering is particular, irreducible and incomparable; there is no such thing as suffering in general, and the Holocaust has to be addressed—if it can be addressed—in its particularity. It is because suffering does not exist in general that the face of my neighbour is visible, creating an ethical demand.

been nonviolent,[9] human life has never been without suffering and human beings have rarely strayed far from the opportunity to inflict gross atrocities on one another (Dresden, Hiroshima, Srebrenica, Rwanda and Darfur would be other recent examples among far too many). Also, neither Lisbon nor Auschwitz brought a swift or complete end to theodic explanations of natural and moral evils, as both, as well as other naturally and humanly caused catastrophes, were subject to theodic explanations of varying kinds (the Jesuit Fr. Malagrida's first thought following the Lisbon earthquake was to explain it as divine punishment for the sins of the city's inhabitants; it took time, distance and reflection for the inadequacies of such views to become widely recognized). There is also the serious risk of Western, colonialist myopia in focusing on Lisbon and Auschwitz; why should conceptual ruptures that have affected modern Western Europe and its intellectual progeny be universalized, as if the perceptions of all humanity should be forced into line?

Lisbon and Auschwitz had the conceptually rupturing effect they did on particular individuals at particular points in time for reasons that can be explained historically, in terms of the particularities of the development of modern—particularly Western European and Anglo-American—philosophical thought. Neiman summarizes the matter thus:

> Lisbon revealed how remote the world is from the human; Auschwitz revealed the remoteness of humans from themselves. If disentangling the natural from the human is part of the modern project, the distance between Lisbon and Auschwitz showed how difficult it was to keep them apart. After Lisbon, the scope of moral categories contracted. Before Lisbon, they could be applied to the world as a whole; it made sense to call earthquakes evils. Afterward moral categories were confined to one small piece of the world, those human beings who may be able to realize them. Auschwitz raised doubts about the sense in which we apply moral categories at all.[10]

---

9. As Breidert puts it, we are living 'on a fiery ball..., whose thin skin is none too sturdy' ('auf ein feuriger Ball..., dessen dünne Haut nicht allzu stabil ist'). More provocatively, 'A generous god could only have allocated such a place to live to one of the creatures driven out of Paradise' (*Erschütterung*, p. 17: 'Nur einem aus dem Paradies vertriebenen Wesen hätte ein gütiger Gott einen solchen Wohnsitz zuweisen können').

10. Neiman, *Evil in Modern Thought*, p. 240. For Breidert, the significance of Lisbon is constituted not in terms of the quantitative vastness of the catastrophe, but by the effect it had on eighteenth century Europe as a cultural, scientific, and intellectual milieu: 'The destruction of Lisbon had a significantly greater effect, at least for European history, because this earthquake shook not only a particular earthly region, but also a cultural, scientific, intellectual world. Nothing more dramatic could have determined the moment of this disaster more effectively' (*Erschütterung*, p. 6: 'Die Zerstörung Lissabons hatte mindestens für die europäische Geschichte eine erheblich größere Wirkung, denn dieses

An explanation for these moments of conceptual rupture must reckon with why a problem of evil could be posed at all in relation to events such as these. This has to do with the deep theological roots of modern Western philosophy, and the ongoing interpenetration of theology and philosophy, which cannot be construed in terms of a simple displacement of theological by 'secular' categories.[11] The place of theological discourse here is conditioned in large part by the rich and complex scriptural traditions of Judaism and Christianity, as shaped by their yet richer and more complex afterlives. The book of Job, in particular, functions as a *Leitmotif* in Neiman's book, and has not only been a source of inspiration or provocation for many who have shaped the contours of modern thought, whether philosophical, theological or psychological, but has, alongside Lamentations and other parts of the scriptural tradition of protest, played an explicit and significant role in some Jewish and Christian responses to the horrors of the Shoah.[12]

The modest purpose of this essay is to wrestle with the question of what all this means for how Scripture is to be read Christianly and with integrity. I am not suggesting that Lisbon and Auschwitz in themselves confront the Christian theologian with a problem to be solved that is somehow ontologically distinct from other examples of the reality of human suffering, nor am I picking up on Neiman's work as if it could somehow be construed as a call for the Christian theologian to offer answers, whether in the mode of explanation or not, to horrors such as these. What I am suggesting is that inasmuch as our discourse in relation to God must be timely if it is to have any point—or rather, if it is to be meaningfully consistent with the *incarnation*, and with the *prophetic*, which together are the *fons et origo* of any Christian claim to say anything at all in and for the world—then it should wrestle with

Erdbeben erschütterte nicht nur eine bestimmte irdische Region, sondern auch eine kulturelle, wissenschaftliche, geistige Welt. Kein Dramatiker hätte den Zeitpunkt dieser Katastrophe wirkungsvoller festlegen können').

11. See esp. Neiman, *Evil in Modern Thought*, pp. 314-28. For Neiman, '[t]he impulse to theodicy is not a relic of monotheism but goes deeper than either. Indeed, it is part of the same impulse that leads to monotheism itself' (p. 318).

12. A study of the reception and effective histories of Job since the dawn of the Enlightenment would need to take in Voltaire, Kant, Herder, Goethe, Blake, Hegel, Kierkegaard, Melville, Dostoyevsky, Nietzsche, Y.L. Perets, Joseph Roth, Kafka, Jung, Vischer, Barth, Borges, Levinas, Wiesel and Žižek, to give but the most truncated of lists. A brief reception history of Job during this period is offered in Stephen Vicchio, *Job in the Modern World* (Eugene, OR: Wipf & Stock, 2006). Breidert quotes a letter written by a German Protestant businessman living in Lisbon at the time of the earthquake, who, having escaped the horror with his wife, three children and very little else, felt able to exclaim, 'Der Herr hats gegeben, der Herr hats genommen, der Name des Herrn sei gelobt!' (Job 1.21; Breidert, *Erschütterung*, pp. 8-9).

questions arising at particular historical moments that seem to lay bare previously unacknowledged limits to our ability to comprehend the world, to find a way of living in the world as if it were our home. We need to wrestle with the questions that define how we experience the world in reasoned, critical conversation with the resources of our native theological language, the densely layered language of Scripture and Tradition (of which Scripture is itself a part).

This critical conversation, however, has to take place in a way that leaves room for the particular hermeneutic of suspicion that belongs to this native language,[13] which is part and parcel of it. It cannot begin from the *a priori* assumption that Scripture and Tradition have the primary function of offering us a language—that is, to borrow Saussure's terminology,[14] a *langue*—with which to shape discrete interventions (*paroles*) that reduce such situations of limit to some *explanation* or other that enables us to go on living. We need to be open to the possibility that theological interpretation might not be about explanation at all, and, moreover, might yield a plurality of conflicting, yet nevertheless faithful, responses. It might, furthermore, allow or even require us to approach Scripture with a hermeneutic of suspicion that is rooted in humility and integrity, a suspicion that turns out not to be an act of hubris against a tradition we would rather control.

We might frame the problem by asking either what it might mean to speak of one benevolent, powerful and supremely knowledgeable creator in the wake of natural catastrophe, or what it might mean to speak of one benevolent, powerful and supremely knowledgeable creator of humanity in the aftermath of gross human wickedness. The first of these was the basis of the formulation of the problem by Pierre Bayle (1647–1706) several decades before Lisbon,[15] the attempt to resolve which Leibniz would term 'theodicy',

---

13. Cf. Walter Brueggemann's language of 'countertestimony' in *Theology of the Old Testament* (Minneapolis: Augsburg Fortress, 1997).

14. Ferdinand de Saussure, *Cours de linguistique générale* (ed. C. Bally and A. Sechehaye, with the collaboration of A. Riedlinger; Paris: Payot, 1916).

15. Pierre Bayle's discussion of the problem of theodicy begins with a stinging critique of a passage from Lactantius (*De ira Dei* 13), which in turn is presented as a response to Epicurus: 'Consider carefully this passage from Lactantius, which contains an answer to an objection of Epicurus. Epicurus says, "God is either willing to remove evil and cannot; or he can and is unwilling; or he is neither willing nor able to do so; or else he is both willing and able. If he is willing and not able, he must then be weak, which cannot be affirmed of God. If he is able and not willing, he must be envious, which is also contrary to the nature of God. If he is neither willing nor able, he must be both envious and weak, and consequently not be God. If he is both willing and able—the only possibility that agrees with the nature of God—then where does evil come from? Or why does he not eliminate it?"' (*Historical and Critical Dictionary: Selections* [trans. and ed. R.H. Popkin and C. Bush; Indianapolis, IN: Bobbs–Merrill, 1965], p. 169; *An Historical*

and this forms the basis of the constellation of intellectual conflicts traced by Neiman. It should not be assumed, however, that to tackle this problem in Christian terms, in dialogue with Scripture, will necessarily yield a *resolution* of the conflict created by the need to reconcile the existence of evil with the existence of an omnipotent, omnibenevolent and omniscient deity; nor should it be assumed that this is even how the issue should be framed in a Christian context.

To be sure, the Jewish and Christian Scriptures contain, and have in their turn inspired, explanations of various sorts that exonerate God, yet arguably at an exorbitant cost in terms of the nexus of divine benevolence and human worth; when does the cost of defending God's justice become untenable, even obscene?[16] If Scripture, however, is taken to function canonically—that is, as *norma normans*, somehow authoritatively shaping our discourse in relation to God—then our response to evil and suffering may involve not simply explanation. It may involve various dimensions of response. It may involve address to God, in worship and thanksgiving, but also in lament, supplication and protest. It may involve engagement with others concerned with the integrity of Godtalk, both in witness and in dispute, proving (i.e., *testing*) the adequacy of our language for God, and of our sense of God's involvement in the world and in our lives. And when the limits of language, even of paradox, are reached, it may leave room for silence before a divine mystery. The response we give should depend not on our desire to impose meaning on both Scripture and human experience, but on how we sense Scripture offering resources for us to understand the context in which we find ourselves, into which, or out of which, we feel ourselves compelled to speak. This is a question of discernment, and all we can say in advance is

---

and Critical Dictionary by Monsieur Bayle [vol. 4; London, 1710], p. 2489; cf. Voltaire, 'Bien, tout est bien', p. 259). Lactantius (c. 250– ca. 325 CE) had argued that God is able to remove evils, but unwilling to do so. He is not, however, envious. He has given wisdom, by which we can know God and thereby attain the highest good, immortality. There is more goodness and pleasure in wisdom than there is annoyance in evils, and unless we first know evil, we cannot know good. Bayle objects stridently to this last point (*Historical and Critical Dictionary*, pp. 170-72), and then proceeds to dismantle the free will defence (pp. 177-79). See further Neiman's discussion in *Evil in Modern Thought*, pp. 116-28.

16. The literature on this problem is vast. An exemplary treatment in relation to the Hebrew Bible is James Crenshaw, *Defending God: Biblical Responses to the Problem of Evil* (Oxford: Oxford University Press, 2005). The anthology, A. Laato and J.C. de Moor (eds.), *Theodicy in the World of the Bible* (Leiden: Brill, 2003), includes a range of more detailed engagements with specific texts and issues. Rolf P. Knierim offers a concise but thorough overview of justice generally in the Hebrew Bible in his 'Third Lecture: Justice in Old Testament Theology', in *The Task of Old Testament Theology: Substance, Method and Cases* (Grand Rapids: Eerdmans, 1995), pp. 86-122.

that a scripturally shaped, Christian response is going somehow to be a witness to a sense of relationship with One who stands in some sense alongside, or over against us, without assuming *a priori* that this response is going to take the form of explanation, justification or judgement.

Two further points need to be made. First, there cannot be a theological hermeneutics that is distinguishable from theology *per se*; they are largely constitutive of one another.[17] Second, theological hermeneutics is not simply one more option for approaching the study of Scripture that can be set up alongside, or over against, other methods of biblical interpretation. A robust use of methodological guidelines is essential to reading Scripture theologically,[18] not least to avoid random and irresponsible fantasies taking the place of sober exegesis, but theological hermeneutics is not *itself* a method that can be placed alongside source criticism, form criticism, redaction criticism and so on, as part of a scholar's toolkit. It is a matter, rather, of the attitude and formation of the interpreter.

Wrestling with God

At issue here are the very nature and possibility of theology. This is because, in the Hebrew Scriptures, it is the situations of limit created by natural catastrophes and humanly enacted moral enormities that forced the language and conceptualities for God that Israel had nurtured and passed on to the brink of bad faith on the one hand, and total collapse on the other. The traditions now embodied in the Hebrew Scriptures had their own paradigms of evil long before Lisbon and Auschwitz, as well as their own paradigms of human righteousness. The Hebrew Scriptures themselves also bear witness to the significance of actual—and arguably fictional—events that produced profound conceptual devastation, forcing the theological resources of ancient Israel and Judah to their very limits.

The destruction of Sodom and the other cities of the wilderness functions in the Hebrew Bible as a paradigm of the sort of disaster that results when

---

17. This is clear from a study of how Scripture has been used in the history of Christian interpretation, when at least until the rise of historical criticism it could, for the most part, be taken as axiomatic that 'all of divine revelation is contained in Scripture and, on the other hand, that in the interpretation of this selfsame body of Scripture all of theological science is encompassed' (Henri de Lubac, *Medieval Exegesis* [vol. 1; trans. M. Sebanc; Grand Rapids: Eerdmans, 1998], p. 24). How such a claim can be upheld in a post-Enlightenment, and now postmodern, intellectual environment without retreating to some form of fideism remains a serious issue for theological hermeneutics.

18. The classic starting point here in a Christian context—at least a Christian context aligned with, or derived from, the traditions of the Western Church—must surely be Augustine's *De doctrina christiana*, though it would be folly to read this work uncritically, or as if post-Enlightenment exegesis did not exist.

YHWH's righteousness can no longer stand the presence of pervasive moral evil.[19] Indeed, Sodom is described as a 'byword' (*shemu'ah*) in Ezek. 16.56, precisely to highlight the fact that the city's destruction should have stood as a warning to Jerusalem not to follow their wickedness: it was a paradigm of moral evil. In the Jeremiah tradition, perhaps because of the place of Shiloh in the memory of Jeremiah's own family,[20] the destruction of Shiloh functions as a paradigm of the sort of destruction YHWH will wreak through human agency on a people that refuses to live faithfully under the terms of their covenant with their God. In the normal run of things, even if they created deep trauma and uncertainty, such disasters seem not to have led to irreversible conceptual rupture, either because they were in the long distant past, ossified as part of a tradition that was authoritative and functioned as a source of analogies for discerning future divine action, or they were in the present or recent past, and indicated some kind of divine displeasure to which Israel had to respond with repentance and intercession. There are clear instances of such intercession in Joel (1.2–2.17), Amos (9.1),[21] Jeremiah (14.1-22), and Haggai (1.4-11; 2.14-19), for example.[22] On an individual level, Noah, Dan'el (or Daniel) and Job stand as paradigms of righteousness, so righteous that their moral integrity *should* be enough to save the lives of others from divinely willed disaster, though in fact, according to Ezekiel, even this would *not* be enough.[23]

---

19. See Deut. 29.20-27; 32.32; Isa. 1.9, 10; 3.9; 13.19; Jer. 23.14; 49.18; 50.40; Ezek. 16.46-50, 53-56; Amos 4.11; Zeph. 2.9; Lam. 4.6. Cf. Jer. 20.16.

20. Jeremiah is identified in Jer. 1.1 as an Elide priest, associated with the line of Abiathar, who was exiled to Anathoth in 1 Kgs 2.26-27 (cf. 1 Sam. 2.27-36) and who was apparently the great-grandson of Eli (cf. 1 Sam. 14.3), the former priest of the destroyed shrine at Shiloh.

21. Amos 9.1 seems to be a vision of an earthquake, whose apparent fulfilment enabled the words of Amos to be regarded as true prophecy (Amos 1.1; Zech. 14.5; cf. Deut. 18.15-22). In Amos 4.6-12 a series of disasters are understood to be warnings, intended to provoke Israel to repentance.

22. The intercessory role of the prophet needs to be correctly understood. It is not simply a matter of bringing the needs of God's people before the throne of God, but of 'standing in the breach' between the people and their God. An excellent account of the prophets of Israel and Judah taking God's part against the people, but equally, taking the people's part in the face of a dangerous God, is Yochanan Muffs, 'Who Will Stand in the Breach? A Study of Prophetic Intercession', in *Love and Joy: Law, Language and Religion in Ancient Israel* (New York: Jewish Theological Seminary of America, 1992), pp. 9-48. Susannah Ticciati has helpfully explored how this construal of prophetic intercession informs our understanding of the role of the 'arbiter' or *mokiakh* in the book of Job (*Job and the Disruption of Identity: Reading beyond Barth* [London: T. & T. Clark, 2005]).

23. Ezek. 14.12-20. In Gen. 6–8, Noah's righteousness is enough to save himself, his wife, his sons, his sons' wives and a menagerie of animals and birds. In Job, paradoxi-

Yet the Hebrew Scriptures also point to events that apparently, in their time, stretched the conceptual resources reflected by Israel's theological language to breaking point in a manner analogous to Lisbon and Auschwitz for the modern West: not for everyone, to be sure, but for particular individuals and groups, whose voices—or the echoes thereof—have found their way into Scripture. On an individual level, the suffering of Job, which ironically takes place *because* he is surpassingly righteous, seems to function as the occasion for testing the limits of Israel's theological resources. More broadly, the fall of Jerusalem to Babylon in 586 BCE was conceptually devastating on many different levels, challenging not only a sense of Zion's inviolability, but the very justice and trustworthiness of Israel's God (whether Job is to be read as an allegory of Judah's suffering in the wake of 586 BCE is by no means clear). The theological uncertainty created by the turmoil in Judah and Jerusalem at the end of the seventh and beginning of the sixth centuries BCE is evident most clearly in the book of Jeremiah, especially in the conflict between Jeremiah and other prophets with whom he disagreed, such as Hananiah. Yet Jeremiah's own voice, as represented in the book to which his name is attached, also appears to bear witness to a profound inner conflict. In Jer. 4.10 (MT),[24] Jeremiah himself seems, at least on the surface, to accuse YHWH of deceiving (*nsh'*, hiphil) his people by announcing 'peace' (*shalom*), when in fact they were faced with a sword. In Jer. 12.1-4, Jeremiah questions the justice of YHWH, which seems to be invisible, and like Job does not receive any clarification on the matter when he addresses his God.[25] In Jer. 15.18, Jeremiah seems to charge YHWH with being untrustworthy, and, judging by v. 19, to have incurred YHWH's anger

---

cally, Job's righteousness is enough to incur the deaths of his children and livestock, and the terrible suffering of himself and his wife.

24. The MT at this point has *wa'omar* ('and I said'), but this may have been written under the influence of Jer. 14.13 (thus *BHS* n.), where Jeremiah addresses YHWH in complaint about the misleading words of 'the prophets', using the same words, *'ahah 'adonay yhwh*. While the majority of Greek witnesses support the reading in the MT, Codex Alexandrinus reads *kai eipan*, which is followed by the Arabic, suggesting a *Vorlage* that read *we'ameru*, 'and *they* said'. It is possible that Codex Alexandrinus reflects an attempt to resolve the apparent anomaly of YHWH's being charged by Jeremiah with deceit, rather than a *Vorlage* different from MT. William McKane solves the apparent problem by suggesting that Jeremiah is quoting fraudulent words spoken by false prophets in the cult, words that YHWH had allowed to be taken as his own: '…the proclamation of *shalom* belongs to the Jerusalem cult and…is made to those who trust in Yahweh. Jeremiah's contention is that Yahweh has permitted this ambiguity whose only outcome can be the deception of the people and in *shalom yihyeh lakem* he reproduces *verbatim* the message of these prophets, represented as Yahweh's word' (*Jeremiah* [ICC; 2 vols.; Edinburgh: T. & T. Clark, 1986, 1996], I, p. 95).

25. Jer. 12.5-6 hardly offer a response that clears up Jeremiah's dilemma.

and (temporary) rejection. In Jer. 20.7, Jeremiah apparently charges YHWH with deceiving (*pth*, piel and niphal)[26] him. The complexity in this particular tradition strongly suggests that the process of discernment that led to the redaction of the Jeremiah tradition(s) should not be regarded without further ado by us as having come to an end: even words honoured by tradition as 'true' prophecy seem to remain shot through with the risk and threat of at least doubt, and perhaps even falsehood.

In spite of this, there is a dominant voice in the Hebrew Bible that emerges from the traumas of 587/586 BCE. This voice now dominates the final forms of the so-called Deuteronomistic History and the book of Jeremiah, as well as the other Latter Prophets, notwithstanding the fact that the tradition-historical complexity of all these works is such that there are many layers to them that, at certain points (such as the Micaiah ben Imlah narrative [1 Kgs 22.1-40], Habakkuk's dialogue with YHWH [Hab. 1.2–2.20], Jeremiah's final 'confessions' [Jer. 20.7-13, 14-18], and Jonah), expose tensions. This dominant voice reflects an attempt to exonerate YHWH and lay the blame on Judah and Jerusalem themselves for this disaster, and it is through the lens of this theodicy that readers of these works are expected by their implied authors to view YHWH's involvement in Israel's history. So powerful was the effect of the destruction of Jerusalem in 586 BCE that it would still be the most obvious metaphor to the authors of *4 Ezra* and *2 Baruch* when they sought to wrestle with the problem of divine justice and integrity anew in light of the fate of Jerusalem and its people at the hands of the Romans in 70 CE.

The Hebrew Scriptures do not formulate the problem of evil the way Bayle, Leibniz, and Voltaire did, of course, and it is worth pondering whether abstract references to a 'problem of evil' or to 'theodicy'—especially when conjoined with the dubious Leibnizian notion of the ultimate goodness of this best of all possible worlds—should be laid aside, not so much as anachronisms, but as misrepresentative abstractions, when we engage with Scripture.[27] The fundamental theological problem that animates much of the Hebrew Scriptures is not what it means to believe in an omniscient, omnipotent, omnibenevolent God in the face of human

---

26. This root is ambiguous, and can mean 'seduce' or 'deceive', or in some cases both, with the possibility of deliberate *double entendre*. I have touched on this problem elsewhere. See my 'In the Name of Love: Resisting Reader and Abusive Redeemer in Deutero-Isaiah', *Bible and Critical Theory* 2.2 (2006), pp. 14.6, 14.12. Theologically, the most troubling occurrences of this root are in connection with a putatively false prophecy inspired by YHWH himself in 1 Kgs 22.20, 21, 22. Walter Moberly's attempts to address the difficulties posed by the Micaiah ben Imlah narrative are valiant, but ultimately rather less than convincing (see further below).

27. Levinas seems to retain the term 'theodicy' for convenience (see below), and I will do the same: the term is inadequate, but a useful shorthand nevertheless.

suffering, but rather what it means to maintain allegiance to the God revealed to Israel's ancestors and bound to Israel in covenant when the evidence of the perceptible world seems to suggest inconsistency, bad faith or even outright cruelty on the part of this God. Another way in which the Hebrew Bible formulates the issue, which relates very strongly to the idea of prophetic intercession,[28] is in connection with the revealed character of God in Exod. 34.6-7: how are the revealed attributes of God borne out in Israel's life?[29]

These are *particular* formulations of the problem, not abstractions. Here history, hermeneutics and theodicy are inextricably intertwined; God's involvement in the world is thought of in Scripture in relation to the extent to which he is experienced as just, and the extent to which Israel's traditions are vindicated in the court of Israel's lived experience in history. For those responsible for the Deuteronomistic History, the Latter Prophets, the historical Psalms, Chronicles, Ezra–Nehemiah and Daniel, in fact for the bulk of the Hebrew Bible, human history is the arena of God's actions, and the suffering of Israel within this arena is to be ascribed to Israel's disobedience to the covenant with their God, and to the response of a compassionate yet just God to their recalcitrance. But for other voices in the Hebrew Bible, all this creates terrible tensions, on both ethical and epistemological grounds. The outcome of this is not just a series of competing resolutions of the problem of divine covenantal justice and Israel's suffering. Rather, the Hebrew Bible presents us with a range of *alternative modes and styles of theology*, that, in the face of the threat of the imminent collapse of Israel's resources for thinking and speaking of God, appear to offer the only possibilities for continuing to speak of God at all.

What is at stake is not so much where the 'truth', if any, lies in the intra-scriptural dialogue, but rather the extent to which ethics exposes the limits of what it seems possible to say about suffering. As the structure of the book of Job shows, with painful irony, the ability to live ethically could very well be grossly threatened by what one could know; how could Job have gone on living had he known the real reason for his suffering, that his exemplary

---

28. See Muffs, 'Who Will Stand in the Breach?'
29. See esp. Num. 14.18; Joel 2.13; Jon. 4.2; Pss. 25.4-11; 86.15; 103.8; 145.8; Neh. 9.17. On the character of YHWH in the Book of the Twelve in particular, see e.g. Raymond C. van Leeuwen, 'Scribal Wisdom and Theodicy in the Book of the Twelve', in L.G. Perdue, B.B. Scott, and W.J. Wiseman (eds.), *In Search of Wisdom: Essays in Memory of John G. Gammie* (Louisville, KY: Westminster/John Knox Press, 1993), pp. 31-49. For a thoughtful treatment of the way the revealed attributes of YHWH are wrestled with in the book of Jonah, see Walter Moberly's essay, 'Jonah, God's Objectionable Mercy, and the Way of Wisdom', in D.F. Ford and G. Stanton (eds.), *Reading Texts, Seeking Wisdom: Scripture and Theology* (London: SCM Press, 2003), pp. 154-68.

righteousness made him an ideal candidate to be used in a wager between YHWH and the Accuser to find out whether disinterested righteousness is possible? It is essential to the structure of the book, and to Job's life as represented within it, that he does not find this out, and in any case, the reasons for *his* suffering offer no insight into the reasons for anyone else's.

The *ethical* affront created by the attempt to *explain* suffering theodically has animated important strands of thought in the wake of the nightmare of Auschwitz. In a now famous short essay,[30] Emmanuel Levinas responds to what he sees as the deeply problematic trend in Western metaphysics to seek an underlying order to explain and justify suffering that would otherwise appear senseless.

> Western humanity has nonetheless sought for the meaning of this scandal [viz., of human suffering] by invoking the proper sense of a metaphysical order, an ethics, which is invisible in the immediate lessons of moral consciousness. This is a kingdom of transcendent ends, willed by a benevolent wisdom, by the absolute goodness of a God who is in some way defined by this supernatural goodness; or a widespread, invisible goodness in nature and history, where it would command the paths which are, to be sure, painful, but which lead to the Good. Pain is henceforth meaningful, subordinated in one way or another to the metaphysical finality envisaged by faith or by a belief in progress.[31]

For Levinas, Auschwitz stands for the ultimate horror that brings an end to such exercises in theodicy. That is because Auschwitz represents, for him, the consequence of the refusal truly to respond to the ethical demand of our neighbour's suffering. Confronted by Auschwitz, explanations that seek some ultimately benign meaning in human suffering can hardly be anything other than bad faith.

The problem this poses for theological hermeneutics—whether within a Jewish or a Christian frame of reference—is the fact that, as Levinas points out, this desire to bring order to otherwise senseless pain by means of explanation is rooted in Scripture.

> But theodicy—ignoring the name Leibniz gave to it in 1710—is as old as a certain reading of the Bible. It dominated the consciousness of the believer who explained his misfortunes by reference to the Sin, or at least by reference to his sins. In addition to the Christians' well-established reference to Original Sin, this theodicy is in a certain sense implicit in the Old Testament,

---

30. Emmanuel Levinas, 'Useless Suffering', in Katz, Biderman, and Greenberg (eds.), *Wrestling with God*, pp. 451-54; repr. from R. Bernasconi and D. Wood (eds.), *The Provocation of Levinas* (London: Routledge, 1988).

31. Levinas, 'Useless Suffering', p. 452. Bayle's objections to earlier theodicies (see above) are not in principle different from the objections of Levinas, though with different results.

where the drama of the diaspora reflects the sins of Israel. The wicked conduct of ancestors, still nonexpiated by the sufferings of exile, would explain to the exiles themselves the duration and harshness of this exile.[32]

For the reader approaching such traditions now, there are the dangerously seductive benefits of emotional distance and the potentially superficial wisdom of hindsight, presented as a *datum* of the canonical shape of the Hebrew Bible. That is, because the Hebrew Bible presents Israel's sins as deserving of divine judgement, it is troublingly easy to take this viewpoint as read, to take it as normative and true, regardless of the reality of the suffering that ensued; Israel sinned, so of course they deserved what they got. What is much harder to acknowledge is the reality of the pain and horror that undoubtedly do lie behind the texts of which the Hebrew Bible is composed. Were we granted the privilege—surely an obscene word under the circumstances—of peeling back the layers of scriptural tradition, we might glimpse what Levinas saw only too clearly in Auschwitz: a gross imbalance, a glaring disproportion between the irreducible realities of human suffering on the one hand, and every attempt to explain it in theodic terms on the other.[33] Crucially, Levinas sees that this cannot be limited to Auschwitz, but points 'in a more general way' to 'the unjustifiable character of suffering in the other person, the scandal which would occur by my justifying my neighbour's suffering'.[34] This leads to the well-known claim

---

32. Levinas, 'Useless Suffering', p. 452.
33. Levinas, 'Useless Suffering', pp. 452-53. Fundamental to the theodicies of the Hebrew Bible is the notion of measure, which raises the problem of what happens when suffering seems to outweigh its supposed cause. The question of measure is an important theme in biblical treatments of suffering rooted in divine justice (see esp. Isa. 40.2; Job 11.6; Ezra 9.13). The disruption of measure is a key element in Job's challenge to accepted theodicies, and forms the basis of Antonio Negri's somewhat idiosyncratic approach to the book in *The Labor of Job: The Biblical Text as a Parable of Human Labor* (trans. M. Mandarini; New Slant: Religion, Politics, Ontology; Durham, NC: Duke University Press, 2009). A brief but excellent treatment of Job as radically disruptive of the possibility of theodicy is David Burrell, *Deconstructing Theodicy: Why the Book of Job Has Nothing to Say to the Puzzle of Suffering* (Grand Rapids: Brazos, 2008). Given that it comes from the pen of a philosopher deeply attached to both the justification of God and the truth value of the various languages of Scripture, the implications of Richard Swinburne's succinct, threefold question as to the nature of the book of Job are worth pondering: 'The Book of Job is obviously connected with the problem of evil, but is it a treatise which seeks to provide a theodicy, or a work which seeks to stimulate the philosophical imagination, or a work which records the story and perplexity of a particular individual? In the first and third cases its truth-value is a function of the truth-value of (some of) the constituent sentences, in the second case not' (*Revelation: From Metaphor to Analogy* [Oxford: Oxford University Press, 2nd edn, 2007], p. 247).
34. Levinas, 'Useless Suffering', p. 453.

that, 'For an ethical sensibility…the justification of the neighbor's pain is certainly the source of all immorality'.[35]

What Levinas advocates, in the end, is a faith that survives the end of theodicy by attending with compassion to the suffering Other.

> Is humanity, in its indifference, going to abandon the world to useless suffering, leaving it to the political fatality—or the drifting—of the blind forces which inflict misfortune on the weak and conquered, and which spare the conquerors, whom the wicked must join? Or, incapable of adhering to an order—or to a disorder—which it continues to think diabolic, must not humanity now, in a faith more difficult than ever, in a faith without theodicy, continue Sacred History, a history which now demands even more of the resources of the *self* in each one, and appeals to its suffering inspired by the suffering of the other person, to its compassion which is a non-useless suffering (or love), which is no longer suffering 'for nothing', and which straightaway has a meaning? At the end of the twentieth century and after the useless and unjustifiable pain which is exposed and displayed therein without any shadow of a consoling theodicy, are we not all pledged—like the Jewish people to their faithfulness—to the second term of this alternative? This is a new modality in the faith of today, and also in our moral certainties, a modality quite essential to the modernity which is dawning.[36]

The challenge laid down by Levinas here needs some unpacking. For one thing, the resources Levinas draws upon are themselves deeply grounded in Scripture, but, aside from a brief excursion into the book of Job to which we will turn in a moment, the full richness and complexity of what Scripture contributes is only faintly in evidence. The command to love one's neighbour,[37] together with the laconic summary of Torah attributed to Hillel in the Babylonian Talmud,[38] are most obviously echoed here, but this only scratches the surface of forms of faithful witness that refuse the temptation to impose order by reducing the pain of human existence to the justification of a righteous and trustworthy deity. For Scripture also, as Anson Laytner and (especially) David Blumenthal have clearly shown, bears witness to the human need to protest before God in the face of what looks like divine negligence, injustice, or cruelty.[39] Zachary Braiterman, likewise, has seen in

---

35. Levinas, 'Useless Suffering', p. 453.
36. Levinas, 'Useless Suffering', p. 454.
37. Lev. 19.18, 34.
38. *B. Shabb.* 31a: 'A foreigner…came before Hillel. He accepted him [for initiation]. He said to him, "That which is hateful to you, do not do to your companion. This is the entire Law, and the rest is commentary. Go and learn."'
39. Anson Laytner, *Arguing with God: A Jewish Tradition* (Northvale, NJ: Jason Aronson, 1990); David R. Blumenthal, *Facing the Abusing God: A Theology of Protest* (Louisville, KY: Westminster/John Knox Press, 1993).

Scripture tendencies toward the justification of God, which he terms *theodic*, and tendencies away from this, which he calls *antitheodic*.[40]

Furthermore, what appear to be the predominant voices in Scripture in a sense themselves create the problem of theodicy by placing interhuman ethics in the context of a certain kind of covenant, in which divine blessing is contingent upon human obedience.[41] This framework, which is stated unequivocally in Deuteronomy, and which dominates the Deuteronomistic History, the Latter Prophets, Chronicles and Ezra–Nehemiah, with further echoes elsewhere, not only encodes Israel's history with a principle of just retribution for human sin, but fails to exclude the logical corollary, which would be to interpret more or less all human suffering in terms of divine retributive intervention, a form of *post hoc ergo propter hoc* reasoning that is exposed in the example of Job's interlocutors in the book of Job.

One of the problems here is with the principle of analogy. In the book of Jeremiah in particular, an awareness of how YHWH has acted at one point in Israel's history—say, in the destruction of Shiloh (Jer. 7.12, 14; 26.6, 9)—somehow determines how YHWH will act at another point in human history. Yet how far could this principle be applied? Job's interlocutors use precisely this model to argue that Job must have sinned and should acknowledge this before God, yet to do this not only involves identifying instances of human suffering as signs of divine retributive intervention, but also involves an act of justifying a righteous and trustworthy deity, precisely the kind of theodicy that so appalled Levinas in the wake of Auschwitz.[42] The fact that much

---

40. Zachary Braiterman, *(God) after Auschwitz: Tradition and Change in Post-Holocaust Jewish Thought* (Princeton, NJ: Princeton University Press, 1998).

41. Richard Rubinstein sought, controversially, to expose the problematic effects of such covenantal theology, and to move beyond a theology of covenant, in *After Auschwitz: History, Theology, and Contemporary Judaism* (Johns Hopkins Jewish Studies; Baltimore, MD: Johns Hopkins University Press, 2nd edn, 1992).

42. It also implies a certain individualism, which is the basis of the responses of both Job and his friends; some*one*, some human, is (or is meant to be) responsible for suffering. Elsewhere in the Hebrew Bible, even when ancestral or communal rather than individual sin are assumed, the focus remains on human responsibility, which may well be the chief burden of the YHWH speeches (Job 38–41); why should YHWH be expected to concur with Job and his friends that human responsibility is the thing that makes the world go round? Breidert sees this individualistic assumption still persisting into the present: 'The widespread inclination at the end of the twentieth century to ascribe responsibility for disasters to human beings also lends support to individualistic fashions. If one ascribes a person's fate wholly and completely to him or herself, because one imputes to them a metaphysical choice (*Wahl*), so everything he or she suffers from outside is a consequence of their own choice (*Wahl*). He or she is then not only the architect of their own happiness, but of their own misery as well' (*Erschütterung*, pp. 2-3: 'Die am Ende des 20. Jahrhunderts [sic] weitverbreitete Neigung, dem Menschen die Verantwortung für

prophetic discernment in the Hebrew Bible revolves around the identification of YHWH's imminent, just, retributive intervention in the course of human history suggests, furthermore, that the irreducibility of human suffering cannot but raise serious questions about the moral integrity of biblical claims to identify the words of true prophets of YHWH.[43] Here epistemology and ethics become entangled in a way that is extraordinarily difficult to resolve: how can true words from God be discerned in situations where the claims of those who presume to speak for God seem to justify God in the face of human suffering in a manner that leads to a morally abhorrent imbalance between human pain and that which explains it? This is not simply a matter of epistemology—how can one know that YHWH has

---

Katastrophen zuzuschreiben, läßt sich auch auf individualistische Weise stützen. Falls man das Schicksal eines Menchen voll und ganz ihm selbst zuschreibt, weil man ihm eine metaphysische Wahl desselben unterstellt, so ist all das, was er von außen erleidet, ein Ergebnis seiner eigenen Wahl. Er ist dann nicht nur seines Glücks, sondern ebenso seines Unglücks Schmied').

43. Cf. Jer. 4.10. Walter Moberly's important study *Prophecy and Discernment* (Cambridge Studies in Christian Doctrine; Cambridge: Cambridge University Press, 2006) discusses the issue of the discernment of true from false prophecy at length in connection with 1 Kgs 22 and the book of Jeremiah (*Prophecy and Discernment*, pp. 41-129; cf. Moberly, 'Does God Lie to his Prophets? The Story of Micaiah ben Imlah as a Test Case', *HTR* 96 [2003], pp. 1-23). Moberly's case is that issues of prophetic discernment cannot be separated from the moral integrity of those who claim to speak for YHWH, and that the apparent inconsistency of YHWH's standing behind even the misleading words of his prophets is mitigated by a deeper moral consistency that is bound to call human injustice to account. Moberly's treatment of Jeremiah in particular is question-begging, on two levels. First, our only access to the moral integrity of the lives and speech of Jeremiah's prophetic opponents is through the book of Jeremiah itself, yet it is surely in the interests of the book's redactors to present Jeremiah and his opponents in a way that justifies Jeremiah and vilifies his opponents, creating a barrier between later readers and those of Jeremiah's contemporaries who would have first been confronted with the challenge of discerning between them. To suggest further that the tradition-historically complex book of Jeremiah is itself the product of a process of discernment (*Prophecy and Discernment*, pp. 41-42 n. 1) may have the ring of truth, but this, too, begs the question why later readers should regard this process of discernment as yielding a trustworthy picture of Jeremiah and his God. Second, Moberly's treatment obscures the fact, which becomes starkly obvious in Lamentations, that the destruction of Jerusalem that Jeremiah is said to have predicted led to extreme human suffering. To be sure, there *are* ways of exonerating Jeremiah and his God here, but it is difficult to escape the implication, which seems unavoidable in light of Levinas, that the redacted and canonized book of Jeremiah explains and justifies the suffering of Jeremiah's (and the redactors') neighbours through explaining and justifying YHWH. My objections to Moberly here in no way, of course, imply that there were no real injustices in the Judah of the late seventh and early sixth centuries BCE that cried out for some sort of rectification.

spoken, and spoken truthfully?—but of ethics: how can one live with the implications of what the prophet claims YHWH has said?

In the tradition-historically complex Deuteronomistic History and the Latter Prophets, the events of Israel's history are interpreted theodically with the benefit of hindsight, which on the one hand suggests the discerning insight that only careful reflection in light of both the unfolding of events and the accumulated wisdom of former faithful generations could bring,[44] but on the other hand erects a barrier between the reader of the final form of the texts and the faces of the compassionate women, who cooked their children in the straits to which YHWH had reduced them.[45] If the post-Auschwitz ethical stance of Levinas were to teach us something here, it should be that we must be wary of treating the final form of the Hebrew Bible as a coherent, monolithic source for an explanatory, covenantal theodicy, instead of seeing *ourselves* as part of an ongoing tradition of discernment that has to be confronted anew with the voices of horror emerging from the destruction of Jerusalem, rather than as privileged recipients of a tradition that gives us the tools to stand in judgement over long dead children whose faces we will never see.

A further issue arises from the phrase 'consoling theodicy'. A core purpose of any theodicy is to offer, whether directly or indirectly, a form of comfort and consolation, that despite the horror that surrounds us, there is a trustworthy order in the world that makes it possible for us to continue to find our home here. But should the position taken by Levinas after Auschwitz not call to account attempts to 'console' a sufferer in his or her pain? Do not such attempts to console at the same time attempt to justify the God who is supposed to stand behind the consolation? The clearest example of this in Scripture, some of the ethical problems of which I have touched

---

44. See, e.g., Christopher R. Seitz, 'What Lesson Will History Teach? The Book of the Twelve as History', in C. Bartholomew, C.S. Evans, M. Healy and M. Rae (eds.), *'Behind' the Text: History and Biblical Interpretation* (Scripture and Hermeneutics Series; Carlisle: Paternoster Press, 2003), pp. 443-67. This idea is also present in Moberly's work and, of course, in that of Brevard Childs.

45. Lam. 4.10. Clear here is the dehumanization inherent in their suffering; they have ceased to be children, and are now food. It is not only in Lamentations that we find this horror, but in the complex layers of the prophetical books. In Ezek. 5.10 fathers eating their own children is part of the judgement of YHWH. It seems meant to horrify the prophet's audience into acknowledging the enormity of Jerusalem's wickedness, and is accompanied by a promise from YHWH never to inflict such punishment again (Ezek. 5.9). In reading these texts, can we now forget that it was precisely the dehumanization of their victims that was the goal of those who implemented the horrors of the Shoah? On this dehumanization, see esp. Terrence Des Pres, *The Survivor: An Anatomy of Life in the Death Camps* (Oxford: Oxford University Press, 1976).

on elsewhere,[46] is Deutero-Isaiah. Isaiah 40 begins with a command to 'console' YHWH's people by announcing that their punishment is almost at an end, and it seems clear that a significant part of the purpose of this section of the Isaiah scroll is both to give comfort to a suffering people, possibly in response to the cries of Zion in Lamentations,[47] and to respond to the claim that YHWH has ignored his people's legal claim.[48] Yet implicit throughout is the claim that this suffering *was* deserved, even if enacted beyond the appropriate measure,[49] and thus the attempt to console Zion has to be read as an implicit justification of YHWH that hides—is perhaps even ignorant of?— the real horror that lies somewhere behind Lamentations.[50]

At this point a word of clarification is necessary. I have been using the word *trustworthy* as if it is tied to the attempt to justify the ways of a righteous God before suffering humanity, but I think that probably will not do. To be sure, in Ezekiel, the prophet, at least as the book presents him, is gravely concerned to show that in the destruction of Jerusalem, YHWH is not acting 'for nothing' (*khinnām* [Ezek. 6.10 (MT); 14.23]), but with just cause. He is thus trustworthy. The knowledge that YHWH is not acting 'for nothing' is meant to 'console' (*nkhm* [14.22, 23]) the prophet's audience. That is, the prophet's audience is meant to find consolation in the fact that although YHWH has brought devastation on Jerusalem, he is nevertheless trustworthy. Using the same language, the book of Job subtly unravels this position without, apparently, making it clear whether this entire complex of ideas is bankrupt or only certain uses of it. At the core of the book is what it means to act 'for nothing', without an ulterior motive. It is the question whether Job fears YHWH for nothing (*khinnam*) that the Adversary uses to provoke YHWH to act against him.[51] The implicit question in Job 1.9 is: 'Is Job's faith *trustworthy*, and does it thus have integrity?' But solving this means that

---

46. Harding, 'In the Name of Love'.

47. Lam. 1.2, 9, 16, 17, 21; 2.13; Isa. 49.13; 51.3, 12, 19; 52.9; 61.2; 66.13; cf. 12.1. See, e.g., Michael Fishbane, *Biblical Interpretation in Ancient Israel* (Oxford: Oxford University Press, 1985), p. 497; Patricia Tull Willey, *Remember the Former Things: The Recollection of Previous Texts in Deutero-Isaiah* (SBLDS, 161; Atlanta: Scholars Press, 1997), pp. 129-31, 155-58, 188; Harding, 'In the Name of Love', pp. 14.7-14.8.

48. Isa. 40.27.

49. Apparently Isa. 40.2. Contrast Job 11.6; Ezra 9.13.

50. I am leaving open here the question of how the literary representation of Zion's suffering in Lamentations relates to what actually happened in Jerusalem in 587–586 BCE.

51. The idea of a 'for nothing' relationship between Job and God has been central to one strand of theological interpretation of Job since at least Wilhelm Vischer. See esp. Vischer, *Hiob: Ein Zeuge Jesu Christi* (Bekennende Kirche, 8; München: Kaiser, 2nd edn, 1934), pp. 4-7; Karl Barth, *Church Dogmatics* 4/3.2 (Edinburgh: T. & T. Clark, 1961), pp. 383-88, 398-408, 421-34, 453-61; Ticciati, *Job and the Disruption of Identity*; 'Does Job Fear God for Naught?', *Modern Theology* 21 (2005), pp. 353-66. See also Ellen van Wolde, *Mr and Mrs Job* (trans. J. Bowden; London: SCM Press, 1997), pp. 139-40.

YHWH himself must act 'without just cause' (*khinnam* [2.3]), as Job clearly recognizes when he confronts his God later on (9.17). The trustworthiness of God, for Job, could no longer be tied to the visibility and transparency of God's righteousness to human beings, if God was to continue to be trusted at all, and not just supposed to be an arbitrary, abusive tyrant. Lacking both a divine perspective and empathy with his suffering friend, and unable to let go of a belief in a trustworthy moral order, Eliphaz can only explain Job's pain in terms of a prior moral wrong: exacting a pledge from his brothers *for no reason* (*ki takhol 'akheyka khinnam* [22.6]).

Here the brief reference to Job at the end of Levinas's essay is perhaps apposite.[52] Levinas points out that Job refuses all theodicy at the same time as remaining in some sense faithful to God on the one hand, and exhibiting a deep awareness of ethics on the other. This, for him, suggests that the purely theodic reading of the Hebrew Bible he had earlier noted could be mitigated. So in the prologue, Job appears to continue to trust his God despite the horrors that have befallen him (and, we should add, his wife, children, household and livestock—but this seems not unduly to bother Job! [2.10]). Yet he refuses to let go of his integrity and thereby collude in the apparent injustice of God (27.5, 6), and it is Job's words, not those his friends uttered in defence of God (13.7), that are ultimately given divine approbation (42.7).

Now it is not clear exactly why YHWH approves Job's words, nor which of Job's words exactly he found so pleasing. But what is clear is that despite the horror to which he was subjected, despite his dehumanisation at the hands of God, and despite the disintegration of the moral order in which he had previously trusted, Job continued to keep open his relationship with God, not by coming up with new explanations for God's work in the world— he never learns exactly what God has done, or why—but by addressing God directly and allowing God to address him. It is somewhere in here that *trust* in God is both maintained and redefined, and the act of *witness* to this counterintuitive, subversive trust opened up as a mode of theology. This is picked up in a recent treatment of the existence of God and the problem of evil by Rowan Williams, who, instead of treating the disjunction between human suffering and a belief in divine justice as something to be resolved at the tribunal of human reason, looks instead at acts of witness to God on the part of those who take *responsibility* for God in situations of gross evil. The main example Williams cites is Etty Hillesum, who perished in Auschwitz in 1943, but who, despite the horror through which she was forced to live, in some sense took responsibility for God, as a witness to his unlikely believability.[53]

---

52. Levinas, 'Useless Suffering', p. 454, n. 3.
53. Rowan D. Williams, *Tokens of Trust: An Introduction to Christian Belief* (Norwich: Canterbury, 2007), pp. 20-24. For Hillesum's own writings, see *Etty: The*

There is a sense in which this is the principal mode of theology adopted by Job too. As Job steels himself to bring God to trial, he exclaims before his well-meaning but misguided comforters that, 'He will kill me, *but* I will await him; I will defend my ways to his face' (*hen yiqteleni lo' 'ayakhel 'akh derakay 'al panayw 'okiakh* [Job 13.15 (Qr)]). That is, Job will continue to keep his relationship with God open, no matter what situation he finds himself in, even if his very life is at stake, and for Williams, Job here stands as an example of one of 'those closest to the risks' who 'are most aware of [God's] presence', in a universe in which 'we are challenged to have confidence in its maker', not because 'he has guaranteed our safety but because he remains there, accessible and free to move things on, even in the most desperate situations'.[54]

This is a tempting way of reading Job. Yet despite my basic sympathy for this position, and while I think Williams is more or less on the right lines, Job's act of trust is a bit more complex than Williams suggests. It is not clear that Job's God *is* accessible in any meaningful sense, at least until chs. 38–41, and it seems rather that Job somehow insists on the requirement of God's accessibility, even when there is no evidence for it. Moreover, and here the intricacies of textual criticism come to have actual theological significance,[55] the MT of Job 13.15 is double-edged. The version Williams is working with is based on the *qere*, but the *ketiv* reads *hen yiqteleni lo' 'ayakhel*, 'He will kill me, I will not hope', which on the face of it does not seem to mean that Job will keep his relationship with God open no matter what, but rather that Job knows his case to be hopeless, believes that God is cruel, and, having nothing to lose, he will bring God to account anyway.

Here there may in fact be no trust in God as such left, unless it be in the following verse, where Job still retains the conviction that no one impious can stand before God, a fact that will be his salvation. What we do still have here is a man at the limit who may no longer have anything that could be called *trust* in his God, but who is nevertheless prepared to take responsibility for God's life in the world when there is no other evidence that a recognisable God is actually at work there. To read Job 13.15 as a statement

---

Letters and Diaries of Etty Hillesum 1941–1943 (ed. K.A.D. Smelik; trans. A.J. Pomerans; Grand Rapids: Eerdmans, 2002). This in some way seems to echo Fackenheim's later retrospective on the new commandment resulting from Auschwitz. Recalling and moving beyond the biblical and later Jewish traditions of protest, Fackenheim sees the religious Jew as bound to continue to wrestle with God, and to bear witness to him, no matter what: 'The fear of God is dead among the nations? We shall keep it alive and be its witnesses! The times are too late for the coming of the Messiah? We shall persist without hope and recreate hope—and, as it were, divine Power—by our persistence!' ('The Commanding Voice of Auschwitz', p. 437).

54. Williams, *Tokens of Trust*, p. 43.
55. This would be true of Jer. 4.10 also (see above).

of *trust* is to run the risk of justifying the one in whom trust is shown, but perhaps it would be truer to say that a certain kind of authentic witness can continue despite the impossibility of trust as such. The idea of a God who *should* show himself to be just thus seems to outlive any evidence that such a God is there.[56]

In the end, confronted by YHWH himself, Job falls silent, but this, too, points us to at least two further important modes of theology. Here it is not so much a situation of suffering as such that causes theology to break down, but the recognition that nothing one could say would be adequate to a direct encounter with an all-encompassing deity who resists description and explanation. The first mode is *irresolvable ambiguity*. Job's last words are, *'al ken 'em'as wenikhamti 'al 'afar wa'efer* (42.6), but these words have resisted all attempts to pin down their meaning definitively.[57] Is Job

---

56. My response to Williams here is against the background of Israel's traditions of 'protest' (Laytner, Blumenthal), 'antitheodicy' (Braiterman), and 'countertestimony' (Brueggemann). My point is to counter what looks like a too simple appeal to trust on the basis that the way human response to God is articulated in the Hebrew Bible is far more complex and multi-faceted. Walter Moberly expresses the complexity of the biblical witness thus: 'Although the OT constantly stresses the importance of trust..., faith..., and obedience...as characterizing the true human response to God, the general canonical presentation is such that these are not to be conceived in any simplistic way, as though life were essentially a matter of "obeying orders". Rather, there is a recurrent portrayal of life under God as containing space for dialogue with God, with room for question and answer. Obedience to God is to be set in the context of an intelligent relationship and not be mindless' ('Lament', in *NIDOTTE*, IV, p. 876).

57. Consequently I cannot offer a single translation that does justice to the problems presented by the text, which are metrical (does the verse scan?), textual (does the text read better when emended, or when one or other of the ancient versions is followed instead of the MT?), philological (what exactly do the words mean in this context, and could they be deliberately ambiguous?), contextual (how does this verse fit into the context of the book of Job?) and theological (what does this verse say about the relationship between Job and YHWH?). Here is a very brief sprinkling of the available options: 'Therefore I will be poured out and melt away, and will become dust and ash(es)' (11QtgJob); 'Therefore I abase myself and melt away, I regard myself [as] earth and ash(es)' (Septuagint); 'Therefore I will keep silence and I will be raised upon dust and ash(es)' (Syriac); 'Therefore I despise my wealth and am comforted concerning my sons, who are dust and ash(es)' (Targum); 'Therefore I rebuke myself and do penance in cinder(s) and ash(es)' (Vulgate); 'Wherefore I abhor *myself*, and repent in dust and ashes' (KJV); 'Therefore I melt away; I repent in dust and ashes' (NEB); '[T]herefore I despise myself, and repent in dust and ashes' (RSV, NRSV); 'Therefore I retract / And repent of dust and ashes' (Norman C. Habel, *The Book of Job: A Commentary* [OTL; Louisville, KY: Westminster Press, 1985], p. 575); 'Therefore I withdraw my case and leave dust and ashes' (Habel, *Job*, p. 578); 'Therefore I despise and I am sorry upon dust and ash' (Edwin M. Good, *In Turns of Tempest: A Reading of Job with a Translation* [Stanford, CA: Stanford University Press, 1990], p. 25; 'Therefore I despise and repent of dust and ashes' (Good, *In Turns of Tempest*, p. 171); 'Therefore I have changed my mind and turn

repenting, and if so, of what? Is he withdrawing his case against God, and if so, why? Is he acknowledging his finitude before the reality of God? Is he somehow consoled by an actual revelation of YHWH's presence? Or is he walking off the stage in disgust at the way he has been treated? By leaving these options irresolvable, the Hebrew text is pointing to the way that theology cannot pin down definitively that to which it can only point.

The second mode is *silence*. When Job responds to the first speech from the whirlwind, he puts his hand on his mouth (40.4; *yadi samti lemo fi*), and after a short response to YHWH in 42.1-6, he says nothing more. But this begs the question of the *quality* of Job's silence. Is it the silence of a victim, bullied into submission? This would be different from the silence of those whose suffering renders them mute,[58] since Job had already moved to the point of being able to speak by the beginning of ch. 3, and it is a response from YHWH that has once more removed his speech. Or is it the silence of the vulnerable,[59] submitting in humility to God without sacrificing integrity

---

away from dust and ashes' (van Wolde, *Mr and Mrs Job*, p. 130); 'Therefore, I recant and relent, Being but dust and ashes' (NJPS); 'Wherefore I demean myself and yield, reduced to dust and ash(es)' (John Gray, *The Book of Job* [The Text of the Hebrew Bible, 1; Sheffield: Sheffield Phoenix Press, 2010], p. 488). Among scholars who acknowledge deliberate, and arguably irresolvable, ambiguity here, see esp. William S. Morrow, 'Consolation, Rejection, and Repentance in Job 42:6', *JBL* 105 (1986), pp. 211-25; and Ellen van Wolde, 'Job 42,1-6: The Reversal of Job', in W.A.M. Beuken (ed.), *The Book of Job* (BETL, 114; Leuven: Leuven University Press, 1994), pp. 223-50. Morrow offers the following three options: 'Wherefore I retract (*or* I submit) and I repent on (*or* on account of) dust and ashes'; 'Wherefore I reject *it* (implied object in v 5), and I am consoled for dust and ashes'; and 'Wherefore I reject and foreswear dust and ashes' ('Consolation', pp. 211-12).

58. On which see, e.g., Dorothee Sölle, *Suffering* (trans. E.R. Kalin; London: Darton, Longman & Todd, 1975), pp. 68-70. This suffering should provoke silent compassion, not explanatory theodicy: 'Respect for those who suffer *in extremis* imposes silence' (p. 69, cf. Job 2.13?).

59. I have in mind here something decidedly distinct from the vulnerability of one bullied and abused, and more akin to the 'spiritual *kenōsis*' explored by Sarah Coakley in '*Kenōsis* and Subversion: On the Repression of "Vulnerability" in Christian Feminist Writing', in *Powers and Submissions: Spirituality, Philosophy and Gender* (Challenges in Contemporary Theology; Oxford: Blackwell, 2002), pp. 3-39 (esp. pp. 32-39): '…this rather special form of "vulnerability" is not an invitation to be battered; nor is its silence a silenc*ing*. (If anything, i[t] builds one in the courage to give prophetic voice.) By choosing to "make space" in this way, one "practises" the "presence of God"—the subtle but enabling presence of a God who neither shouts nor forces, let alone "obliterates"… this special "self-emptying" is not a negation of self, but the place of the self's transformation and expansion into God' (pp. 36-37). Coakley's essay makes no mention of Job in this connection, and it is not yet clear to me how much mileage there is in this notion as a position from which to revisit Job's silence; Job's God can hardly be said not to shout, force or obliterate, and there is the risk of whitewashing Job's relationship with

or empowered personhood, open to seeing God anew without the shackles of ideology? Is it a silence that refuses to continue trying to box God in, instead returning to *living* in a way that is not dependent on the necessary predictability and transparency of God? (Job 42.10-17).[60] Is it a silence caught between a sense of responsibility to a tradition of religious language and thought that has been brought into question, and a realisation that the implications of a radically new situation cannot yet be—perhaps can *never* be—assimilated?[61] Is it a silence that points to the radical collapse of language before a reality that language cannot contain? Again, all this is left open.

Lament and Ambiguity

What has been left hanging so far is the question of the extent to which a distinctively *Christian* theological hermeneutics can offer clarity of any sort on the kinds of Godtalk that might be possible at the limits of human experience. This is not the same as asking whether a single, univocal Christian viewpoint is possible, not simply because this would be to collapse the matter back into the sphere of explanation, but because it is not obvious, to me at least, that the locus of the unity of Christian truth is to be sought in *univocity*. It is, rather, to be sought in the mystery of a person, the person of Jesus Christ, who is also the locus of the unity of Scripture Christianly understood, and, in some sense, the figure who gives history as such a sense of unity.[62]

We are on potentially shaky ground here. It could be objected that an appeal to mystery is simply a fudge, a rather pathetic evasion before a devastating ethical challenge. It could also be objected that this appeal to the mystery of Christ is itself explanatory in character. It may be that this cannot

---

God in just the way I criticized Rowan Williams for advocating above, but there is surely room here for further reflection on the quality of Job's silence.

60. Perhaps I am echoing here the return to life of Dr Sussman in the Coen Brothers' film *A Serious Man*. Sussman is reduced to a state of existential angst and confusion—as, later, is the unfortunate Larry Gopnik when Rabbi Nachtner relates the story to him—when he finds the words *hoshi'eni* ('save me') inscribed, inexplicably, on the back of a goy's teeth. There is no answer to how these words got there, so Sussman gives up the quest and goes back to life.

61. Fackenheim compared the relative silence of Jewish theologians confronted with the immediate aftermath of the Holocaust with the silence of Job: 'A well-justified fear and trembling, and a crushing sense of the most awesome responsibility to four thousand years of Jewish faith…has kept Jewish theological thought, like Job, in a state of silence' ('The Commanding Voice of Auschwitz', pp. 70-71).

62. Cf. Christopher Seitz, *Prophecy and Hermeneutics: Toward a New Introduction to the Prophets* (Studies in Theological Interpretation; Grand Rapids: Baker Academic, 2007), p. 7.

ultimately be avoided, if the life, death, resurrection and ascension of Jesus Christ do indeed tell us something fundamental about the way the world is, the way we are and where we are heading. Let me nevertheless make the effort by pointing to the cry of desolation from the cross in the Gospels of Matthew and Mark. In this cry Jesus exemplifies—indeed *embodies*—a mode of theology that is central to the Hebrew Bible but that has only relatively recently been revisited by Christian scholars.[63] He embodies the mode of theology that comes to us as lament. The cry of desolation from the cross teaches us that this mode of theology, this lament, can in certain extreme situations be the only authentic mode of witness to God left. It can reject every suggestion of the ongoing presence or ultimate justice of God, while refusing to let the matter of God disappear from the world. Theological hermeneutics is here richly interwoven with the implications of the incarnation.

In Mk 15.34 / Mt. 27.46, Jesus cries out an address to God, in Aramaic, that appears to correspond to Ps. 22.2.[64] This psalm opens with a cry of abandonment; the psalmist's suffering connotes for him wilful divine absence. The psalmist's words reflect both physical distress and social ostracism, his ostracisation being directly connected with the claim that his God is absent and untrustworthy (Ps. 22.8-9). The psalm as a whole, which is a lament with a rather complex structure, incorporates not only the experience of suffering, but also the experience of salvation from distress and the thanksgiving that follows. The psalm is used, in the Catholic tradition, during the Triduum Sacrum, where it accompanies the Stripping of the Altar on Holy Thursday. The shape of Holy Week demands that all the horror of the last hours of the life of Jesus be experienced as redeemed by the joy of the Resurrection; yet we should not move too quickly from Holy Thursday, through Good Friday, to Easter Sunday without giving the ghastly emptiness of Holy Saturday, bleak and devoid of Christ's sacramental presence, its due.[65]

---

63. The works of Claus Westermann and Walter Brueggemann have been fundamental here. See esp. Westermann, 'The Role of Lament in the Theology of the Old Testament', *Int* 28 (1974), pp. 20-38; Brueggemann, 'From Hurt to Joy, from Death to Life', *Int* 28 (1974), pp. 3-19; *The Message of the Psalms: A Theological Commentary* (Minneapolis: Augsburg, 1984); 'The Costly Loss of Lament', *JSOT* 36 (1986), pp. 57-71; *Theology of the Old Testament*. To some extent this section of my argument fleshes out Moberly's excellent treatment in 'Lament', p. 883.

64. This is certainly how it has generally been taken, and the connection between Ps. 22.2 and the cry of desolation is the basis for the liturgical singing of Ps. 22 at the Stripping of the Altar on Holy Thursday, and during the Liturgy of the Word at the Celebration of the Passion of the Lord on Good Friday.

65. Indeed, the Resurrection only makes sense in relation to the suffering and absence that precede it. Paul Fiddes writes helpfully that '...the resurrection of Jesus does not

Elsewhere in the Psalter, of course, divine absence can appear to have neither a reason nor an end (Ps. 88). In other places still, the experience of divine absence can connote inexplicable abandonment (Ps. 80) or even YHWH's apparent unfaithfulness to his covenant with Israel (Ps. 44). None of these passages offers a divine perspective on the meaning or significance of human suffering—and we should not be too quick to suggest that the narratorial voice in texts such as 2 Kgs 17.7-23 or Jer. 25.3-11 do, in fact, reflect a divine perspective on Judah's history—but psalms such as these offer, rather, a means of *addressing* God, and thereby of taking responsibility, in some way, for God's presence in the world. God seems to be absent, but his witnesses refuse the option of abandoning him, and by their very address to an apparently absent God, they bear witness to him, and to what they believe is, or should be, his desire to be in the thick of the human quest for justice in history.

In Psalm 22, Jesus is embodying God in the midst of an extreme situation of suffering that somehow unites him with the experience of estrangement and alienation from God that led the ancient psalmists to cry out, and with the experience of gross human abuse that led some of the psalmists, and some of the prophets, to cry to heaven for vengeance. Here God becomes part of human history in connection not with a tradition of theodicy, of a drive for an explanation that exonerates God at all costs, but rather with a tradition of lament and protest. The mortifying act by which we are justified *by* God is not one that should lead to our justification *of* God. God does not simply answer the cry of the suffering, as if from a position of detachment, but embodies it.

There is a risk in this reading of the cry of desolation, in that because the death of Jesus is, in terms of Christian teaching, redemptive, acknowledging the embodiment of God in the context of such extreme suffering might lead to the belief that suffering as such has a definable, predetermined purpose, but that would bring us back dangerously close to the kind of theodicy Levinas rejects. More disturbingly, it would raise the dangerous spectre of supersessionism:[66] the Christian revelation has superseded its Jewish

---

simply cancel the cross, wiping it out as if it were a mistake. If it did, the cross of Jesus would have nothing to say to suffering and dying people; we would not identify ourselves with it, and there would be no Christian tragedy for a tragic world. The resurrection makes the cross of Jesus eternal in the life of God; that is, the particular experience of death which God endured in the death of Jesus is preserved in the life of God just as all experience of the world enriches his being' (*The Creative Suffering of God* [Oxford: Clarendon Press, 1988], p. 266).

66. Not only fideism (cf. n. 17 above), but (if anything much more seriously) supersessionism, present very serious dangers for Christian theological hermeneutics that theologians need to work hard to negotiate and, if possible, resolve.

precursor, and the suffering of Jesus offers the *real* key to the passages of human suffering in the Hebrew Bible, as well as the suffering of Auschwitz. As part of this, it would lead to the implication that these gross sufferings had some kind of purpose.[67] To make such a claim without further ado would be, once again, to obliterate the face of the sufferer, of the compassionate woman who boiled her children, of the children murdered by their starving, dehumanized parent. It would also be implicitly to deny that the traditions embodied in the Hebrew Bible had any integrity of their own. What if we were to invert this claim? It would not, then, be so much that in the face of Zion's children we see the dying Christ, who explains and thus redeems all, but that in the face of the dying Christ we see Zion's children, their suffering irreducible and beyond explanation.[68]

To illustrate the ethical scandal of finding purpose in suffering, especially in light of the crucifixion, a well-known passage from Elie Wiesel's harrowing account of his experience of Auschwitz is apposite. Wiesel here is recalling a hanging he witnessed at Buna during his incarceration there:

> The SS seemed more preoccupied, more disturbed than usual. To hang a young boy in front of thousands of spectators was no light matter. The head of the camp read the verdict. All eyes were on the child. He was lividly pale, almost calm, biting his lips. The gallows threw its shadow over him.
> This time the Lagerkapo refused to act as executioner. Three SS replaced him.
> The three victims mounted together onto the chairs.
> The three necks were placed at the same moment within the nooses.
> 'Long live liberty!' cried the two adults.
> But the child was silent.
> 'Where is God? Where is He?' someone behind me asked.
> At a sign from the head of the camp, the three chairs tipped over.
> Total silence throughout the camp. On the horizon, the sun was setting.

---

67. On this danger, cf. Sölle, *Suffering*, p. 146 ('Wherever one compares the incomparable...there, in a sublime manner, the issue is robbed of clarity, indeed the modern horror is justified'); Surin, *Theology and the Problem of Evil*, pp. 123-24, 132 (responding to Sölle and Moltmann). It is not clear to me that Sölle manages adequately to maintain her position here. Her claim is that 'the God who causes suffering is not to be justified even by lifting the suffering later. No heaven can rectify Auschwitz. But the God who is not a greater Pharaoh has justified himself: in sharing the suffering, in sharing the death on the cross' (*Suffering*, p. 149). But does not the latter claim somehow entail the former? The difficulty here may be with the very constraints of using any language of justification, and in fact, her position may not be that different from the one I hold (see the next note). If so, Surin's criticism of Sölle might be a little too harsh.

68. That is, the events of 587–586 BCE are the *interpretans*, the cross is the *interpretandum*, rather than *vice versa* (cf. Surin's reformulation of Sölle's Christian response to Auschwitz in his *Theology and the Problem of Evil*, pp. 123-24).

> 'Bare your heads!' yelled the head of the camp. His voice was raucous. We were weeping.
>
> 'Cover your heads!'
>
> Then the march past began. The two adults were no longer alive. Their tongues hung swollen, blue-tinged. But the third rope was still moving; being so light, the child was still alive....
>
> For more than half an hour he stayed there, struggling between life and death, dying in slow agony under our eyes. And we had to look him full in the face. He was still alive when I passed in front of him. His tongue was still red, his eyes were not yet glazed.
>
> Behind me, I heard the same man asking:
>
> 'Where is God now?'
>
> And I heard a voice within me answer him:
>
> 'Where is He? Here He is—He is hanging here on this gallows...'
>
> That night the soup tasted of corpses.[69]

Coming to this text from the perspective of a concern for Christian theological hermeneutics should involve humility and a spirit of repentance, for at least two reasons. First, one of the two Gospels that contains the cry of desolation from the cross also contains a passage that, through its tortuous history of reception, use and effect, has been implicated in the complex historical process that made this hanging possible (I refer, of course, to Mt. 27.25: 'Then the people as a whole answered, "His blood be on us and on our children"' [NRSV]). Secondly, entangled in a fallen world as we are, we ourselves are implicated in processes whose ends are scarcely less egregious than this. What we cannot do is use a text such as Mk 15.34 to soften the horror of what Wiesel witnessed and endured, or to construct a model for exonerating God. What it should provoke instead is a sense of radical compassion that leads to a commitment to view the kinds of horrors to which Jesus and the executed child were subjected as ones that we are not willing to accept in our world. These are not the sort of horrors we should be

---

69. Elie Wiesel, *Night* (trans. S. Rodway; London: Penguin Books, 1981; 1st edn London: McGibbon & Kee, 1960), pp. 76-77. Jürgen Moltmann famously, but not unproblematically, cited the last part of this passage in an important treatment of the idea of divine self-abasement (*The Crucified God: The Cross of Christ as the Foundation and Criticism of Christian Theology* [trans. R.A. Wilson and J. Bowden; London: SCM Press, 1974], p. 274). Integral to the shaping of Moltmann's *theologia crucis* is the work of Abraham Joshua Heschel (chiefly *The Prophets* [2 vols.; New York: Harper & Row, 1962], but see also his *God in Search of Man: A Philosophy of Judaism* [New York: Farrar, Straus & Giroux, 1955]), which stresses God's pathic self-involvement in the history of Israel, and shares a great deal with Muffs's treatment of prophetic intercession ('Who Will Stand in the Breach?'). On this passage from Wiesel, see *inter multa alia*, and from varying perpsectives, Surin, *Theology and the Problem of Evil*, pp. 112-32; Fiddes, *Creative Suffering of God*, pp. 3-5; Thomas G. Weinandy, *Does God Suffer?* (Edinburgh: T. & T. Clark, 2000), pp. 3-4 (and the several additional works cited therein).

prepared to live with, or to which we are prepared to adapt ourselves, and where we do live with them, and where we do so adapt ourselves—as in fact we do, to our shame—we need to be called to account.

There is, of course, an ambiguity in what Wiesel wrote, an ambiguity that might echo the sort of double-edgedness we find in Jer. 4.10 and Job 13.15. To say that God is here, hanging on the gallows as a dying child, can be taken either to point to the pathic self-involvement of God in the life of his people in the world, or to the death of one's sense of God when confronted with such an affront to the idea of a God who has any care for justice. Neither the words themselves, nor the immediate context in which they appear, can resolve that ambiguity, which is significant because it means the words can be taken to mean different things at different points in one's wrestling with the ethical dilemma to which they point. A theological interpretation of Scripture should take this kind of ambiguity seriously as a mode of theology.

Conclusion

If there is any coherence to what I have been arguing, it is that despite the overwhelming predominance of an approach to history in the Hebrew Bible that sees that fate of Israel as the outworking of divine justice, thus binding history and theodicy inextricably together, such an explanatory approach to the world's suffering—and Israel's—is not to be regarded as normative. This does not exhaust the resources of Scripture for shaping faithful witness to God. The Hebrew Bible probes the ethical integrity of Israel's theological language with great intensity, especially in Jeremiah's confessions, the Psalms of Lament, Lamentations and Job, potentially leaving the reader with the impression that nothing that is said of God in Scripture can be taken for granted, or assumed to be the word of God, even when the tradition in which we stand seems to endow them with such authoritative, even prophetic, status. We are dealing with human words that seek haltingly, even if sometimes eloquently, to speak faithfully of Israel's covenant God. In terms of God's involvement in the mess of history, the demands of ethics, particularly in the wake of horrors such as Auschwitz—we could add Cambodia, Rwanda, Darfur and any number of others, leading to a list without end that would itself risk obscuring the scandal and particularity of each—seem to make the justification of human suffering by appeal to the ultimate goodness of God abhorrent (this is without even beginning to tackle the ethical and theological problems with relating 'natural' evil and suffering rather than 'moral' evil—notwithstanding the problems with this modern distinction—to the goodness, knowledge and power of God). Yet there is a sense in which it may be possible to refuse theodicy—with Job, some of the voices in

Lamentations,[70] and Levinas—while recognizing the embodiment of God on the cross, demanding an ethical response that refuses adaptation to a world in which a cross can be allowed to have place.

---

70. See Miriam Bier's essay in the present volume for a thoughtful treatment of Lamentations, as well as her recent doctoral thesis, '"Perhaps There Is Hope": Reading Lamentations as a Polyphony of Pain, Penitence, and Protest' (PhD thesis, University of Otago, Dunedin, 2012).

13

RESPONSE:
THEOLOGICAL INTERPRETATION ON DISPLAY:
TRAJECTORIES AND QUESTIONS

Joel B. Green

The recovery of theological interpretation has attracted its critics, with indictments generally coming from two different arenas. On the one hand, theological interpretation is incriminated for its departure from the interests and procedures accredited by biblical scholars and biblical scholarship in the modern era. Simply put, theological interpretation is not *real* scholarship; it does not exemplify the *Wissenschaft* we have come to expect from the biblical studies academy. On the other hand, theological interpretation, we often hear, is overly preoccupied with defining itself. It spends too much time in theoretical conversation about what it is and is not. We have had enough methodological throat-clearing, we are told; it is time to show what theological interpretation looks like.

The juxtaposition of these two accusations indicates why theological interpreters spend, and must continue to spend, as much time as they do reflecting methodologically on the commitments and sensibilities that might be characteristic of theological interpretation.[1] Biblical scholars have generally been shaped by their graduate programs and profession to pursue historical questions—and, even when asking theological questions, to define these first and foremost in historical terms. Biblical scholars have generally been content, and even preferred, to call themselves *historians* (and not *theologians*). Having had their theological hands tied behind their backs for so long, then, biblical scholars, once liberated to participate in the church's theological vocation, find their theological muscles atrophied. And for their part, theologians, having abdicated serious engagement with the Bible to the specialists, now find themselves puzzling over how to work with (and not simply talk about) Christian Scripture, the church's book, without parroting the dispositions and procedures of modern biblical scholarship that led to the

---

1. I have discussed these issues more fully in Joel B. Green, *Practicing Theological Interpretation: Engaging Biblical Texts for Faith and Formation* (Grand Rapids: Baker Academic, 2011), pp. 1-12.

great divide between biblical studies and systematic theology in the first place. If the customary paths of biblical scholarship in the west over the past two or three centuries seem to lead us inexorably into the aridity of a theological desert, away from the church that turns to the Bible for its religious fecundity and toward the allegedly dispassionate and objective readings of the so-called secular university, then theological interpreters require different interpretive itineraries. Other routes, some ancient and others fresh, must be explored and mapped, and this hermeneutical cartography requires methodological attention.

The indictment against theological interpretation that it is overly concerned with theory is problematic on other grounds, too. A constellation of publications has made a strong beginning at placing theological readings of Scripture on display. These have appeared in journals like *Journal of Theological Interpretation* and *Ex auditu*; in book series like Studies in Theological Interpretation (Baker Academic) and Journal of Theological Interpretation Supplement Series (Eisenbrauns); and in four commentary series: Two Horizons New Testament Commentary (Eerdmans), Two Horizons Old Testament Commentary (Eerdmans), Brazos Theological Commentary on the Bible (Brazos), and Belief (Westminster John Knox). Indeed, those who want to see theological interpretation in practice need look no further than the three dozen or so biblical commentaries written by theologians and biblical scholars and published in these four series over the past decade. What they will find is that theological interpretation is not and will never be a 'method' like source criticism or narratology, but is instead a still-emerging set of commitments and practices. In fact, with so many theological commentaries having been published in recent years, the case could easily be made that it is worth stopping for a moment to engage self-reflexively with the results of our work thus far. Critical reflection on theological commentary might fruitfully inquire into whether we are on a desirable trajectory in our shared work.

For such reasons as these, we should not be surprised that the essays collected here sometimes reflect on the nature of theological interpretation. As they do, they demonstrate that theological interpreters are still finding their way. Nevertheless, it is also heartening to see the degree to which these essays actually work with biblical texts theologically; indeed, some essays explicitly tie their ruminations on the nature of theological interpretation to their theological exegesis of Scripture. This has led to the identification of what is probably the defining characteristic of theological interpretation. I refer to the way these essays identify theological interpretation less as a critical method and more as an interpretive practice.

Readers would be hard pressed to discern in this collection a common commitment to particular exegetical techniques, as though the work of theological interpretation could be captured in a series of procedures or steps. More visible would be an understanding of engagement with biblical texts characterized as a *practice*, that is, as *interpretive activity shaped by particular contexts, arising from certain dispositions, and oriented toward a certain telos*. With respect to *context*, for example, we find that theological interpretation is located ecclesially, though not in a way that neglects theological concerns that extend beyond the church. With regard to *dispositions*, we can identify among these essays such emphases as love, humility, hearing, openness to transformation, and prayer. And with regard to *teleology*, we repeatedly find that theological interpretation has as its goal the ecclesial and personal formation of God's people.

Thinking about theological interpretation in this way leads to a series of corollaries. For example, some hermeneutical approaches and exegetical methods are more appropriate than others, and some have to be rethought from the ground up. In the latter category, particular attention has been drawn to modern historical criticism, not only because of its atheistic underpinnings but also because of its presumptive reduction of 'truth' and 'meaning' to the historically verifiable. To mention another corollary, this approach to theological interpretation embraces the church's faith, including its creedal traditions, as essential to the task of biblical studies. Biblical interpretation in this key sees itself as a theological enterprise, one that is learning to be as much at home when interacting with the church's theologians, past and present, as it is while contemplating the significance of regulations governing marriage and divorce in the Roman Empire. Theological interpretation does not stand over against the church, as though it might find its home outside the church's theological commitments. Rather, theological interpretation exercises its prophetic and pastoral roles from within the church. This is true even if it remains the case that theological interpreters continue to struggle with how best to understand the role of the church's Rule of Faith in theological exegesis. One more illustrative corollary: with theological interpretation of the Bible, we surrender the quest for the holy grail of biblical studies in the modern era, namely, disinterested neutrality, embracing instead a thoroughgoing commitment to the self-involving nature of our work. This does not require that we sacrifice intellectual honesty and self-reflexive criticism, but accentuates the contextual and traditioned character of our interpretive practices.

No one essay is home to all of these emphases, of course. Nor do these essays speak with a single voice with regard to any of them. Rather, a close reading of this collection heightens our awareness of such key points of conversation as these regarding the nature of theological interpretation.

At the same time that these essays lead us to recognize some of the more distinct landmarks on the terrain of theological interpretation, other important issues have attracted comparatively little attention. An emphasis on the *practice* of theological interpretation might fail to dislodge exegetical activity from its predominately anthropological base, for example. If, theologically, we recognize that we turn to the Bible to attune our ears to God's address and if we recognize that Christian formation, whether of persons or of ecclesial communities, is divine work after all, then our conversation needs to extend beyond what we human beings bring to the table of biblical interpretation. Particularly, we require more reflection on the role of the Holy Spirit in theological interpretation. Although we can celebrate in these pages an initial interest in the pneumatology of biblical interpretation, this is a matter that generally remains very much underdeveloped.

Another concern has to do with the degree to which theological interpretation remains or might be seen as an 'add on' to what have become the more standard approaches to reading the Bible. We discern here and there vestiges of a kind of linear hermeneutic, that is, a hermeneutic that moves from the descriptive work of biblical studies to the application of that work by theologians. This can take the form of a baton-passing enterprise, as though in a relay race the biblical scholar would run her part of the course in order then to pass the results of her work to the theologian or homiletician. It can also take the form of a costume change, where the biblical scholar does his work, then adopts a fresh, a different persona in order now to take on the interests and tasks of a theologian or preacher. Whether this really is theological interpretation might be debated, but it hardly seems to represent the approaches to biblical studies taken by our ancestors, for whom studying the Bible simply was a theological, catechetical, and homiletical enterprise. The question that needs more engagement overall is how the whole enterprise of biblical studies and how the whole enterprise of theological studies might find themselves transformed, down to the roots, by the practice of theological interpretation.

Finally, this collection of essays does not go very far toward addressing what is surely one of the most pressing questions for theological interpretation today, namely, What does it mean to read a two-testament Christian Scripture? To be sure, for most practitioners, the *raison d'être* of the contemporary renaissance of theological interpretation has been the major fault line separating biblical studies and systematic or constructive theology. But even early efforts at spanning this chasm exposed a network of other fractures, the most prominent being the relationship between the Old and New Testaments. Of the various proposals championed today,[2] none receive explicit attention here; indeed, the opposite is typically on display, as each essay remains largely focused on a single biblical book or on a single

---

2. For summaries of and critical engagement with recent proposals, see Christopher R. Seitz, *The Character of Christian Scripture: The Significance of a Two-Testament Bible* (Studies in Theological Interpretation; Grand Rapids: Baker Academic, 2011).

pericope within that book. This is less a criticism of this essay collection, however, and more a placeholder for ongoing reflection among theological interpreters.

One of the encouraging aspects of this essay collection, and of the colloquium from which much of its substance is drawn, is its interdisciplinary character. I have often observed that my mother would be surprised to hear that biblical studies and ethics were different 'things', but this is the nature of the increasingly specialized world of 'theology'. Whatever else it does, theological interpretation resists this kind of compartmentalization, inviting into an often demanding and sometimes unruly interchange between theologians and ethicists and historical theologians, Old Testament scholars and New Testament scholars, professors of philosophy and of communication, and more. This is just the sort of gathering represented in these pages. And, for theological interpreters, this is cause for celebration.

14

Response: Reading as Formation

Murray A. Rae

Advocates of the theological interpretation of Scripture are generally agreed that theological interpretation should not be construed as a hermeneutical method or as an exegetical tool. It is variously described rather as an attitude or a disposition giving rise to a particular set of practices that are apparent most especially in the worshipping community of faith. Academic interest in theological interpretation stems largely from the conviction that those practices in that context yield readings of Scripture that are more faithful to the reality of Scripture itself—more faithful, that is, than readings undertaken without the prayerful expectation that through Scripture we are encountered by the living God. This expectation, variously expressed through the essays in this volume, presumes that reading Scripture is a formative process in and through which God is at work shaping a people to be his witness in the world. The phenomenon of Scripture, accordingly—its formation, its transmission and its reception—is best understood in terms of the divine economy, summary statements of which are called 'the rule of faith'.

Appeals to the rule of faith as a guide to the interpretation of Scripture have commonly been regarded in the modern era of biblical studies as illegitimate. Ernst Troeltsch's sharp distinction between 'historical and dogmatic method in theology', developed in his famous 1898 essay, stands as a classic statement of the conviction that application of the rule of faith in biblical interpretation constitutes an imposition upon the text of a dogmatic framework that distorts or obscures the meaning of the text itself.[1] This disparagement of the rule of faith is typically accompanied by efforts to remove the Bible from its ecclesial setting and strong resistance to the dogmatic identification of the texts of the Bible as a canon.[2] As we have

---

1. Ernst Troeltsch, 'Historical and Dogmatic Method in Theology', in *Religion in History* (Minneapolis: Fortress Press, 1991), pp. 11-32.
2. See, for instance, the work of Philip Davies, *Whose Bible Is It Anyway?* (London: T. & T. Clark, 2nd edn, 2004).

seen in the foregoing essays, however, proponents of theological interpretation, by contrast, typically regard the reading of Scripture as a participation in the divine economy, consider the community of faith to be the proper and primary locus of interpretation and recognize the unity of the canonical books to be a function both of their narrative content and of their divine use. It is important to point out, however, as several essayists do, that confession of the unity of Scripture does not preclude there being multiple legitimate interpretations of single texts. That the unity of Scripture is a function of divine use demands, in fact, that the uses to which God may put particular texts be left open. We cannot say in advance of the Spirit's continuing work that the meaning of a text is determined once and for all, not even by authorial intention, albeit authorial intention, so far as we are able to recognize it, requires careful consideration.

The matters briefly referred to here are recurring themes in this book. While theological interpretation is not itself a method for interpreting Scripture but rather a disposition giving rise to certain practices, it is possible nevertheless to identify some consistent features in the approach to Scripture taken by this book's twelve contributors. The first is that the reading of Scripture is both a communicative and a formative act. To read Scripture in the context of faith is to be drawn into communion with God, with Scripture's authors and with the community of interpreters extensive in time and space who have discovered in Scripture the communicative presence of God. The content of the communicative and formative act varies widely of course. As James Harding and Miriam Bier remind us, it can sometimes take the form of protest, of lament, of outrage at the apparent absence of God. But even the outrage and the protest, even the demand that God should be held accountable, constitutes, in the end, a testimony of faith, precisely because of its implication that despite all the evidence to the contrary, we live in a world created by God and proclaimed by him to be good. Theological interpreters of Scripture are those who become, through their reading and proclamation of Scripture, participants in this faith-filled outrage and demand, and who attest that their participation in Scripture's drama has become a means by which they are chastened, comforted, justified and transformed.

The attention given by Harding and Bier to the texts of penitence, of protest and of lament helpfully draws out as well the bi-directional nature of the communication involved in reading Scripture. Theological interpretation is concerned, certainly, with the question, 'What does God have to say to us?', but also with the question of what we have to say to God. Scripture invites a straightforward honesty in penitence and a boldness in prayer, in protest and in lament, that liturgical convention and the selectivity of the lectionary often dissuade us from. Faithful theological interpretation of

Scripture, if it is to help us enter into the full richness and depth of the communicative event that Scripture is, has at times to overcome, not only the resistance of cultured despisers, but also of misguided piety.

That the reading of Scripture is a formative act focuses attention on the outcomes to which theological interpretation is directed. Matthew Easter suggests that the theological interpretation of Scripture is directed toward the formation of disciples. Or as John McDowell puts it, we become 'followers not users of the text'. Marianne Meye Thomson likewise draws attention to the continuing capacity of Matthew's Gospel, for a case in point, not only to *describe* discipleship, but to *form* in its readers 'the faith and practice of disciples of Jesus'. Paul Trebilco explains that reading Scripture in the context of faith is itself a participation in God's work. Readers have a place in the story Scripture tells. Faithful interpretation of Scripture, therefore, is not demonstrated by a conceptual account of what a text may mean, however accurate it may be, but by lives lived in accordance with the reality to which Scripture testifies, namely, the divine economy. Quoting Paul Ricoeur, Allan Bell observes that 'an interpretation is not authentic unless it culminates in some form of appropriation'.[3] Articulating a similar point but with richer nuances, Tim Meadowcroft reminds us, through an exegesis of Jn 14.15-26, that we are to become 'keepers of the Word'. In this same text, Jesus explains that keeping his commandments is the fruit of love, and promises that the disciples will be equipped for this commission by the indwelling Spirit whom Jesus himself will send. Theological interpretation is simply a description of the kind of reading that is directed, above all, towards these ends. The goal is not mastery of the text, but attentiveness to and participation in the creative and redemptive work of God.

It is apposite to recall here that the essential content of the creative and redemptive work of God is described in variant forms through the Christian tradition, beginning in Scripture itself, by the rule of faith. The rule of faith is not, therefore, an imposition upon the text, but an attempt to tell in brief and summary form, the story told by Scripture itself. The rule of faith highlights, in other words, the central features of the divine drama toward which Scripture testifies. Joel Green argues, therefore, with particular reference to Luke's account of Jesus' ascension, that the rule of faith helps us to see in particular texts what we might otherwise miss if we were not cognisant of the wider story in which the particular text has its place. We must read *with* Scripture, Green contends, because Scripture interprets itself. Myk Habets cites T.F. Torrance in support of this view: 'It is when we

---

3. Paul Ricoeur, *Paul Ricoeur: Hermeneutics and the Human Sciences—Essays on Language, Action and Interpretation* (ed. and trans. John B. Thompson; Cambridge: Cambridge University Press, 1981), p. 178; cited by Allan Bell in Chapter 4, above.

interpret different passages and statements in the light of the whole that their real meaning and force become apparent'.[4]

A further, utterly vital, point to be made in relation to Scripture's testimony to the creative and redemptive work of God is that the story Scripture tells is nothing less than a description of how reality itself is constituted. Taking up the concern of Seth Heringer's essay, Scripture is to be understood as a theological account of history, a theological account of all that happens and all that is. As Heringer points out, this recognition renders deeply problematic the heavy reliance that modern biblical interpreters have placed upon a method of historical enquiry that deliberately excludes any theological explanation of what takes place in history. Precisely by virtue of this exclusion, the historical critical method renders itself incapable of agreeing with what the biblical writers have to say. Heringer helpfully draws to our attention the fact that theological interpretation and historical critical method, as presently conceived, cannot easily coexist. Because the proponents of theological interpretation generally share a commitment to the reliability of Scripture's witness to God at work in history, however, they have a deep interest in whether a historiography can be found that is able to recognize that work. Without such recognition, I suggest, the fruitfulness of historical, critical enquiry when applied to the biblical texts will be severely limited.

One of the hurdles to be overcome in quest of an historiography suitable for the task of discerning where God is at work in the world is the modernist conviction that the field of knowledge and truth has limits determined by our own epistemic capacities. Put crudely, but accurately nevertheless, this conviction entails that if our tools of historical enquiry cannot establish that, for paramount instance, God raised Jesus from the dead, then we need to find some other explanation to account for the disciples' mistaken, fanciful or mythic belief that God did just that. An alternative possibility, however, is that our epistemic capacities are inadequate to the task of 'seeing what really happened'. It may be that we have need of God's assistance to see and understand. This is a possibility set forth by several contributors to this book. God is involved in our reading of Scripture, it is proposed, and without openness to that involvement, we cannot hope to understand. Habets, guided by T.F. Torrance, refers to the epistemological role of the Spirit. The divine presence through Word and Spirit 'renders Scripture an abiding and authoritative Word of God to humanity'.[5] We have to do, through the reading of Scripture, with the self-communication of God that yields an

---

4. Thomas F. Torrance, *The Christian Doctrine of God: One Being Three Persons* (Edinburgh: T. & T. Clark, 1991), p. 38; cited in Chapter 3, above.

5. Myk Habets, in Chapter 3, above.

understanding of things that is given rather than grasped and requires a mind genuinely open to possibilities beyond its own capacity to conceive.

We thus return to the point with which we began. Prayerful expectation that God will address us through Scripture and recognition that through Scripture we are given words with which to address God are fundamental characteristics of theological interpretation and attitudes commensurate, it is contended, with the reality of Scripture itself.

BIBLIOGRAPHY

Albrektson, Bertil, *Studies in the Text and Theology of the Book of Lamentations with a Critical Edition of the Peshitta Text* (STL, 21; Lund: C.W.K. Gleerup, 1963).
Alter, Robert, *The Five Books of Moses: A Translation with Commentary* (New York: Norton, 2004).
Anderson, Kevin L., *'But God Raised Him from the Dead': The Theology of Jesus' Resurrection in Luke–Acts* (Paternoster Biblical Monographs; Milton Keynes: Paternoster Press, 2006).
Andriessen, P.C.B., 'La communauté des "Hébreux": Etait-elle tombée dans le relâchement?', *NRTh* 96 (1974), pp. 1054-66.
Aquinas, Thomas, *Summa contra gentiles* (trans. Joseph Rickaby; London: Burns & Oates, 1905).
Arichea, D.C., 'Translating Hymnic Materials: Theology and Translation in 1 Timothy 3.16', *BT* 58 (2007), pp. 179-85.
Attridge, Harold W., *The Epistle to the Hebrews* (Hermeneia; Philadelphia: Fortress Press, 1989).
Augustine, *De doctrina christiana* (trans. R.P.H. Green; Oxford and New York: Oxford University Press, 1995).
—*On Christian Doctrine* (ed. P. Schaff; 2 vols.; Nicene and Post-Nicene Fathers, first series; Grand Rapids: Eerdmans, 1956).
Avemarie, Friedrich, and Hermann Lichtenberger (eds.), *Auferstehung—Resurrection* (WUNT, 135; Tübingen: Mohr Siebeck, 2001).
Bakhtin, M.M., *Problems of Dostoevsky's Poetics* (trans. Caryl Emerson; Minneapolis: University of Minnesota Press, 1984).
Balla, Peter, *Challenges to New Testament Theology: An Attempt to Justify the Enterprise* (Tübingen: Mohr Siebeck, 1997; repr., Peabody, MA: Hendrickson, 1998).
Barrett, C.K., *The Pastoral Epistles in the New English Bible, with Introduction and Commentary* (New Clarendon Bible; Oxford: Clarendon Press, 1963).
Barth, Karl, *Church Dogmatics* 1/2 (Edinburgh: T. & T. Clark, 1956).
—*Church Dogmatics* 4/3.2 (Edinburgh: T. & T. Clark, 1961).
—*The Epistle to the Romans* (trans. of 6th ed. by Edwyn C. Hoskyns; Oxford: Oxford University Press, 1968).
—*The Knowledge of God and the Service of God according to the Teaching of the Reformation* (London: Hodder & Stoughton, 1938).
Bartholomew, Craig, 'Before Babel and after Pentecost', in Bartholomew, Greene and Möller (eds.), *After Pentecost*, pp. 131-70.
Bartholomew, Craig, Colin Greene and Karl Möller (eds.), *After Pentecost: Language and Biblical Interpretation* (Carlisle: Paternoster Press; Grand Rapids: Zondervan, 2001).

Barton, J., 'Beliebigkeit', in Y. Sherwood (ed.), *Derrida's Bible (Reading a Page of Scripture with a Little Help from Derrida)* (New York: Palgrave MacMillan, 2004), pp. 301-303.
Bassler, J.M., *1 Timothy, 2 Timothy, Titus* (AbNTC; Nashville: Abingdon Press, 1996).
Bauckham, Richard, *God Crucified: Monotheism and Christology in the New Testament* (Grand Rapids: Eerdmans, 1998).
—*Jesus and the God of Israel:* God Crucified *and Other Studies on the New Testament's Christology of Divine Identity* (Grand Rapids: Eerdmans, 2008).
—'The Throne of God and the Worship of Jesus', in *Jesus and the God of Israel*, pp. 152-81.
Bayle, Pierre, *Historical and Critical Dictionary: Selections* (trans. and ed. R.H. Popkin and C. Bush; Indianapolis, IN: Bobbs–Merrill, 1965); translated from *An Historical and Critical Dictionary by Monsieur Bayle* (vol. 4; London, 1710).
Beale, G.K., *We Become What We Worship: A Biblical Theology of Idolatry* (Downers Grove, IL: InterVarsity Press, 2008).
Bell, Allan, 'Re-constructing Babel: Discourse Analysis, Hermeneutics and the Interpretive Arc', *Discourse Studies* 13 (2011), pp. 519-68.
Benson, Bruce Ellis, *Graven Ideologies: Nietzsche, Derrida and Marion on Modern Idolatry* (Downers Grove, IL: InterVarsity Press, 2002).
Benson, Bruce Ellis, James K.A. Smith and Kevin J. Vanhoozer, 'Introduction', in Bruce Ellis Benson, James K.A. Smith, and Kevin J. Vanhoozer (eds.), *Hermeneutics at the Crossroads* (Bloomington: Indiana University Press, 2006), pp. xiii-xviii.
Berlin, Adele, *Lamentations* (OTL; Louisville, KY: Westminster/John Knox Press, 2002).
Bier, Miriam, '"Perhaps There Is Hope": Reading Lamentations as a Polyphony of Pain, Penitence, and Protest' (PhD thesis, University of Otago, Dunedin, 2012).
Billings, J.T., *The Word of God for the People of God: An Entryway to the Theological Interpretation of Scripture* (Grand Rapids: Eerdmans, 2010).
Bird, Michael F., *Are You the One Who Is to Come? The Historical Jesus and the Messianic Question* (Grand Rapids: Baker, 2009).
Black, C.C., 'Exegesis as Prayer', *Princeton Seminary Bulletin* NS 23 (2002), pp. 131-45.
Blair, H.A., *A Creed before the Creeds* (London: Longmans, Green & Co, 1955).
Blumenthal, David R., *Facing the Abusing God: A Theology of Protest* (Louisville, KY: Westminster/John Knox Press, 1993).
Boase, Elizabeth, *The Fulfilment of Doom? The Dialogic Interaction between the Book of Lamentations and the Pre-Exilic/Early Exilic Prophetic Literature* (LHB/OTS, 437; New York: T. & T. Clark, 2006).
—'The Many Voices of Lament: An Exploration of the Book of Lamentations', *AJL* 10 (2005), pp. 3-26.
Bockmuehl, Markus, 'The Church in Hebrews', in Markus Bockmuehl and Michael B. Thompson (eds.), *A Vision for the Church* (Festschrift J.P.M. Sweet; Edinburgh: T. & T. Clark, 1997), pp. 133-51.
— *Seeing the Word: Refocusing New Testament Study* (Studies in Theological Interpretation; Grand Rapids: Baker Academic, 2006).
Bori, Pier Cesare, *The Golden Calf and the Origins of the Anti-Jewish Controversy* (Atlanta: Scholars Press, 1990).
Bowie, Andrew, *Aesthetics and Subjectivity: From Kant to Nietzsche* (Manchester and New York: Manchester University Press, 2nd edn, 2003).

Bracke, John, *Jeremiah 30–52 and Lamentations* (WestBC; Louisville, KY: Westminster/John Knox Press, 2000).
Braiterman, Zachary, *(God) after Auschwitz: Tradition and Change in Post-Holocaust Jewish Thought* (Princeton, NJ: Princeton University Press, 1998).
Braun, Herbert, *An die Hebräer* (HNT, 14; Tübingen: Mohr Siebeck, 1984).
Breidert, Wolfgang (ed.), *Die Erschütterung der vollkommenen Welt: Die Wirkung des Erdbebens von Lissabon im Spiegel europäischer Zeitgenossen* (Darmstadt: Wissenschaftliche Buchgesellschaft, 1994).
Briggs, Richard S., *The Virtuous Reader: Old Testament Narrative and Interpretive Virtue* (Studies in Theological Interpretation; Grand Rapids: Baker Academic, 2010).
Brown, R.E., *The Gospel according to John (xiii–xxi): Introduction, Translation, and Notes* (AB, 29A; Garden City, NY: Doubleday, 1970).
Bruce, F.F., *The Epistle to the Hebrews* (NICNT; Grand Rapids: Eerdmans, rev. edn, 1990).
Brueggemann, Walter, 'The Costly Loss of Lament', *JSOT* 36 (1986), pp. 57-71.
— 'From Hurt to Joy, from Death to Life', *Int* 28 (1974), pp. 3-19.
—*Genesis* (Interpretation; Atlanta: John Knox Press, 1982).
—*The Message of the Psalms: A Theological Commentary* (Minneapolis: Augsburg, 1984).
—'Some Aspects of Theodicy in Old Testament Faith', *PRSt* 26 (1999), pp. 253-68.
—*Theology of the Old Testament* (Minneapolis: Augsburg Fortress, 1997).
Brunner, Peter, 'The Ascension of Christ: Myth or Reality?', *Dialog* 1.2 (1962), pp. 38-39.
Buckwalter, H. Douglas, *The Character and Purpose of Luke's Christology* (SNTSMS, 89; Cambridge: Cambridge University Press, 1996).
—'The Divine Saviour', in Marshall and Peterson (eds.), *Witness to the Gospel*, pp. 107-23.
Bultmann, Rudolf, *History of the Synoptic Problem* (trans. John Marsh; Oxford: Basil Blackwell, 1963).
Burnett, Gary W., *Paul and the Salvation of the Individual* (BIS, 57; Leiden: Brill, 2001).
Burrell, David B., *Deconstructing Theodicy: Why the Book of Job Has Nothing to Say to the Puzzle of Suffering* (Grand Rapids: Brazos, 2008).
—'Distinguishing God from the World', in Brian Davies (ed.), *Language, Meaning and God: Essays in Honour of Herbert McCabe, OP* (London: Geoffrey Chapman, 1987), pp. 75-91.
Calvin, John, *Calvin's New Testament Commentaries* (ed. D.W. Torrance and T.F. Torrance; 12 vols.; Grand Rapids: Eerdmans, 1959–72).
—*Commentaries on the Last Four Books of Moses* (trans. Charles William Bingham; Grand Rapids: Eerdmans, 1964).
—*Commentary on a Harmony of the Evangelists: Matthew, Mark, and Luke* (trans. William Pringle; Ages Digital Library Edition).
—*Institutes of the Christian Religion* (ed. J.T. McNeill; trans. F.L. Battles; Library of Christian Classics; 1559 repr.; Philadelphia: Fortress Press, 1960).
Campbell, Douglas A., *The Deliverance of God: An Apocalyptic Rereading of Justification in Paul* (Grand Rapids: Eerdmans, 2009).
Cargas, Harry James, and Elie Wiesel, *Harry James Cargas in Conversation with Elie Wiesel* (New York: Paulist Press, 1976).

Carson, D.A., *The Gospel according to John* (Leicester: Inter-Varsity Press, 1991).
Childs, Brevard S., 'Toward Recovering Theological Exegesis', *ExAud* 16 (2000), pp. 121-29.
Coakley, Sarah, '*Kenōsis* and Subversion: On the Repression of "Vulnerability" in Christian Feminist Writing', in *Powers and Submissions: Spirituality, Philosophy and Gender* (Challenges in Contemporary Theology; Oxford: Blackwell, 2002), pp. 3-39.
Colyer, Elmer M., *The Nature of Doctrine in T.F. Torrance's Theology* (Eugene, OR: Wipf & Stock, 2001).
Congdon, D.W., 'The Trinitarian Shape of πίστις: A Theological Exegesis of Galatians', *JTI* 2 (2008), pp. 231-58.
Crenshaw, James, *Defending God: Biblical Responses to the Problem of Evil* (Oxford: Oxford University Press, 2005).
Curtis, E.M., 'Idol, Idols', in *ABD*, III, p. 379.
Davies, J.G., *He Ascended into Heaven: A Study in the History of Doctrine* (Bampton Lectures, 1958; London: Lutterworth Press, 1958).
Davies, M., *The Pastoral Epistles* (NTG; Sheffield: Sheffield Academic Press, 1996).
Davies, Oliver, 'Reading the Burning Bush: Voice, World and Holiness', *Modern Theology* 22 (2006), pp. 439-48.
Davies, Philip, *Whose Bible Is It Anyway?* (London: T. & T. Clark, 2nd edn, 2004).
Davis, Ellen F., and Richard B. Hays (eds.), *The Art of Reading Scripture* (Grand Rapids: Eerdmans, 2003).
Davis, Stephen T., 'The Meaning of Ascension for Christian Scholars', *Perspectives* 22.4 (2007), pp. 13-19.
Dawson, Gerrit Scott, *Jesus Ascended: The Meaning of Christ's Continuing Incarnation* (London: T. & T. Clark, 2004).
Day, Peggy L., 'The Bitch Had It Coming to Her: Rhetoric and Interpretation in Ezekiel 16', *BI* 8 (2000), pp. 231-54.
Dean-Otting, Mary, *Heavenly Journeys: A Study of the Motif in Hellenistic Jewish Literature* (JU, 8; Frankfurt am Main: Peter Lang, 1984).
Demarest, B. 'Creeds', in S.B. Ferguson and D.F. Wright (eds.), *New Dictionary of Theology* (Leicester: Inter-Varsity Press, 1988).
Dennert, Brian C., 'John Calvin's Movement from the Bible to Theology and Practice', *JETS* 54 (2011), pp. 345-65.
Des Pres, Terrence, *The Survivor: An Anatomy of Life in the Death Camps* (Oxford: Oxford University Press, 1976).
DeSilva, David, *Perseverance in Gratitude: A Socio-Rhetorical Commentary on the Epistle 'to the Hebrews'* (Grand Rapids: Eerdmans, 2000).
Dibelius M., and H. Conzelmann, *The Pastoral Epistles* (Hermeneia; Philadelphia: Fortress Press, 1972).
Dobbs-Allsopp, F.W., *Lamentations* (Interpretation; Louisville, KY: John Knox Press, 2002).
—'Tragedy, Tradition, and Theology in the Book of Lamentations', *JSOT* 74 (1997), pp. 29-60.
Dobbs-Allsopp, F.W., and Tod Linafelt, 'The Rape of Zion in Thr 1,10', *ZAW* 113 (2001), pp. 77-81.
Donelson, L.W., *Colossians, Ephesians, First and Second Timothy, and Titus* (WestBC; Louisville, KY: Westminster/John Knox Press, 1996).

Donne, Brian K., 'The Significance of the Ascension of Jesus Christ in the New Testament', *SJT* 30 (1977), pp. 555-68.
Dunn, James D.G., 'The Ascension of Jesus: A Test Case for Hermeneutics', in Avemarie and Lichtenberger (eds.), *Auferstehung—Resurrection*, pp. 301-22.
—'Demythologizing the Ascension—A Reply to Professor Gooding', *IBS* 3 (1981), pp. 15-27.
—'Demythologizing—The Problem of Myth in the New Testament', in I. Howard Marshall (ed.), *New Testament Interpretation: Essays on Principles and Methods* (Grand Rapids: Eerdmans, 1977), pp. 285-307.
Dunnill, John, *Covenant and Sacrifice in the Letter to the Hebrews* (SNTSMS, 75; Cambridge: Cambridge University Press, 1992).
Eagleton, T., *Ideology: An Introduction* (London: Verso, 1991).
Easter, Matthew C., '"Let Us Go to Him": The Story of Faith and the Faithfulness of Jesus in Hebrews' (PhD thesis, University of Otago, Dunedin, 2011).
Eissfeldt, Otto, *The Old Testament: An Introduction* (trans. Peter R. Ackroyd; Oxford: Basil Blackwell, 1965).
Ellingworth, Paul, *The Epistle to the Hebrews* (NIGTC; Grand Rapids: Eerdmans, 1993).
Elvey, Anne F., *The Matter of the Text: Material Engagements between Luke and the Five Senses* (Sheffield: Sheffield Phoenix Press, 2011).
Enslin, Morton S., 'The Ascension Story', *JBL* 47 (1928), pp. 60-73.
Fackenheim, Emil, 'The Commanding Voice of Auschwitz', in Katz, Biderman, and Greenberg (eds.), *Wrestling with God*, pp. 434-38; repr. from *God's Presence in History: Jewish Affirmation and Philosophical Reflections* (Deems Lectures, 18; New York: New York University Press, 1970).
Fairclough, Norman, *Critical Discourse Analysis: The Critical Study of Language* (Harlow: Pearson Education, 2nd edn, 2010).
Farrow, Douglas, *Ascension and Ecclesia: On the Significance of the Doctrine of the Ascension for Ecclesiology and Cosmology* (Grand Rapids: Eerdmans, 1999).
— *Ascension Theology* (London: T. & T. Clark, 2011).
—'The Doctrine of the Ascension in Irenaeus and Origen', *Arc: The Journal of the Faculty of Religious Studies, McGill University* 26 (1998), pp. 31-50.
Fee, G.D., *1 and 2 Timothy, Titus* (NIBC; Peabody, MA: Hendrickson, 1988).
Feldman, Jerome A., *From Molecule to Metaphor: A Neural Theory of Language* (Cambridge, MA: The MIT Press, 2006).
Ferguson, D.S., 'Kerygma', in W. Elwell (ed.), *Evangelical Dictionary of Theology* (Grand Rapids: Baker Academic, 2nd edn, 2001), pp. 653-54.
Fernández, Víctor M., 'La vida sacerdotal de los cristianos según la carta a los Hebreos', *RevistB* 52 (1990), pp. 145-52.
Fiddes, Paul S., *The Creative Suffering of God* (Oxford: Clarendon Press, 1988).
— *Participating in God: A Pastoral Doctrine of the Trinity* (London: Darton, Longman & Todd, 2000).
Fiore, B., *The Pastoral Epistles: First Timothy, Second Timothy, Titus* (SP; Collegeville, MN: Liturgical Press, 2007).
Fishbane, Michael, *Biblical Interpretation in Ancient Israel* (New York: Clarendon Press; Oxford: Oxford University Press, 1985).
Fitzmyer, Joseph A., *The Gospel according to Luke: Introduction, Translation, and Notes* (AB, 28–28a; 2 vols.; Garden City, NY: Doubleday, 1981/85).

Flannery, Frances *et al.* (eds.), *Experientia*. I. *Inquiry into Religious Experience in Early Judaism and Early Christianity* (SBLSymS, 40; Atlanta: Society of Biblical Literature, 2008).
Fletcher-Louis, Crispin H.T., *Luke–Acts: Angels, Christology and Soteriology* (WUNT, 2.94; Tübingen: Mohr Siebeck, 1997).
Ford, D.F., and G. Stanton (eds.), *Reading Texts, Seeking Wisdom: Scripture and Theology* (London: SCM Press, 2003).
Fowl, S.E., *Engaging Scripture: A Model for Theological Interpretation* (Malden, MA: Blackwell, 1998).
—'Introduction', in Fowl (ed.), *The Theological Interpretation of Scripture*, pp. xii-xxx.
—*Philippians* (THNTC; Grand Rapids: Eerdmans, 2005).
—*The Story of Christ in the Ethics of Paul: An Analysis of the Function of the Hymnic Material in the Pauline Corpus* (JSNTSup, 36; Sheffield: Sheffield Academic Press, 1990).
—*Theological Interpretation of Scripture* (Cascade Companions; Eugene, OR: Cascade, 2009).
Fowl, Stephen (ed.), *The Theological Interpretation of Scripture: Classical and Contemporary Essays* (Oxford: Blackwell, 1997).
Frame, John M., *The Doctrine of the Knowledge of God: A Theology of Lordship* (Phillipsburg, NJ: Presbyterian & Reformed, 1987).
France, R.T., *The Gospel of Mark: A Commentary on the Greek Text* (Grand Rapids: Eerdmans, 2002).
Fretheim, Terence E., 'The Book of Genesis: Introduction, Commentary, and Reflections', in Leander E. Keck (ed.), *The New Interpreter's Bible* (12 vols.; Nashville: Abingdon Press, 1994), I, pp. 321-674.
Fuhrer, Georg, and Werner Foester, '*sōtēr*', in *TDNT*, VII, pp. 1003-21.
Gallagher, Eugene V., 'Conversion and Community in Late Antiquity', *JR* 73 (1993), pp. 1-15.
Gibbs, Raymond W., Jr, *Embodiment and Cognitive Science* (Cambridge: Cambridge University Press, 2006).
Goldingay, John, *Psalms*. I. *Psalms 1–41* (BCOTWP; Grand Rapids: Eerdmans, 2006).
Good, Edwin M., *In Turns of Tempest: A Reading of Job with a Translation* (Stanford, CA: Stanford University Press, 1990).
Gooding, D.W., 'Demythologizing Old and New, and Luke's Description of the Ascension: A Layman's Appraisal', *IBS* 2 (1980), pp. 95-119.
— 'Demythologizing the Ascension—A Reply', *IBS* 3 (1981), pp. 46-54.
González, Justo L., *Luke* (Belief; Louisville, KY: Westminster/John Knox Press, 2010).
Gordis, Robert, *The Song of Songs and Lamentations: A Study, Modern Translation and Commentary* (New York: Ktav, 1974).
Gorman, Michael, *Elements of Biblical Exegesis: Revised and Expanded Edition* (Peabody, MA: Hendrickson, 2009).
Gottwald, Norman K., 'The Book of Lamentations Reconsidered', in *The Hebrew Bible in its Social World and in Ours* (Atlanta: Scholars Press, 1993), pp. 165-73.
—*Studies in the Book of Lamentations* (SBT, 14; London: SCM Press, 1954).
Grässer, Erich, 'Die Gemeindevorsteher im Hebräerbrief', in Gerhard Müller and Henning Schröer (eds.), *Vom Amt des Laien in Kirche und Theologie* (Festschrift Gerhard Krause; Berlin: W. de Gruyter, 1982), pp. 67-84.
Gray, Bryan J., 'Towards Better Ways of Reading the Bible', *SJT* 33 (1980), pp. 301-15.

Gray, John, *The Book of Job* (The Text of the Hebrew Bible, 1; Sheffield: Sheffield Phoenix Press, 2010).
Gray, Patrick, *Godly Fear: The Epistle to the Hebrews and Greco-Roman Critiques of Superstition* (AcBib, 16; Atlanta: SBL, 2003).
Green, Barbara, *How Are the Mighty Fallen? A Dialogical Study of King Saul in 1 Samuel* (JSOTSup, 365; London: Sheffield Academic Press, 2003).
Green, Joel B., *Practicing Theological Interpretation: Engaging Biblical Texts for Faith and Formation* (Grand Rapids: Baker Academic, 2011).
—'"Salvation to the End of the Earth" (Acts 13.47): God as Saviour in the Acts of the Apostles', in Marshall and Peterson (eds.), *Witness to the Gospel*, pp. 83-106.
— *Seized by Truth: Reading the Bible as Scripture* (Nashville: Abingdon Press, 2007).
Green, J.B., and S. McKnight (eds.), *Dictionary of Jesus and the Gospels* (Downers Grove, IL: InterVarsity Press, 1992).
Green, Joel B., and Max Turner (eds.), *Between Two Horizons: Spanning New Testament Studies and Systematic Theology* (Grand Rapids: Eerdmans, 2000).
—'New Testament Commentary and Systematic Theology: Strangers or Friends', in Green and Turner (eds.), *Between Two Horizons*, pp. 1-22.
Gregory, Brad S., 'Anabaptist Martyrdom: Imperatives, Experience, and Memorialization', in John D. Roth and James M. Stayer (eds.), *A Companion to Anabaptism and Spiritualism, 1521–1700* (Brill's Companions to the Christian Tradition, 6; Leiden: Brill, 2007), pp. 467-506.
Gregory of Nazianzus, *Oration 2*, in Philip Schaff (ed.), *Nicene and Post-Nicene Fathers of the Christian Church.* II/7. *Cyril of Jerusalem, Gregory Nazianzen* (Edinburgh: T. & T. Clark, 1893).
Grudem, Wayne A., 'Perseverance of the Saints: A Case Study from Hebrews 6:4-6 and the Other Warning Passages in Hebrews', in Thomas R. Schreiner and Bruce A. Ware (eds.), *Still Sovereign: Contemporary Perspectives on Election, Foreknowledge, and Grace* (Grand Rapids: Baker Academic, 2000), pp. 133-82.
Guinan, Michael D., 'Lamentations', in R.E. Brown, J.A. Fitzmyer, and R.E. Murphy (eds.), *The New Jerome Biblical Commentary* (London: Chapman, 1990), pp. 558-62.
Gundry, R.H., 'The Form, Meaning and Background of the Hymn Quoted in 1 Timothy 3:16', in W.W. Gasque and R.P. Martin (eds.), *Apostolic History and the Gospel: Biblical and Historical Essays Presented to F.F. Bruce on his 60th Birthday* (Exeter: Paternoster Press, 1970), pp. 203-22.
Gurewicz, S.B., 'The Problem of Lamentations 3', *ABR* 8 (1960), pp. 19-23.
Guthrie, George H., 'Hebrews', in G.K. Beale and D.A. Carson (eds.), *Commentary on the New Testament Use of the Old Testament* (Grand Rapids: Baker Academic, 2007), pp. 919-95.
Habel, Norman C., *The Book of Job: A Commentary* (OTL; Louisville, KY: Westminster/John Knox Press, 1985).
Habets, Myk, *The Anointed Son: A Trinitarian Spirit Christology* (Eugene, OR: Pickwick, 2010).
—'Beyond Henry's Nominalism and Evangelical Foundationalism: Thomas Torrance's Theological Realism', in T.J. Meadowcroft and M. Habets (eds.), *Gospel, Truth, and Interpretation: Evangelical Identity in Aotearoa New Zealand* (Auckland: Archer, 2011), pp. 205-40.

— 'Reading Scripture and Doing Theology with the Holy Spirit', in Myk Habets (ed.), *The Spirit of Truth: Reading Scripture and Constructing Theology with the Holy Spirit* (Eugene, OR: Pickwick, 2010), pp. 89-106.

Hagner, Donald A., *Matthew* (2 vols.; WBC, 33A–33B; Dallas, TX: Word Books, 1993).

Hanson, A.T., *The Pastoral Epistles* (NCB; Grand Rapids: Eerdmans, 1982).

Harding, James E., 'In the Name of Love: Resisting Reader and Abusive Redeemer in Deutero-Isaiah', *Bible and Critical Theory* 2.2 (2006), pp. 14.1-14.15.

Harland, P.J., 'Vertical or Horizontal: The Sin of Babel', *VT* 48 (1998), pp. 515-33.

Haroutunian, Joseph, 'The Doctrine of the Ascension: A Study of the New Testament Teaching', *Int* 10 (1956), pp. 270-81.

Hart, Trevor, 'Tradition, Authority, and a Christian Approach to the Bible as Scripture', in Green and Turner (eds.), *Between Two Horizons*, pp. 183-204.

—'The Word, The Words and the Witness: Proclamation as Divine and Human Reality in the Theology of Karl Barth', in *Regarding Karl Barth: Toward a Reading of his Theology* (Downers Grove, IL: InterVarsity Press, 1999), pp. 28-47.

Hauerwas, Stanley, *Matthew* (BTCB; Grand Rapids: Brazos, 2006).

Hays, Richard, 'Can Narrative Criticism Recover the Theological Unity of Scripture?', *JTI* 2 (2008), pp. 193-212.

— 'Reading the Bible with Eyes of Faith: The Practice of Theological Exegesis', *JTI* 1 (2007), pp. 5-21.

Heater, Homer, 'Structure and Meaning in Lamentations', in R.B. Zuck (ed.), *Vital Old Testament Issues: Examining Textual and Topical Questions* (Vital Issues Series; Grand Rapids: Kregel, 1996), pp. 150-59.

Heim, Knut M., 'The Personification of Jerusalem and the Drama of her Bereavement in Lamentations', in R. Hess and G. Wenham (eds.), *Zion, City of our God* (Grand Rapids: Eerdmans, 1999), pp. 129-69.

Heltzel, Peter, 'Thomas Torrance', in *Dictionary of Modern Western Theology* (http://people.bu.edu/wwildman/WeirdWildWeb/courses/mwt/dictionary/mwt_themes785; cited 28 August 2012).

Heschel, Abraham J., *God in Search of Man: A Philosophy of Judaism* (New York: Farrar, Straus & Giroux, 1955).

—*The Prophets* (2 vols.; New York: Harper & Row, 1962).

Hesselink, John I., 'A Pilgrimage in the School of Faith—An Interview with T.F. Torrance', *Reformed Review* 38 (1984), pp. 49-64.

Hillers, Delbert, *Lamentations: A New Translation with Introduction and Commentary* (AB, 7A; New York: Doubleday, 2nd edn, 1992).

Hillesum, Etty, *Etty: The Letters and Diaries of Etty Hillesum 1941–1943* (ed. K.A.D. Smelik; trans. A.J. Pomerans; Grand Rapids: Eerdmans, 2002).

Himmelfarb, Martha, *Ascent to Heaven in Jewish and Christian Apocalypses* (Oxford: Oxford University Press, 1993).

Horton, Michael S., 'Hellenistic or Hebrew? Open Theism and Reformed Theological Method', *JETS* 45 (2002), pp. 317-41.

— 'A Vulnerable God apart from Christ? Open Theism's Challenge to the Classical Doctrine of God', *Modern Reformation Magazine* 10.3 (2001), pp. 30-38.

Houlden, J.L., 'Beyond Belief: Preaching the Ascension', *Theology* 94 (1991), pp. 173-80.

—*The Pastoral Epistles* (PNTC; Harmondsworth: Penguin Books, 1976).

House, Paul R., *Lamentations* (WBC, 23B; Nashville: Thomas Nelson, 2004).

Huey, F.B., *Jeremiah and Lamentations* (NABC, 16; Nashville: Broadman, 1993).
Hultgren, A.J., and R. Aus, *I–II Timothy, Titus, II Thessalonians* (Augsburg Commentary on the New Testament; Minneapolis: Augsburg, 1984).
Hunsinger, George. 'Beyond Literalism and Expressivism: Karl Barth's Hermeneutical Realism', in *Disruptive Grace: Studies in the Theology of Karl Barth* (Grand Rapids: Eerdmans, 2000), pp. 210-25.
—'The Dimension of Depth: Thomas F. Torrance on the Sacraments of Baptism and the Lord's Supper', *SJT* 54 (2001), pp. 155-76.
Insole, Christopher, 'Anthropomorphism and the Apophatic God', *Modern Theology* 17 (2001), pp. 475-83.
Irenaeus, *Against Heresies* (trans. and ed. Dominic J. Unger; rev. John J. Dillon; ACW, 55; Mahwah, NJ: Paulist Press, 1992).
Jantzen, Grace, *Power, Gender and Christian Mysticism* (Cambridge: Cambridge University Press, 1995).
Jenson, Robert W., *Ezekiel* (BTCB; Grand Rapids: Brazos, 2009).
—'The Hidden and Triune God', *IJST* 2 (2000), pp. 5-12.
—'On the Ascension', in Michael Welker and Cynthia A. Jarvis (eds.), *Loving God with our Minds: The Pastor as Theologian: Essays in Honor of Wallace M. Alston* (Grand Rapids: Eerdmans, 2004), pp. 331-40.
Johnson, Andy, 'Resurrection, Ascension and the Developing Portrait of the God of Israel in Acts', *SJT* 57 (2004), pp. 146-62.
Johnson, Keith E., 'Augustine's "Trinitarian" Reading of John 5: A Model for the Theological Interpretation of Scripture?' *JETS* 52 (2009), pp. 799-810.
Johnson, Luke Timothy, *The First and Second Letters to Timothy: A New Translation with Introduction and Commentary* (AB, 35A; New York: Doubleday, 2001).
—*Hebrews: A Commentary* (NTL; Louisville, KY: Westminster/John Knox Press, 2006).
—*Letters to Paul's Delegates: 1 Timothy, 2 Timothy, Titus* (New Testament in Context; Valley Forge, PA: Trinity Press International, 1996).
Jüngel, Eberhard, *God as the Mystery of the World: On the Foundation of the Theology of the Crucified One in the Debate between Theism and Atheism* (trans. Darrell L. Guder; Edinburgh: T. & T. Clark, 1983).
Käsemann, Ernst, *The Wandering People of God* (trans. Roy A. Harrisville and Irving L. Sandberg; Eugene, OR: Wipf & Stock, 1984).
Katz, S.T., S. Biderman and G. Greenberg (eds.), *Wrestling with God: Jewish Theological Responses during and after the Holocaust* (Oxford: Oxford University Press, 2008).
Kelly, J.N.D., *A Commentary on the Pastoral Epistles* (BNTC; London: A. & C. Black, 1963).
Kierkegaard, Søren, *For Self-Examination: Recommended for the Times* (trans. Edna and Howard Hong; Minneapolis: Augsburg, 1940).
Klauck, Hans-Josef, 'Moving in and Moving out: Ethics and Ethos in Hebrews', in Jan G. van der Watt (ed.), *Identity, Ethics, and Ethos in the New Testament* (BZNW, 141; Berlin: W. de Gruyter, 2006), pp. 417-43.
Klein, Hans, *Das Lukasevangelium* (KEK; Göttingen: Vandenhoeck & Ruprecht, 2006).
Knierim, Rolf P., 'Third Lecture: Justice in Old Testament Theology', in *The Task of Old Testament Theology: Substance, Method and Cases* (Grand Rapids: Eerdmans, 1995), pp. 86-122.
Knight, G.W., *The Pastoral Epistles: A Commentary on the Greek Text* (NIGTC; Grand Rapids: Eerdmans, 1992).

Koester, Craig R., 'Conversion, Persecution, and Malaise: Life in the Community for Which Hebrews Was Written', *HvTSt* 61 (2005), pp. 231-51.
—*Hebrews* (AB, 36; New York: Doubleday, 2001).
Kooij, Arie van der, 'The City of Babel and Assyrian Imperialism: Genesis 11:1-9 Interpreted in the Light of Mesopotamian Sources', in André Lemaire (ed.), *Congress Volume: Leiden, 2004 (Papers from the XVIIIth Congress of the International Organisation for the Study of the Old Testament, Leiden, 2004)* (VTSup, 109; Leiden: Brill, 2006), pp. 1-17.
Köstenberger, A.J., *John* (Grand Rapids: Baker Academic, 2004).
—*The Mission of Jesus and the Disciples according to the Fourth Gospel: With Implications for the Fourth Gospel's Purpose and the Mission of the Contemporary Church* (Grand Rapids: Eerdmans, 1998).
Kox, Willem, Wim Meeus and Harm't Hart, 'Religious Conversion of Adolescents: Testing the Lofland and Stark Model of Religious Conversion', *Sociological Analysis* 52 (1991), pp. 227-40.
Kraŝovec, Jože, 'The Source of Hope in the Book of Lamentations', *VT* 42 (1992), pp. 223-33.
Krause, D., *1 Timothy* (Readings; London: T. & T. Clark, 2004).
Laato, A., and J.C. de Moor (eds.), *Theodicy in the World of the Bible* (Leiden: Brill, 2003).
Ladd, G.E., *A Theology of the New Testament* (Grand Rapids: Eerdmans, 1993).
Lake, Kirsopp, 'The Ascension', in F.J. Foakes-Jackson and Kirsopp Lake (eds.), *The Acts of the Apostles. V. Additional Notes to the Commentary* (Beginnings of Christianity, 1; London: Macmillan, 1933), pp. 16-22.
Lanahan, William F., 'The Speaking Voice in the Book of Lamentations', *JBL* 93 (1974), pp. 41-49.
Lane, William L., *Hebrews 1–8* (WBC, 47A; Nashville: Thomas Nelson, 1991).
—*Hebrews 9–13* (WBC, 47B; Dallas, TX: Word Books, 1991).
—'Living a Life of Faith in the Face of Death: The Witness of Hebrews', in Richard N. Longenecker (ed.), *Life in the Face of Death: The Resurrection Message of the New Testament* (Grand Rapids: Eerdmans, 1998), pp. 247-69.
Larkin, William J., Jr, 'The Spirit and Jesus "on Mission" in the Postresurrection and Postascension Stages of Salvation History: The Impact of the Pneumatology of Acts on its Christology', in Amy M. Donaldson and Timothy B. Sailors (eds.), *New Testament Greek and Exegesis: Essays in Honor of Gerald F. Hawthorne* (Grand Rapids: Eerdmans, 2003), pp. 121-39.
Lash, Nicholas, 'Considering the Trinity', *Modern Theology* 2 (1986), pp. 183-96.
Lau, A.Y., *Manifest in Flesh: The Epiphany Christology of the Pastoral Epistles* (WUNT, 2.86; Tübingen: Mohr Siebeck, 1996).
Laytner, Anson, *Arguing with God: A Jewish Tradition* (Northvale, NJ: Jason Aronson, 1990).
Lee, Archie Chi Chung, 'Mothers Bewailing: Reading Lamentations', in Caroline Vander Stichele and Todd C. Penner (eds.), *Her Master's Tools? Feminist and Postcolonial Engagements of Historical-Critical Discourse* (Atlanta: SBL; Leiden: Brill, 2005), pp. 195-210.
Lee, Nancy, *The Singers of Lamentations* (Biblical Interpretation Series, 60; Leiden: Brill, 2002).

Leithart, Peter J., 'Womb of the World: Baptism and the Priesthood of the New Covenant in Hebrews 10.19-22', *JSNT* 78 (2000), pp. 49-65.
Levering, Matthew, *Ezra and Nehemiah* (BTCB; Grand Rapids: Brazos, 2007).
Lévi-Strauss, Claude, *La pensée sauvage* (Paris: Librairie Plon, 1962).
Levinas, Emmanuel, 'Useless Suffering', in Katz, Biderman, and Greenberg (eds.), *Wrestling with God*, pp. 451-54.
Lienhard, Joseph T. (ed.), *Ancient Christian Commentary on Scripture, Old Testament.* III. *Exodus, Leviticus, Numbers, Deuteronomy* (Downers Grove, IL: InterVarsity Press, 2001).
Linafelt, Tod, 'Surviving Lamentations', in A. Brenner and C.R. Fontaine (eds.), *A Feminist Companion to Reading the Bible: Approaches, Methods, and Strategies* (Sheffield: Sheffield Academic Press, 1997), pp. 344-57.
—*Surviving Lamentations: Catastrophe, Lament, and Protest in the Afterlife of a Biblical Book* (Chicago: University of Chicago Press, 2000).
—'Zion's Cause: The Presentation of Pain in the Book of Lamentations', in *Strange Fire: Reading the Bible after the Holocaust* (New York: New York University Press, 2000), pp. 267-79.
Lindars, Barnabas, *The Theology of the Letter to the Hebrews* (Cambridge: Cambridge University Press, 1991).
Lofland, John, and Rodney Stark, 'Becoming a World-Saver: A Theory of Conversion to a Deviant Perspective', in Charles Y. Glock (ed.), *Religion in Sociological Perspective: Essays in the Empirical Study of Religion* (Belmont, CA: Wadsworth, 1973), pp. 28-47.
Lohfink, Gerhard, *Die Himmelfahrt Jesu: Untersuchungen zu den Himmelfahrts- und Erhöhungstexten bei Lukas* (SANT, 26; Munich: Kösel, 1971).
Longman, Tremper, III, *Jeremiah, Lamentations* (NIBC, 14; Peabody, MA: Hendrickson, 2008).
Loughlin, Gerald, *Telling God's Story: Bible, Church and Narrative Theology* (Cambridge: Cambridge University Press, 1996).
Lubac, H. de, *Medieval Exegesis* (vol. 1; trans. M. Sebanc; Grand Rapids: Eerdmans, 1998).
— 'Spiritual Understanding', in Fowl (ed.), *The Theological Interpretation of Scripture*, pp. 3-25.
Luz, Ulrich, *Matthew 1–7* (trans. Wilhelm C. Linss; Minneapolis: Fortress Press, 1989).
MacKinnon, D.M., *Themes in Theology: The Three-Fold Cord: Essays in Philosophy, Politics and Theology* (Edinburgh: T. & T. Clark, 1987).
MacLeod, D.J., 'Christology in Six Lines: An Exposition of 1 Timothy 3:16', *BSac* 159 (2002), pp. 334-48.
Magee, G.S., 'Uncovering the "Mystery" in 1 Timothy 3', *TJ* NS 29 (2008), pp. 247-65.
Maile, John F., 'The Ascension in Luke–Acts', *TynBul* 37 (1986), pp. 29-59.
Malina, Bruce J., *Christian Origins and Cultural Anthropology: Practical Models for Biblical Interpretation* (Atlanta: John Knox Press, 1986).
— 'The Individual and the Community-Personality in the Social World of Early Christianity', *BTB* 9 (1979), pp. 126-38.
Mandolfo, Carleen R., *Daughter Zion Talks Back to the Prophets: A Dialogic Theology of the Book of Lamentations* (Semeia, 58; Atlanta: SBL, 2007).

—'Dialogic Form Criticism: An Intertextual Reading of Lamentations and Psalms of Lament', in R. Boer (ed.), *Bakhtin and Genre Theory in Biblical Studies* (Atlanta: SBL, 2007), pp. 69-90.
— 'Lamentations', in Gail R. O'Day and David L. Petersen (eds.), *Theological Bible Commentary* (Louisville, KY: Westminster/John Knox Press, 2009), pp. 237-39.
Manson, William, *Jesus and the Christian* (London: James Clarke, 1967).
Marion, Jean-Luc, *God without Being* (trans. Thomas A. Carlson; Chicago: University of Chicago Press, 1991).
Marley, A.G., *T.F. Torrance: The Rejection of Dualism* (Edinburgh: Handsel, 1992).
Marohl, Matthew J., *Faithfulness and the Purpose of Hebrews: A Social Identity Approach* (PTMS; Eugene, OR: Pickwick, 2008).
Marshall, Christopher D., 'One for All and All for One: The High Priesthood of Christ, the Church, and the Priesthood of Believers in Hebrews', *Journal of the Christian Brethren Research Fellowship* 129 (1992), pp. 7-13.
Marshall, I.H., '1 Timothy, Book of', in Vanhoozer (ed.), *Dictionary for Theological Interpretation of the Bible*, pp. 801-804.
— *The Pastoral Epistles* (ICC; Edinburgh: T. & T. Clark, 1999).
Marshall, I.H., and David Peterson (eds.), *Witness to the Gospel: The Theology of Acts* (Grand Rapids: Eerdmans, 1998).
Mathewson, Dave, 'Reading Heb. 6:4-6 in Light of the Old Testament', *WTJ* 61 (1999), pp. 209-25.
McCabe, Herbert, *God Still Matters* (London: Continuum, 2002).
—*The Good Life: Ethics and the Pursuit of Happiness* (London: Continuum, 2005).
McClendon, J.W., Jr, *Doctrine: Systematic Theology*, II (Nashville: Abingdon, 1994).
McDowell, J.C., 'Silenus' Wisdom and the "Crime of Being": The Problem of Hope in George Steiner's Tragic Vision', *Literature and Theology* 14 (2000), pp. 385-411.
McGrath, Alister E., 'Stratification: Levels of Reality and the Limits of Reductionism', in *The Order of Things: Explorations in Scientific Theology* (Oxford: Blackwell, 2006), pp. 97-116.
—*T.F. Torrance: An Intellectual Biography* (Edinburgh: T. & T. Clark, 1999).
McKane, William, *Jeremiah* (ICC; 2 vols.; Edinburgh: T. & T. Clark, 1986, 1996).
McKnight, Scot, 'The Warning Passages of Hebrews: A Formal Analysis and Theological Conclusions', *TJ* 13 (1992), pp. 21-59.
Meadowcroft, T.J., *The Message of the Word of God: The Glory of God Made Known* (BSTBT; Leicester: Inter-Varsity Press, 2011).
—review of *Theological Interpretation of the Old Testament: A Book-by-Book Survey*, ed. K.J. Vanhoozer, *Colloquium* 41 (2009), pp. 223-25.
Meek, E. Lightcap, *Loving to Know: Introducing Covenant Epistemology* (Eugene, OR: Cascade, 2011).
Metzger, Bruce M., 'The Meaning of Christ's Ascension', in J.M. Myers, O. Reimherr, and H.N. Bream (eds.), *Search the Scriptures: New Testament Studies in Honor of Raymond T. Stamm* (Gettysburg Theological Studies, 3; Leiden: Brill, 1969), pp. 118-28.
— *A Textual Commentary on the Greek New Testament* (Stuttgart: Deutsche Bibelgesellschaft, 2nd edn, 2002).
Meyer, Paul W., 'The Problem of the Messianic Self-Consciousness of Jesus', *NovT* 4 (1960), pp. 122-38.
Micou, R.W., 'On ὤφθη ἀγγέλοις, I Tim. iii. 16', *JBL* 11 (1892), pp. 201-205.

Míguez-Bonino, José, 'Genesis 11:1-9—A Latin American Perspective', in Priscilla Pope-Levison and John R. Levison (eds.), *Return to Babel: Global Perspectives on the Bible* (Louisville, KY: Westminster/John Knox Press, 1999), pp. 13-16.
Miller, Charles William, 'Reading Voices: Personification, Dialogism, and the Reader of Lamentations 1', *BI* 9 (2004), pp. 393-408.
Miller, John B.F., *Convinced That God Had Called Us: Dreams, Visions and the Perception of God's Will in Luke–Acts* (BIS, 85; Leiden: Brill, 2007).
Mintz, Alan, *Ḥurban: Responses to Catastrophe in Hebrew Literature* (New York: Columbia University Press, 1984).
Moberly, Walter, 'Does God Lie to his Prophets? The Story of Micaiah ben Imlah as a Test Case', *HTR* 96 (2003), pp. 1-23.
—'Jonah, God's Objectionable Mercy, and the Way of Wisdom', in Ford and Stanton (eds.), *Reading Texts, Seeking Wisdom*, pp. 154-68.
—'Lament', in W.A. van Gemeren (ed.), *New International Dictionary of Old Testament Theology and Exegesis* (5 vols.; Carlisle: Paternoster Press, 1997), IV, p. 876.
—*Prophecy and Discernment* (Cambridge Studies in Christian Doctrine; Cambridge: Cambridge University Press, 2006).
—'What Is Theological Interpretation of Scripture?', *JTI* 3 (2009), pp. 161-78.
Molnar, Paul D., *Divine Freedom and the Doctrine of the Immanent Trinity: In Dialogue with Karl Barth and Contemporary Theology* (London: T. & T. Clark, 2002).
—'God's Self-Communication in Christ: A Comparison of Thomas F. Torrance and Karl Rahner', *SJT* 50 (1997), pp. 294-96.
Moloney, F.J., *The Gospel of John* (Collegeville, MN: Liturgical Press, 1989).
Moltmann, Jürgen, *The Crucified God: The Cross of Christ as the Foundation and Criticism of Christian Theology* (trans. R.A. Wilson and J. Bowden; London: SCM Press, 1974).
—*The Trinity and the Kingdom of God: The Doctrine of God* (trans. M. Kohl; London: SCM Press, 1981).
Montague, G.T., *First and Second Timothy, Titus* (CCSS; Grand Rapids: Baker Academic, 2008).
Moore, Michael S., 'Human Suffering in Lamentations', *RB* 90 (1983), pp. 534-55.
Morrow, William S., 'Consolation, Rejection, and Repentance in Job 42:6', *JBL* 105 (1986), pp. 211-25.
Mosser, Carl, 'Rahab outside the Camp', in Richard Bauckham *et al.* (eds.), *The Epistle to the Hebrews and Christian Theology* (Grand Rapids: Eerdmans, 2009), pp. 383-404.
Motyer, J.A., 'Idolatry', in J.D. Douglas *et al.* (eds.), *New Bible Dictionary* (Leicester: InterVarsity Press, 2nd edn, 1982), pp. 503-505.
Moule, C.F.D., 'The Ascension—Acts i.9', *ExpTim* 68 (1956–57), pp. 205-209.
—'The Individualism of the Fourth Gospel', *NovT* 5 (1962), pp. 171-90.
Mounce, W., *The Pastoral Epistles* (WBC, 46; Nashville: Thomas Nelson, 2000).
Muffs, Yochanan, 'Who Will Stand in the Breach? A Study of Prophetic Intercession', in *Love and Joy: Law, Language and Religion in Ancient Israel* (New York: Jewish Theological Seminary of America, 1992), pp. 9-48.
Murphy-O'Connor, J., 'Redactional Angels in 1 Tim 3:16', *RB* 91 (1984), pp. 178-87.
Needham, Nick, 'Christ Ascended for Us—Jesus' Ascended Humanity and Ours', *Evangel* 25.2 (2007), pp. 42-46.

Negri, Antonio, *The Labor of Job: The Biblical Text as a Parable of Human Labor* (trans. M. Mandarini; New Slant: Religion, Politics, Ontology; Durham, NC: Duke University Press, 2009).

Neiman, Susan, *Evil in Modern Thought: An Alternative History of Philosophy* (Princeton, NJ: Princeton University Press, 2002).

Newsom, Carol A., 'Bakhtin, the Bible, and Dialogic Truth', *JR* 76 (1996), pp. 290-306.

Neyrey, Jerome H., 'Dyadism', in Pilch and Malina (eds.), *Biblical Social Values*, pp. 49-52.

—'Group Orientation', in Pilch and Malina (eds.), *Biblical Social Values*, pp. 88-91.

Nicole, Roger R., 'Some Comments on Hebrews 6:4-6 and the Doctrine of the Perseverance of God with the Saints', in Gerald F. Hawthorne (ed.), *Current Issues in Biblical and Patristic Interpretation* (Festschrift Merrill C. Tenney; Grand Rapids: Eerdmans, 1975), pp. 355-64.

Noth, Martin, *Exodus: A Commentary* (London: SCM Press, 1962).

O'Connor, Kathleen M., *Lamentations and the Tears of the World* (Maryknoll, NY: Orbis Books, 2002).

O'Grady, John F., 'Individualism and Johannine Ecclesiology', *BTB* 5 (1975), pp. 227-61.

O'Keefe, John J., and R.R. Reno, *Sanctified Vision: An Introduction to Early Christian Interpretation of the Bible* (Baltimore, MD: The Johns Hopkins University Press, 2005).

Olhausen, W., 'A "Polite" Response to Anthony Thiselton', in Bartholomew, Greene and Möller (eds.), *After Pentecost*, pp. 121-30.

Oord, T.J., *The Nature of Love: A Theology* (St Louis, MO: Chalice Press, 2010).

Osborne, Grant R., 'A Classical Arminian View', in Herbert W. Bateman IV (ed.), *Four Views on the Warning Passages in Hebrews* (Grand Rapids: Kregel, 2007), pp. 86-128.

—*The Hermeneutical Spiral: A Comprehensive Introduction to Biblical Interpretation* (Downers Grove, IL: InterVarsity Press, 1991).

Ostler, Nicolas, *Empires of the Word: A Language History of the World* (London: HarperCollins, 2005).

Painter, J., 'World', in Green and McKnight (eds.), *Dictionary of Jesus and the Gospels*, pp. 889-90.

Palatty, Paul, 'The Ascension of Christ in Luke–Acts', *Bible Bhashyam* 12 (1986), pp. 166-81.

Palmer, D.W., 'The Literary Background of Acts 1.1-14', *NTS* 33 (1987), pp. 427-38.

Parker, Harold M., 'Domitian and the Epistle to the Hebrews', *Iliff Review* 36 (1979), pp. 31-43.

Parry, Robin A., *Lamentations* (THOTC; Grand Rapids: Eerdmans, 2010).

Pelikan, Jaroslav, *Acts* (BTCB; Grand Rapids: Brazos, 2005).

—*The Vindication of Tradition* (New Haven, CT: Yale University Press, 1984).

Pervo, Richard I., *Acts: A Commentary* (Hermeneia; Minneapolis: Fortress Press, 2009).

Petersen, Norman R., *Rediscovering Paul: Philemon and the Sociology of Paul's Narrative World* (Philadelphia: Fortress Press, 1985).

Pham, Xuan Huong Thi, *Mourning in the Ancient Near East and the Hebrew Bible* (JSOTSup, 302; Sheffield: Sheffield Academic Press, 1999).

Philips, Dietrich, 'The Church of God, c. 1560', in Williams and Mergal (eds.), *Spiritual and Anabaptist Writers*, pp. 228-60.

Pilch, John J., and Bruce J. Malina (eds.), *Biblical Social Values and their Meanings: A Handbook* (Peabody, MA: Hendrickson, 1993).
Placher, William C. *Mark* (Belief; Louisville, KY: Westminster/John Knox Press, 2010).
Placher, William C., and Amy Plantinga Pauw, 'Series Introduction', in William C. Placher, *Mark* (Belief; Louisville, KY: Westminster/John Knox Press, 2010), pp. ix-xi.
Plantinga, Alvin, and Nicholas Wolterstorff (eds.), *Faith and Rationality: Reason and Belief in God* (Notre Dame, IN: University of Notre Dame Press, 1983).
Popper, Karl R., *The Logic of Scientific Discovery* (London: Hutchinson, 1959).
Porter, Stanley E., 'Foreword', in Michael F. Bird, *Are You the One Who Is to Come? The Historical Jesus and the Messianic Question* (Grand Rapids: Baker, 2009), pp. 7-10.
Posner, Michael I., and Marcus E. Raichle, *Images of Mind* (New York: Freeman, 1997).
Pseudo-Dionysius, 'The Divine Names', in *Pseudo-Dionysius: The Complete Works* (trans. Colm Luibheid and Paul Rorem; New York: Paulist Press, 1987).
Rae, Murray A., *History and Hermeneutics* (London: T. & T. Clark, 2005).
—'Texts in Context: Scripture and the Divine Economy', *JTI* 1 (2007), pp. 23-45.
Rae, M.A., J.E. Goldingay, C.J.H. Wright, R.W. Wall and K. Greene-McCreight, 'Christ in/and the Old Testament', *JTI* 2 (2008), pp. 1-22.
Ramachandran, V.S., *A Brief Tour of Human Consciousness* (New York: Pi, 2004).
Re'emi, S. Paul, 'The Theology of Hope: A Commentary on the Book of Lamentations', in R. Martin-Achard and S.P. Re'emi, *Amos and Lamentations: God's People in Crisis* (Grand Rapids: Eerdmans; Edinburgh: Handsel, 1984), pp. 73-134.
Renkema, Johan, 'Theodicy in Lamentations?', in Laato and de Moor (eds.), *Theodicy*, pp. 410-28.
Reno, R.R., *Genesis* (BTCB; Grand Rapids: Brazos, 2010).
Ricoeur, Paul, *The Conflict of Interpretations: Essays in Hermeneutics* (ed. Don Ihde; Evanston, IL: Northwestern University Press, 1974).
—*Essays on Biblical Interpretation* (ed. Lewis S. Mudge; Philadelphia: Fortress Press, 1980).
—*Figuring the Sacred: Religion, Narrative, and Imagination* (ed. Mark I. Wallace; trans. David Pellauer; Minneapolis: Fortress Press, 1995).
—*From Text to Action: Essays in Hermeneutics*, II (trans. Kathleen Blamey and John B. Thompson; Evanston, IL: Northwestern University Press, 1991).
—*Interpretation Theory: Discourse and the Surplus of Meaning* (Fort Worth, TX: Texas Christian University Press, 1976).
—*On Translation* (trans. Eileen Brennan; London: Routledge, 2006).
—*Paul Ricoeur: Hermeneutics and the Human Sciences: Essays on Language, Action and Interpretation* (ed. and trans. John B. Thompson; Cambridge: Cambridge University Press, 1981).
—*The Philosophy of Paul Ricoeur: An Anthology of his Work* (ed. Charles E. Reagan and David Stewart; Boston: Beacon Press, 1978).
Rigby, Cynthia L., 'Divine Sovereignty, Human Agency, and the Ascension of Christ', *QR* 22 (2002), pp. 152-65.
Rosner, Brian, *Greed as Idolatry: The Origin and Meaning of a Pauline Metaphor* (Grand Rapids: Eerdmans, 2007).
Rowe, C. Kavin, *Early Narrative Christology: The Lord in the Gospel of Luke* (BZNW, 139; Berlin: W. de Gruyter, 2006).

Rubinstein, Richard, *After Auschwitz: History, Theology, and Contemporary Judaism* (Johns Hopkins Jewish Studies; Baltimore, MD: Johns Hopkins University Press, 2nd edn, 1992).
Ryken, Philip Graham, *Jeremiah and Lamentations: From Sorrow to Hope* (Preaching the Word; Wheaton, IL: Crossway, 2001).
Saarinen, R., *The Pastoral Epistles with Philemon and Jude* (BTCB; Grand Rapids: Brazos Press, 2008).
Sæbø, Magne, 'Who Is "The Man" in Lamentations 3? A Fresh Approach to the Interpretation of the Book of Lamentations', in A.G. Auld (ed.), *Understanding Poets and Prophets: Essays in Honour of George Wishart Anderson* (Sheffield: JSOT Press, 1993), pp. 294-306.
Salevao, Iutisone, *Legitimation in the Letter to the Hebrews: The Construction and Maintenance of a Symbolic Universe* (JSNTSup, 219; London: Sheffield Academic Press, 2002).
Salters, Robert B., *Jonah and Lamentations* (OTG; Sheffield: Sheffield Academic Press, 1994).
Sarisky, Darren, 'T.F. Torrance on Biblical Interpretation', *IJST* 11 (2009), pp. 332-46.
Sarna, Nahum M., *Genesis* (The JPS Torah Commentary; Philadelphia: Jewish Publication Society, 1989).
Saussure, Ferdinand de, *Cours de linguistique générale* (ed. C. Bally and A. Sechehaye, with the collaboration of A. Riedlinger; Paris: Payot, 1916).
Schaff, Philip (ed.), *The Creeds of Christendom* (rev. David Schaff; 3 vols.; Grand Rapids: Baker, 6th edn, 1983 [1889]).
Schneemelcher, Wilhelm, 'The Acts of Peter', in Wilhelm Schneemelcher (ed.), *New Testament Apocrypha* (rev. Edgar Hennecke; 2 vols.; Louisville, KY: Westminster/ John Knox Press, 1992), II, pp. 271-321.
Scholer, John M., *Proleptic Priests: Priesthood in the Epistle to the Hebrews* (JSNTSup, 49; Sheffield: Sheffield Academic Press, 1991).
Schüssler Fiorenza, Elisabeth, 'Der Anführer und Vollender unseres Glaubens: Zum theologischen Verständnis des Hebräerbriefes', in J. Schreiner (ed.), *Gestalt und Anspruch des Neuen Testaments* (Würzburg: Echter Verlag, 1969), pp. 262-81.
—*In Memory of Her: A Feminist Theological Reconstruction of Christian Origins* (New York: Crossroad, 1983).
Schweid, Eliezer, 'Is the Shoah a Unique Event?', in Katz, Biderman, and Greenberg (eds.), *Wrestling with God*, pp. 219-29; originally published in *Iyyun* (1988), pp. 271-85 [Hebrew].
Schweizer, E., *The Good News according to Mark* (Atlanta: John Knox Press, 1970).
—*Lordship and Discipleship* (London: SCM Press, 1960).
—'Two New Testament Creeds Compared: 1 Corinthians 15.3-5 and 1 Timothy 3.16', in W. Klassen and G.F. Snyder (eds.), *Current Issues in New Testament Interpretation: Essays in Honor of Otto A. Piper* (New York: Harper & Brothers, 1962), pp. 166-77.
Segal, Alan F., 'Heavenly Ascent in Hellenistic Judaism, Early Christianity and their Environment', *ANRW* 2.23.2 (1980), pp. 1333-94.
—*Paul the Convert: The Apostolate and Apostasy of Saul the Pharisee* (New Haven, CT: Yale University Press, 1990).

Seitz, Christopher R., *The Character of Christian Scripture: The Significance of a Two-Testament Bible* (Studies in Theological Interpretation; Grand Rapids: Baker Academic, 2011).
—*Prophecy and Hermeneutics: Toward a New Introduction to the Prophets* (Studies in Theological Interpretation; Grand Rapids: Baker Academic, 2007).
—'What Lesson Will History Teach? The Book of the Twelve as History', in C. Bartholomew, C.S. Evans, M. Healy and M. Rae (eds.), *'Behind' the Text: History and Biblical Interpretation* (Scripture and Hermeneutics Series; Carlisle: Paternoster Press, 2003), pp. 443-67.
Simons, Menno, 'The Cross of the Saints, c. 1554', in John Christian Wenger (ed.), *The Complete Writings of Menno Simons* (Scottdale, PA: Herald, 1956), pp. 581-622.
—'Reply to Gellius Faber, 1554', in Wenger (ed.), *The Complete Writings of Menno Simons*, pp. 623-781.
Simpson, E.K., *The Pastoral Epistles: The Greek Text with Introduction and Commentary* (London: Tyndale, 1954).
Sleeman, Matthew, *Geography and the Ascension Narrative in Acts* (SNTSMS, 146; Cambridge: Cambridge University Press, 2009).
Smith, D.M., *The Theology of the Gospel of John* (Cambridge: Cambridge University Press, 1995).
Söding, Thomas, 'Gemeinde auf dem Weg: Christsein nach dem Hebräerbrief', *BK* 48 (1991), pp. 180-87.
Sölle, Dorothee, *Suffering* (trans. E.R. Kalin; London: Darton, Longman & Todd, 1975).
Stark, Rodney, *The Rise of Christianity: A Sociologist Reconsiders History* (Princeton, NJ: Princeton University Press, 1996).
Steiner, George, *Language and Silence: Essays 1958–1966* (Harmondsworth: Penguin Books, 1967).
Stiebert, Johanna, 'Human Suffering and Divine Abuse of Power in Lamentations', *Pacifica* 16 (2003), pp. 195-215.
Still, Todd, 'Christos as Pistos: The Faith(fulness) of Jesus in the Epistle to the Hebrews', *CBQ* 69 (2007), pp. 747-55.
Strauss, David Friedrich, *The Life of Jesus Critically Examined* (1840 repr.; ed. Peter C. Hodgson; trans. George Eliot; Life of Jesus Series; Philadelphia: Fortress Press, 1972).
Strecker, G., *Theology of the New Testament* (New York: W. de Gruyter, 2000).
Surin, Kenneth R., *Theology and the Problem of Evil* (Signposts in Theology; Oxford: Blackwell, 1986).
Swinburne, Richard, *Revelation: From Metaphor to Analogy* (Oxford: Oxford University Press, 2nd edn, 2007).
Tabor, James D., 'Heaven, Ascent to', in *ABD*, III, pp. 91-94.
Thiselton, Anthony C., *New Horizons in Hermeneutics: The Theory and Practice of Transforming Biblical Reading* (Grand Rapids: Zondervan, 1992).
Thomas, C. Adrian, *A Case for Mixed-Audience with Reference to the Warning Passages in the Book of Hebrews* (New York: Peter Lang, 2008).
Thomas, Heath, 'Poetry and Theology in Lamentations: An Investigation of Lamentations 1–3 Using the Aesthetic Analysis of Umberto Eco' (PhD thesis, University of Gloucester, 2007) [rev. version: *Poetry and Theology in the Book of Lamentations: The Aesthetics of an Open Text* (Hebrew Bible Monographs, 47; Sheffield: Sheffield Phoenix Press, 2013)].

Thompson, Marianne Meye, *Colossians and Philemon* (THNTC; Grand Rapids: Eerdmans, 2005).
—*The Promise of the Father* (Louisville, KY: Westminster/John Knox Press, 2000).
Ticciati, Susannah, 'Does Job Fear God for Naught?', *Modern Theology* 21 (2005), pp. 353-66.
—*Job and the Disruption of Identity: Reading beyond Barth* (London: T. & T. Clark, 2005).
Torrance, Alan J., 'The Bible as Testimony to our Belonging: The Theological Vision of James B. Torrance', in G.S. Dawson (ed.), *An Introduction to Torrance Theology* (London: T. & T. Clark, 2007), pp. 103-19.
— 'Can the Truth Be Learned? Redressing the "Theologistic Fallacy" in Modern Biblical Scholarship', in Markus Bockmuehl and Alan J. Torrance (eds.), *Scripture's Doctrine and Theology's Bible* (Grand Rapids: Baker, 2008), pp. 143-63.
Torrance, Thomas F., *The Apocalypse Today* (London: James Clarke, 1960).
—'The Christian Apprehension of God the Father', in A.F. Kimel (ed.), *Speaking the Christian God: The Holy Trinity and the Challenge of Feminism* (Grand Rapids: Eerdmans, 1992), pp. 120-43.
—*The Christian Doctrine of God: One Being Three Persons* (Edinburgh: T. & T. Clark, 1991).
—'The Deposit of Faith', *SJT* 36 (1983), pp. 1-28.
—*Divine Meaning: Studies in Patristic Hermeneutics* (Edinburgh: T. & T. Clark, 1995).
—*God and Rationality* (1971 repr.; Eugene, OR: Wipf & Stock, 1997).
—'"The Historical Jesus": From the Perspective of a Theologian', in W.C. Weinrich (ed.), *The New Testament Age: Essays in Honor of Bo Reicke* (2 vols.; Macon, GA: Mercer University Press, 1984), II, pp. 511-26.
—*Incarnation: The Person and Life of Christ* (ed. Robert T. Walker; Milton Keynes: Paternoster Press; Downers Grove, IL: InterVarsity Press, 2008).
—*Karl Barth: An Introduction to his Early Theology 1910–1931* (1962 repr.; Edinburgh: T. & T. Clark, 2000).
—*Karl Barth: Biblical and Evangelical Theologian* (Edinburgh: T. & T. Clark, 1990).
—'The Lamb of God', in *When Christ Comes and Comes Again* (London: Hodder & Stoughton, 1957), pp. 47-60.
—'The Place of Christology in Biblical and Dogmatic Theology', in *Theology in Reconstruction* (Grand Rapids: Eerdmans, 1965), pp. 128-49.
—*Preaching Christ Today* (Grand Rapids: Eerdmans, 1994).
—*Reality and Evangelical Theology* (Downers Grove, IL: InterVarsity Press, 2nd edn, 1999).
—*Space, Time and Resurrection* (1976 repr.; Edinburgh: T. & T. Clark, 1998).
—'The Stratification of Truth', in *Reality and Scientific Theology* (Edinburgh: Scottish Academic Press, 1985), pp. 131-59.
—*Theological Science* (Oxford: Oxford University Press, 1969).
—*Theology in Reconciliation: Essays towards Evangelical and Catholic Unity in East and West* (London: Geoffrey Chapman, 1975).
—*Transformation and Convergence in the Frame of Knowledge: Explorations in the Interrelations of Scientific and Theological Enterprise* (Grand Rapids: Eerdmans, 1984).
—'Trinity Sunday Sermon', *Ekklesiastikos pharos* 52 (1970), pp. 191-99.
—'Truth and Authority: Theses on Truth', *ITQ* 39 (1972), pp. 215-42.

Towner, P.H., *The Goal of our Instruction: The Structure of Theology and Ethics in the Pastoral Epistles* (JSNTSup, 34; Sheffield: JSOT Press, 1989).
—*The Letters to Timothy and Titus* (NICNT; Grand Rapids: Eerdmans, 2006).
Trebilco, P.R., *The Early Christians in Ephesus from Paul to Ignatius* (WUNT, 166; Tübingen: Mohr Siebeck, 2004).
Treier, Daniel J., *Introducing Theological Interpretation of Scripture: Recovering a Christian Practice* (Grand Rapids: Baker Academic, 2008).
Trible, P., *Texts of Terror: Literary-Feminist Readings of Biblical Narratives* (Philadelphia: Fortress Press, 1984).
Troeltsch, Ernst, 'Contingency', in James Hastings (ed.), *Encyclopedia of Religion and Ethics* (12 vols.; Edinburgh: T. & T. Clark, 1911), IV, pp. 87-89.
—'Historical and Dogmatic Method in Theology', in *Religion in History* (Minneapolis: Fortress Press, 1991), pp. 11-32.
—'Modern Philosophy of History', in *Religion in History* (Minneapolis: Fortress Press, 1991), pp. 273-320.
Tull Willey, Patricia, *Remember the Former Things: The Recollection of Previous Texts in Second Isaiah* (SBLDS, 161; Atlanta: Scholars Press, 1997).
Turner, Denys, *Marxism and Christianity* (Oxford: Blackwell, 1983).
— 'On Denying the Right God: Aquinas on Atheism and Idolatry', *Modern Theology* 20 (2004), pp. 141-61.
Turner, Max, 'Holy Spirit', in Green and McKnight (eds.), *Dictionary of Jesus and the Gospels*, pp. 341-51.
—*Power from on High: The Spirit in Israel's Restoration and Witness in Luke–Acts* (JPTSup, 9; Sheffield: Sheffield Academic Press, 1996).
—'The Spirit of Christ and "Divine" Christology', in Joel B. Green and Max Turner (eds.), *Jesus of Nazareth: Lord and Christ: Essays on the Historical Jesus and New Testament Christology* (Grand Rapids: Eerdmans, 1994), pp. 413-36.
—'"Trinitarian" Pneumatology in the New Testament? Towards an Explanation of the Worship of Jesus', *AsTJ* 57–58 (2002–2003), pp. 167-86.
Turner, M.M.B. 'The Spirit of Christ and Christology', in H.H. Rowdon (ed.), *Christ the Lord: Studies in Christology Presented to Donald Guthrie* (Leicester: InterVarsity Press, 1982), pp. 168-90.
Uehlinger, Christoph, *Weltreich und 'eine Rede': Eine neue Deutung der sogenannten Turmbauerzählung (Gen 11, 1-9)* (Göttingen: Vandenhoeck & Ruprecht, 1990).
Van Leeuwen, Raymond C., 'Scribal Wisdom and Theodicy in the Book of the Twelve', in L.G. Perdue, B.B. Scott, and W.J. Wiseman (eds.), *In Search of Wisdom: Essays in Memory of John G. Gammie* (Louisville, KY: Westminster/John Knox Press, 1993), pp. 31-49.
Vandrunen, David, 'Iconoclasm, Incarnation and Eschatology: Toward a Catholic Understanding of the Reformed Doctrine of the "Second" Commandment', *IJST* 6.2 (2004), pp. 130-47.
Vanhoozer, Kevin J., *Biblical Narrative in the Philosophy of Paul Ricoeur: A Study in Hermeneutics and Theology* (Cambridge: Cambridge University Press, 1990).
—'From Speech Acts to Scripture Acts', in Bartholomew, Greene, and Möller (eds.), *After Pentecost*, pp. 1-49.
—'Imprisoned or Free? Text, Status, and Theological Interpretation of the Master/Slave Discourse of Philemon', in A.K.M. Adam, Stephen E. Fowl, Kevin J. Vanhoozer and Francis Watson, *Reading Scripture with the Church: Toward a Hermeneutic for Theological Interpretation* (Grand Rapids: Baker, 2006), pp. 51-93.

—'Interpreting Scripture between the Rock of Biblical Studies and the Hard Place of Systematic Theology: The State of the Evangelical (Dis)union' (delivered at Renewing the Evangelical Mission Conference, Gordon–Conwell Theological Seminary, 13–15 October, 2009).
—'Introduction: What Is Theological Interpretation of the Bible?', in Vanhoozer (ed.), *Dictionary for Theological Interpretation of the Bible*, pp. 19-25.
—*Is There a Meaning in This Text? The Bible, the Reader and the Morality of Literary Knowledge* (Leicester: Apollos, 1998).
Vanhoozer, Kevin J. (ed.), *Dictionary for Theological Interpretation of the Bible* (Grand Rapids: Baker Academic, 2005).
Verbrugge, Verlyn D., 'Towards a New Interpretation of Hebrews 6:4-6', *CTJ* 15.1 (1980), pp. 61-73.
Verhey, Allen, and Joseph S. Harvard, *Ephesians* (Belief; Louisville, KY: Westminster/ John Knox Press, 2011).
Vicchio, Stephen, *Job in the Modern World* (Eugene, OR: Wipf & Stock, 2006).
Viladesau, Richard, *Theological Aesthetics: God in Imagination, Beauty and Art* (Oxford: Oxford University Press, 1999).
Vischer, Wilhelm, *Hiob: Ein Zeuge Jesu Christi* (Bekennende Kirche, 8; Munich: Kaiser, 2nd edn, 1934).
__ *The Witness of the Old Testament to Christ*. I. *The Pentateuch* (trans. A.B. Crabtree; London: Lutterworth Press, 1949).
Volf, M., *After our Likeness: The Church as the Image of the Trinity* (Grand Rapids: Eerdmans, 1998).
Voltaire, 'Bien, tout est bien', in *Oeuvres complètes de Voltaire: Dictionnaire philosophique*, I (Paris: Furne, 1835), pp. 258-61.
Walker, Peter, *Jesus and the Holy City: New Testament Perspectives on Jerusalem* (Grand Rapids: Eerdmans, 1996).
Walker, Robert T., 'Editor's Introduction', in Thomas F. Torrance, *Atonement: The Person and Work of Christ* (ed. Robert T. Walker; Downers Grove, IL: InterVarsity Press, 2009), pp. lvii-lx.
—'Editor's Introduction', in Torrance, *Incarnation*, pp. xxi-lii.
Wall, R.W., 'Reading the Bible from within our Traditions: The "Rule of Faith" in Theological Hermeneutics', in Green and Turner (eds.), *Between Two Horizons*, pp. 88-107.
Wallis, Ian G, *The Faith of Jesus Christ in Early Christian Traditions* (SNTSMS, 84; Cambridge: Cambridge University Press, 1995).
Walton, Steve, 'Ascension of Jesus', in Joel B. Green (ed.), *Dictionary of Jesus and the Gospels* (Downers Grove, IL: InterVarsity Press, 2nd edn, in press).
Ward, Graham, 'In the Daylight Forever? Language and Silence', in Oliver Davies and Denys Turner (eds.), *Silence and the Word: Negative Theology and Incarnation* (Cambridge: Cambridge University Press, 2002), pp. 159-84.
Watson, Francis, *Text, Church and World: Biblical Interpretation in Theological Perspective* (Edinburgh: T. & T. Clark, 1994).
Webster, John, *Holiness* (Grand Rapids: Eerdmans, 2003).
—*Holy Scripture: A Dogmatic Sketch* (CIT; Cambridge: Cambridge University Press, 2003).
—'Reading Scripture Eschatologically', in Ford and Stanton (eds.), *Reading Texts, Seeking Wisdom*, pp. 245-56.

—'T.F. Torrance on Scripture' (keynote address at the annual meeting of the T.F. Torrance Theological Fellowship, Montreal, 6 November 2009).
Weinandy, Thomas G., *Does God Suffer?* (Edinburgh: T. & T. Clark, 2000).
Wenger, John Christian (ed.), *The Complete Writings of Menno Simons* (Scottdate, PA: Herald, 1956).
Wenham, Gordon J., *Genesis 1–15* (WBC, 1; Nashville: Thomas Nelson, 1987).
Westcott, B.F., *The Gospel according to St John* (1880 repr.; London: James Clark, 1958).
Westermann, Claus, *Genesis 1–11: A Commentary* (trans. John J. Scullion; Minneapolis: Augsburg; London: SPCK, 1984).
—*Lamentations: Issues and Interpretation* (trans. Charles Muenchow; Minneapolis: Fortress Press, 1994).
—'The Role of Lament in the Theology of the Old Testament', *Int* 28 (1974), pp. 20-38.
Wiesel, Elie, *Night* (trans. S. Rodway; London: Penguin Books, 1981; 1st edn London: McGibbon & Kee, 1960).
Wiles, Maurice, 'Scriptural Authority and Theological Construction: The Limitations of Narrative Interpretation', in Garrett Green (ed.), *Scriptural Authority and Narrative Interpretation* (Philadelphia: Fortress Press, 1987), pp. 42-58.
Williams, George Huntston (trans.), 'Trial and Martyrdom of Michael Sattler', in Williams and Mergal (eds.), *Spiritual and Anabaptist Writers*, pp. 138-44.
Williams, George Huntston, and Angel M. Mergal (eds.), *Spiritual and Anabaptist Writers* (LCC, 25; London: SCM Press, 1957).
Williams, Rowan D., *On Christian Theology* (Oxford: Blackwell, 2000).
—*Tokens of Trust: An Introduction to Christian Belief* (Norwich: Canterbury, 2007).
Wilson, Stephen G., 'The Ascension: A Critique and an Interpretation', *ZNW* 59 (1968), pp. 269-81.
Wolde, Ellen van, 'Job 42,1-6: The Reversal of Job', in W.A.M. Beuken (ed.), *The Book of Job* (BETL, 114; Leuven: Leuven University Press, 1994), pp. 223-50.
—*Mr and Mrs Job* (trans. J. Bowden; London: SCM Press, 1997).
—*Words Become Worlds: Semantic Studies of Genesis 1–11* (Leiden: Brill, 1994).
Wolterstorff, N., *Art in Action: Toward a Christian Aesthetic* (Carlisle: Solway, 1980).
Wright, N.T., *The New Testament and the People of God* (Minneapolis: Fortress Press, 1992).
— *The Resurrection of the Son of God* (Christian Origins and the Question of God, 3; Minneapolis: Fortress Press, 2003).
—'Resurrection: From Theology to Music and Back Again', in J. Begbie (ed.), *Sounding the Depths: Theology through the Arts* (London: SCM Press, 2002), pp. 193-212.
Wyschogrod, Edith, *An Ethics of Remembering: History, Heterology, and the Nameless Others* (Chicago: University of Chicago Press, 1998).
—'Eating the Text, Defiling the Hands: Specters in Arnold Schoenberg's Opera *Moses und Aron*', in John D. Caputo and Michael J. Scanlon (eds.), *God, the Gift and Postmodernism* (Bloomington: Indiana University Press, 1999), pp. 245-59.
Wyschogrod, Michael, 'Faith and the Holocaust', in Katz, Biderman, and Greenberg (eds.), *Wrestling with God*, pp. 286-94.
Yeago, David S., 'The New Testament and the Nicene Dogma: A Contribution to the Recovery of Theological Exegesis', in Fowl (ed.), *The Theological Interpretation of Scripture*, pp. 87-100.
Yoder, John Howard, *The Legacy of Michael Sattler* (Scottdale, PA: Herald, 1973).

—*The Royal Priesthood: Essays Ecclesiological and Ecumenical* (Grand Rapids: Eerdmans, 1994).

Young, Norman H., 'Suffering: A Key to the Epistle to the Hebrews', *ABR* 51 (2003), pp. 47-59.

Yu, Ning, 'Metaphor from Body and Culture', in Raymond W. Gibbs, Jr (ed.), *The Cambridge Handbook of Metaphor and Thought* (Cambridge: Cambridge University Press, 2010), pp. 247-61.

Zachman, R.C., *Image and Word in the Theology of John Calvin* (Notre Dame, IN: University of Notre Dame Press, 2007).

Zwiep, A.W., *The Ascension of the Messiah in Lukan Christology* (NovTSup, 87; Leiden: Brill, 1997).

—'Assumptus est in caelum: Rapture and Heavenly Exaltation in Early Judaism and Luke–Acts', in Avemarie and Lichtenberger (eds.), *Auferstehung—Resurrection*, pp. 323-49.

INDEXES

INDEX OF REFERENCES

OLD TESTAMENT

Genesis
6–9	80
6–8	231
9.1	80
10	80
10.18	80
11	71
11.1-9	75-76, 79-82, 84-93
24.3	117
24.7	117

Exodus
10.11	208
12.37	208
32	96-97, 100-13
33.13	203
33.18	102
33.19-23	102
34.6-7	234

Leviticus
4.12	160
16.27	160
19.18	237
19.34	237

Numbers
13–14	161
14.18	234
24.3	208
24.15	208

Deuteronomy
8.2	123
18.15-22	231
22.5	208
28	207
29.20-27	231
32.6	117
32.32	231

Joshua
7.14	208
7.17	208
7.18	208

Judges
5.30	208

1 Samuel
2.27-36	231
14.3	231

2 Samuel
7.12-14	117
7.14	117
8.13	86
22.3	154
23.1	208

1 Kings
2.26-27	231
12.28	103
22	239
22.1-40	233
22.20	233
22.21	233
22.22	233

2 Kings
2.1-18	141-42
17.7-23	248

1 Chronicles
17.13	117
22.10	117
23.3	208
24.4	208
26.12	208

2 Chronicles
36.23	117

Ezra
9.13	236, 241

Nehemiah
9.17	234

Esther
2.22	203

Job
1.9	241
2.3	242
2.10	242
2.13	245
3.3	208
3.23	208
4.17	208
9.17	242
10.5	208
11.6	236, 241
13.7	242

Job (cont.)		68.17-18	145	66.13	241
13.15	243-44, 251	80	248		
		86.15	234	Jeremiah	
14.10	208	88	248	1.1	231
14.14	208	94.12	208	3.4-5	117
16.21	208	103.8	234	3.19	117
22.2	208	103.13-18	118	4.10	232, 239, 243, 251
22.6	242	110	143		
27.5	242	119	199	4.14	140
27.6	242	127.5	208	7	205
33.17	208	128.4	208	7.12	238
33.29	208	136.23	117	7.13	80
34.7	208	145.8	234	7.14	238
34.9	208			12.1-4	232
34.34	208	Proverbs		12.5-6	232
38–41	238, 243	6.34	208	14.1-22	231
38.3	208	24.5	208	14.13	232
40.4	245	28.3	208	15.18	232
40.7	208	30.1	208	15.19	232-33
42.1-6	245	30.19	208	20.7-13	233
42.6	244			20.7	233
42.7	242	Isaiah		20.14-18	233
42.10-17	246	1.9	231	20.16	231
		1.10	231	22.20	216
Psalms		3.9	203, 231	22.22	216
2.7	117	6.9-10	16	22.30	208
18.26	208	8.17	154	23.14	231
19	143	8.18	154	25.3-11	248
22	155, 247-48	12.1	241	26.6	238
		12.2	154	26.9	238
22.2	247	13.19	231	30.6	208
22.8-9	247	22.17	208	30.14	216
22.15	156	40	241	31.9	117
22.16	156	40.1-3	212	31.22	208
22.21-22	156	40.2	236, 241	31.31-34	40
22.23	155-56	40.8	38	41.16	208
22.24-47	156	40.27	241	43.6	208
24	143	49.13	241	44.20	208
25.4-11	234	51.3	241	49.18	231
34.9	208	51.12	241	50.40	231
37.23	208	51.19	241		
40.5	208	52.9	241	Lamentations	
44	248	61.2	241	1–2	208, 210, 218-19
47	143	63.16	117		
51.6	179	64.8	117	1	207
68	143	66.1	138	1.1-9	213

1.2	241	*Ezekiel*		APOCRYPHAL/DEUTERO-	
1.5	213	5.9	240	CANONICAL BOOKS	
1.8	213, 216	5.10	240	*Tobit*	
1.9	213, 241	6.10	241	10.13	117
1.10-11	213	14.12-20	231	12.15	149
1.10	216	14.22	241	12.19	149
1.12-16	213, 215	14.23	241	13.4	117
1.12	213, 216	16.33	216		
1.13	216	16.36	216	*Judith*	
1.14	213	16.37	216	9.12	117
1.16	241	16.46-50	231		
1.17	213, 241	16.53-56	231	*Wisdom of Solomon*	
1.18-22	213	16.56	231	17.4	203
1.18	207-208, 213-19	23.5	216	18.18	203
		23.9	216		
1.19	216	23.22	216	*Sirach*	
1.20-22	220-21	26.1-21	38	23.1	117
1.20	213, 215				
1.21	213, 241	*Daniel*		*2 Maccabees*	
1.22	213, 215-16	8.15	208	3.7	202
				7.1-42	140
2.2	217	*Joel*		8.27-29	140
2.11	220	1.2–2.17	231	11.29	202
2.13	218, 241	2.13	234		
2.17	217			*3 Maccabees*	
2.21	217	*Amos*		6.2-3	117
3	206-207, 209-10, 212, 218-19	1.1	231		
		4.6-12	231	NEW TESTAMENT	
		4.11	231	*Matthew*	
		9.1	231	1.21	126
3.1	208			2.3	121
3.8	217	*Jonah*		3.2	120
3.11-17	220	4.2	234	3.14	126
3.22-25	208			3.17	117
3.25-39	220	*Habakkuk*		4.1-11	127
3.26-30	208	1.2–2.20	233	4.17-18	114
3.27	208			4.17	120
3.39	208	*Zephaniah*		4.23	120
3.42	208, 213	2.9	231	5–7	115
3.43	217			5.3	120
3.44	217	*Haggai*		5.4	108
3.60-66	221	1.4-11	231	5.10	120
4.6	231	2.14-19	231	5.14	188
4.10	240			5.16	118
4.21-22	221	*Zechariah*		5.20	114-15
5	220	14.5	231	5.21	9
				5.43-48	115

Matthew (cont.)		16.24	114, 122,	27.46	155, 247		
5.45	118		124, 165	27.53	203		
5.48	114, 118	16.25	122	28.16-20	182		
6.1	118	17.5	117	28.17	128		
6.4	118	18.1-6	122	28.18-20	119		
6.6	118	18.14	123	28.19-20	128		
6.8	118	18.20	67-69	28.19	128		
6.9-15	115	18.21-35	122				
6.9	116	18.21-22	126	*Mark*			
6.10	123	18.23-35	126	1.2	181		
6.14-15	126	19.13-15	122	1.15	17		
6.25-26	118	19.16	163	1.16-20	16		
6.31-32	118	19.21-26	122	2.13	16		
6.33	120	19.21	114, 124	3.13-19	13		
7.9-11	124	20.1-16	122	3.13-14	16		
7.13-14	127	20.22	67	4.1-20	12-24, 61-		
7.21	114, 123	21.5	121-22		64		
8.11	188	21.31-32	114	4.14	120		
8.22	114	21.31	123	4.35-41	33		
9.2-5	126	21.32	123	6.3	65		
9.8	128	22.34-40	114	6.30-44	33		
9.9	114	24.14	188	8.34-38	165		
9.10	126	25.31-46	126	10.17	163		
9.13	126	26.7	121	12.35-37	65		
9.35	120	26.12	121	13.27	188		
10.7	120	26.26	125	15.24	156		
10.38	114, 124,	26.28-29	128	15.34	155, 247,		
	165	26.28	126		250		
11.4-5	120	26.29	119	16.19	131		
11.10	181	26.39	119, 123				
11.19	179	26.41	127, 183	*Luke*			
11.20	119	26.42	119, 123	1.32	147		
11.25-26	118	26.45	126	1.35	147		
11.25	116-17	26.53	119	1.52-53	147		
11.29	126	26.54	123	1.76	147		
12.50	123	26.56	123	2.52	67		
13.19	120	26.66	121	3.21	138		
13.24-30	120	27.4	127	3.22	147		
13.36-43	120	27.11	121	5.8	147		
13.44-46	120	27.24	127	6.35	147		
13.47-50	120	27.25	127, 150	7.24	181		
13.51	114	27.27-30	121	7.29	179		
14.13-21	125	27.29	121	7.35	179		
15.33-37	125	27.35	156	8.8	91		
16.21-22	127	27.36	121	8.21	149		
16.23	127	27.37	121	8.28	147		
		27.42	121	8.35	147		

Index of References

9.16	138, 147	24.32	83	19.24	156
9.23-25	165	24.33	131	19.28	156
9.28-36	135	24.34	180	20.17	130
9.31	135	24.36	131, 149		
9.35	147	24.37	149	*Acts*	
9.51	135, 137, 147, 150, 182	24.39	149	1	131
		24.41-43	149	1.1-14	135
		24.47	182	1.1	150
9.52	181	24.49	138, 141-42	1.2	137, 180, 182
9.54	138				
10.15	138, 147	24.50	131-32	1.3	132
10.21	117, 138	24.51	131, 147	1.4-5	142
10.29	179			1.4	142
10.39	147	*John*		1.5	142
11.13	138	1.1	38	1.6-8	138
11.16	138	1.4	203	1.8	138, 142, 188
14.7-10	147	1.5	203		
14.11	147	1.9	203	1.9-11	131-33, 135, 137, 139-41
14.27	165	1.13	65		
15.7	138	1.14	178		
15.18	138	1.19-51	51	1.9	138, 149
15.21	138	1.29	188	1.10	138
17.15	147	2.22	199	1.11	138, 150, 182
17.29	138	2.23–3.15	66-67		
18.13	138, 147	3.6	183	1.22	182
18.14	147	3.16-17	188	2	92
18.18	163	3.16	192	2.1-13	142
18.22	138	4.42	188	2.2	138
20.4-5	138	4.43-54	64-65	2.5	138
20.46	147	6.63	178	2.14-41	91
22.19	125	8.11	120	2.16-21	140
22.41	147	12.47-49	199	2.17	141
22.42	66-67	12.47	188	2.23-24	180
22.59	150	14.15-26	191, 194-203, 260	2.23	150
23.5	150			2.24-36	141
23.34	156	14.23	192	2.32	150
23.49	150	15.4-10	195	2.33	140-41
23.55	150	15.10	194	2.36	141
24	131, 135, 149	15.12-14	195	2.38-40	141
		15.13	192	3.11-15	180
24.1	131	15.17	194	3.21	138
24.6	150	15.18-25	194	4.10-12	180
24.13	131	15.26-27	200	4.12	149
24.15-16	149	16.12-14	19	5.31	140
24.21	131	16.27	192	7.2	181
24.23	181	17	23	7.49	138
24.31	149	17.6	199	7.55-56	138

Acts (cont.)		1 Corinthians		Colossians	
8.5-25	144	1.18-31	191	1.5-6	182
9.3	138	2.1-9	180	1.18	175
9.17	180-81	3.16-17	175	1.22	178
10.11	138	3.16	174	1.23	188
10.16	138	11.24-25	125	1.24	175
10.30	149	12.28	175	2.5	183
10.39-40	180	14.19	175	2.8-15	180
11.5	138	14.26	173	2.15	181
11.9	138	15.5-8	180-81	3.16-17	173
11.10	138	15.22	66		
13.31	150, 180-81			*1 Thessalonians*	
		2 Corinthians		1.8	188
13.47	188	2.14	188		
16.17	142	3.2	188	*1 Timothy*	
17.24-29	40	5.19	188	1.15	179, 182
17.24	117	6.16	175	1.18	174
17.34	40			2.1–3.13	174
19.27	176	*Galatians*		2.4-6	182
19.28	176	1.22	175	3.4	174
19.34	176	2.20	179	3.5	174
19.35	176	3.3	183	3.9	176
20.34-43	180	4.4	66	3.12	174
22.6	138	4.23	66	3.14-15	171-72, 174-76
23.15	202	4.24	66		
23.22	202	4.29	66, 183	3.16	171-90
24.1	202			4.1-5	175-76
25.2	202			4.11	174
25.15	202	*Ephesians*		5.4	174
26.16	180	1.20-21	180	6.2	174
		1.21	181	6.5	175
Romans		2.14	178		
1.3	178	2.21	174	*2 Timothy*	
1.4	180	2.22	174	1.9	179
1.8	188	4.7-8	130	1.16	174
1.13	66	5.18-20	173	2.18	175
1.16	45			3.8	175
3.4	179	*Philippians*		4.4	175
8.3	178-79	1.22	179	4.19	174
8.4-6	183	1.24	179		
8.13	183	2.5-11	180	*Titus*	
8.32	172	2.6-11	34	1.11	174
9.5	178	2.6	172	2.14	172
9.17	188	2.7-8	179		
10.18	188	2.7	66		
11.15	188	4.10-20	34		
12.2	12				

Index of References

Hebrews		10.23	159	13.18	153, 160	
1.2	158, 160	10.24	159	13.19	153, 157	
1.3-4	181	10.25	157, 162-	13.20	158	
2.1	158-59		23	13.21	158	
2.3	158	10.26	158	13.22-25	157	
2.9	155	10.32-34	153, 157	13.22	158	
2.10-18	155	10.33	165	13.23	153, 157-	
2.10	155, 161	10.35	159		58	
2.11-17	155	10.39	158	13.24	157, 160	
2.13	154-56	11.40	158			
2.14	178	12.1-3	151, 154,	*James*		
2.18	155		165	2.25	181	
3.1	158-59	12.1-2	159			
3.6	158-59	12.1	152, 158-	*1 Peter*		
3.7–4.11	161		59	1.29	179	
3.12-13	162	12.2	152, 154-	2.1-19	200	
3.12	159		55, 160,	2.22-24	172	
3.13	159		166-67	3.18	178, 183	
3.14	159	12.3	153, 154,	3.21	180	
4.1-2	161		159	3.22	172, 181	
4.1	159	12.4	153-54			
4.2	161-62	12.7	159	4.1	178	
4.11	158, 162	12.9	158	5.9	188	
4.13	158	12.12	158			
4.14	159	12.13	158	*2 Peter*		
4.15	158	12.14-15	159	1.19-21	200	
4.16	159	12.15	161	3.10-13	185	
5.7	178-79	12.25	158-59	3.16	200	
5.11	158	12.28	159-60			
6.1-2	163	12.29	158	*1 John*		
6.1	158	13.2-3	160	3.5	179	
6.4-6	163	13.2	159	3.8	179	
6.4-5	163	13.3	153	4.2	178	
6.11-12	158, 160	13.6	158	4.14	188	
6.19	160	13.7	153, 158-			
6.20	158		60	*2 John*		
7.14	158	13.9	159	7	178	
7.26	158	13.10	160			
9.8	160	13.13-14	163	*Revelation*		
9.14	158, 160	13.13	151, 159-	5.8-14	181	
9.24	158, 203		60, 165-66	7	67	
9.26	160, 179	13.14	166	11.19	181	
10.15	158	13.15-16	160	12.1	181	
10.19	160	13.15	159	12.3	181	
10.20	158, 178	13.16	159	22.7	200	
10.22	159-60	13.17	158-60			

INDEX OF AUTHORS

Adam, A.K.M. 98
Albrektson, B. 204-205, 208, 210
Alston, W.M. 137
Alter, R. 80-81
Anderson, K.L. 140
Andriessen, P.C.B. 152-53
Arichea, D.C. 182
Attridge, H.W. 153-55, 161-62, 165
Aus, R. 172
Avemarie, F. 134, 136

Bakhtin, M. 207, 219
Balla, P. 29
Bally, C. 228
Barrett, C.K. 177, 187
Barth, K. 5, 19, 27, 32, 53-55, 57-60, 62, 97, 241
Bartholomew, C.G. 70, 77, 93, 196, 240
Barton, J. 196
Bassler, J.M. 172, 174-75
Bateman, H.W. 162
Bauckham, R. 63, 141, 165
Beale, G.K. 100, 102, 109, 156
Begbie, J. 5
Bell, A. 71, 260
Benson, B.E. 101, 108, 110
Berlin, A. 208, 211, 216
Bernasconi, R. 235
Beuken, W.A.M. 245
Bhaskar, R. 56
Biderman, S. 205, 225, 235
Bier, M. 252, 259
Billings, J.T. 170-71, 183
Bird, M.F. 63
Black, C.C. 6, 191
Blair, H.A. 172
Blumenthal, D.R. 237, 244
Boase, E.C. 206-207, 210-11, 216, 218
Bockmuehl, M.N.A. 44, 95, 160-61
Boer, R. 217
Bonhoeffer, D. 9
Bori, P.C. 103
Bowie, A. 107
Bracke, J. 209
Braiterman, Z. 207, 211-12, 237-38, 244
Braun, H. 152-53

Bream, H.N. 130
Breidert, W. 223-24, 226-27
Briggs, R.S. 11-12
Brown, R.E. 202, 209
Bruce, F.F. 154
Brueggemann, W. 79-80, 85-86, 90-91, 207, 228, 244, 247
Brunner, P. 136
Buckwalter, H.D. 134, 140
Bultmann, R. 14, 33
Burnett, G.W. 156
Burrell, D.B. 101, 236
Bush, C. 228

Campbell, D.A. 164
Caputo, J.D. 104
Cargas, H.J. 105
Carson, D.A. 156, 199
Childs, B.S. 50, 240
Coakley, S. 245
Colyer, E.M. 54, 56-58, 62, 69
Congdon, D.W. 5
Conzelmann, H. 172, 177, 180, 186-87
Cranfield, C.E.B. 14
Crenshaw, J. 229
Curtis, E.M. 100

Davies, B. 101
Davies, J.G. 135, 143
Davies, M. 174, 182
Davies, O. 96, 106
Davies, P. 258
Davis, E.F. 1, 21
David, S. 136
Davidson, I. 49
Dawson, G.S. 51, 146
Days, P.L. 209
Dean-Otting, M. 133-34
Demarest, B. 6
Dennert, B.C. 47
Derrida, J. 196
Des Pres, T. 240
DeSilva, D. 154
Dibelius, M. 172, 177, 180, 186-87
Dillon, J.J. 143, 171

Dobbs-Allsopp, F.W. 206, 208, 211-12, 215-16, 218
Donaldson, A.M. 134
Donelson, L.W. 185
Donne, B.K. 146
Douglas, J.D. 100
Dunn, J.D.G. 136
Dunnill, J. 152

Eagleton, T. 98
Easter, M.C. 156, 260
Eissfeldt, O. 208
Ellingworth, P. 154
Elvey, A.F. 83
Elwell, W. 199
Enslin, M.S. 131-32
Evans, C.S. 240

Fackenheim, E. 225, 243, 246
Fairclough, N. 80
Farrow, D. 130-31, 145
Fee, G.D. 175-77, 179
Feldman, J.A. 148
Ferguson, D.S. 199
Fernández, V.M. 160
Fiddes, P.S. 193, 247-48, 250
Fiore, B. 179
Fishbane, M. 80, 241
Fitzmyer, J.A. 131, 209
Flannery, F. 133.
Fletcher-Louis, C.H.T. 149
Foakes-Jackson, F.J. 131
Foester, W. 149
Ford, D.F. 111, 234
Fowl, S.E. 2, 12, 21, 24, 26, 33-34, 43-46, 49-50, 60, 98, 172, 176, 178, 180-81, 184-85
Frame, J.M. 55
France, R.T. 20
Fretheim, T.E. 81, 86
Fuhrer, G. 149

Gallagher, E.V. 164
Gasque, W.W. 177
Gibs, R.W. 148
Glock, C.Y. 164
Goldingay, J.E. 3, 155
González, J.L. 36-37, 39-40
Good, E.M. 244
Gooding, D.W. 136

Gordis, R. 213
Gorman, M.J. 46
Gottwald, N. 204-206, 208, 210, 215
Grässer, E. 153
Gray, B.J. 50, 61-62
Gray, J. 245
Gray, P. 152
Green, B. 220
Green, G. 95
Green, J.B. 6, 21, 26, 33, 47, 140-41, 170, 195, 198, 253, 260
Greenberg, G. 205, 225, 235
Greene, C.J.D. 70, 77, 93, 196
Greene-McCreight, K. 3
Gregory, B.S. 168
Grudem, W.A. 163
Guinan, M.D. 209
Gundry, R.H. 177-79, 181, 187, 189
Gurewicz, S.B. 208
Guthrie, G.H. 156

Habel, N.C. 244
Habets, M. 4, 6, 57, 260-61
Hagner, D.A. 120
Hanson, A.T. 176
Harding, J.E. 233, 241, 259
Harland, P.J. 85, 90
Haroutunian, J. 146
Hart, H. 164
Hart, T.A. 47, 58-59
Hartman, N. 56
Harvard, J.S. 35
Hastings, J. 30
Hauerwas, S. 37
Hawthorne, G.F. 163
Hays, R.B. 1, 4, 5, 16-18, 21, 25, 46
Heater, H. 209, 214
Healy, M. 240
Hebb, D. 148
Heim, K.M. 214
Heltzel, P. 55
Hennecke, E. 144
Henry, C.F.H. 4
Herringer, S. 261
Heschel, A.J. 250
Hess, R. 214
Hesselink, J.I. 60
Hillers, D. 208, 211
Hillesum, E. 242-43
Himmelfarb, M. 133-34

Hodgson, P.C. 132
Holmgren, F.C. 209
Horton, M.S. 55
Houlden, J.L. 133, 146-47, 178
House, P.R. 209, 218
Huey, F.B. 209
Hultgren, A.J. 172, 175, 189
Hunsinger, G. 55

Ihde, D. 77
Insole, C. 106

Jantzen, G. 94-95
Jarvis, C.A. 137
Jenson, R.W. 35-36, 38, 42, 106, 137
Johnson, A. 141
Johnson, K.E. 49
Johnson, L.T. 153-55, 180, 186
Jüngel, E. 96-97

Käsemann, E. 151, 165
Katz, S.T. 205, 225, 235
Keck, L.E. 81
Kelly, J.N.D. 176, 182
Kierkegaard, S. 94
Kimel, A.F. 55
Klassen, W. 185
Klauck, H.-J. 152
Klein, H. 131
Knierim, R.P. 229
Knight, G.A.F. 209
Knight, G.W. 180, 182, 187
Koester, C.R. 152-55, 162
Kooij, A. van der, 79
Köstenberger, A.J. 195, 200
Kox, W. 164
Krašovec, J. 209
Krause, D. 186-88

Laato, A. 216, 229
Ladd, G.E. 200
Lake, K. 131
Lanahan, W.F. 208, 214
Lane, W.L. 152-56, 161-62, 163
Larkin, W.J. 134
Lash, N. 97
Lau, A.U. 179, 187
Laytner, A. 237, 244
Lee, A.C. C. 210-11
Lee, N. 208

Leithart, P.J. 160
Lemaire, A. 79
Levering, M. 37-38
Lévi-Strauss, C. 78
Levinas, E. 205, 233, 235-40, 242, 248, 252
Levison, J.R. 90
Lichtenberger, H. 134, 136
Lienhard, J.T. 109
Linafelt, T. 210-11, 215-16, 220
Lindars, B. 158
Lofland, J. 163-64
Lohfink, G. 131, 133
Longenecker, R.N. 152
Longman, T. 213, 218-19
Loughlin, G. 94-95
Lubac, H. de 19-20, 230
Luz, U. 115

MacKinnon, D. 97, 103, 105-10, 112
MacLeod, D.J. 177
Magee, G.S. 176
Maile, J.F. 139
Malina, B.J. 157
Mandolfo, C.R. 206, 211-12, 217
Manson, W. 62, 64
Marion, J.-L. 108-109
Marley, A.G. 56
Marohl, M.J. 157-58
Marshall, C.D. 160
Marshall, I.H. 134, 136, 140, 172-73, 175, 177-82, 186-88
Martin, R.P. 177
Mathewson, D. 163
McCabe, H. 110-11, 113
McClendon, J.W. 8-9
McDowell, J.C. 110, 260
McGrath, A.E. 56, 60
McKane, W. 232
McKnight, S. 163, 195, 198
Meadowcroft, T.J. 3-4, 191, 260
Meek, E.L. 193-94
Meeus, W. 164
Mergal, A.M. 167-68
Metzger, B.M. 130, 136, 141, 154, 162
Meyer, P.W. 62
Micou, R.W. 182
Míguez-Bonino, J. 90
Miller, C.W. 215-16
Miller, J.B.F. 132
Mintz, A. 215

Index of Authors

Moberly, R.W.L. 1-2, 11-12, 233-34, 239, 244, 247
Möller, K. 70, 77, 93, 196
Molnar, P.D. 53, 57
Moloney, F.J. 200
Moltmann, J. 193, 249-50
Montague, G.T. 176
Moor, J.C. de 216, 229
Moore, M.S. 205
Morrow, W.S. 245
Mosser, C. 165
Motyer, J.A. 100
Moule, C.F.D. 132, 156
Mounce, W. 177
Muffs, Y. 231, 234, 250
Müller, G. 153
Murphy, R.E. 209
Murphy-O'Connor, J. 177, 180
Myers, J.M. 130
Needham, N. 146
Negri, A. 236
Neiman, S. 224-29
Newsom, C.A. 220
Neyrey, J.H. 157
Nicole, R.R. 163
Noth, M. 103-104

O'Connor, K.M. 208, 212, 217-18, 220
O'Day, G.R. 211
O'Grady, J.F. 156
O'Keefe, J.J. 131
Olhausen, W. 196
Oord, T.J. 192
Osborne, G.R. 47, 162
Ostler, N. 90

Painter, J. 198
Palatty, P. 139
Palmer, D.W. 133
Parker, H.M. 153
Parry, R.A. 209, 211, 219
Pauw, A.P. 27
Pelikan, J. 8, 40
Penner, T.C. 210
Perdue, L.G. 234
Pervo, R.I. 131
Peterson, D. 134, 140, 211
Peterson, N.R. 157
Pham, X.H.T. 214
Pilch, J.J. 157

Placher, W.C. 27, 32-33
Plantinga, A. 55
Polanyi, M. 60
Pope-Levison, P. 90
Popkin, R.H. 228
Popper, K. 79, 87
Porter, S.E. 63-64
Posner, M.I. 148

Rae, M.A. 2-3, 5, 7, 27, 41-42, 92, 220, 240
Rahner, K. 53
Raichle, M.E. 148
Ramachandran, V.S. 148
Rawden, H.H. 141
Re'emi, S.P. 209
Reimherr, O. 130
Renkema, J. 216
Reno, R.R. 27, 30-32, 34-35, 131
Ricoeur, P. 50, 70-79, 82-84, 87-89, 92-93, 112, 260
Riedlinger, A. 228
Rigby, C.L. 146
Rosner, B. 96
Roth, J.D. 168
Rowe, C.K. 140
Rubinstein, R. 248
Ryken, P.G. 208-209

Saarinen, R. 175, 189
Sæbø, M. 208
Sailors, T.B. 134
Salevao, I. 153
Salters, R.B. 208, 215
Sarisky, D. 57
Sarna, N.M. 86
Saussure, F. de, 228
Scanlon, M.J. 104
Schaff, D. 130
Schaff, P. 130
Schneemelcher, W. 144
Scholer, J.M. 160
Schreiner, J. 152
Schreiner, T.R. 163
Schröer, H. 153
Schüssler Fiorenza, E. 152, 196
Schweid, E. 225
Schweizer, E. 15, 184
Scott, B.B. 234
Sechehaye, A. 228
Segal, A.F. 133, 164

Seitz, C.R. 240, 246, 256
Sherwood, Y. 196
Simpson, E.K. 172, 187
Sleeman, M. 139
Smelik, K.A.D. 243
Smith, D.M. 192, 200
Smith, J.K.A. 110
Snyder, G.F. 185
Söding, T. 158
Sölle, D. 225, 245, 249
Stanton, G. 111, 234
Stark, R. 163-64
Stayer, J.M. 168
Steiner, G. 97, 100-108, 110, 112
Stiebert, J. 212, 217
Still, T. 155
Strauss, D.F. 132
Strecker, G. 177, 179, 185
Surin, K.R. 225, 249
Swinburne, R. 236

Tabor, J.D. 133
Tenney, M.C. 163
Thiselton, A.C. 70
Thomas, C.A. 153, 163
Thomas, H. 219
Thompson, J.B. 72, 260
Thompson, M.B. 160
Thompson, M.M. 26, 117, 260
Ticciati, S. 231, 241
Torrance, A.J. 51, 95
Torrance, D.W. 68
Torrance, J.B. 51
Torrance, T.F. 46-69, 260-61
Towner, P.H. 172, 176, 179-80, 183, 186, 188
Trebilco, P.R. 174, 260
Treier, D.J. 1, 21, 44-45
Trible, P. 98
Troeltsch, E. 28-30, 33-34, 39-40, 258
Tull Willey, P. 206, 241
Turner, D. 98, 106
Turner, M. 26, 47, 140-41, 170, 195
Turner, M.M.B. 141

Uehlinger, C. 85, 90
Unger, D.J. 143, 145, 171

van Leeuwen, R.C. 234
Vander Stichlele, C. 210

Vandrunen, D. 102
Vanhoozer, K.J. 1, 3, 12, 17, 21, 43, 45-46, 59, 70, 77-78, 98, 110, 112, 180, 197
Verbrugge, V.D. 161
Verhey, A. 35
Vicchio, S. 227
Viladesau, R. 101, 104
Vischer, W. 1, 241
Volf, M. 194

Walker, P. 165
Walker, R.T. 43, 49-50, 59
Wall, R.W. 3, 47, 170
Wallis, I.G. 153
Walson, S. 140
Ward, G. 105-107
Ware, B.A. 163
Watson, F. 21, 44, 98
Watt, J.G. van der, 153
Webster, J. 9, 11-12, 58-61, 99, 111
Weinandy, T.G. 250
Weinrich, W.C. 53
Welker, M. 137
Wenger, J.C. 167, 169
Wenham, G.J. 81, 85, 214
Westcott, B.F. 202
Westermann, C. 85-86, 205, 210-11, 214-15, 247
Wiesel, E. 105, 249-51
Wiles, M. 95-97, 112
Williams, G.H. 167-68
Williams, R.D. 113, 242-44, 246
Wilson, S.G. 132
Wiseman, W.J. 234
Wolde, E. van, 86, 241, 244-45
Wolterstorff, N. 55, 198
Wood, D. 235
Wright, C.J.H. 3
Wright, N.T. 5, 137, 144, 193
Wyschogrod, E. 104-105, 108, 112
Wyschogrod, M. 225

Yeago, D.S. 50
Yoder, J.H. 168-69
Young, N.H. 153
Yu, N. 148

Zachman, R.C. 100, 102, 104
Zuck, R. 209
Zwiep, A.W. 133-34

www.ingramcontent.com/pod-product-compliance
Lightning Source LLC
Chambersburg PA
CBHW071957220426
43662CB00009B/1174